Harvest of Hate

The Nazi Program for the
Destruction of the Jews of Europe

Revised and Expanded Edition

Léon Poliakov

Foreword by
Reinhold Niebuhr

HOLOCAUST LIBRARY
New York

Originally published as *Bréviare de la haine*,
Paris, Calmann Lévy, 1951
First English edition published by Syracuse University
Press in 1954

Copyright © 1979 by Léon Poliakov
Publication of this book was made possible
by a grant from Benjamin and Stefa Wald
Library of Congress Catalog Card Number: 78-71294

Cover Design by Luba Krugman Gurdus

Printed in the United States of America
By Waldon Press Inc., NYC

To the memory of my master and friend

JACOB GORDIN

Contents

vii

Foreword

This study of the Nazi policy of cruelty, sadism, and extermination against the Jews, the Slavs and other "enemies"of the Germans, is a very important document for several reasons. It gives us the moral and spiritual background of this policy of frightfulness. By the diligent analysis of cabinet minutes, correspondence between Nazi officials and their diaries, it shows the official character of this cruelty. Even the revelations of an occasional twinge of conscience in unlikely quarters is significant because it reminds us that these were actually human beings which were thus corrupted by the religion of hatred.

This is such a sorry chapter both in the history of mankind and in that of Germany that there is a general inclination to forget the chapter. Its scrupulously recorded history therefore has another important function. Different people will draw different conclusions from this tragic story. But it is better, as the author has done, to let history speak for itself in order that any reader may gather such lessons from it as his competence or inclination will allow. Some will emphasize the shattering fact that a civilization which boasted of its refinements could nevertheless prompt a rebellion against its standards which reached such unfathomed depths of inhumanity. Others will emphasize the lesson contained in the author's title and call attention to the evil consequences of a systematic indoctrination of hatred in a population.

My personal conviction is that the tragedy is too enormous to permit us to treat it as a fund for whatever moral lessons we desire to teach. I think one must read it with a contrite sense, transcending all moral lessons, that it was our humanity which was capable under certain historical conditions, of sinking to this inhumanity. We will no doubt be diligent to avoid recreating the historical conditions which made these noxious fruits possible. We will be assiduous in our lessons on the brotherhood of mankind. But these lessons must not allow us to exhaust the meaning of this terrible record of human depravity.

REINHOLD NIEBUHR
Professor of Christian Ethics,
Union Theological Seminary

Author's Introduction

This book is devoted to the most tragic page in Jewish history—the extermination in cold blood of six million Jewish men, women, and children, with the result that in a few short years the total number of the European Jews was reduced by two-thirds. Such bloodletting is without precedent in European history; the Nazi enterprise was unique in its very principle. But to treat this subject is also to treat a part of the history of contemporary Germany, for in the actual event the Jews were chiefly passive victims; the active role, that of the protagonist in the tragedy, fell to the German people as a group, acting under the stimulus of leaders of their own choice. When one reflects that we are dealing here with a highly civilized nation that for many years was a torch-bearer of Western society, one realizes that we are concerned with an anti-Semitic problem that is intrinsic to our entire Western civilization, an aberrant and pathological phenomenon that lay at the very center of the 1939–45 catastrophe; the general interest of mankind, as well as the more particular question of the future of the European community, demand that we study closely the Nazi war on the Jews.

Such insights into these matters, however, as the subject suggests will only be briefly touched on in these pages; our main purpose is to compile a documentary and psychological record. With this record in hand, the reader may then judge for himself and draw his own conclusions.

One thing needs saying. Some of the documents cited in this book are so disconcerting and improbable that some readers may be tempted to question their authenticity. For have we not already seen the appearance of publications in which doubt is cast on the number of Jewish victims and on a great many other things? We therefore think it useful to state the following: The majority of the quotations given, especially those of German origin, come either from the Nazi archives captured by the Allies or from the records of the Nuremberg Tribunal (wherever possible, to forestall objections, we have quoted the executioners rather than the victims); the original records are now either at The Hague or in Washington, as the case may be. In all the polemics that raged around the Nuremberg trials, the authenticity of these records was never questioned even by the most rabid detractors of Allied justice. Photostatic reproductions or certified copies of these documents, as well as originals from other sources, are located in the Centre du Documentation Juive Contemporaine in Paris, an institution established by its late president, M. Schneersohn, in 1943; without the Centre's help this work would have been impossible.

Foreword to Revised Edition (1974)

This book was first published a quarter of a century ago. Rereading the original text to see where alterations were needed, I came across many passages which I felt I might have written differently today. In retrospect, some of the opinions I held in 1949 and 1950 seem a little naïve to me now. In other instances, I felt I might have kept a tighter rein on emotions which are considered unacceptable in historians. But then I wonder whether the book really would have gained by such changes.

Under the circumstances, I decided to leave my 1951 text essentially unchanged. The only major alterations come toward the end of the book. I am giving less space to the attitude of the Vatican. As long as Pope Pius XII was alive, discussions of his silence during the Holocaust era were tempered by circumspection. (François Mauriac was the first Catholic author to touch upon that question in his courageous preface to the first French edition of this book.) But after that, the subject was debated with increasing vehemence, culminating in the worldwide scandal set off in 1962, after the death of Pius XII, by Rolf Hochhuth's Deputy. This theatrical catharsis put an end to the great debate, and frankly, I do not see why that Pope's attitude should rate more commentary or sterner condemnation than the passivity that characterized the Christians of his generation in general. At most, the former is a symbol of the latter.

Near the end of the book, where I discuss the response of the Jews to the Holocaust, I have deleted one final paragraph. In that paragraph, I had expressed the thought that the Jews would find peace at last in their own homeland. However, history seems to have decreed otherwise.

CHAPTER ONE

The Beginnings

THINK BACK to 1933, the year of Hitler's coming to power. Two months after Marshal Hindenburg entrusted Adolf Hitler with the task of forming a government, the first measures against the German Jews were put in force. As a prelude to the restrictive measures, a mass boycott of Jewish business was organized on April 1, 1933, by a semi-official committee headed by Julius Streicher. On April 7, the first two laws were published: except for veterans, and civil servants and lawyers appointed prior to August 1, 1914, Jews were to be excluded from the public service and the bar. A law, announced on April 22, barred payment from social security funds to Jewish doctors. In rapid order came a series of other legislative and administrative measures which eliminated Jews from all phases of German national life. On September 15, 1935, with the promulgation of the Nuremberg racial laws, German anti-Semitism acquired a new and highly characteristic note.

These measures provoked various reactions abroad, such as protest meetings, the formation of leagues and committees, and the publication of Brown Books. These protests were neither clear nor unanimous, for they quite naturally reflected the conflicting interests of different groups. Often they collided with a latent anti-Semitism. Official action was lacking because governmental chancelleries were bent on appeasement. Practically no one suspected the sinister events that these discriminatory measures foreshadowed —least of all the Jews.

It was not apparent from the then known principles of the Nazi party or from the writings of the Nazi leaders that mass extermination was contemplated. The word "Jews" appears on almost every page of *Mein Kampf*, but it is silent about the fate reserved for

1

them under National Socialism. The official program of the party was only slightly more explicit. It provided that:

4. None but members of the nation may be citizens of the State. None but those of German blood, whatever their creed, may be members of the nation. No Jew, therefore, may be a member of the nation.
5. Anyone who is not a citizen of the State may live in Germany only as a guest and must be regarded as being subject to foreign laws.

More precisely the commentaries on the program required:

3. The eviction of Jews and non-Germans from all responsible posts in public life.
4. Cessation of immigration of Jews from the East as well as that of all parasitic foreigners; the expulsion of Jews and undesirable aliens.

Only Julius Streicher and Joseph Goebbels, among the Nazi leaders, had occasion to express publicly their sanguinary intentions during these first years of the regime.

Streicher (in a speech):

It is wrong to believe that the Jewish question can be settled without bloodshed: the only possible solution is a bloody one.[1]

Goebbels (in an interview):

'Death to the Jews' has been our war cry for fourteen years. Let them die.[2]

But one finds sentiments of this kind being regularly expressed by the more belligerent anti-Semitic propagandists in every country.

Did Hitler and his chief lieutenants dream at that time of wiping the Jewish people from the face of the earth? There is not the slightest evidence of it. No document or testimony then current or since discovered gives any indication of such intentions. My own opinion leans very much to the negative. From an ideological point of view the Nazi theodicy demanded the existence of an Enemy, that *Gegenreich* (Anti-Reich) which polarized so well the cherished national aggressiveness. "If the Jew did not exist, we should have to invent him," the aphorism cited by Rauschning (1) was no idle

(1) Hermann Rauschning, former National Socialist head of the Danzig government, is a rare and almost unique example of a very high Nazi dignitary breaking with the regime as early as 1935. A refugee abroad—all the while

flash of wit. For a long time the Jews would be needed for the building of the Third Reich. From the practical point of view, what purpose would be served by extermination? It was so much more economical to confine the Jews to some area and put them to the hardest labor. Thus the Nazis would hold valuable hostages. "The Jews are Germany's best safeguard," Hitler told Rauschning. "They will be Germany's benefactors!" [3] And Alfred Rosenberg was to speak, at the Nuremberg trial, of the "chivalrous" solution of the Jewish question.

At the time of which we speak, physical extermination certainly was not being considered in the party inner circle. However, everybody was free to think his own thoughts. If the primitive psychopath, Julius Streicher, was only dreaming of blood and massacres, another cold fanatic, Reinhard Heydrich, Chief of Police, was perhaps already giving the matter serious thought. Certainly, the testimony of Dieter Wisliceny (2) would seem to indicate that he was. Among all the Nazi leaders, Streicher and Heydrich were apparently the only ones whose thoughts were already turned in the direction of extermination.

To say that the Nazis arrived at genocide as it were in spite of themselves, carried away by the demons they had unleashed, is only further to accentuate the problem. When the accused at Nuremberg, faced with the facts, swore "they had known nothing about it," for the most part they lied. But when they cried out, "We did not want that," they were no longer lying. For such is the history of most crimes. It reminds us that the Nazis, however criminal they may have been, were only men.

BASIS AND MEANING OF NAZI ANTI-SEMITISM

The fate of the German Jews rapidly worsened. The initial series of measures had banished them from the liberal professions, civil

dodging assassination or the firing squad—he published revelations and analyses (*The Revolution of Nihilism, Hitler Told Me*) whose exceptional accuracy has been confirmed by the course of events.

(2) Dieter Wisliceny, one of the principal agents of the *Judenreferat* (Jewish section) of the Gestapo. Wisliceny was condemned to death and executed at Bratislava in 1947. In prison he wrote several memoirs that contain information of great interest.

administration, and teaching. Jewish businesses were subjected to ever stricter boycotts. Except in isolated instances, however, they suffered no physical mistreatment, and Goebbels could proclaim, *"Man krümmt den Juden kein Haar!"* ("Not a hair of the Jews has been touched.") But the subsequent measures startle the imagination; no other civilization has known anything quite like them. In the fall of 1935, the Nuremberg laws forbade sexual relations between Germans and Jews on pain of severe penalties. The first and basic law was that of September 15, 1935, "for the protection of the German blood and honor."

> Deeply conscious that the purity of German blood is the necessary condition for the continued existence of the German people, and inspired by an inflexible will to assure the existence of the German nation for all times, the Reichstag has unanimously adopted the following law, which is hereby promulgated.
>
> 1. Marriage between Jews and subjects of German or cognate blood is forbidden.
>
> 2. Extramarital relations between Jews and subjects of German or cognate blood are forbidden.
>
> 3. Jews may not employ in their houses women of German or cognate blood under forty-five years of age.
>
> 4. Jews are forbidden to fly the German national colors. They may, however, fly the Jewish colors; the exercise of this right is protected by the State.
>
> 5. Infractions of (1) are punishable by solitary confinement at hard labor. Infractions of (2) will be punished by imprisonment or solitary confinement at hard labor.

Ordinances and regulations bearing on the case of *Mischlinge,* or persons of mixed blood, followed a few weeks later.

These laws have a deep significance; they touch closely upon the essence of the Nazi phenomenon and were crucial for the success of the Third Reich. Without them the extermination of the Jews might not have been possible. We shall refer to these laws, as well as certain later ones, as "sacral" measures, in contrast to the first anti-Jewish ordinances, which may be called "profane." The latter were discriminatory devices which we often find employed against minorities, non-Jewish as well as Jewish, particularly for economic reasons. But the "sacral" measures were completely original, and indispensable to the success of Hitler's project. To understand this, a short digression is necessary.

World domination. . . . "Today Germany belongs to us, tomorrow
the whole world!" sang the young SS troopers. Hitler's ambitions
were limitless. No mere political program or national aspiration,
no matter how well their German character lent itself to his purposes, could spur the people to attain Hitler's aims. Was not the
defeat of 1918, to which he often referred, a warning to him? Did
not Adolf Hitler dream of an entirely new man, of a German youth
that was "cruel, violent, harsh, with the strength and beauty of wild
beasts"? [4] The innumerable confused aspirations, the latent dy-
namisms and personal disappointments, the national "inferiority
complex"—all these different elements and tendencies were to be
fused into a single collective force. Hitler dreamed of eradicating
Christianity and replacing it with a new cult and morality, "a strong
and heroic faith . . . in a God indistinguishable from blood and
destiny." [5] The Pan-German doctrines, race theories, and simple
superstitions that were so widespread in Germany supplied the
"Great Simplifier" with the raw material for an easy, effective dogma.
Only a faith, a religion with enthusiasm and spirit of sacrifice in it,
with "the dynamogenic influence it exercises over consciences," to
use Emile Durckheim's expression, could enable him to reach his
goal. Such a collective state of mind alone could provide Hitler with
the religiously obedient and fanatically subservient men he needed
behind him. With remarkable sureness of insight and a true understanding of the German mind, the Führer shaped such a religion.

That Nazism was primarily a religion has often been stated. To
show that this is true would lead us too far afield. Let us simply
state that the three necessary characteristics of a religion—the perception of a higher power, the submission to that power, and the
establishment of relations with it [6]—were indisputably a part of
Nazism. The racial soul, the blood and its mysterious appeal, was
the higher power realized concretely in the people (*Volk*). Submission to the Führer, its guiding light, was unconditional and
absolute. He alone could infallibly discern the commandments of
the racial soul; he alone was the high priest who knew how to
express the divine will.

The mysteries of the racial soul, blood, and *Volk* would remain
vague and indefinite abstractions so long as they were not made
tangible to the faithful by opposing to them an anti-race. an exist-

ing and clearly embodied anti-people. "If the Jew did not exist, we should have to invent him," [7] because a devil was indispensable to the Nazi religion. The Jew, principle of impurity and evil, symbolized the devil. This Manichean duality was essential. The existence of a devil assured a better understanding of the god; hatred of the unclean stimulated adoration of the divinity. The religion of the Master Race was perfectly suited for inspiring complete fear and submission in the faithful.

And so we see Nazi commentators ponderously discussing the question whether the Jews were an "anti-people" or a "pseudo-people." (3)

To make the symbol even more convincing, to make the devil more real, he had to be invested with a sacred horror. Why were the Jews chosen to represent the devil? Their silent presence "among the nations" had always assured the hatred of the mob; theirs was the role of the scapegoat upon which were vented the ill feelings aroused by economic jealousy, etc. To this feeling, already strong in Germany, Hitler added some reasons of his own. Jewish internationalism and individualism were obvious obstacles to Nazi plans. In the eyes of the neo-pagans, the chosen people symbolized the dishonored morality of the Gospels and the Judeo-Christian tradition. All this fitted so perfectly that it has been possible to speak of a true "complicity between assassin and victim." The stronger the horror, the more absolute faith and adoration would be. To stimulate faith it was necessary to couple hostility toward the Jew with the holiest images: mother and wife. Whence the appeal to sexuality (and the pornographic filth of Der Stürmer) (4). Such is the deep meaning of the sacral laws of Nuremberg and the severe penalties accompanying them.

The new ideas served their purpose and quickly penetrated the popular mind. Not only was the Jew impure, but contact with him defiled; this applied to everything that belonged or was associated with him. There was a Jewish science and a Jewish art; and there were also cafes where Jews were not wanted and streets that were forbidden to them. Extending the Nuremberg laws to Jewish-owned

(3) Gegenvolk or Scheinvolk. Cf. Weinreich, Hitler's Professors, p. 184 ff.
(4) A weekly appearing in Nuremberg; it was the personal organ of Julius Streicher, Gauleiter of Franconia.

animals, village municipal councils forbade Jews the use of the communal bull for their cows. Even their goats were untouchable for the communal billy goat, and veterinarians refused to clip their dogs. Local authorities, competing with the state, issued regulations that tried to outdo the Nuremberg laws; even private individuals entered into this rivalry. Did the wife of a party member buy from a Jew? Her husband would be expelled from the party. His explanation that it was "not he, but his wife, who had bought ten pfennigs' worth of post cards from the Jew Cohn," was judged insufficient.

The courts liberally dealt out prison terms and sentences of solitary confinement. (By 1936 Streicher considered these sentences inadequate and demanded the introduction of capital punishment; his wish was granted in 1939.) Statutory law specified that kissing or simple bodily contact constituted defilement. "Race defilement is worse than murder!" exclaimed the president of a court when commenting on his verdict. *Das Schwarze Korps,* the SS newspaper, pointed out to its members that every German had the right to arrest any Jew whom he saw in public with a German woman, "employing force if necessary. There is no need, however, to bind him except in extreme cases." The statutory law of the tribunals exonerated the German from all responsibility in case of error (5).

Certain procedures, processions, exposure in the pillory, and *autos-da-fé* of "Jewish and degenerate" books recalled medieval practices. Others, like the astonishing law of August 26, 1938, which ordered all Jews to take the name Israel, all Jewesses the name Sarah, smacked of primitive magic. (However, sorcerers and medicine men make use of the magic power of names to work cures as well as to cast evil spells; these modern sorcerers limited themselves to the latter end.) All this was accompanied by a press campaign whose violence and obscenity are difficult to convey except by quotation from the texts themselves. Julius Streicher's *Der Stürmer,* which ran to several hundred thousand copies and was aimed particularly at children, took the lead. "A skillful and amusing campaign," the Führer said. "Where does Streicher get all his ideas?" [8]

Robert Kanters expressed it well:

(5) "When Have I the Right to Arrest Somebody?" *Das Schwarze Korps,* August 7, 1938.

By the multiplication of these tabus, the division of the world into sacred and profane is always present to the mind of a German; he lives almost continually in a religious atmosphere. From the simplest to the most important act, from entering a cafe to marrying, he can do nothing without first taking care to recognize the barrier that separates the two worlds. If he makes a mistake, he will have against him not only the vague sanctions of public opinion, but also the sanctions prescribed by law and the State. A work contract, a marriage, anything can be invalidated and annulled by the courts, if it is found to contain any attack on the purity of things sacred. . . . This trait marks in striking fashion the contrast between a world without zeal and a life imbued with faith.[9]

In this way the minds and souls of millions of Germans were more or less suffused with a sense of sacred horror. If only a minority hated the Jew to the point of wanting to kill him, the majority that was not fundamentally anti-Semitic could stand by and let the Jew be killed because of the general disrespect in which he was held. "It [the majority] had learned to avert its eyes; it is the fate of the Jews, not ours."[10] An old Wehrmacht guard, apparently taken aback when a prisoner told him he was Jewish, replied, "But why do you tell me this? In your place I would rather die of shame than admit it." (6) Such were the conditions that made genocide possible. Without these psychological presuppositions the few thousand SS troops of the "Jewish section" or in the "action groups," even with the help of 300,000-400,000 Waffen-SS men, could never have assassinated 6,000,000 human beings. The connivance of the German people and the Wehrmacht was also needed.

As we shall see later, when it came to the extermination of their own, Germans were not so passive. Hitler's attempt, in the first years of the war, to eliminate the "useless mouths" of Germany, the feeble-minded and the insane, had to be abandoned in face of the strong popular opposition; for once in his career Hitler was forced to back down, and abandoned his ambitious program of "euthanasia."

THE TRAGEDY OF THE GERMAN JEWS

The Jewish communities in the countries of the Dispersion lived and developed according to their own laws. Spain served Judaism

(6) This was a personal experience of the author's during the French campaign in June 1940.

as its principal homeland during the Middle Ages, succeeded until recently by Poland. But it was in Germany that the "assimilated" Jewish minorities seemed to have sent down their deepest roots; the first Jewish settlements in the Rhine region date from the third and fourth centuries. Did the German Jews assimilate so successfully because, unlike the French and English Jews, they had never been expelled from their country? Or was it because the subtlety and sharp flavor of the Jewish intellect were a welcome contrast to the heaviness and flatness of the average German mind? Whatever the cause, their assimiliation was deep, their adherence to German interests complete, and their contribution to all phases of German life greater than anywhere else. (Indeed, assimilation sometimes led them to copy the excesses and chauvinistic arrogance of the German national character to the point where a type was created whom Jews elsewhere called "Jäcke." (7) —Doesn't Jewish wit declare that every country has the Jews it deserves?)

The contribution of the German Jews is easily shown in a few figures, facts, and symbols. Of the forty-four Nobel prizes awarded to Germans, eight went to Jews and four to half-Jews, although the percentage of Jews in the German population was only 0.8. Let us recall a few famous names: in philosophy, Hermann Cohen, Edmund Husserl, Georg Simmel; in the physical sciences, Albert Einstein, Heinrich Hertz, Fritz Haber, Georg Cantor; in medicine, Sigmund Freud (Vienna), August Wassermann, Paul Ehrlich; in music, Giacomo Meyerbeer, Felix Mendelssohn and Gustav Mahler; in literature, Heinrich Heine, Jacob Wassermann, and the Austrians Stefan Zweig and Franz Werfel; and in politics, Karl Marx, Ferdinand Lassalle, Ludwig Bamberger and Walter Rathenau. These last remind us that it is in the Jewish tradition to be attracted to critical and reforming tendencies and to make common cause with the disinherited.

The 12,000 Jewish soldiers killed in 1914–18 indicate the attachment of the German Jews to their national ideal; the suicide of Albert Ballin, famous shipowner and friend of William II, at the time of the November 9, 1918, surrender, symbolizes their patriotism. The fate of Walter Rathenau, the powerful industrialist who

(7) This appellation was particularly common in Israel, where it humorously referred to the pedantic and pretentious German Jew.

during World War I conceived and instituted the first planned economy of our times, enabling Germany to go on fighting, provides a more significant example. The negotiator of the Rapallo Treaty and Minister of Foreign Affairs fell victim to the bullets of pre-Nazi assassins in 1923. The tormented soul of this greatly gifted man sought relaxation in poetry and metaphysics. Torn by doubt, he reached the point in his attitude toward Judaism where he sighed over "the Oriental horde camped on the Brandenburg sands."

Demographically, the 525,000 German Jews were traditionally concentrated in the cities and for the most part engaged in commerce and the liberal professions. But their percentage in such occupations was far below what was attributed to them in the tireless anti-Semitic propaganda (commerce 3.3; liberal professions 2.3; the peak in law was 8.1; in medicine, 7.1). Of their total number, 29 per cent were employees, 7 per cent workers. Their religious communities in the big cities were prosperous and, like German life in general, better and more solidly organized than in other Western countries. As in these other countries, however, only a minority of Jews belonged to them. Since the beginning of the nineteenth century, conversions as well as mixed marriages had become more and more numerous. (8) These few indications reveal how heterogeneous and developed was German Judaism.

The rise of Hitlerism dismayed the German Jews to such a degree that their demographic curve, which rose by 29,000 between 1910–25, fell by 69,000 between 1925–33. Their dismay, however, did not reach the point where they emigrated in appreciable numbers. Their ties to their native land were strong and their imagination incapable of embracing the thought of genocide. Once the persecutions began, their reactions were varied and characteristic.

The first tendency was to adapt to the new conditions. The extreme expression of this was the creation of a "Union of National German Jews" (Verband National-Deutscher Juden) headed by Max Naumann. This organization hoped for nothing less than the

(8) From 1900 on, the number of conversions was more than 400 per year; 12 per cent of the marriages were mixed (S. Grayzel, *A History of the Jews*, p. 708).

reconciliation of the Nazi program and the "German future" with the aspirations of the truly "national" and German Jews. This pitiful attempt misfired. The masochism of Naumann and his friends found no favor in the eyes of the Nazis and their association was quickly dissolved. This episode tells us a great deal about the psychological drama of the German Jews; it would be quite wrong to attribute it solely to the instinct for self-preservation. Is it not, in a sense, an echo of the torment of Walter Rathenau and many others? Though they did not go to such extremes, most German Jews showed themselves incapable of understanding their new situation. They believed it to be a transitory matter, a mere misunderstanding; their showing themselves faithful through every trial would dissipate such misunderstanding. They thought it a wise move to bear public witness to their unswerving loyalty to the German fatherland. After Hitler's accession to power, they even went so far as to praise the new government for its moderation and wisdom.

"Spreading false news . . . will create difficulties and tarnish the reputation of our German homeland," the Jewish community of Berlin cabled the Chief Rabbi of Great Britain in April 1933. "We beg you to put a stop to all acts of propaganda and boycott." [11] The German Jewish Veterans Association handed the United States Ambassador, "in the patriotic interest, but also in the name of truth," an even more energetic protest aimed at American public opinion. Alfred Tietz, director of one of the biggest Berlin stores, cabled "to his friends and clients": "Complete security of life and property assured. Calm and order reign everywhere, threatened only by false and senseless propaganda."

These naive attempts at "appeasement," which the German government at first promoted, soon ceased. "German Jews must put pressure on their people abroad, otherwise they'll be sorry!" Goebbels wrote.[12] The sponsors of such ventures soon saw that it was hopeless to expect to placate the beast. Their endeavors served only to emphasize the weakness of the victims; the Nazis soon convinced themselves they needed no such "character testimonials."

It took time, however, for German Jewry to accept the fact that it was definitely and irrevocably outlawed from the national community, and that expatriation was the only remaining solution. During the first years of the Hitler regime, the emigration of German

Jews was insignificant. The only ones to leave were political figures or journalists immediately threatened by prison or the concentraion camp. Attachment to the fatherland was one reason for this general indecision, another being the enormous difficulties that emigration presented. Not only had it already become difficult to obtain a visa for a foreign country, but an emigrant found himself stripped of nine-tenths of his possessions by a complex series of financial regulations. (9) Condemned by his country and robbed of his fortune, the unfortunate German Jewish emigrant also suffered from the general hostility shown abroad to holders of German passports ornamented with the swastika. Only Palestine received the emigrants with open arms; 40 per cent of them settled in that tiny country. The fate of the emigrés was so precarious that many of them dreamed of returning to Germany; but after the promulgation of a regulation dated March 1935, those who returned were immediately interned in a concentration camp. Twenty-five thousand German Jews left Germany in the first half of 1933; 50,000 between July 1, 1933, and September 15, 1935; and 100,000 during the following two years.

Those who remained were the first European Jews to travel the painful road of forced isolation and withdrawal into themselves which in all countries preceded the deportations. There was the further circumstance that they received hardly any moral consolation or material aid from their fellow citizens, and in no way benefited from that solidarity which elsewhere would unite them in common opposition to the oppressor. The essentially moral drama of the German Jew thus has a particularly heart-rending quality.

Take, for example, the Jew who directed an athletic club in a little Würtemberg city. In August 1933, he committed suicide, leaving the following note:

My friends! Here is my last farewell!
A German Jew cannot go on living knowing that the movement from which national Germany expects its salvation considers him a traitor. I leave without any feelings of hatred. I have only one burning desire: that reason may return.

(9) On all capital transferred abroad after 1931, the German treasury levied an "exodus tax" of 25 per cent. The other 75 per cent could not be transferred except in the form of the "blocked mark" (*Sperrmark*), whose exchange value was only about one-sixth that of the free mark.

Unable to engage in any activity for which I am suited, I am trying
to arouse my Christian friends by my suicide. May this make you see
what the German Jews are going through. How I would have preferred to give my life for my country! Do not mourn for me; try
rather to make others understand and help the truth to win out.
In this way you will honor me.

Your Fritz.

"Fritz Rosenfelder is sensible; he hangs himself!" wrote the local
paper. "We are content, and see no objection to all those like him
saying goodbye to us in the very same way." [13]

German Jews committed suicide by the hundreds; their despair
is best indicated by the paradoxical inversion of their "demographic
pyramid" due to a precipitous drop in the birth rate. In 1933 the
Jews counted as many old people over sixty as children under fifteen; in 1939 the percentage of old people was four times that of
children.

The few privileges still reserved to Jewish veterans were renounced by the best among them. They followed the example of
an illustrious holder of the Iron Cross, Professor James Franck,
Nobel Prize Winner for Physics, who wrote to the rector of the
University of Göttingen as early as April 1933:

> I have asked the Minister to relieve me of my functions. I shall try
> to pursue my scientific research in Germany. We Germans of Jewish
> origin are treated like enemies of the fatherland. They demand that
> our children grow up knowing that they never will be Germans.
> Veterans will be permitted to continue serving the State. I refuse to
> benefit from this favor, although I understand the point of view of
> those who believe it their duty to persevere in their tasks.[14]

However, the few exceptions made in favor of veterans or those
who had assumed their duties before 1914 were abolished after
September 1937.

An almost incalculable number of new measures, covering all
aspects of professional or private activity, made the fate of the
German Jews worse month by month. Their complete enumeration
here would be impossible as well as tedious. Jews were barred from
the benefits of the social security laws and unemployment insurance,
and subjected to special taxes and levies. The ingenuity of the Nazis
knew no bounds, extending even to classifying unwed Jewish

mothers as persons living alone, in order to make them subject to the tax on bachelors. Harassed by a stubborn boycott, Jewish businesses were increasingly jeopardized; they lived on their savings or off the tiny percentage allowed them from the sale price of their businesses. A growing number were reduced to living from subsidies provided by Jewish philanthropic agencies; by March 1937, 60,000 of the 150,000 Jews remaining in Berlin had already reached this stage. The almost insignificant emigration of the first years began to swell despite all difficulties.

German Jews were thus taught that no renunciation, no platitude, no heroism was of any help, and that they would have to abandon once and for all their dream of remaining German, in spite of, and against, everything. Man, however, needs something spiritual to belong to, a group and a country of his own. The best of the German Jews followed the advice ironically given them by the Nazis ("The Jews . . . may fly the Jewish colors"—paragraph 4 of the first Nuremberg law), and resolutely turned to Judaism. There was a renewal of Jewish life in Hitler Germany; the young became enthusiastic Zionists, studied Hebrew, and prepared to leave for Palestine; older people returned to the synagogue or immersed themselves in books, seeking the consolation of the mind. Thus animated by an often intense spiritual life, there arose the first of those "closed societies" which seemed to form an inevitable stage between the past life and extermination.

At this time the German Jews were still free to move about; until the end of 1938 (if they had been politically neutral) they were rarely molested. The avalanche of measures that barred them from the life of the country was promulgated by the Ministry of Justice and executed by the Ministry of the Interior. Goering's Gestapo intervened only in "political" cases; this, however, was given the broadest possible interpretation, even embracing the cases of emigrants returning to Germany. Himmler was still only the head of the nascent SS; it was not until the end of 1936 that a "Department for Jewish Questions" was set up side by side with the Security Department of the SS (*Sicherheitsdienst,* or SD). In the past these matters had come under the jurisdiction of the department concerned with the "Free Masons." It was apparently an insignificant occurrence when the study of Zionist and Palestinian questions was confided to a young SS junior officer named Adolf Eichmann at the beginning of 1937. The principal aim of the new department was the study of all the questions involved in preparing for a mass emigration of the Jews.

THE CRUCIAL MONTH OF NOVEMBER 1938

After the Anschluss with Austria (March 1938), anti-Jewish measures, both "profane" and "sacral," were enacted at an increased tempo. Needless to say, the first thing done was to bring Austria into line regarding anti-Jewish legislation; this was carried out with all the more brutality as the ground covered in Germany over five years had to be made up in a few weeks. Among these new measures was one requiring the registration of Jewish-owned property, a prelude to mass confiscations (April 26, 1938). Others included the requirement that every Jew or Jewess use the name of Israel or Sarah (August 18, 1938), the abolition of the last exceptions favoring lawyer veterans (September 27, 1938), and finally the requirement that passports and identity papers be stamped with the letter "J" (October 7, 1938). One week later, Goering declared at an informal gathering that the time had come to settle the Jewish question. The Jews would have to disappear from the economy and leave Germany. But of course the emigrants would not be permitted to take any currency with them. "If necessary, we will organize ghettos in the big cities." [15]

The very day on which the Hitler government ordered the stamping of Jewish passports, the Polish government prescribed another kind of stamp for its nationals living abroad. Lacking this special stamp placed on their passports by the consulates, such nationals were to lose their Polish nationality. But the Polish consulates had been instructed not to renew the passports of Jews who had been abroad for more than five years. More than 20,000 Polish Jews who had lived in Germany for many years thus found themselves stateless overnight. (This time, as the Gestapo ironically stressed, it was at the suggestion of the Reich's Ministry of Foreign Affairs that· Himmler ordered the immediate arrest and expulsion of all Polish Jews residing in Germany.) In the city of Vienna alone, 3,135 Jews were arrested and sent to Poland.

But the Warsaw government refused to let them enter Polish territory. The first displaced persons of our time, thousands of Jewish men, women, and children, had to camp for long weeks in a no man's land along the border in the region of Zbonszyn, in freezing weather, while waiting for the governments to agree on their fate.

Among these unfortunates was the Grynspan family, from Hanover, whose son, young Herschel Grynspan, lived with his uncle in Paris. This young seventeen-year-old was pious, a bit of a mystic, somewhat *exalté*. On November 6, he bought a revolver and learned how to use it. Then he went to the German Embassy in Paris and shot, as an expiatory victim, the diplomat who received him, the embassy counsellor, Ernst vom Rath; vom Rath died of his wounds two days later.

Such was the rapid sequence of events that is called "the Grynspan Affair"; it came so opportunely for the Nazis that it has been supposed that an *agent provocateur* armed Grynspan. In Germany, the Party was preparing to celebrate November 9, the anniversary of the first Hitler "putsch" at Munich in 1923. The celebrations turned into "spontaneous" manifestations of vengeance. The following lines are taken from a very curious Nazi report prepared three months afterwards by the Party's supreme judge, Major Walter Buch,[16] which describes the genesis of the demonstrations.

> On the evening of November 9, 1938, Comrade Goebbels notified the party chiefs, gathered in friendly reunion at the old Munich city hall, that anti-Jewish demonstrations had occurred in the provinces of Hesse and Magdeburg. Some Jewish stores had been destroyed and synagogues burned. He so informed the Führer, who decided that such demonstrations did not have to be prepared or organized by the party since they were spontaneous, but there was no reason to oppose them.
> The oral instructions of the Minister of Propaganda were certainly interpreted by all the chiefs present to mean that the party did not wish to appear publicly as instigator of the demonstrations, but that it did want them organized and carried out. It is in this sense that these instructions were immediately telephoned to their respective provinces (*Gauen*) by most of the comrades present.

"On November 10, 1938, at 1:20, the attached telegram from the *Geheime Staatspolizei* (Gestapo) was sent to all police bureaus," the report continues. This telegram, signed by Heydrich, stated that anti-Jewish demonstrations "were to be expected" to take place during the night of November 9-10. It advised the police commissioners to get in touch "with the political authority of their province" and to see to it that German life and property were not threatened, that Jewish stores and apartments were not plundered during the attacks, and that foreigners were not molested even if they were Jews. Within these limits, the commissioners were not to oppose the manifestations in any way, confining themselves to surveillance. "As soon as the night's events make police inspectors available, there will be an opportunity to arrest as many Jews, preferably those who are rich, as the jails can hold. Male Jews who are in good health, and not too old, are to be arrested first. After the arrests, immediate contact is to be made with the nearest concentration camps for the speedy jailing of the Jews."

The pogroms that immediately started had nothing in common with the sadistic eruptions and isolated brutalities of the preceding years. To the profane or sacral measures were now added physical ones, carried out in wholesale fashion. The next day Heydrich submitted an accounting to Goering.

> At this time, the extent to which Jewish stores and apartments were sacked cannot yet be established. The figures already known are: 815 stores demolished, 29 warehouses burned, 171 houses set on fire; this represents only a part of the havoc. The great majority of the reports that have reached us are limited to such generalizations as "destruction of numerous stores" or "destruction of the majority of stores." One hundred ninety-one synagogues have been set on fire and 76 completely destroyed; 20,000 Jews have been arrested, along with 7 Aryans and 3 foreigners; 36 Jews have been assassinated, 36 seriously wounded.[17]

The following day, at a conference called by Goering, Heydrich was already talking of 7,500 stores destroyed. The Buchenwald archives show that between November 10-13, 10,454 Jews were received in this camp alone, where they were treated with the customary sadistic refinements. They were made to pass the night in the open winter air, beaten and tortured all day long, while a loud speaker shouted: "Any Jew who wants to hang himself is asked please to put a piece of paper with his number in his mouth, so that we may know who he is."

This orgy of destruction did not unduly alarm the German people, who were witnesses to it from beginning to end. It occurred in the midst of an almost general indifference. "The reaction of the German people to the pogroms of the fall of 1938 shows how far Hitler has led them in five years and how much he has degraded them," wrote Rauschning in 1939.[18] And Karl Jaspers observed: "In November 1938 when the synagogues were burning and the Jews were deported for the first time . . . the generals were present; in every city the commandant could have intervened. . . . They did nothing." [19]

The night of November 9-10 was a turning point. For the German Jews it meant an extraordinary aggravation of their fate; if extermination was still far from the minds of the Nazi chiefs, they could at least convince themselves that every brutality and excess was henceforth permitted. On the "mental attitudes" which the Nazis instilled in their men, the previously cited report of Walter Buch contains highly instructive details.

Since assassination and rape were not included in the instructions cabled by the Gestapo, a number of civil magistrates wished to open investigations; the party cut them short by referring all such cases to its extraordinary jurisdiction, of which Buch was chief justice. Of the 91 cases investigated, Buch examined 16.[20] In 13 he decided not to continue the investigation. These involved murder. The men, he argued, may have misinterpreted their orders; moreover, *they may have had to conquer the greatest mental inhibitions in order to do what they did.* . . . They should be honored for having overcome them. Was not the Sixth Commandment, "Thou shalt not kill," an obstacle to the development of a "hard, violent, and cruel" youth?

Did this mean that all "mental inhibitions" were to be suppressed? Not at all. In cases 1 and 3, rape was involved. Buch decided that the guilty persons should be referred to ordinary justice; they had been expelled from the Party. If in other times and places a Cossack or soldier raped or defiled a Jewess during a pogrom, he might be prosecuted. But here the Nazis prosecuted their own people for having dishonored *themselves* with the crime of racial defilement; *their acts were based on egoistic or criminal motives.* The inhibition, the tabu, had to be unbreakable.

In this way they sought to attain total obedience. We see a systematic attempt to reverse "mental attitudes" completely. This was a new cult, a disconcerting morality, calling to mind the bloody practices and hieratic hecatombs of the Aztecs. . . . How to punish men who only did what the party demanded? "Each man carried out not the apparent will of the party leadership, but its clearly perceived will, although confusedly expressed. He cannot be punished for that," very judiciously concluded the remarkable report of the Parteirichter (party judge) Walter Buch.

The Nazis now had to take stock and, on November 12, Goering called a council of ministers for that purpose in the sumptuous new building of the Ministry of Aviation. The tone of the meeting was highly characteristic. I quote rather lengthy extracts from the typed minutes, which read like a play (they bring *Ubu-roi* (10) irresistibly to mind, so true is it that nature often imitates art). Most of the dignitaries of Nazism were present: Goering (presiding), Goebbels, Frick (Interior), Heydrich, Dalüge (police), Funk (Economics), Schwerin-Krosigk (Finances). And if the Führer was absent, his spirit hovered over the assembly, as Goering's first words show.

> *Goering:* Gentlemen, today's meeting is of decisive importance. I have received a letter which Bormann sent me by order of the Führer, asking that the Jewish question be treated in its entirety and settled in some way. Yesterday the Führer telephoned me to point out again that decisive measures must be undertaken in a coordinated manner.
>
> What we have here is above all a great economic problem, and it will be necessary at this point to apply the lever.

The first part of the conference concerned the rapid and complete dispossession of the Jews from their businesses, factories, and real estate. Then the question arose as to how the damage caused by recent events would be paid for, how to keep the Jews from becoming insurance beneficiaries, especially where a foreign company was involved. This required the summoning of an insurance expert. While awaiting his arrival, Goebbels spoke.

> *Goebbels:* In almost every German city synagogues have been burned. The land on which they stood can be used in many different

(10) The farce by Alfred Jarry, produced in Paris in 1896.

ways; some cities want to convert the land into parks; others want to build on it.

Goering: How many synagogues were actually set afire?

Heydrich: One hundred and one synagogues were burned, 76 demolished; 7,500 stores were destroyed.

Goebbels: I believe this gives us an opportunity to dissolve the synagogues. All those not completely intact must be demolished by the Jews themselves. The Jews must pay for it. The Berlin Jews are ready to do so. The synagogues burned in Berlin will be pulled down by the Jews. . . . This should become the guiding line for the entire Reich. . . .

Moreover, I think it necessary to issue an ordinance forbidding Jews to attend German theaters, movies, and circuses. I think, the way the theater situation is nowadays, we can afford it. The theaters are crowded anyhow; you can scarcely find a seat. I am of the opinion that it is not possible to allow Jews to sit beside Germans. Later on we could perhaps consider putting one or two movies at their disposition, where they would show Jewish films.

Furthermore, they must be removed from public view where their presence is provocative. For example, it is still possible today for a Jew to use the same sleeping car compartment as a German. The Minister of Communications should publish an ordinance introducing compartments for Jews, to be used only when all Germans are seated, and without the Jews being able to mix with the Germans. If there aren't enough seats, they must remain standing outside in the corridor.

Goering: I find it more sensible to give them a special section.

Goebbels: Not when the train is crowded.

Goering: Just a minute. There will be only one Jewish car. If it is full, the other Jews must stay at home.

Goebbels: And suppose—let's take the Munich express, for example—suppose there are not enough Jews; there are two Jews on the train, and the other cars are crowded. These two Jews, then, have a car to themselves. We should therefore announce that Jews cannot sit until all Germans are seated.

Goering: I wouldn't go to the trouble to announce it, but I'd give the Jews a car or a section to themselves. If the train is really full, as you say, believe me, I don't need a law. The Jew will be thrown out, even if he has to sit by himself in the toilet for the whole trip.

Goebbels: . . . Another ordinance should forbid Jews to visit German spas, beaches, and summer resorts. . . . I wonder if it isn't necessary to keep Jews out of German parks. Nowadays, packs of Jews stroll through the Grunewald! (11) It is a constant provocation; we

(11) A park located west of Berlin.

constantly have incidents. What the Jews do is so exasperating that there are constant brawls.

Goering: Well, we'll set aside a certain part of the park for the Jews. Alpers will take care of putting animals there that look like Jews; the stag has just the hooked nose for it.

Goebbels: Next, Jews must not sit around in German gardens. In this connection, I want to point out the whispering campaign by Jewish women in the squares of the Fehrbelliner Platz. There are Jews who don't look much like Jews. They sit down next to German mothers and German children and begin to gripe and stink up the air.

Goering: They don't admit that they are Jews.

Goebbels: That's particularly dangerous. I think it necessary to restrict the Jews to certain squares—certainly not the nicest ones—and to say that the Jews have the right to sit on these benches. They will be specially marked: "For Jews Only." Otherwise, there's no place for them in German squares.

Finally, we must consider the following: There are actually still cases of Jewish children attending German schools. I think this is impossible. It is out of the question for my boy to sit beside a Jew in a German high school while he is being taught German history. It is absolutely necessary to bar Jews from German schools. Let them take care of raising their children in their own community.

Goering: I request permission to bring in Herr Hilgard, who represents the insurance companies. He is waiting outside. When we have finished with him, he can leave and we shall pick up our discussion.

Hilgard entered. Goering told him that since the German people had caused important material damage in their justifiable anger, it was feared that this damage might be borne in part by the insurance companies, that is, by a section of the German community. It would be easy to issue an ordinance according to which the companies would not be obliged to pay for such damage; but the "burning" question was how to avoid letting precious currency escape if these companies had been reinsured abroad.

There followed a long technical discussion. It appeared that the cases were very different, that in many of them the "Aryan" building had been destroyed or damaged along with the "Jewish" business within it, with only the Jew insured. Hilgard stated that the number of broken windows equaled two years of Belgian production (Belgium was the sole supplier of plate glass for windows); we also find a few details on the pillage.

Hilgard: The most important case is that of the Margraf jewelry shop, located at Unter den Linden. This store is covered for all kinds of damage. Damage of 1.7 million marks has been declared, the store having been completely pillaged.

Goering: Dalüge and Heydrich, you must recover all those jewels for me. Get some mass round-ups going!

Dalüge: They have already been ordered and there will be continual check-ups. Yesterday afternoon they jailed 150 people. . . .

Heydrich: We have already arrested hundreds of pillagers and are in the process of recovering the stolen objects.

Goering: And the jewels?

Heydrich: It is difficult to say. Some were thrown into the street and picked up. The same with the furs. The crowd fell upon the sables and other things; they are hard to recover. Often children filled their pockets, it was a game. In the future, we should not allow the Hitler Youth to be called on without the Party's knowing it.

There followed an enumeration of the losses. "I would rather you had slaughtered 200 Jews than destroyed such valuable property," Goering sighed. A solution was easily found for the insurance: the companies would pay only in cases where Aryans suffered damage.

Goering: The Jew declares the damage. He receives the insurance, but it is confiscated. The end result is that the insurance companies make a profit, since they do not have to settle certain accounts. Herr Hilgard, you have a right to smirk!

Hilgard: I see no reason to do so. Not having to pay a damage does not constitute a profit.

Goering: Please! If you have a legal obligation to pay five million, and if an angel appears before you in my rather corpulent form and says: "You can keep one million"—by God, isn't that a profit? . . . You're smirking all over. You have made a rebbes. (12)

After Hilgard left the conference, discussion continued on the problems of "Aryanization" of buildings, industrial concerns, stocks, registered or bearer securities. But Heydrich reminded them that these economic measures did not solve the essential problem.

Heydrich: Despite the expulsion of the Jews from the economy, the essential problem still remains one of forcing the Jews to leave Germany. May I make a few suggestions?

(12) Berlin slang for "profit." This word goes back, curiously enough, to the Hebrew *ribbit* ("interest").

We have organized a center for Jewish emigration at Vienna, thanks to which we have been able to evacuate 50,000 Jews from Austria, while in the old Reich only 19,000 Jews could be expelled during the same period.

Goering: Chiefly because you collaborated with the local leaders of the "green frontier." (13) That's the essential thing.

Heydrich: They were minimum figures, Marshal. Clandestinely. . . .

Goering: The story has made the rounds of the world press. On the first night the Jews were expelled into Czechoslovakia. The next morning the Czechs sent them off to Hungary. From there they went back again to Germany and Czechoslovakia. They went back and forth. Finally they landed on an old flat-bottomed ship on the Danube. As soon as they landed, they were driven out.

Heydrich: There were barely 100 Jews involved in that. . . . At least 45,000 have been evacuated legally.

Goering: How was that possible?

Heydrich: We did that by demanding that rich Jews who wish to emigrate pay us certain sums which we collected from the Jewish community. This money has made it possible for us to expel a certain number of poor Jews. The problem was not to make the rich Jews leave, but to evacuate the Jewish mob.

Goering: What are you thinking of, my children? It's no use forcing hundreds of thousands of poor Jews to leave if it costs too much. . . .

All the ministers agreed: The evacuation of the Jews would be a long-drawn-out affair. Meanwhile, it was necessary to isolate the Jews completely.

Heydrich: I should like to make some suggestions about isolating them, purely of a police nature, but important for their psychological effect on public opinion. For example, identifying Jews; every Jew will have to wear a special badge! It is a measure that will facilitate many others, particularly in our relations with foreign Jews.

Goering: A uniform!

Heydrich: A badge! . . . In this way we can avoid trouble that arises when foreign Jews are mistaken for local Jews.

. . . As for the question of ghettos. From the police point of view, I think it impracticable to set up a ghetto in the form of a special quarter for the Jews. Such a ghetto, where all Jewry would be collected, would be impossible to supervise. It would be the den of criminals, an epidemic center, etc. Today the German population is forcing the Jews to concentrate in designated houses, for we do not

(13) Slang expression for illegal passage over the border.

want to live in the same house with a Jew. The surveillance of Jews by the vigilant eye of the whole population is better than their concentration by the thousands in special quarters where I cannot have their daily life watched by uniformed civilians.

Goering: And special cities?

Heydrich: If I put them in isolated cities, we will still have the danger of crime centers. . . .

The ministers discussed the question of ghettos at length. How would the Jews live? How would they feed themselves? Would the stores be kept by Jews—but it had been decided to drive them from business once and for all—or by Germans, a course which would have the disadvantage of multiplying undesirable contacts? The question remained open. Heydrich continued:

. . . I propose furthermore that the Jews be deprived of all personal privileges, such as drivers' licenses; forbidden to own automobiles, for a Jew does not have the right to menace Aryan lives; to be restricted in their places of residence . . . likewise in the case of hospitals. A Jew can't lie in the same hospital with Aryans.

Goering: But that must be done step by step.

Heydrich: The same goes for public transportation.

Goering: Aren't there any Jewish hospitals and sanatoria? (*Cries:* Yes, there are!) All these things must be investigated thoroughly. They must be done away with one after another.

Heydrich: I only wanted to ask for an agreement in principle so that we can begin to arrange these matters.

Goering: One more question, gentlemen. What would you say if I proclaimed today that a fine of one billion would be imposed on the Jews as a contribution?

Burckel: The Viennese would be very pleased.

Goebbels: I wonder if the Jews won't be able to escape by putting money aside. . . . ?

The ministers discussed the best way to make this last impossible, as well as technical procedures for levying the fine.

Goering: I would like to put it as follows: As punishment for their infamous crimes, etc., the German Jews, as a collectivity will have levied on them a contribution of one billion. That is going to hit home. The pigs won't commit a second murder so quickly. I must say it again: I shouldn't care to be a Jew in Germany!

Von Krosigk: That is why I wanted to emphasize what Herr Hey-

drich said at the beginning. We must do everything to send the Jews
abroad, with the help of an agreement on our exports. The important
thing is not to keep their proletariat at home. That would be a terrible
burden. (*Frick:* And a danger!) I can imagine that the prospect of
being driven into ghettos will not be a very pleasant one. The goal
must then be, as Heydrich said: "Clear out what we can!"

Goering: The second point is this: If the Reich should later in some
foreseeable future become involved in a war, it goes without saying
that we in Germany shall have to consider settling our accounts in a
big way with the Jews. Furthermore, the Führer is now finally going
to take an offensive tack with the powers that are raising the Jewish
question so as to arrive at a solution of the Madagascar question.
He explained it to me on November 9. That's the only way to do it.
He wants to say to the other countries: "Why are you always talking
about the Jews? Take them!" We can also make another proposal:
The rich Jews can buy a vast territory for their co-religionists in North
America, in Canada, or elsewhere. . . .[21]

Gentlemen, I thank you.

(Meeting ended at 2:40)

Such were the ideas on the Jewish question exchanged by the
high dignitaries of the Third Reich in the month of November
1938.

THE LAST YEAR OF PEACE

The Jewish emigration center of which Heydrich spoke so highly
had been set up in Vienna in April 1938. Immediately after the
Anschluss, Heydrich had gone to Austria to organize the Gestapo
bureaus. Among the civil servants who accompanied him as a
"specialist on Jewish questions" was the Obersturmführer (SS Lieutenant) Adolf Eichmann, who has already been mentioned. Eichmann suggested to Heydrich the idea of uniting in a single Gestapo department the numerous administrative offices concerned
with emigration (police, interior, finance). In this way emigration
would be speeded up. Heydrich accepted Eichmann's suggestion
and put him in charge of the new "central bureau for emigration";
we have seen how he praised himself for the creation of the new
organization. In January 1939, a "Central Reich Bureau for Jewish
Emigration" was organized for all of Germany on the Viennese
model; it was always under Heydrich's thumb, though its actual
direction was confided to Eichmann. In March 1939, Eichmann was

sent to Prague to head the "Central Bureau for the Jewish Question in Bohemia and Moravia." His jurisdiction thus grew progressively larger.

The German Jews numbered 350,000 in September 1937. In the course of the next two years, nearly 115,000 departures took place. But the annexation of Austria and the Sudeten raised the total number of Jews within the limits of the Third Reich to more than 350,-000.

The wishes of the Jews, ruined, abased, and marked for destruction as they were, played only a negligible role in their migrations at this time. Emigration of course had now become their supreme hope, but it depended on two factors: the good will of other countries in letting them in, and the good will of Germany in letting them out.

Surely one of the most characteristic phenomena of our time is the denial of asylum to those persecuted for religious or political reasons. History has known nothing like it. The Jews driven from Spain found shelter in the Sultan's empire and in the Netherlands Republic; the Huguenots fleeing France settled in the colonies of the New World, or in the Prussian Kingdom; but "displaced persons" are an essentially modern phenomenon. Countries did not grant visas to poverty-stricken German Jews, or gave them only with extreme reluctance. In response to public opinion and following various interventions, President Franklin D. Roosevelt of the United States called an international conference on July 6, 1938, at Evian, to do something about this problem. But the only result of the Evian conference was the creation of a permanent intergovernmental committee with headquarters in London; its representatives regularly went to Berlin to arrange for the financing of emigration through property requisitioned from the Jews. But these attempts failed because the powers of the intergovernmental committee were very limited, and the nations making it up, divided in their counsels and their minds, did not really know what they wanted.

The Nazis knew very well what they wanted. First of all, as certain remarks of Goering at the November 12 conference show us, there was the financial consideration: how to prevent the departure of the Jews from causing "a weakening of the German economic body." For this reason they were not permitted to take out any property or money. The only form of financing that suited the Nazis was suggested by the fertile brain of Hjalmar Schacht: the freeing of a certain percentage of funds, which would leave Germany in the form of German export goods. In this way Germany would not lose its currency and would open new trade outlets for itself. But the Western states refused to agree to this dumping of German goods on their markets. Quite paradoxically, the only agreement of this kind that Germany was able to conclude was with the Jewish Agency for Palestine. (How true it is that open adversaries often find it easier to agree!) (14)

This agreement, called *Haavara*, was severely criticized in Palestine, and was even boycotted by part of the population. It was also much discussed in Germany; a note from the Ministry of Foreign Affairs, dated March 10, 1938, reveals that the bureaus of the Ministry had been working for more than a year toward a denunciation of the treaty. The reasons, indicated in the note of March 10, 1938, are as follows:

1. The *Haavara* accord is, in view of the strict foreign exchange legislation, the only possibility open to German Jews for transferring their capital abroad.
2. The influx into Palestine of German capital in Jewish hands will facilitate the building up of a Jewish state, which runs counter to German interests; for this state, instead of absorbing world Jewry, will someday bring about a considerable increase in world Jewry's political power (as is the case with the Vatican State vis-a-vis political Catholicism). (A similar concept was formulated by the Führer in *Mein Kampf*).
3. Germany is not interested in facilitating the emigration of rich Jews who take their capital with them. Germany is far more interested in a *mass* Jewish emigration.[22]

We glimpse here the second reason why emigration ultimately failed, why the all-powerful Führer paid scant attention to the projected exodus. It was not a simple financial question. The mere departure of the German Jews, whatever Heydrich might think, could not satisfy the enormous potential of hatred accumulated by the

(14) Remember that Jewish immigration to Palestine was regulated by England. The number of "workers" certificates was set at 1,500 per month, while the number of certificates for "capitalists" (£1,000) was unlimited.

Nazis. This potential would have had to find other channels if all the German Jews had been allowed to emigrate. As another report of the Ministry of Foreign Affairs stated in January 1939,[23] "The Jewish question will not be solved for Germany even when the last Jew has left German soil."

This same report indicated in its last paragraphs why the departure of the poor Jews was an essential goal:

> Experience will teach the populations [of other countries] what the Jewish danger means. The poorer the Jewish immigrant, the heavier he will burden the country of immigration, and the more vigorously this country will react in a way favorable to German interests.
>
> The goal of German action is a future international solution of the Jewish question that will not be inspired by false pity for the "persecuted religious minority," but dictated by the mature comprehension of all nations of the danger Judaism represents for the national existence of peoples.

What this future solution would be, the reader will discover in the next chapter. Meanwhile the report announced with satisfaction the results already attained. "A wave of anti-Semitism can be seen in all countries toward which the tide of Jewish emigration is directed. It is the task of German foreign policy to heighten this wave." An enumeration followed:

> Reports from the United States speak of numerous anti-Semitic manifestations by the population. It is significant that the number of listeners to the well-known anti-Semitic "radio-priest" Coughlin has reached twenty million. The Montevideo legation reported last December 12 that there has been a steady influx of Jewish immigrants over the past month. There is no doubt that anti-Semitism is increasing.

The situation in Greece, France, the Netherlands, and Norway was then complacently reviewed. "These examples can easily be multiplied with the aid of other diplomatic reports." Here we have a second essential characteristic of the policy followed by the Nazis: to facilitate the exodus of Jews only when it benefited the international schemes of the Nazis. The gains that Hitlerian policy ingeniously derived from "the Jewish question" were decidedly many and varied.

Now the different measures envisaged by Goering, Goebbels, and Heydrich on November 12, 1938, followed at a dizzy pace. First, the economic measures: an ordinance decreeing the complete and final eviction of Jews from business, dated the same day; the imposition on the Jews of a collective fine of one billion marks, decreed on November 14. On November 15 an ordinance of the Ministry of Education banned Jewish children from German schools. This was followed by a police ordinance of November 28 dealing with "the appearance of Jews in public places." Taking a new step forward, it provided that "restrictions in space and time might be imposed on the Jews, forbidding them to frequent certain areas or to show themselves in public at certain times." The establishment of ghettos was not far off. The same theme was repeated in an ordinance by Goering on December 28: "Access to pullmans and diners is forbidden to Jews; likewise, access to restaurants and hotels frequented by members of the party." This ordinance introduced rather complex measures designed "to achieve, if possible, a concentration of Jews in specified buildings." The previously mentioned report of the Ministry of Foreign Affairs states:

> The reprisals following the assassination of Counsellor of Legation vom Rath have so well accelerated the process that Jewish retail trade —foreign enterprises excepted—has completely disappeared. The liquidation of Jewish industry and wholesale business, as well as Jewish real estate, is so advanced that shortly it will be impossible to speak of Jewish property in Germany.

At this time the Jewish communities of Germany were supervising the clearing of synagogue ruins; almost everywhere the sites were transformed at Jewish expense into squares "for Aryans," in accordance with Goebbels' wish. A few months later, on the eve of the war, a basic law regulated the status of Jews. It decreed the establishment of a "Union of Jews of the Reich" to which all German Jews or stateless persons had to belong, and on which devolved the responsibility for the education of Jewish children, social security, and the problems of emigration (Law of July 4, 1939). The Union was placed under the surveillance of the Ministry of the Interior and the Police; it served as a model for similar institutions subsequently created in all the occupied countries. Ghettoization thus advanced rapidly.

Such was the situation of the German Jews on the eve of World War II. Repeating Goering's veiled threats of a "big accounting," the Führer exclaimed in 1939, in the course of his annual January 30 speech:

Europe will not find peace until the Jewish problem has been settled. An accord may be reached on this question between nations that otherwise would not so easily arrive at an understanding. There still exists sufficient available land on this globe. . . . On this day, which will remain a memorable one for other than German people, I should like to add the following: Often in my life, ever since I began my struggle for power, I have been a prophet, and I have often been ridiculed, especially by the Jewish people. I think that the resounding laughter of the German Jews has since stuck in their throats.

Today I am going to play the prophet again. If international Jewry should succeed, in Europe or elsewhere, in precipitating nations into a world war, the result will not be the bolshevization of Europe and a victory for Judaism, but the extermination in Europe of the Jewish race.

CHAPTER TWO

Persecution Unleashed

IT WOULD CERTAINLY BE A MISTAKE to regard Hitler's "prophecies" as being based on an exact plan which the Nazis had already drawn up. Nothing was further from his nature; yet the speech of January 30, 1939, indicates the two alternative "solutions" as they would present themselves to him more or less consciously: "Either Europe and the world shall bow to my wishes, and I will send all the Jews to some deserted island; or they will try to resist me, in which case the accursed race shall be annihilated." As soon as the war really became total in 1941, as soon as the Führer felt that he had definitely burned his bridges and a new Munich was impossible, the Nazis turned to the second solution. We have not yet reached this point in our narrative; during the period now under examination, each new Nazi success was followed by the hatching of a new "solution" along territorial lines. The invasion of Poland produced the idea of a Jewish reservation in the region of Lublin; the invasion of France, the "Madagascar plan." But these plans were never put into execution; meanwhile events followed one another in their implacable course.

With the outbreak of war, the situation of the Jews rapidly worsened. Now their fate was decided not by legislative acts, but by police measures, a change that marked an essential stage in the evolution of the Nazi totalitarian state. In 1936, the SS Reichsführer, Heinrich Himmler, was named chief of the German police, thus giving him control over the Gestapo. He entrusted its administration to Reinhard Heydrich, the chief of the SD. By thus placing the state police and party organization in the same hands, they were in effect merged. This state of affairs was officially confirmed after the declaration of war when, on September 27, 1939, the different

31

state and party services under Heydrich were joined in a single administrative unit, the RSHA (Reichssicherheithauptamt—Principal Service for the Security of the Reich). The RSHA was at the same time an SS administration and an essential service of the Ministry of the Interior. It included seven bureaus, of which the Gestapo was the fourth; section b of the fourth bureau (*Amt* IVb) dealt with "Jewish questions" and "evacuation problems." Section b was directed by Adolf Eichmann, who in the meantime had been promoted to SS commander (Hauptsturmführer). As we shall see, his power and freedom of action were far greater than his rank and position would suggest; he generally dealt directly with Heydrich, or even with Himmler, over the heads of his immediate superiors.

Himmler's bureaus were the principal agencies entrusted with the "Jewish question"; but in the nature of things they were never at any time the only ones. Physical measures—deportations, exterminations—were now to be taken on a large scale; but the profane and sacral measures enumerated in the preceding chapter continued to be applied in Germany and the countries that were successively occupied. In the latter, the "protectors"—the governors-general, the military, or others—were the authority that watched over the introduction and application of these measures. In the "satellite" nations, which kept a semblance of independence, this function fell to the German diplomatic representatives. "Protectors" and diplomats collaborated more or less actively with the murderous endeavors of Himmler's representatives and Eichmann's envoys. This cooperation confronts one almost everywhere with the terrible problem of the moral responsibility of large sections of the Wehrmacht, and the leading groups of German society itself, a problem which we shall return to at the end of this book. It explains why of the nineteen accused at Nuremberg, as many as sixteen were found guilty of crimes against humanity and racial persecution (only Hess and the two navy men, Raeder and Donitz, were exonerated). The same state of affairs obtained at every level of the Nazi hierarchy. By its very organization, by the principle of the "delegation of sovereignty," the regime gave full license to the repressed desires and lust for power that played a leading role in the genocidal system and the martyrdom of the Jews. Countless officials in all kinds of positions competed with one another to "solve the Jewish question"—as, for example, the young SS man (mentioned in the verdict of the Nuremberg tribunal) who on his own initiative assassinated fifty Jewish workers in his custody in September 1939; the three-year sentence imposed on him by the Wehrmacht (later suspended by amnesty) sought to excuse him by explaining that he had been driven "by a spirit of youthful adventure." [1]

PLAN FOR A "RESERVATION" AT LUBLIN

The lightning conquest of Poland in September 1939 brought the largest and most vital Jewish community in Europe under the Nazi thumb. The more than three million Jews living in Poland since the fourteenth and fifteenth centuries had created a culture which spread into all countries of the Jewish Dispersion, and had for the most part kept intact the faith of their fathers as well as the customs and traditions developed over the centuries. Now they were in the hands of the Nazis, and the latter were in a position to seek a "solution to the Jewish question" on a large scale.

THE "WILD" DEPORTATIONS

All sorts of plans were advanced. Remember that only a small part of the conquered territories had been annexed by the Reich, the largest part being formed into a "Government General," under the administration of Hans Frank. Let me cite, for curiosity's sake, a plan prepared by an expert from Alfred Rosenberg's "Foreign Policy Bureau," (*Aussenpolitisches Amt*—APA), Councillor Wetzel. Even though he foresaw the immediate expulsion of all Jews from the annexed territories into the Government General, Wetzel envisaged, for Jews in the government itself, "greater liberties than those enjoyed by the Poles in the domain of culture and economics, since many administrative and economic measures could be undertaken with their support." This unexpected gentleness is explained by "the task of the German Administration, which will be to set Poles and Jews against each other; and the Jews do not have any real strength to draw upon of the kind represented by the Polish national ideology. It is unnecessary to add," continued Wetzel, "that a sanitary state for the Jews does not interest us; it is still a valid principle for us that their multiplication must be checked by every means." [2]

But all this is quite unimportant. Of all the Nazi bureaus, Rosenberg's "ideological" laboratories were probably those which had the least influence. Even before the end of the Polish campaign, the dreaded Heydrich had personally taken charge of the matter; on September 21, 1939, he sent his instructions to the SS chiefs assigned to Poland.

Just before sending his hunting dogs into the conquered territories Heydrich had told them: "You must distinguish between the final aim, whose attainment will take considerable time, and the steps necessary for reaching it, which can be applied within a short time." The document of September 21, 1939 [3] has a short introduction referring to an SS conference held that very day in Berlin, and recalls that the measures planned at the conference "are to be considered top secret." Then Heydrich sketched the main points of his plan.

The first condition for attaining the "final goal" was the concentration of the Jews of the countryside in the cities. Insofar as possible, the rural districts were to be emptied of Jews; in the rest of the territory cities with railroad connections were to be chosen for concentration points. All Jewish communities with fewer than five hundred members were to be dissolved and incorporated into the neighboring urban concentration centers.

The second paragraph of the document gave instructions on how to create a Jewish Council in each Jewish community, "composed, insofar as possible, of outstanding personalities and the rabbis who have remained." These councils were to be "entirely responsible for the punctual execution of all present and future instructions," and in particular for concentrating the Jews in places provided for this purpose. (The latter step would be justified by charging the Jews with "active participation in guerrilla attacks and acts of pillage.")

"In general, all measures will be taken in close cooperation with the civil and military authorities," the third paragraph pointed out. However, it also listed different economic reasons for delaying the execution of these measures.

Next, the circular indicated what statistical and economic information the SS chiefs would have to collect (e.g., would it be pos-

sible to maintain certain enterprises after the evacuation of the
Jews who operated them?). First of all, it ordered a general census
of Jews, urging the "unreserved cooperation of all SD and police
forces in order to reach the goal fixed." At the end of the text was
a list of the different administrations to which a copy had been sent.

Two points in these instructions are of special interest. There was
a "final goal" that was to be achieved. What was that goal? Not
extermination yet; we are still only in 1939. A passage from the
document gives the key; in the territory "east of Cracow" the Jews
would not be touched. In other regions, they were to be grouped
near railroad stations, obviously in order to facilitate their eventual
evacuation. To what destination? Obviously, to the "region east of
Cracow." However, Heydrich was not completely sure of his ground,
for—and this is the second point to be remembered—the document
contains certain reservations and references to the "requirements
of the civil administration." (In fact, in the months to follow the
Jews were to be the prize of an incessant battle waged between
the RSHA on the one side, and the civil and military authorities,
especially the Governor General Hans Frank, on the other.)

Such was the plan for solving the Jewish question by grouping
all Jews under Nazi control in the Lublin region, on the Russian
border. This project for creating a "Jewish reservation" received
some publicity in the German press at the time. A territory was
chosen, bounded it seems (the information is incomplete and contradictory) by the Vistula, the San, and the Russian border, where
Jews were to engage in colonization work under SS supervision.
Police wheels were immediately set in motion. From Vienna, from
Prague, from Stettin, convoys of Jews were dispatched to the "reservation." The minutes of a conference called by Heydrich in January 1940 state that 78,000 Jews had already been transferred by
that date; the evacuation of 400,000 more was forecast for the following months.[4] The convoys were got together by the police without the knowledge of the civil or military authorities.

But it soon appeared that this method of "chaotic deportations"
(*wilde Deportationen*) sowed disorder and upset the economic life.
It provoked the indignation of the generals:

> These unplanned evacuations have prevented any census being
> taken and any systematic use of Jewish labor, while filling the big city

ghettos (Warsaw, especially) with a miserable proletariat. . . . The continuation of these population transfers menaces the social and economic future of the region and is an immediate danger to the health of the economy.[5]

The deportations seriously hurt the prestige of Frank, who publicly declared on March 8, 1940:

> There exists in the Government General no power that is higher, stronger in influence, and with greater authority than the Governor General. . . . This includes the SS. There is no State within the State; we are the representatives of the Führer and the Reich here.[6]

Goering was asked to arbitrate this sharpening conflict of authority. By a decision of February 12, 1940, confirmed by an order of March 23, 1940, he forbade all such "evacuations" until further notice.

But the RSHA did not consider itself beaten. It secretly continued the "chaotic deportations" of small groups. The following document is interesting for the vivid picture it gives of such a deportation, and also for the state of mind it reveals. At the beginning of 1940, the Polish Jews still thought it possible to appeal to the humanity of the Nazis. The following is an anonymous letter sent to Lammers, chief of the Chancellery of the Reich, which the latter forwarded to Himmler.

THE DEPORTATIONS CONTINUE

The following report comes from the Joint Polish-Jewish Aid Commission, which is collaborating in the Government General with the American Quakers, the delegate from the Red Cross, and the regional authorities of the administration for occupied Polish territory. It is an urgent appeal to the human conscience and to the world's sense of responsibility.

Cracow
March 14, 1940

Despite the protests of the Government General against the hasty and chaotic deportation of German Jews to eastern Poland, these evacuations have continued by order of the SS Reichsführer.

On March 12, 1940, the 160 Jews of Schneidemühl were deported in boxcars to the region of Lublin. Other convoys are expected there. The deportees had to abandon all their possessions. They were not even allowed to take suitcases. The women had to leave their purses.

Some deportees had their coats taken away, especially those who had tried to put on several to protect themselves the better against the cold. They were not able to take any money, not even the twenty zlotys granted to the Stettin deportees. Nor were they able to take either food, bedding, or dishes. They arrived at Lublin owning only what they were wearing on their backs.

The deportees have been sent to the villages of Piaski, Glusk, and Belcyca, twenty-five to thirty kilometers from Lublin. There they found the deportees from Stettin, or those of them who were still alive. Men, women, and children have had to walk to these villages on roads covered with deep snow in a temperature of −22° (centigrade). Of the 1,200 deportees from Stettin, 72 died during a march that lasted more than fourteen hours. The majority died from exposure. Among others, a mother who was carrying a three-year-old child in her arms, trying to protect him from the cold with her own clothes, was found dead, frozen in this position. The half-frozen body of a five-year-old girl was found wearing around her neck a cardboard sign with the words, "Renate Alexander, from Hemmerstein, Pomerania." This child was visiting relatives in Stettin and was included in the deportation; her mother and father stayed in Germany. Her hands and feet had to be amputated at the Lublin hospital. The bodies of the deportees who had died of exposure were piled on sleds and buried in the Jewish cemeteries at Piaski and Lublin.

The Government General (district governor Zörner) has refused all responsibility for these occurrences, and for their consequences. Marshall Goering has been informed of the situation.[7]

The deportations stopped only in the summer of 1940, after the French campaign, when the RSHA turned its attention to quite a different quarter.

Note that, as a parallel to these deportations to the east, the "Center for Jewish Emigration" was trying to expel German Jews to other destinations. Legal emigration had become almost impossible; a small stream of emigrants nevertheless continued to flow, especially from Austria, via Italy, to the lands across the sea. A few illegal convoys, established with Eichmann's help, tried to go down the Danube by boat, with Palestine as their destination, but the British government refused to let these visaless travelers enter the Jewish National Homeland. This is not the last time that we shall confront the bitter paradox of the Gestapo's pushing the Jews toward their salvation, only to have His Majesty's democratic government bar the way to the future victims of the crematory ovens.

The Fate of the Polish Jews

The actual fate of the Polish Jews, needless to say, had nothing in common with the subtle notions developed by Councillor Wetzel. The policy adopted by the Nazis could only correspond to the procedures and practice followed in Germany, but with a violence intensified by the harshness of a military and police occupation operating in a hated country. On the other hand, certain sacral measures, such as the Nuremberg laws, were never introduced into a territory which the Nazis considered to be inhabited by an inferior race. In this area, the Nazis were satisfied with measures of a more superficial symbolism, such as the obligation imposed upon the Jews to yield the sidewalks to Germans, whom, on the other hand, they were forbidden to greet. What we have here is a triangle whose three sides are the occupiers, the natives, and the Jews. The persecutions took the form generally found in the occupied countries, except for a difference in tempo. The measures were publicized in the form of ordinances of the Government General, all signed by Hans Frank.

The general policy conformed to Heydrich's program of isolating the Jews, concentrating them in the ghettos, and using them for forced labor, until circumstances permitted their "total" evacuation. It was inspired by a bestial and irrational hate, but this did not prevent it from making systematic use of the Jewish Councils created at German instigation. We have already seen them make their appearance in Germany itself in 1939, where they served as means for assuring the application and regulation of the measures decreed by the Germans.

After October 26, 1939, the obligation to perform forced labor was established in principle. The general census prescribed on October 28 permitted stamping the Jews' identity cards, and on November 23, the latter were forced to wear a white arm band "at least ten centimeters wide." (1) On December 11, changes in residence were forbidden, and a curfew was instituted between 9:00 P.M. and 5:00 A.M. The next day, another decree specified that all Jews between fourteen and sixty years of age were subject to forced

(1) In the "annexed territories" Jews were made to wear two yellow stars, "sewed on their garment, on the left side in front, on the right in back."

labor "for a period of two years, which period may be prolonged if the educational aims pursued have not been reached." The use of the railroads was forbidden to Jews on January 26, 1940; this ban was extended to all means of public transportation on February 20, 1941. A series of minor ordinances, similar to those introduced in Germany, in a few weeks' time forbade Jews to frequent public establishments and theaters, ousted them from the schools and universities, barred them from the liberal professions and all phases of economic life, deprived them of the benefits of social legislation, and "Aryanized" their businesses and industries. Jews were authorized only to engage in manual labor. Finally, a systematic policy of ghettoization was instituted. The Lodz ghetto was the first to be set up. "Since the immediate evacuation of 320,000 Jews from Lodz (2) is impossible," the provincial governor decided on December 10, 1939, "they will be concentrated in an exactly delimited section." [8] This measure, applied in February 1940, involved the moving of two hundred thousand Jews and some tens of thousands of Poles. In November 1939, the Jewish community of Warsaw had also been notified that a ghetto would be established for it. But this was only a pretext for the SS to extort a huge contribution. The threat was left hanging for several months; there were still too many reasons against establishing ghettos, which interfered considerably with commerce and industry. The Warsaw ghetto was not created until November 1940.

The Wehrmacht report previously quoted had this to say about the anti-Jewish measures in general, and ghettoization in particular:

These different ordinances . . . have destroyed the economic bases of Jewish life. Thus, according to a report of the Warsaw Rüko (*Rüstungs-Kommando*—"Command for Arms Inspection") dated January 29, 1941, this "solution of the Jewish question" has had serious consequences in Warsaw. The creation of a Jewish quarter right in the center of the city ruthlessly split up important economic units. Prohibiting the crossing of this quarter caused losses in time and material (combustible). Two thousand Aryan businesses were moved out and 4,000 Jewish concerns were moved in. The number of Jews in this

(2) Remember that Lodz was part of the "annexed territories" and was baptized "Litzmannstadt."

section is 400,000, to which were added 200,000 from outside. The bureaus of the municipal administration have issued 60,000 permits authorizing entry into the area.

Despite such complications and difficulties, of which we are giving only one example, the policy of the total expulsion of the Jews from the economic life has been continued. . . . This despite the fact that the civil administration could not deny that the Jew was practically irreplaceable in certain areas of economic life.[9]

Such considerations could only slow up the process, but they could not block it. In the large cities, the ghettos were surrounded by walls; elsewhere the ghettos were restricted sections at whose entrance signs in German announced: "Danger of Epidemic; Enter at Your Own Risk!" Early in 1941, ghettoization was an accomplished fact in Poland. On October 15, 1941, the death penalty was decreed for any Jew found outside the ghetto. Among other consequences, these restrictions on the Jews condemned them to slow death by starvation. "That we have condemned one or two million Jews to death should be said in passing; if the Jews do not die of hunger, the measures will be intensified." (Hans Frank's diary, August 24, 1942.) [10] The endless list of legal measures culminated in a few edicts decreeing that the Jew was no longer subject to the civil or penal law. He could no longer bring suit; the courts had no jurisdiction in his case. He was put outside the law; the misdemeanors or crimes he committed came only under the jurisdiction of the police and the SS. (Ordinances of December 4, 1941 and November 9, 1942.) [11]

This was only to give legal expression to a reality that had been affirmed from the first day of the invasion of Poland. The Germans —SS, ordinary soldiers, or civilians—quickly understood that they could do anything, or almost anything, to the Jews. All they had to do, as individuals, was to show some active interest in the "Jewish question." And the "activists" were legion; the intensive training had done its work. The checks placed on excesses in Germany by an administration maintaining an external appearance of public order were no longer in effect under military occupation; the very sight of a Polish Jew, in his traditional dress, provoked Nazi passions.

The individual excesses were a worse torture for the Jews than the slow pressure of the "legal measures." Facing three million dis-

armed victims were a million soldiers and policemen belonging to
a people who had been taught that they had complete freedom to
commit any act of cruelty or persecution. Every barbarity would be
considered a good deed; their exploits would be celebrated by the
press and glorified in the movies. "Polish Jews Are Put to Work,"
"Settling Accounts with the Jews of Warsaw," were the slogans.
The results were not long in appearing.

The SS set the example, though they were far from holding a
monopoly. There were certain classic procedures. Cutting off the
beards and earlocks of Jews was a widespread entertainment; it
was also the thing to be pulled about in a cart by a victim. How
many Germans sent their families photographs preserving these
deeds for posterity! Another amusement consisted of breaking into
a Jewish apartment or house and forcing young and old to undress
and dance, arm in arm, to the sound of a phonograph. Following
this with rape was optional, as one risked being tried for the "crime
of race defilement." Staider spirits, combining business and pleasure, seized pedestrian Jewesses in the street in order to make them
clean their quarters or barracks (business) with the victims' underwear (pleasure).

The gamut of individual invention was endless. During the
search of a Jewish tradesman's house in Warsaw, the SS found a
dress coat in a closet. An idea was immediately born: the unfortunate Jew was forced to put on the coat, thrown outside, and
chased down the street, beaten by horsewhips. Jewish girls, arrested haphazardly in the street, had to wash the feet of their jailers and then drink the dirty bath water.[12]

Thousands of such cases were duly recorded in the trials and in-
terrogations of the inquiry commissions on war crimes, while tens
of thousands of others will never be known. But why go on with
such a catalogue? It would also be tedious to list the thousands of
individual murders committed at that time; moreover, they pale
before the systematic genocide of the following years. Let us content ourselves with citing the case of eight Jews taken by German
soldiers from the center of Warsaw on Good Friday, 1940, and
murdered in the outskirts of the city.[13]

The self-destructive effects of such a sanguinary eruption were
understood from the first by certain Germans, especially the high

officials. The lines that follow are taken from a report by General Johannes Blaskowitz, Oberbefehlshaber Ost (Supreme Commander in the East), submitted to von Brauchitsch in February 1940, that is, the fifth month of the occupation: [14]

> The methods and means of slaughter employed are most damaging [for us], complicating the problem, and making matters far worse than they might have been if a sensible and systematic course of action had been taken. The results are:
> a. Enemy propaganda is furnished with material more effective than any that could possibly have been thought up. What foreign radio broadcasts have mentioned up to now is only a minor portion of what has actually happened. There is reason to foresee that the outcry from foreign countries can only increase, resulting in serious political damage —all the more since the atrocities really have taken place and cannot be denied by any manner or means.
> b. The violence publicly perpetrated against the Jews is not only provoking in the basically pious Polish people a deep disgust with their perpetrators; it is also creating a profound pity for the Jewish population, to whom the Poles were more or less *hostile* until now. Our sworn enemies in the East, the Poles and the Jews, supported by the Catholic Church, will rapidly form a coalition on every front out of hatred for their tormenters.
> c. We need not mention again the unhappy role played by the Wehrmacht, forced to be a passive witness to these crimes, whose reputation with the Polish population is suffering irreparably.
> d. But the worst effect that the present situation will have on the German people is the unlimited brutalization and moral depravity which will spread like an epidemic through the most valuable German human material.
> If the high officials of the police and the SS continue to call for violence and brutality, brutal men will soon reign supreme. With disconcerting speed depraved birds of a feather find one another out and band together in order to satisfy their pathological and bestial instincts—as they are now doing in Poland. They can barely be kept in hand; for they have good reason to feel that they have official sanction and justification to commit the most horrible of acts.

Blaskowitz's reasoning was based exclusively on opportunistic considerations, excluding any invocation of general humanitarian or moral principles. The same "style" may be found in other such documents. Was this the inevitable moral deformation suffered by "specialists," or a calculated employment of the only arguments acceptable to the regime?

To Blaskowitz's report were added those of General Ulex, commanding the Southern Region, and of Major von Tschammer und Osten, liaison officer to the Government General, as well as descriptions of about thirty specific examples of atrocities. There is very little to add to the lucid judgment of these high German officers. Need we add that their protests had no effect?

THE "MADAGASCAR PLAN"

While the fate of the Jews grew steadily worse, the German armies were celebrating their 1940 triumphs. With the enormous perspectives opened to the Nazis after the collapse of France, a plan long cherished by some of them seemed possible of achievement. In their hands they felt they held the key to the "final solution of the Jewish question."

As noted previously, Goering had mentioned the "Madagascar Question" during the astonishing meeting of November 12, 1938. Himmler had been dreaming of it since 1934, as one witness testified.[15] Putting all the Jews on a large island—moreover a French island—would satisfy the Nazi love of symbolism. At any rate, the idea was put forth by the Minister of Foreign Affairs after the armistice of June 1940; it was taken up enthusiastically by the RSHA, and accepted by Himmler as well as by the Führer himself. (3) Great inventions always have several originators; other more or less famous dignitaries can claim the honor of fathering this "philanthropic" solution. For example, Philip Bouhler, chief of the Führer's personal chancellery, who, if we can believe his adjutant, Viktor Brack, hoped to become the governor of the island.[16]

(3) What was Hitler's personal attitude on this subject at that time? We have seen that he was interested in this "solution" in November 1938. For the period in question we have no document or testimony of absolute value. Abetz stated that the Führer had told him in August 1940 that "all the Jews were to get out of Europe." According to Ribbentrop, their destination was to be Madagascar. (Interrogation of Ribbentrop at the Nuremberg trial.) A report written for the latter in February 1942, points out in connection with the "Madagascar project" that "in the mind of the Führer, this question has been superseded by events"—seeming to imply that it had been on the agenda during the preceding period. It is difficult to imagine that the RSHA could have undertaken any considerable preparatory work unbeknownst to the Führer, or against his wish.

However, Rademacher, head of the "Jewish section" (Referat D
111) of the Ministry of Foreign Affairs, could exult that his plan
was at least partially worked out. We shall examine this question
in some detail; it permits one a deeper penetration into the caverns
where the Nazi "thousand-year" plans were being elaborated.

Franz Rademacher, an ambitious young jurist, former volunteer
in the "Ehrhardt" brigade (1923), and member of the Party since
1932, entered the Ministry of Foreign Affairs in 1937. He was appointed secretary of the legation at Montevideo; he left this post
in April 1940 to return to Germany. His eagerness to do great
things was rewarded with the offer of the directorship of a bureau
of internal affairs, the Referat D 111, which had just been created at
the Wilhelmstrasse. On June 3, 1940, he set down on paper a few
notes for submission to Ribbentrop dealing with the "National-
Socialist war aims in regard to the Jewish question." These aims
were clear: the Jews had to leave Europe. Rademacher only wondered whether all the Jews had to be evacuated, or whether it
would be better "to make a distinction between western and eastern Jews."

> The more prolific eastern Jews, a reservoir of Talmudism for the
> Jewish intellect, might remain as hostages in German hands [Lublin?],
> thus paralyzing the American Jews. The western Jews must be thrown
> out of Europe [Madagascar?].[17]

Such grandiose considerations were followed by the expression of
the more modest hope that the Referat D 111 might be enlarged for
this job: "one clever young consulate secretary, and one stenographer."

This last wish seems to have been granted, since a "plan for the
solution of the Jewish question" came out of the Referat D 111 at
the beginning of July, followed a few weeks later by "notes on the
creation of an inter-European bank for the utilization of Jewish
funds in Europe." Approved by Ribbentrop, the file was sent to
the RSHA, where it received an enthusiastic welcome. The appropriate service of the RSHA drew up a detailed plan for evacuating
the Jews and settling them in Madagascar, and the plan was approved by the SS Reichsführer.[18] Responsibility for the details of
the operation was to be Adolf Eichmann's, as chief of the agency
charged with the tasks of Jewish emigration.

The following is an outline of Rademacher's ideas: By the peace treaty, Germany would have Madagascar entrusted to her as a mandate. Ports and supply areas for the German navy would be established in the principal roadsteads, and military air bases built in the interior. The "militarily unusable" part of the island would be placed in the hands of an administrator directly responsible to the SS Reichsführer. "From the German point of view it means creating a super-ghetto: the security police alone have the necessary experience in this domain."

This is how Rademacher pictured the administration of the "super-ghetto." "The Jews are to govern themselves; they are to have their own mayors, police, post offices, and railroads. . . . But the political administration will stay in German hands. . . . Thus, the Jews will remain as hostages in our hands, guaranteeing a suitable attitude on the part of their American co-religionists." This would be killing two birds with one stone, for "we shall be able to utilize for our propaganda the magnanimity which Germany is showing by granting cultural, economic, and administrative freedom to the Jews, while at the same time we emphasize that our sense of responsibility prevents us from allowing independence to a race which for thousands of years has not known independence."

The financing of the operation was also anticipated. The Jews as a whole were to be responsible for the economic status of the island. Their possessions in Europe would be transferred to a bank specially created for this purpose, which would finance the emigration and settling of the Jews, and sell land to them.

It was still necessary to have a few facts about Madagascar itself. Here, Rademacher (despite his secretary and stenographer) seems to have fallen down, since he rather lamely attached to his plan two typed sheets copied from *Meyers Konversations-Lexicon*, a popular German encyclopedia (vol. 7-8, 1939 edition).

The RSHA did better. SS Lieutenant Dannecker, future chief of the Paris "Jewish service," was charged with the problem of documentation. To this end he betook himself to Paris and there conducted an inquiry at the Ministry of Colonies.[19] The "Madagascar Plan" file of the RSHA (August 1940) made the following proposals:

Attached . . . are preliminary studies on the project to transfer about 4,000,000 Jews to Madagascar: An overseas solution of insular character is preferable to any other, in order to avoid permanent contacts between the Jews and other people.

a) First of all, all bureaus in charge of the operation have to make a survey of the Jews under their jurisdiction. They are responsible for such preliminary measures as preparing documents for individual Jews, confiscating and evaluating their property, and setting up convoys. The first convoys must include principally farmers, construction specialists, artisans, and manual laborers with their families, as well as doctors. These must serve as an advance guard to prepare the way for the masses to come later.

b) Each Jew can take up to 400 pounds of baggage. The farmers, artisans, and doctors *must* take along whatever tools and professional instruments they have. Cash and precious objects will be subject to current regulations.[20]

The work began. Dieter Wisliceny stated that Eichmann worked actively on his plan up until the summer of 1941. He surrounded himself with maritime experts in order to prepare a plan for transportation; the latter was to be assured by a pool of ships provided by the big German steamship companies, with embarkation at the principal North Sea and Mediterranean ports. At the same time, he tried to have all Jewish fortunes confiscated for the "central funds." (4) Eichmann sent representatives into the occupied or controlled countries to gather statistics on the number, age, professional distribution, etc., of the Jews. These detailed statistics were later to serve another aim, as we shall see. The machinery was ready to start with the conclusion of peace. A huge propaganda campaign, prepared by Alfred Rosenberg and his collaborators at the Institute of Studies on Jewish Questions established at Frankfurt in March 1941, began with the announcement that the last Jew would soon leave the European continent. But the peace treaty was late in coming.

Operations in France and Adjacent Countries

Nearly 600,000 Jews lived in the occupied western countries: France, Belgium, the Netherlands, and Luxemburg. Occupied

(4) In October 1941 a law stripping German Jews abroad of their nationality stipulated that "their confiscated property shall be used to settle the problems related to the final solution of the Jewish question." (*Reichsgesetzblatt,* I, 722)

France and Belgium were placed under military administration; the Netherlands were governed by Seyss-Inquart, Reich Commissioner; whereas Luxemburg was annexed to the Reich. The fate of the Jews followed the same pattern in each of these territories, despite notable differences in detail. The situation was quite different from that in Poland, and the Nazi policy dealt with it in quite a different manner. But the first reaction of Heydrich and Eichmann was to use the new territories as a kind of "first stage" for expelled German Jews, while awaiting the annexation of Madagascar.

The first impetus was given by the expulsion of the Jews from Alsace-Lorraine, practically completed at the beginning of October 1940.[21] Then followed "Operation Bürckel," which gives an exact measure of the real power of the RSIIA and Section IVb. With the consent of Joseph Bürckel, Gauleiter of the Baden section, but without notifying either the Ministry of the Interior or any other authority, the SS deported 6,300 Jews of the Baden area on October 22, 1940, depositing them on the border of the French Free Zone. Another 1,125 Jews from the Palatinate and the Saar basin were added to the convoy. The deportees had been notified a half-hour in advance. The operation was "total," including the occupants of homes for the aged; one of the exiles was ninety-seven years old. The Vichy government placed the deportees in camps at Gurs and Rivesaltes, at the foot of the Pyrenees, where they found several thousand compatriots, the "scum of the earth" in Arthur Koestler's phrase, who had been arrested time after time by the police of every country and regime. (5) Vichy protested through the Armistice Commission. The Ministry of Foreign Affairs pigeonholed the protest and Rademacher worked hard to mislay the text, in order not to create complications for the RSHA and Bürckel. But the deportations, which Heydrich and Eichmann hoped to extend to the 270,000 Jews still in the Reich and in Bohemia and Moravia, were not continued.[22] It was unwise to offend the Vichy government too much.

For questions of high policy now entered into the considerations. In 1940, when Hitler hoped for a quick peace, discretion was still

(5) By the Gestapo (because of their race), by the police of the Third Republic (because of their nationality), and by Vichy (because of their religion).

essential in a Western Europe completely exposed to the eyes of the world on the Atlantic side, a discretion long ago forgotten in the East. In France especially, the situation called for pacificatory measures. Hitler sent Abetz, who promised to win over the French, as minister plenipotentiary to Paris. The Nazis reasoned that anti-Jewish measures taken by the France of the New Order would create a feeling of allegiance and establish a bond of solidarity among the French, whereas measures directly imposed by the occupier ran the risk of seeming an act of enemy oppression. It was a matter of "keeping the French people from reacting against everything German," as one of the SD officials in France put it.[23] So for a long while the Nazis in France struggled to have these measures carried out by "French hands." In Belgium, the sequence of events generally followed the French pattern, although it is necessary to distinguish between the Walloon region and Flanders. In Holland and Luxemburg, the situation was somewhat different; the Nazis hoped sooner or later to inculcate the native "people of the German stock" with the racist gospel, and then take them into the ranks of the Master Race.

On the other hand, in France (and in Walloon Belgium) the Nazis felt they were dealing with a somewhat alien people, in their eyes evidently degenerate, but toward whom they confusedly felt an unavowable but persistent sense of inferiority. Politically, the Nazis aimed at keeping them weak and divided; otherwise, they did not care and let the French stew in their inferior biological juices. Sometimes, however, they feared shocking the French human feelings too much. Beside, the Jews were far fewer in the invaded territories of the west than in the east; they enjoyed equality of rights with other citizens; and they lived scattered about among the population, from whom they were in no way distinguishable by dress or physical appearance. From this one can understand why the persecution, especially in the beginning, took a different form in the west, and why anti-Jewish measures may have been more difficult, tardy, and seemingly not so cruel.

In France, anti-Jewish measures had the peculiarity of being carried out by two different authorities: the German military government, in the occupied zone, and the Vichy government, whose legislation was valid for all of France. This was a rickety harness, in which the enraged Hitler mare was struggling to drag along a Vichy nag. Vichy anti-Semitism was the product of a cross between the xenophobia so characteristic of certain sections of the French middle class, and an old, traditionally reactionary, clerical anti-Semitic doctrine that supposedly found its inspiration in the medieval theologians, and sought supporting authority in the *Summa Theologica* of St. Thomas Aquinas. The Germans forced nothing on Vichy; they advised, "they made suggestions," even going so far as to "let the French have a glimpse of the abrogation of the German measures, in order to stimulate their initiative in the Jewish Question." [24] The Vichy government went along willingly, and even with real zeal when German policy conformed to its own doctrine. Pétain and Xavier Vallat (the first Commissioner General for Jewish Questions) were the recognized exponents of this policy. Pétain even took the precaution of getting advice from the Holy See on the timeliness of the Vichy measures, and the very precise reply from his ambassador doubtlessly soothed his conscience: "Never has anything been said to me in the Vatican which might suggest, on the part of the Holy See, criticism or disapproval of the legislation and ordinances in question." (6)

Other high Vichy officials, Pierre Laval especially, saw the Jews as counters to bargain with. By yielding to the demand for handing over foreign Jews in the Free Zone, for example, they hoped to obtain some other advantage, perhaps a modification of the demarcation line. They even tried to "exchange" foreign Jews for French Jews; Knochen, head of the SD in France, drew a sinister moral from this:

> Jews of French nationality, arrested for not wearing the star or for other infractions, should be deported. Bousquet [Undersecretary of Police in the Vichy Government] stated . . . that the French police would not cooperate in this. To our reply that this would be carried out by German forces, the French police answered by organizing a raid and arresting 1,300 foreign Jews. These Jews were handed over to the German police with a request to deport them instead of the French Jews. It goes without saying that both categories of Jews are going to be deported.[25]

(6) Report dated September 7, 1941, from Léon Bérard, French Ambassador to the Holy See, to Marshal Pétain, on the "questions and difficulties which could result from the measures taken with reference to the Jews." For the attitude of the Vatican, *see* p. 294.

Let us note, in conclusion, that within the limit of its doctrine the assistance given by Vichy to the Germans was essential. It assured the isolation of the Jews from the rest of the French population—a necessary precondition for genocide—as a result of the census, the *numerus clausus,* and other preliminary operations. In addition it relieved the occupiers of the bother of police operations, which were carried on in both the Free and Occupied zones by the French police. Nothing will ever be able to wash away the stigma of this deliberate complicity from Vichy, even though Vallat, for example, who was as much a Germanophobe as he was an anti-Semite, violently opposed the Germans on other occasions. The latter finally had him replaced by an outright madman (Darquier de Pellepoix), who lent himself better to their practices. (7)

The Jews in France undeniably benefited from the existence of a "free" zone, and from its relatively more benign regime. The example of countries like Denmark, or even Bulgaria (whose Jews were saved almost in their entirety), shows the possibilities for action that remained to regimes or governments, no matter how subordinated or subjected, when the leaders sincerely rejected all complicity.

On October 3, 1940, Vichy published a "Jewish law" that barred Jews from public functions, from the press, etc. In April 1941 the "General Commissariat for Jewish Questions" was established. This organization, directed by X. Vallat, intended to adopt most of the Nazi profane measures excluding Jews from social and economic life, and "Aryanizing" their trade and industry. Sacral measures never were undertaken in France, for they clashed with the clerical

(7) Dannecker, the first commissioner of IVb in France, prepared a report of his last conversation with Vallat. Here is a characteristic extract.

I pointed out to Vallat that his delaying tactics proved to me, once more, that he did not really want the separation of Jews from non-Jews. Vallat answered in an unheard-of tone: ". . . I am an older anti-Semite than you. Moreover, I could be your father." I answered that he could not talk to me that way, since our conversation was official.

In the course of the conversation, Vallat had also deliberately used the term "invasion"; at my insistence he substituted the word "occupation."

Toward the end of the interview, when Vallat became bold enough to observe that he could not tolerate my treating him as a subordinate, I declared: "I cannot tolerate such language, the more so since this statement is without any foundation. I deem this reproach to be a piece of incredible impertinence and I consider the meeting ended."

inspiration of the official anti-Semitism; consequently there were no Nuremberg laws. Vichy set the example for the physical measures taken in France. Since one of the cornerstones of its ideology was the distinction between French Jews and foreign Jews, more than 30,000 of the latter, "superfluous in the French economy," were interned in camps from the summer of 1940. The strongest were enlisted in "work battalions," following the German custom in Poland. The SS pointed to the French example in justification of their own deeds; Knochen did not fail to cite it when, at the beginning of 1941, he demanded the internment of the Jews in the occupied zone. (8).

As we have said, the Germans went slowly at first. True, after August 1940 the military government forbade the return of Jews who had taken refuge in the south of France during the exodus. This measure was instigated by Abetz, who at the same time proposed driving all the Parisian Jews into the Free Zone.[26] But the military government did not follow his suggestion. As in Poland, the military often showed a certain detachment from the anti-Jewish actions, though their lack of sacred fire did not prevent them from playing their part in the carrying out of a series of progressive measures; these began at the end of September 1940 (on the Jewish New Year's Day) with an order requiring Jews to register in the commissariats; their papers were stamped, their business indicated on a separate sheet. The tempo quickened in December, when a representative from Section IVb, SS Lieutenant Dannecker, Eichmann's delegate at the SD in France, installed himself in Paris with his staff.

(8) Letter from Knochen to the head of the military administration in France, dated February 28, 1941:

The anti-Jewish evolution of the first months has clearly shown that French anti-Semitism is aimed especially at foreign elements. The French government has taken account of this by issuing on October 4, 1940, a law making possible the internment of foreign Jews in concentration camps. . . . At the present time the establishment of camps seems indicated (in the Occupied Zone). Two considerations lead us to this conclusion:

1. The principal support of pro-English and pro-Gaulist propaganda probably comes from foreign Jews.

2. It seems almost impossible to develop in the French an ideological anti-Jewish feeling, whereas the offer of economic advantages would more easily produce sympathy for the anti-Jewish struggle. (The internment of nearly 100,000 foreign Jews living in Paris would give many Frenchmen a chance to lift themselves into the middle class.)

In July 1941, Dannecker compiled a ninety-six-page veritable handbook detailing his conception of his own activities, "in the hope that this study might be useful and suggestive for the work of other staffs." [27] At this stage, all efforts tended essentially toward the forced isolation of the Jews, their total segregation from the rest of the French population. The latter were to be subjected to ceaseless propaganda. Dannecker tells in detail how he called into being the "Anti-Jewish Institute" of Paris, an indispensable instrument "for giving a French twist to anti-Jewish propaganda." It is interesting to see how easily this simple SS Lieutenant succeeded in overcoming the little resistance he met from the military government. "After the internment of 3,600 Polish Jews (by virtue of a French law and after some pressure from us), and the arrest of the Jew, Alphonse Weill, the French Jews gave in," he announced; in November 1941, "the General Union of French Israelites" was founded as a counterpart of the Polish "Jewish Council." Henceforth, all measures were taken at Dannecker's instigation. The internment of 3,600 Polish Jews took place in May 1941; two other roundups of the same size followed in August and September of the same year. The sinister Drancy camp was established adjacent to Paris and, in March 1942, deportation to the east began. That same month, a curfew from 8:00 P.M. to 6:00 A.M. was ordered for Jews in the Occupied Zone, who could no longer change their residence. The yellow star was introduced in June 1942, and served to identify Jews in public; in July of the same year an ordinance barred them from theaters, movie houses, and other public places, even stores. At this time, their dispossession was complete, and their pauperization imminent. The difficulties which blocked the creation of an actual ghetto in France (beside, it would be very difficult to concentrate all the Jews in Paris), as well as the solidarity and extensive assistance given the Jews by the rest of the French population, made more bearable the fate of those who escaped the mass roundups. These raids were not discontinued, however, especially after the die had been cast in Berlin in 1942.

DRAMA OF THE FRENCH JEWS

While the hour of final tragedy was approaching, the fate of the French Jews was being decided in the Free Zone and to some extent even in the Occupied Zone (9) by the measures instituted by Vichy. How much Vichy followed its own bent is indicated by the fact that, on certain points, its legislation went beyond that of Berlin. Certain categories of Jews, who were not considered such from the German point of view, and whose lives were never threatened, had their rights and patrimony reduced by the Vichy regulations. (10) Of course, except for a few madmen, homicide did not enter into the plans of the ideologists of the "French State" or of those who inspired Marshal Pétain's policies. They in no way denied the humanity of the Jews. They were even inclined to admit that in exceptional and individual cases a Jew might deserve the title of citizen and Frenchman. But, as a general rule, they tended to exclude them from the national community by such means as denationalization and banishment from the various professions, etc. When one remembers the support that a large part of the French people gave the Marshal's government during the first two years of the occupation and the approval they accorded his acts, one can understand the moral sufferings of the isolated Jewish minority.

Certainly this did not compare with the tragedy of German Jewry. The colors of the drama were less harsh; we have here a purgatory and not a hell. Although accused, the Jews had not yet been finally condemned. The very expressions used in the legislation decreeing their humiliation often provided for exceptions. Such mitigating circumstances as "unusual services, war exploits and official citations, residence in France for more than five generations," show that the French Jew might hope to be treated as an equal by

(9) Most of the Vichy anti-Jewish measures were applicable all over France.

(10) Consider this memo from the Commissariat for Jewish Questions (Law of Persons; March 10, 1944): "I think it necessary to draw your attention to the fact that the decision taken in January 1943, at Vichy by the Law on Persons, a decision which granted the status of non-Jew to all Georgians of the Mosaic faith under its jurisdiction, must be considered null and void. . . .

"The German authorities exempt Georgians of Jewish faith from wearing the star because they consider them as not of pure Jewish blood.

"Nevertheless, it does not seem that this exemption from wearing the star must *ipso facto* entail the removal of the temporary administrators whom you would have considered it necessary to appoint to administer the property of Georgians of the Mosaic faith. Better still, I think it must be decided that, in all cases, Georgians of the Mosaic faith must be subject to a measure of aryanisation."

proving his outstanding merit, by surpassing his countrymen on
every occasion. This flagrant injustice deeply hurt the French Jews,
who in addition were humiliated in all sorts of petty ways. (Thus,
a circular from the Commissariat on Jewish Questions specified
that "the Commissioner General has noticed that in the correspondence of certain services, Jews were called 'Israelites.' At the Commissariat General for Jewish Questions, a Jew must be called a
Jew, and not be described in writing as 'Mr. Levy' or 'Mr. Dreyfus,'
but as 'the Jew Levy' or 'the Jew Dreyfus.' The term 'Israelite' shall
be used only in religious references.") [28]

Only by vain protests could the French Jews express their dis-
illusionment. Many moving letters were addresssed to Marshal
Pétain. "I believe I have the right and duty to protest . . . because
I recognize neither the right nor the power of anyone to set limits
to the love I have for my fatherland, a love which is part of the
patrimony of my heart and mind, shelters no one can violate," [29]
wrote General Boris, the oldest ranking officer among the Jews
expelled from the French army. A scout leader, Marc Haguenau, a
future Resistance martyr, wrote as follows to the Commissioner on
Jewish Questions:

> I submit this personal protest, along with that of so many of my
> Jewish and non-Jewish countrymen, to tell you of my sadness at the
> fact that an exceptional law should be passed for one category of
> Frenchmen. I count in my family too many generations of French
> Israelites, who have lived under all regimes—monarchies, empires,
> republics—not to be capable of judging in a completely French spirit
> what a backward step this is for our country, as regards the respect
> for all spiritual values in which I was raised, and to which I remain
> attached.
> I would have considered it contrary to my dignity not to make this
> brief and useless declaration.[30]

Such protests most often went unanswered; sometimes the Marshal's office replied, in rather ambiguous terms. Such was the
Marshal's answer to the protest from the chief rabbi of Paris about
the crimes perpetrated in December 1941 against the Paris synagogues by men from Deloncle's MSR party:

> The Marshal has noted your letter of December 11 and has in-
> structed me to thank you for it. . . . The present times are too trou-

bled and too confused to permit a sure judgment right now. History will appreciate your protest at its true value.[31]

But more characteristic is this brief correspondence, which shows that the Jew received a complete pardon from his earthly judges only when he had left for a better world.

January 27, 1941

Dear Marshal Pétain:

I have just read the following in a local paper: "In applying the law of December 3, 1940, M. Peyrouton has relieved (among others) Cohen, *chef de cabinet* at the Prefecture of the Côte-d'Or."

M. Peyrouton should have made inquiries before taking this step; he would have discovered that officer-candidate Cohen was killed on May 20 and buried at Abbeville.

He followed in the glorious tradition of his cousins, our only sons, who died for France in 1914–18, one as a *chasseur-alpin,* the other as an officer in the 7th Engineers, at the ages of twenty-four and twenty-five. Their spirits must have trembled with horror at such treatment.

Vichy, January 31, 1941

Civil Office of Marshal Pétain

Madam,

The Marshal has read the letter you sent him concerning your nephew.

He was all the more moved because one of his colleagues was with M. J. Cohen on May 20, 1940, a few hours before he was hit.

Marshal Pétain will ask the Minister of the Interior to reconsider the action taken with reference to your nephew.[32]

IN OTHER EUROPEAN COUNTRIES

In Belgium, with only 90,000 Jews, anti-Jewish measures were taken at the same rate as in occupied France, with only an occasional variation in detail. The first decree banned the ritual slaughtering of animals (October 27, 1940). At the end of 1941, Jewish children were excluded from the schools. The smallness of the country and the ease of surveillance made the fate of the Belgian Jews more precarious than that of the French Jews.

For these reasons the situation was still worse in the Netherlands, where the number of Jews exceeded 150,000. Anti-Jewish action reached a pitch of intensity at the beginning of 1941. The first deportations took place in February 1941; in this same month the segregation of the Jews was commenced with an order forbidding them all contact with the Dutch authorities. Sacral measures followed, the Nuremberg laws being introduced in May. The series of interdictions was completed in May 1942; it had gone much faster than in France and included laws against Jews' buying fruits and fish, against Jews' riding bicycles, and forbidding Jews to enter non-Jewish houses.

Refinements were thus introduced in the Netherlands which were unknown even in Poland. In addition, a policy of ghettoization was successfully carried out, with all the Dutch Jews being concentrated in three districts of Amsterdam as early as March 1942. A parallel might be drawn between this extreme virulence and the private grudge Hitler seemed to hold against the Dutch people: Had he not planned, in 1941, to deport all of them to the eastern section of the Government General? (11)

Other countries and other territories were now to be brought under the German yoke, some by brutal conquest, others after stealthy and progressive penetration. Here we encounter a new and paradoxical aspect of the Jewish tragedy: In the countries which took part in the Resistance, the fate of the Jews was almost immediately sealed with the advent of the Germans; whereas the regimes which submitted to and were allied with the Reich almost always followed an anti-Semitic policy of their own, within the limits of the autonomy allowed them, thus preserving at least a part of the threatened Jewish population. In the occupied territories, only a few months, a year at the most, separated invasion from deportation. The IVb "teams" moved in, armed with peremptory orders from Berlin, and vied with one another to hasten the introduction of a sequence of anti-Jewish measures that became classic. As for the satellite countries, they were caught in a web which we have already seen being spun in Vichy France under the protection of Pétain. With some notable differences in detail, the general tempo was the same in Catholic Hungary and in Orthodox Rumania, where from 1937 on the Patriarch Miron Christea, a future prime minister, had been exhorting his faithful to combat "the Jewish parasites." In Rumania, where Hitler's methods seem to have been most firmly implanted, a very complete "statute on the Jews" which included the Nuremberg laws had been promulgated in the summer

(11) For details of this project, see p. 279.

of 1940. Under Conducator (Führer) Antonescu's regime, bloody pogroms took place in January 1941, resulting in several thousand victims; and at the beginning of the war against Russia, more than 300,000 Jews from the provinces of Bukovina and Bessarabia were deported to "Transnistria" in the newly conquered region. But the Jews of Rumania proper, though stripped of all their rights and reduced to a state of extreme misery, managed in their majority to survive. The Hungarian Jews lived in relative security until the German military occupation in March 1944. For complex reasons, chief among which was the attitude of the population, the Bulgarian satellite saw the least amount of persecution of the Jews; whereas Monseigneur Tiso's Slovakia and Ante Pavelitch's Croatia had little to learn from their Nazi masters.

AGONY OF THE GERMAN JEWS

It seems strange that nearly 300,000 Jews could continue to live in Germany while hostilities were raging. Yet no radical changes occurred in their lot until the fall of 1941—so true is it that genocide is not a movement of collective fury (a necessary but insufficient condition), but must be set in motion by a determined will guided by exact orders. It is even possible to declare that with the help of habit and the infinite resources of the human soul, these last years proved more bearable for many a German Jew than the preceding years with their sudden and overwhelming trials.

This is not to say that the Nazi machine had finally slowed down. It seemed to be an inexhaustible Nazi necessity to legislate against the Jews, so much so that they continued to pass laws long after Germany had literally been "purified" of Jews. (One wonders what course the Nazis would have taken when the Jewish devils, having shed their carnal envelopes [and been transformed into phosphate and soap] were nothing but a spectral legion. We shall see that, in 1944, there was actual alarm at this prospect.) Thus, "the political situation having completely changed," the wearing of the yellow star (which Hitler had hesitated to introduce in 1938) became obligatory in the Reich on September 1, 1941. This made the observance of the ritual tabus easier; shortly afterward, Germans were absolutely forbidden to appear in public with Jews. "As for those who cannot understand these elementary principles of National Socialism," like the Jews, they would be interned in camps.[33] The sequence continued: Jews were forbidden to use any public conveyance, to stop in the street, to stroll or window shop, to own domestic animals, and the like.

Particular mention should be made of food rationing. By a series of decrees the ration for Jews was steadily reduced until it consisted only of potatoes, vegetables, bread and rye flour, and skimmed milk for nursing children.[34] Customs officials were instructed to properly mark packages sent from neutral countries to addressees "with a Jewish name" so that their contents might be deducted from the recipients' monthly ration.[35]

Finding a general legal basis for the concept of the Jewish "subman" was a preoccupation of the German legislators at this time. The same attempt had been made in Poland; but in this case the legal experts of the Berlin Chancellery were trying to be very thorough and exact. The attempt to squeeze a racial ideology into the mold of classic legalism sometimes ended in strange impasses. Thus a proposed law on the general status of Jews forbade their testifying under oath (what is the oath of a Jew worth?); but "the inability of the Jew to take an oath must not work to his advantage," and so "the testimony of Jews will be treated, for penal purposes, like a deposition made under oath." [36] As was customary, the Ministry of Justice sent the plan to all the departments concerned, and the Wehrmacht Command remarked, with a last glimmer of logic, that "this regulation would lead to an unjustified overvaluation of unsworn Jewish testimony as against the unsworn testimony of witnesses who could take an oath." [37] The law was progressively modified and reduced to its simplest expression: In the first paragraph it specified that the police alone had authority in Jewish crimes and felonies; in the second paragraph, that the Reich was the sole heir to their possessions. (When it was promulgated in July 1943, there was no longer a single Jew at liberty in Germany except for those married to Aryans.) [38]

On the other hand, there were still some Germans who were "incapable of understanding the elementary principles of National Socialism." Statistics from the Ministry of Justice indicate 189 convictions for "crimes against the race" in 1941, and 109 in 1942.[39]

To recall the people to their better nature, legal spectacles were staged from time to time, such as the trial of Israel Katzenberger, condemned to death at Nuremberg in March 1942, for having engaged in "substitute acts" (*Ersatzhandlungen*) with a German woman. (12) "Racial contamination is worse than murder!" exclaimed Rothaug, president of the tribunal, to the audience. "Whole generations extending into the far distant future are affected by it!" And, in fact, were not the Jews finding more and more insidious means for tarnishing the Master Race? Witness this note found in the archives of the Ministry of Justice, meant for the Führer himself:

> After the birth of her child, a pure-blooded Jewess sold her mother's milk to a pediatrician, hiding the fact that she was Jewish. Babies of German blood were nourished on this milk in a maternity hospital. The accused woman will be tried for fraud. The purchasers of the milk have been wronged, for the milk of a Jewish woman cannot be considered nourishment for German children. The accused woman's impudent attitude is another insult. The investigation of the affair, however, has been suspended in order not to disturb the parents, who are unaware of these facts. I shall discuss with the Minister of Health the hygienic and racial aspects of the question.[40]

The keepers of the racial Grail did not wish to publicize this case out of consideration for parental feeling. But in the case of young Herschel Grynspan, who had been handed over to the Germans by the Vichy government in the summer of 1940, a spectacular public

---

(12) The following is an extract from the verdict:

Katzenberger Lehmann, Israel, called Leo, merchant and president of the Israelite religious community of Nuremberg, and Seiler, Irene, proprietress of a photography shop in Nuremberg.

Both placed under arrest pending investigation, for crime against the race and perjury. At the court's public session on March 13, 1942. . . .

In terms of the law for the protection of the blood extra-marital sexual relations, apart from coition, must be understood as being any kind of sexual activity with a person of the opposite sex which is intended to serve and satisfy the sexual needs of at least one of the partners, by means other than coition. The acts acknowledged by the accused consisted of Katzenberger's having pulled Seiler to him, kissed her, caressed her hips through her clothes—acts vulgarly known as "petting." It is evident that the only motive for these acts is sexual desire. Even if the Jew has done no more than perform these "substitute acts" on the person of Seiler he has been guilty of a crime against race. . . . (NG 154)

trial was prepared. The case had been scheduled for the month of
May 1942, and was to last several days; a number of witnesses were
to be subpoenaed, including a few French witnesses, among them
Georges Bonnet, the former Minister of Foreign Affairs. However,
at the last moment the trial was canceled. (13)

The "Jewish question" continued to be the principal theme of
Nazi propaganda. No Nazi leader could open his mouth in public
without expatiating on this inexhaustible subject; no less than five
learned societies were laboring to deepen its ideological foundations, consecrating it with the seal of German erudition. (14) One
of these learned scholars, Lieutenant-Colonel Meyer-Christian,
pointed out some new and disconcerting facts in March 1944:

> Young officers of twenty declare upon inquiries that they have
> never yet consciously seen a Jew. Consequently they find no interest,
> or only slight interest, in the Jewish problem, as it has been presented
> to them up to now. . . . Therefore the danger arises that the speeches
> of the Führer, who always begins his political messages with a de-
> tailed summary (*Abriss*) of the Jewish problem, lose much of their im-
> pact for the younger generation.[41]

It would indeed seem to be the case that Nazi anti-Semitic propaganda had reached its saturation point in 1938. Perhaps it was simply desensitization; on the other hand, human reactions are sometimes unpredictable and follow contradictory paths. When one
wonders what the existence of the German Jews was like during
these last years, it is well to recall that even in the Third Reich
there was a number of instances of individuals showing sympathy
for the Jews—these advances were timid, certainly, and isolated,
but they made the agony more bearable.

In the fall of 1941, the first of a series of deportations began that
would empty Germany of all Jews. Only the *Mischlinge*, as well as

(13) Grynspan had threatened to "sabotage" the trial by publicly revealing
his supposed homosexual relationships with vom Rath. The trial was canceled
at Hitler's personal intervention. (NG 179)

(14) The Reichsinstitut für Geschichte des neuen Deutschlands, sponsored
by Streicher and Hess; the Institut zum Studium der Judenfrage, sponsored
by Goebbels; the Institut zur Erforschung des jüdischen Einflusses auf das
deutsche kirchliche Leben, sponsored by the Ministry of Religion; the Institut
für deutsche Ostarbeit, sponsored by Frank; and Alfred Rosenberg's Institut
zur Enforschung der Judenfrage. (*Hitler's Professors,* by Max Weinreich, Yivo,
1946)

"those married to Aryans," were temporarily exempted. Their fate was the subject of endless debate in the course of several interministerial meetings held during 1942. It is worth quoting the arguments developed by one of the participants who was against the deportation of half-Jews:

> The fact is that in deporting half-Jews, German blood is being sacrificed. I have always considered it biologically very dangerous to introduce German blood into the enemy camp. This blood will only produce personalities who will place at the service of the enemy those precious qualities inherited with their German blood. The half-Jews' intelligence and excellent education, linked to their ancestral Germanic heritage, make them natural leaders outside of Germany and, consequently, dangerous enemies. . . . Therefore I prefer to see half-Jews die a natural death inside Germany, although from three to four decades may be necessary to achieve this purpose.[42]

These lines were not meant to be funny. They bear the signature of one of the highest officials of the regime, Wilhelm Stuckart, Secretary of State in the Ministry of the Interior and an SS general. Be that as it may, it was finally decided in principle to include half-Jews in the deportations, but to allow them the possibility of withdrawing on condition that they "voluntarily" asked for sterilization. Thus the perpetuation of a "third race" would be avoided. The "one-fourth Jews" ("second generation *Mischlinge*") were considered members of the German race, provided they did not "physically resemble Jews" or "give reason to believe that they feel and act like Jews." [43]

Those married to Aryans were also to be deported. But first there had to be a divorce, made to appear as spontaneous as possible, since forced annulments might excite the emotions of the German side of the families.[44] This subtle consideration entailed procedures and delays which in the end permitted most of those married to Aryans to avoid deportation.

CHAPTER THREE

Pillage and Enslavement

MANY WRITERS HAVE TRIED to see anti-Semitism as the result of intergroup economic rivalries. Marxist writers try to reduce it to an aspect of the class struggle, the Jews, an obsolete class of small merchants and middlemen, being doomed to extinction by the implacable dialectic of history. The truth is certainly more complex; but economic considerations played so important and varied a role in the unfolding events that it is necessary to examine this aspect of the problem. If the enslavement of the Jews recalls in many ways the Hegelian dialogue between the master and the slave, their deliberate and premature assassination confutes the Hegelian logic. But before this point was reached, their spoliation had to be complete. The non-Jews benefited from the Jew's property, from the manpower he could furnish, and from his knowledge. Refinements were later developed to the point where his very body was exploited for its fats and phosphates. The thoroughness with which the Jews were pillaged may be seen in a particularly striking manner in certain Nazi documents. ("Operation Reinhard," for example, which will be discussed later, embraced the transfer of Jewish population, utilization of their manpower, confiscation of their goods and property, recovery of debts, etc.) The spoliation was so grandiose that it is difficult to find a name for it. This is true less of its quantitative aspect, which the best experts put at nearly $9,-000,000,000,[1] than its qualitative aspect, which we shall try to examine in certain of its very characteristic forms.

It is well known how National Socialism benefited from the German inflation of 1923 and the 1929 crisis. The disappointed, the embittered, the unemployed, were its principal backers. The legends about the huge Jewish fortunes found an enthusiastic and credulous audience. Thenceforth ruined members of the middle class and intellectuals without a future were to be seduced by the prospect which the elimination of the German Jews seemed to open for them.

Their hopes were partially satisfied in 1933, 1934, and 1935. "Aryan" lawyers and doctors profited from the elimination of their Jewish colleagues; boycotts, voluntary or forced, were beginning to have a favorable influence on the balance sheets of numerous Aryan businesses. However, the total elimination of the Jews from industrial and commercial activity came later, in the crucial month of November 1938. We have noted above how in October 1938 Goering proclaimed that "the Jews must disappear from the German economy!" At this point new claimants appeared, more voracious and infinitely more dangerous than respectable business and professional men.

The night of October 9-10, 1938, opened the way for direct action on a large scale. Henceforth, slow economic strangulation would be inseparable from pillage pure and simple; the latter became increasingly the rule. Caution was tossed aside: SA and SS men now had free rein and law gave way to the leveled revolver; the SA and SS men used the one or the other indifferently. They lacked *savoir-faire*, but they had confidence, support, and large appetites.

The procedures which a conscientious and methodical Nazi could use are listed in the conclusions of an inquiry commission established by Goering to examine Aryanizations in Franconia, Julius Streicher's stamping grounds. Ayranization was accomplished, in principle, with the naming of a temporary administrator, who was to manage, and sell if need be, Jewish stores or factories. The big Nazis soon grasped the possibilities that their prestige and position afforded them in connection with these Aryanizations. Streicher's own adjutant, SA Oberführer Hanns König, organized the Aryanization of a half-dozen plants and factories in three or four days, bought them at one-tenth their value through straw men, and resold them the next day at a 200 to 400 per cent profit. These operations were carried on shamelessly in broad daylight, and so an inquiry commission was sent from Berlin at the insistence of the Ministry of Economics. A few sales were canceled; a few too enterprising SA or SS men were removed.[2] But it became general practice.

Joseph Bürckel, the first gauleiter of Vienna, described the situation in a report sent to Goering on November 19, 1938: [3]

> The old members of the party have been saying to one another: "We have suffered a great deal under this system, we have fought hard and now we have a right to reparations." This conception of reparations and Aryanization that the Austrian Party members have has been defeating the purpose of Aryanization and reparations. I have fought against this point of view from the beginning. I have said to the men, "Your demand that the biggest Jewish business be given to the best National-Socialist fighter is madness. You are hurting the German economy and your own comrades, for their professional inability will quickly lead them to ruin, and that is not a fitting reward for a fighter's career." I finally gave flat orders to separate Aryanization from reparations in the future. . . . Then the events of November 9-10 happened. At Vienna, the police gave orders to raze all Jewish property. It is evident that this order has nullified all my educational work.

What we have here is an evolution in which the political gangster came to the fore without displacing the commercial profiteer. According to a report by Funk, the total property to be Aryanized in Germany was estimated at nearly 7,000,000,000 Reichsmarks.[4] The biggest businesses were acquired by such well-established enterprises as Krupp, I. G. Farben, and Siemens. New names, however, competed with them; the publishing houses of Ullstein and Mosse passed into the hands of Franz Eher, the Nazi press octopus. The group of profiteers, little and big, grew continually until it came to include in one way or another almost the entire German people; the whole population profited from the general enrichment, either by direct and personal seizure, or by specific participation in numerous and different distributions. This becomes clearer later on in the war.

In the conquered countries of the east and west, the dispossession of the Jews was carried out under military occupation, which meant that it was a hundred times more ruthless. Decrees and ordinances were issued as soon as a territory was occupied; these played an essential part in the west, but in Poland their role was minor. It is enough to mention the ordinance of September 29, 1939, which announced the seizure of the property of "Jews absent from their homes" in the Government General; one year later (September 17, 1940), all Jewish possessions and capital above 1,000 marks were definitively confiscated. A *Fideicommissariat,* created on November 15, 1939, had the task of Aryanizing Jewish enterprises. The major businesses were taken over by the state; the army requisitioned the warehouses. The concentration of Jews in crowded ghettos set certain limits to this total dispossession. But pillage and direct extortion continued.

Here is some testimony on the way in which the plans were carried out. One witness relates:

> In the first three months of the occupation, the looting usually stopped short of the furniture. Later, however, the Nazis went systematically from house to house, and laid hands on whatever they could find. Bed-rooms, dining-rooms, even lavatories were stripped. Jews were accosted on the street and forced to help pile up the spoils into waiting cars. Nor was the pillage confined to private dwellings. Shops, factories, warehouses and cultural institutions fared no better. . . .[5]
>
> If such thievery was a regular thing, really huge operations took place from time to time. Thus, in Cracow, on December 3, 1939, large military detachments surrounded the Jewish quarter at eleven o'clock at night. Sentries were posted in front of the houses to prevent the inhabitants from leaving. The next morning, at eight, all the houses were ransacked from top to bottom. The official pretext was a search for currency, jewels, and cash.
>
> Officers did not hesitate to confiscate for their personal use such things as silk stockings, shoes, bedding, and even food. The search continued the next day and did not stop until half past two in the afternoon.[6]

General Blaskowitz confirmed this in his previously mentioned report: "All police searches and confiscations are accompanied by theft and pillage. . . . It is well-known that merchandise of all kinds is distributed or sold by detachments of the police and the SS." [7]

Another practice was to give a Jewish community twenty-four hours to collect a sum of money or to hand over a certain quantity of specified merchandise. Large industries were confiscated by the administration of the Government General and distributed to the

big German trusts, ostensibly for them to manage. Small factories
and businesses were parceled out to the *Volksdeutsche* ("ethnic
Germans") of Poland. When the ghettos were set up, the *Volksdeutsche* were able to take possession of Jewish apartments and
furniture. As Blaskowitz said:

> Given this state of affairs, it is naturally not surprising that the
> individual German is taking every occasion to get rich. And he can
> do it without danger, because when everybody steals, the individual
> thief does not have to be overly afraid of punishment.

The circle of those who benefited from the spoliation of the Jews
was thus progressively enlarged: it included the administration and
the army, the big trusts, tradesmen who came from the Third Reich,
"ethnic" Germans, SS men, and individual pillagers. The SS men
played a very active role in all this and became more and more the
principal profiteers.

In the west, however, the spoliations were carried out within the
framework of the new laws. Essentially, this meant freezing bank
accounts and Aryanizing businesses, industries, and real estate.
In France, for example, more than 70,000 Aryanizations took place
between 1940 and 1944. The choice properties—large industries,
the Rothschild mansions, etc.—were reserved for emissaries of
the trusts and the army; the rest was given over to collaborators in
the invaded countries under the management of the General Commissariat for Jewish Questions. A host of temporary administrators,
intermediaries, shady dealers, and profiteers sprang up. The policy
had been well planned; for once, the Germans seem to have been
shrewd psychologists. Knochen, chief of the SD in France, summed
it up:

> It is plainly almost impossible to cultivate in Frenchmen an anti-
> Jewish feeling based on ideological grounds, whereas the offer of eco-
> nomic advantages could more easily create sympathy for the anti-
> Jewish struggle. . . .
> The internment of nearly 100,000 Jews living in Paris could give
> many Frenchmen the chance to pull themselves up into the middle
> classes.[8]

Nothing could be clearer. Though the economic motives, however large their part may have been in the formation of Nazi anti-

Semitism, were largely irrelevant to Hitlerism's religious fervor, they furnish an essential key to the behavior of individuals in the conquered countries.

"Ideological" Pillage

We shall now examine more closely an organization specializing in pillage. Its development is typical. Created for an ideological purpose, *Einsatzstab Rosenberg* ("Rosenberg's Special Staff") rapidly enlarged its field of action to embrace the hunt for "cultural treasures" and ended up by pillaging apartments on a large scale.

Alfred Rosenberg's Special Staff

The Einsatzstab was created by an order from Hitler in January 1940, and was financed directly from the party treasury. Its powers were defined and expanded by another order from Hitler dated March 1, 1942. In a memorandum meant for internal use,[9] its aims were defined as follows:

> [To create] an arsenal of material that will furnish scientific and technical bases for the struggle against our ideological adversary. For this purpose we must establish a library dealing with all the problems of Judaism, Free Masonry, and Bolshevism, as well as archives of films, posters, records, photographs, paintings, and all objects helpful in teaching the spiritual basis and tactics of our ideological adversary.

Superfluous "spiritual weapons, of no use to the planned collection," were to be destroyed immediately. "The undersigned does not believe that restricting the Reichsleiter by fixing precise aims is indicated: the Einsatzstab must remain flexible in its choice of objectives," adds the author of the memorandum. Another document [10] relates in detail the struggles which the Einsatzstab had to undergo in order to have its rights recognized, especially by the Wehrmacht. The problems involved its legal status, gasoline and provisions, ranks and uniforms, access to canteens, and the assignment of postal-zone numbers. The Einsatzstab was especially concerned over "the ill will which the majority of the services have been displaying to our special situation and which they oppose to our tasks." In the world of Nazi clans, the Einsatzstab, a hybrid half-military, half-civilian organism, seems to have been especially unpopular. The SS men reacted against the competition of the "archivists of Reichsleiter Rosenberg." SS General Veesenmayer, promoted to Nazi pro-consul of Hungary in March 1944, forbade them access to Hungarian territory. "I am familiar with the Einsatzstab, having seen it at work in the Balkans, particularly at Agram; that's enough for me," he declared to the representative of the special staff.[11]

The first task of the Einsatzstab consisted of getting together a library representative of the "ideological adversary" and of drawing on the books appertaining to the Jews for this purpose, at the same time destroying most of them. Here matters become interesting. One might think that tearing up millions of volumes would have been the first concern of the Nazis, who were constantly in search of raw material. But nothing of the sort happened. An immense project, stretching over all of Europe, ended in the concentration of a collection of nearly 6,000,000 volumes in a chateau near Frankfort. This later fell intact into the hands of the American army. (1) Hebraica, Talmuds, and prayer books constituted its principal items. After reviewing the wealth of the large European Jewish libraries, J. Pohl, one of the librarians, proudly concluded: "As far as Jewish literature is concerned, this library holds collections such as have never before been assembled in Europe or elsewhere. The library will be developed (as part of the organization of the New Order in Europe) not only for Europe but for the entire world." [12] Thus, while the Jew was "evacuated from Europe," or rather exterminated, Jewish thought, carefully (piously, one might say) preserved, was to be put at the disposal of the best Nazi minds. More simple beings were prudently kept away from it. (2)

(1) The identification, classification, and restitution of these books has taken more than two years, and has occupied nearly 150 employees. (See our article on this subject, "Récupération des livres voltés," *Le Monde juif*, January 1947.)

(2) In this connection, one of the officials of the Einsatzstab, whose duty it was to collect books (in Germany itself this was done by agents of the Ministry of Finance), tells the following story:

I have found that important libraries have been stored in certain offices. The books were on loan to the officials. In one office a book was on loan which told the story of a man who had replaced his sick head with a

Rosenberg's men rapidly extended their activity to less exclusive but more lucrative domains: "cultural treasures" in general, that is to say, works of art belonging to Jews. This aspect of their work has been treated in detail in an excellent work to which the reader is referred. (3) The Einsatzstab had to fight hard against other claimants to this booty, especially the German Embassy in France. Thanks to the support of the all-powerful Goering, for whom the most precious works were reserved, the Einsatzstab finally won out. The loot, destined for the principal Nazi leaders and the German museums, was all-inclusive:

> During the period between March 1941 and July 1944, the general staff for the plastic arts sent to the Reich 29 large shipments consisting of 137 freight cars loaded with 4,174 cases of works of art. . . . By July 15, 1944, 21,903 works of art were inventoried, including 5,281 paintings, pastels, watercolors, and drawings; 684 miniatures, paintings on glass or on enamel; 583 sculptures, terra cotta, medallions; 2,477 precious furnishings. . . . The artistic and material value of the objects seized cannot be expressed in figures.[13]

In April 1943, on the occasion of the Führer's birthday, Rosenberg sent him "an album containing the photographs of the most precious paintings from the Jewish collections which have been placed in safekeeping in accordance with your orders," and he ended with this compliment: "I shall take the liberty of sending you twenty other albums of photographs in the hope that this brief relaxation with beautiful objects of art, which are so dear to you, may bring a ray of beauty and of joy into the seriousness and grandeur of your present life." [14]

It should be added that the military authorities in France tried to block this pillage. Vichy, "concerned with protecting the national artistic patrimony," protested ceaselessly; the Marshal's men ex-

---

wooden one manufactured by a carpenter. When asked how he was and what he was doing, this man answered: "I'm feeling fine now; I've become a party orator." I've not been able to find out anything about the author or the editor of this book.

This incident leads me to suggest that the contents of books should be verified by a delegate of the party before they are loaned. (Letter from the director of the Neuwied bureau to the central Einsatzstab at Berlin, January 26, 1943.)

(3) *Le Pillage par les Allemands des oeuvres d'art et des bibliothèques appartenant à des Juifs en France,* Paris, Editions du Centre, 1947.

pressed a fervor in this cause that no execution or deportation had
been able to arouse. "This question . . . is one of those which cause
the most bitterness in the long run, since the nation will long remember it," Admiral Darlan wrote on August 11, 1941; (4) he
begged the military administration, "which was generally very con-
siderate . . . to preserve its good reputation in History." The Einsatzstab had constructed (in support of its demands) a theory:

> Jewry is putting all its strength into the struggle against the German
> people. . . . Today's Rembrandt represents in practice the financing
> of tomorrow's anti-German fight. That is why it is just as much to be
> considered war booty as the weapons of the soldiers who are its mili-
> tary instruments. (5)

The legal experts of the Gestapo at Paris's Hotel Majestic balked
at such ideas. The military caste had its traditions. "Logically, that
would lead to the dispossession of all the nationals of the occupied
countries who are ill-disposed toward the occupation authorities,
and consequently, of almost all the inhabitants," remarked one of
them (report cited above). These scruples evidently remained a
dead letter. "I am the first jurist of the state!" cried Goering in a
rage when his subordinates brought him up to date on the question.[15]

From the evacuation of "cultural treasures," it was only a step
to the systematic plundering of Jewish apartments; this step was
taken several months later, and entitled "Action M" (möbel =
furniture). An Einsatzstab activity report gives the following details:

> The requisitioning of Jewish apartments was carried out as follows:
> In most cases, in Paris, for example, so-called "inventory officials"
> went from house to house to find out whether there were any apart-
> ments abandoned by Jews. In Paris alone, 20 "inventory officials" seized
> more than 38,000 apartments. They enlisted all the equipment and

(4) This quotation and those which follow are taken from an important
manuscript that gives a detailed account of the pillaging of art works in
France. The unknown author was, from every indication, one of the judges
in the German military administration. The document may be found in the
archives of the CDJC.
(5) Note from von Behr, director of the Einsatzstab in France, dated January 27, 1941. It is quoted in the report mentioned above.

personnel of the Union of Parisian Furniture Movers, which had to furnish a daily quota of up to 150 trucks and 1,200 to 1,500 French workmen.[16]

The report complained that the German authorities, far too few in number, "had not been able to prevent sabotage by the French workmen, which was considerable." Another method was then used: "Two large assembly camps were set up and, to supply the manpower, the SD put 700 Jews interned in these camps at our disposal." However, "despite strict surveillance, sabotage could not be avoided."

The balance sheet of the operation, which had the city of Paris and the Netherlands as its principal fields of activity, showed 736 train loads of furniture, each consisting of 40 freight cars, from Paris, and 586 barges, loaded with 248,525 tons of furniture, from the Low Countries.

All over Europe, the apartments of the deported Jews stimulated an inexhaustible cupidity. It was Rosenberg again, now Minister for the Territories of the East, who personally asked Albert Speer in January 1942, to set aside apartments for officials of the new ministry. "I can well understand your desire," answered the future Minister of Armaments, "but I must first hold a large number of apartments for war victims. The evacuation of Jews has been stopped, for reasons having to do with the railroads, until April; so I face great difficulties. While asking you to treat the matter confidentially, I promise to place fifteen apartments at your disposal in the next few months." [17]

The claimants were, in fact, very numerous. There was, for example, Secretary of Legation Rademacher, the author of the Madagascar Plan, who wrote to his superiors in the personnel bureau: "I have succeeded, privately, in obtaining a promise that a Jewish apartment will be liberated for me by special measure, provided I repair it at the cost of 700 RM. . . . In view of the present crisis, I see no other way of finding a suitable apartment at a reasonable price. I do not have the 700 RM, and in this situation I am requesting a special grant of 700 RM." [18] Nothing better illustrates this mentality than a sentence from a communication by another Nazi diplomat, Counsellor of Legation Carlthéo Zeitschel. Attached to the Paris embassy, Zeitschel wrote to the SD to notify it that a

"German-Jewish emigrant" was secretly moving his furniture. "Unfortunately, I did not learn of this until today, but there still seem to be a few cases left in the apartment." And the diplomat added: "Perhaps we can still 'swipe' something" (*"Vielleicht kann man noch etwas schnappen?"*).[19]

ENSLAVEMENT

The exploitation of Jewish manpower was another source of substantial revenue for the Third Reich and its officials. The idea of punishment was maintained, but it was modified by the growing economic power of the SS, a development which the war speeded up.

With the dizzy rise of Himmler, the SS men increased their influence and power. By giving big industrialists, bankers, and other important people high rank in their hierarchy, they infiltrated every phase of German life; they became in fact a state within the state. A desire to make the organization financially self-supporting, the growing appetite of leaders and rank-and-file alike, caused a new development to take place which had its beginnings in the first concentration camps. Owners of an ever growing number of slaves, they exploited to the full the advantage given them by their absolute police power over this "human material."   It was a matter of "laying hands on all anti-social elements which no longer have a right to live in the National Socialist State, and of turning their work potential to the advantage of the entire nation."[20] The concentration camps became a source of enormous profit. Thus began the translation into practical terms of Hitler's apocalyptic views on the structure of the society of the future; and thus an SS economic empire was created which in a few years developed into an octopus trust. For the greater glory of the Führer, the men of the New Order turned themselves into business men. A new SS department came into being, created by Himmler on April 20, 1939; it took definitive form in March 1942 as the SS Central Administrative and Economic Office (WVHA—*Wirtschafts-Verwaltungshauptamt SS*). SS General Oswald Pohl was placed at its head. The aim of the WVHA, says a report,[21] was to "to utilize the labor of the prisoners on a large scale"; the report added:

The most splendid idea and the finest task are worthless if it is impossible to find men capable of carrying them out. This rule is applicable in politics, and is particularly valid in private economy.

Complaints followed that the new men were "flocking into the SS and wearing the black uniform for material considerations and so as to do administrative work." Thus, while the older members of the party and the SS were enriching themselves, the new recruits were being attracted by the innumerable positions opening up. The lack of manpower in wartime Germany accelerated this growth of slave labor. The number of slaves in concentration camps finally reached several million. (6)

The first contingents of slave laborers were not limited to Jews, though they made up the major part of them. Their exploitation followed two different patterns: they were either hired out to public or private industry, or employed in factories owned by the SS. In the Government General alone, in March 1943, 52,000 Jewish slaves were employed in SS plants that included iron works, quarries, textile factories, a glass works, a brush factory, and many brick yards, all grouped under the trade name of OSTI (Eastern Industries).[22] Where the SS hired out slave labor, a fee of 0.70 to 1 RM per day was paid by the employer; the SS itself always provided the guards. The life the slaves lived did not depend on the kind of work they did but varied with local conditions and political changes. Places where there were slave labor concentrations were especially preferred by German industry as sites for new plants. (7)

The enslavement of Jews went on in various ways. After the invasion of Poland, men and women were rounded up by the thousands on the streets and made to clean the streets, clear ground, and perform a thousand different kinds of forced labor. The ordinances of September 25 and December 12, 1939, furnished the legal

(6) The American tribunal in Germany estimated the number at 3.5 million. (Trial of Oswald Pohl and accessories, session of April 8, 1947). This figure seems to us far below the actual number. On the other hand, it should be noted that the reference is to the total number of slave laborers between 1939 and 1945: according to the same source, only 1.2 million were still alive shortly before the end of the war.

(7) As was the case when I. G. Farben set up the famous Buna factory at Auschwitz.

framework for using Jewish labor in digging ditches and building
canals, and, later, fortifications. Hundreds of work camps sprang up
all over the territory. Their way of life differed little from that of
the concentration camps.

Blows, refined torture, hunger, and cold undermined the prisoners' resistance and in a short while brought sickness and death.
"Why are we here?" wrote a young boy assigned to the construction
of a mine on the Polish-German border.[23] "A hundred Jewish boys
of fifteen, seventeen, and twenty, miserable and unhappy. Many of
us have seen our own families killed. Apparently just to make us
suffer. We are exposed to the jeers and mockery of the German
brutes. On top of the blows: hunger. We were warned that if they
found any bread on us beyond the ration, we would be shot. Fifteen days later there were only sixty-five of us left out of one hundred."

Work and death became almost synonymous, since the camps
were a perverse blend of both. (In Chapter VII we shall see what
Heydrich had to say about this.) The general intent of the Nazis
in all this remained about the same, whether, as at first, they supported the idea of deporting the Jews to the tropics, or whether
they decided to exterminate the Jews on the spot. What they
wanted was to make the Jews suffer. The system they created was
dominated by this sadistic desire, which soon erupted and against
all economic logic sought satisfaction for itself in total genocide.

In the case of the Jews, the human wastage was all the greater
and the attrition the more rapid because of their inexperience in
and unsuitability to hard physical work. There were cases of contractors and foremen trying to make conditions more bearable.
Their efforts were wasted; threats like those contained in the following circular from Himmler, dated August 13, 1943, forced the
offenders back into line.

Various sources have indicated that the attitude of certain German
administrations toward the Jews has taken a disturbing course in the
occupied eastern territories. . . . Unfortunately, personal relations between Germans and Jewish women have been going beyond those limits
which, for racial and ideological reasons, ought to be scrupulously
observed. Because of an ill-advised use of Jewish manpower, the repu-

tation of the greater German Reich and the position of its representatives are being damaged. . . . Consequently, I desire . . . to see the following instructions given:

1. Jews and other people of a similar class are to be assigned only to physical labor. Their employment at office work is prohibited.

2. It is forbidden to use Jews for general or personal services . . . of any kind.

3. All private relations with Jews, Jewish women, and people of a similar class, as well as all relations superfluous to the needs of the service, are forbidden.[24]

It was the fate of this miserable "human material" to be crushed between the millstones of Nazi ideological fury and the Third Reich's bizarre economic forms. Moreover, a keen competition went on between the hirers of slave labor and the slave owners for the ever diminishing supply. The SS was jealous of private industry. In June 1943 the OSTI attempted to have the Jews in the Lodz ghetto assigned to its organization. "As for Lodz," wrote SS General Globocnik, chief hangman of Poland, to Hitler, "I propose to send its well-qualified workmen and machines to the Poniatowa work camp in order to build it up, and to transfer all production from Lodz to Poniatowa. Lodz will thus be liquidated, for only a part of the 78,000 Jews there are working on war production."[25] The plan was not followed up, though another attempt at it was made in January 1944.[26] In the same document, Globocnik complains of the ill-will of his competitors: "Lodz was packed with labor battalions so as to prevent its evacuation, whereas the same battalions could have been sent on to us, automatically liquidating Lodz."

The document that concludes this section affords us a somewhat deeper view into the functioning of the system. It concerns the difficulties that a middling employer of slave labor, a construction engineer, experiences in dealing with the SS slave owners. He had failed to pay the hire regularly; but more important, he had committed the major crime of having corresponded directly with the Jewish Council of Lodz whence his slaves had come. He was just an ordinary person, neither an SS man nor a member of the Party. His business was going badly and he complained; the tone of the letter is extraordinarily revealing. The fate of the slaves can easily be imagined.

Engineer Rudolph Lautrich
Hohensalza (Posnania)
To the Administrator of the Lodz Ghetto

Hohensalza, July 15, 1943

Subject: Jews' Clothing
See: letter of July 8, 1943.

Please excuse me if I have committed an error in writing a letter to
the Jewish Elder [*Judenältester*] concerning the sending of clothing
and underwear for the Jews working for me.

The rags are literally falling off the bodies of many of these Jews,
and are held together only by strings. Many have neither underwear
nor shoes. The letter was handed to me with the rest of the mail and
I inadvertently signed it. At the age of sixty, I am directing this shop
(as well as another) and I am the only German here, so that an
error like this is easily explained.

In the matter of the hire due for the Jews, I immediately wrote to
my headquarters in Posnania, where the chief accountant is located
whom I send the bills to, and who is responsible for the chief pay-
ments.

I take the liberty of observing that I have 211 Jews in my shop, 54
men and 157 women. Though I have succeeded in turning these men
into acceptable workmen, it is only thanks to my inflexible firmness.
I must admit that this is not so in the case of the women. Only one-
third of the latter do enough work to cover my expenses; for the rest I
have to go into my own pocket.

During the winter the men turned out work worth only 0.80 RM a
day because of the cold and the shortness of the work day. This sum
is spent on their maintenance, so that there is nothing left for the
hire. I thus have to pay the hire for the winter without being able to
keep the Jews busy, and when the work season does come the Hohensalza county government comes along and takes the Jews away from
me to work them elsewhere. Just before winter begins these Jews come
back in an awful condition and it is I who have to pay their maintenance and hire for the winter.

Is it right for a private businessman to have to maintain the work
material [*Arbeitsmaterial*] at his own expense, and then put it at the
disposition of the administration on order without compensation?

I beg you to give a favorable answer to my letter of June 21, 1943,
and I assure you that I shall do my utmost to carry out my promises
punctually.

Heil Hitler!

(Signed)   Engineer Robert Lautrich [27]

A few months later, Engineer Lautrich's worries ended. His
"work material" was sent to a better world.

THE ULTIMATE PILLAGE

If the wholesale extermination of the slaves was economic nonsense, the SS at least made up for it by a skillful exploitation of the retail possibilities of the operation. That was the meaning of the "Operation Reinhardt."

When Reinhard Heydrich, chief of the RSHA and Reichsprotektor of Bohemia-Moravia, was assassinated in Prague in May 1942, the extermination of the Jews was already proceeding at top speed all over Europe. Heydrich's death seems to have been the signal for a speed-up. Operation Reinhard was first of all a colossal expiatory contribution levied in advance on the Polish Jews. (It was not important that the assassination in Prague was the work of non-Jewish Czech patriots; the Jews, by definition, were held responsible.) Himmler, obsessed as he was with the dark Germanic past, may well have been behind this grandiose *Wehrgeld;* the whole operation is quite in keeping with the delirious imagination of the Nazis. And the madness was organized with the efficiency of a Taylor system.

The man whom Hitler had put at the head of the undertaking, SS Brigadeführer Globocnik, divided Operation Reinhard into four parts: "evacuation," "use of manpower," "recuperation of non-real property (*Sachverwertung*)," and "recovery of hidden assets." [28] By "hidden assets" Globocnik meant "machines, raw material, etc., which have passed into Aryan hands . . . permitting interested persons to get rich at little expense." These assets were valued at 15,-000,000 RM. In addition there were Jewish credits in Poland and foreign countries (the SS thought of everything). Of this amount 11,000,000 zlotys had already been recovered. But it was in connection with the recovery of non-real property, in the broadest meaning of the term, that the economic shrewdness of the SS was able to find its greatest scope, especially since the hour of the ultimate pillage was at hand.

A note dated September 26, 1942, listed seventy-eight categories of recoverable objects under ten headings from (a) to (j). [29] The liquid assets—currency and "precious metals, jewels, precious stones, gold or gold fillings and teeth taken from Jews"—were sent to the Reichsbank. There they were deposited in the "Reinhard

Fund," which furnished the commercial operations of the WVHA.[30] The money was put in a separate account, under the fictitious name of "Max Heiliger" [31] (Max the Saint; the supreme mockery for the victims). The "watches, alarm clocks, fountain pens, mechanical pencils, hand or electric razors, scissors, flashlights, billfolds," were to be distributed or sold to the troops on the big Nazi holidays, like the "Feast of the Winter Solstice." [32] "Linen, clothing and men's shoes were to be sorted and valued," the same for "children's clothing, including shoes, to be sent, after payment, to the Vomi. (8) The revenue will come back to the Reich."

We are concerned here with headings (d) and (e). The note recommended that "strict attention be paid to seeing to it that the Jewish star is removed from all the clothing and outer garments to be distributed"—a necessary precaution if there ever was one. The good reputation of the SS outfitters was at stake. A few months later, the "Winter Aid for the German People" complained that "most of the clothing is stained, and covered in places with filth and bloodspots. When 200 dresses were sent to the city of Posnania, the Jewish star had not been removed from 51 of them." [33] For this reason the Winter Aid wanted to return the merchandise. Those were not bloodstains but rust spots, the SS answered. This gruesome correspondence was to continue for several weeks; finally the Winter Aid accepted the clothes in their existing condition but demanded that the SS see to it that the stars were removed. This was no isolated case. A circular from WVHA pointed out to the camp commanders in July 1942, that "the concentration camps have sent packages of clothing . . . in some cases containing articles stained with blood and full of bullet holes. Some of the packages arrived in a damaged condition, so that people outside the service could see their contents." [34]

The enumeration continued: "(f) mattresses, woolen or cotton blankets, cloth remnants, shawls, umbrellas, canes, bottles, thermos bottles, baby carriages, combs, pipes, suitcases and strong boxes; (g) bed sheets, cushions, towels, table cloths, silverware; (h) eyeglasses and monocles; (i) furs." The total product of Operation

(8) Vomi: *Volksdeutsche Mittelstelle*—an organization intended to look after the "ethnic Germans" from the eastern countries, once again incorporated in the Reich.

Reinhard was valued at 180,000,000 RM by Globocnik, "according to the attached conservative estimate, the real value being probably twice as much." [35] According to this estimate, 42,000,000 in jewels and precious objects, and 6,000,000 in currency, were deposited to the account of the WVHA in the Reichsbank. More than 160,000 watches, 7,000 alarm clocks, 29,000 pairs of glasses, were officially "recovered," 1,901 carloads of clothing, linen, and various objects, were earmarked for repatriated *Volksdeutsche* and sent to the Reich. No one will ever be able to estimate the sum of the thefts and "private" recoveries carried on during Operation Reinhard .

As a final touch, Pohl, chief of the WVHA, was named administrator of all Jewish property, real and non-real, in the Government General in September 1942.[36] Farther east, emissaries of the WVHA were attached to each of the "flying commandos" assigned to the extermination of the Jews in the USSR.[37] For Jews deported from western or southeastern Europe, the ultimate spoliation generally took place at Auschwitz itself. The clothing or baggage they had been able to bring filled the thirty-five warehouses of the "Canada" —the nickname the prisoners gave this area of the camp had been picked up by the SS themselves. At certain times, 2,000 to 3,000 privileged prisoners were assigned to sorting the piles of linen, clothes, shoes, and an incalculable quantity of different objects.[38] Among other things there were glasses, artificial limbs, and women's hair; this was the very last stage of the death industries, in which the bones were turned into phosphate and the human fat into soap. The bureaucratic organization of the operation staggers the imagination, even more than does its pure horror. Even the Jews of dead and gone generations made their modest contribution to the prosperity of the Third Reich. In many German cities, the municipalities sold the gates and funeral monuments of the Jewish cemeteries; tombstones in the Government General were used for paving the streets.[39]

Still more gruesome examples could be given—but what is the use? We are confronted here with an attempt at a total reversal of values; everything that was blameworthy, repulsive, and odious had become not merely neutral but praiseworthy and noble. Men gave free rein to their instincts; all barriers were swept away; every mind was bent on self-aggrandizement. Everything they did was well done. "We have written a glorious page in our history," Himmler said, when talking about the exterminated Jews, and he continued: "We have taken everything they owned." [40]

The majority of the records on Operation Reinhard refer to Jewish property as "goods stolen, concealed, and hoarded by the Jews." (9) A circular dated September 26, 1942, formally prescribed the future use of these terms. It was necessary to ease the consciences of German officials and business connections of the SS and to give them a certain amount of self-justification.

But inversely, certain profits derived from apparently lucrative operations seem to have been only the secondary consequences of actions primarily aimed at consolidating the moral basis of the anti-Jewish undertakings. When the Jews handed over by the satellite countries were deported, the Nazis tried to collect a fee for each one from the satellite governments. Slovakia agreed to pay 500 RM for each "evacuated" Jew. Vichy France and Bulgaria refused.[41] There is certainly more to this curious German demand than a desire to increase the state's revenue; what they want is a certificate of work well done from the country "cleansed" of its Jews. The relations of the Third Reich with its satellites illustrates many aspects of the Jewish question. Involved in this problem are such things as the value that the troubled Nazi conscience attached to public opinion in the "New Europe"; the tendency to share responsibility; as well as a propaganda effort such as Knochen contemplated. When the works of art were looted in France, Rosenberg suggested answering the Vichy protest approximately as follows: The French should be grateful to us for having cleansed them of their Jews. Let them keep the Jewish money and property and let us keep their paintings. (10)

(9) *Jüdisches Diebes-, Hehler- und Hamstergut.*
(10) From "An Account of the Principles of the Special Headquarters of Reichsleiter Rosenberg *in re* the Protest of the French Government of July 25, 1941, Against the Seizure of Art Objects Belonging to Jews":
    The French government wrongly invokes the arrangement according to which the possessions of these Jews were, after the withdrawal of their French nationality, for the most part, seized and placed at the disposal of the National Aid. This possibility of disposing of Jewish possessions was not acquired by the French government under its own power, but only through the victory of the German army. The French state has every reason to be

Within this framework, whenever it seemed to serve their political aims, the Nazis invited other peoples to share in the spoils.

Hundreds of thousands of their own nationals profited personally from the pillage. In his work on Auschwitz,[42] the historian P. Friedman reports the case of an SS wife who wrote her husband not to hesitate sending her bloodstained linen, as she could certainly wash out the bloodstains herself. But as a general rule, such hysterical extremes can be ignored in what had become a routine business. As Blaskowitz wrote, "When the group steals, the individual thief need not fear punishment." Especially in the east, getting rich at the expense of the Jew had become a daily activity. But it was during the mass anti-Jewish "actions" that the looters had their field day. In what follows a German official in White Russia describes the looting that took place during the "liquidation" of the Sluzk ghetto.[43]

> In conclusion, I must point out that, at the time of the action, the police battalion pillaged in an unprecedented manner, not only Jewish homes, but White Russian homes, as well. They took anything that was usable, like shoes, copper, leather, textiles, gold, and valuable objects. According to stories told by soldiers who were eyewitnesses, watches were publicly torn from the wrists of Jews and rings brutally pulled from their fingers. A military administrator reported that a Jewish girl was asked to go out and get 5,000 rubles as the condition for her father's being freed. This girl ran about madly trying to find the money.

It became an established practice to have an official distribution of the loot after the liquidation of a ghetto. The spoils were handed out freely or sold at a ridiculously low price by the detachment commander. Frequently the men submitted a list of what they needed (*Wunschliste*).[44] (For a sample of one such *Wunschliste*, see p. 83.)

To be sure, above all the SS as well as the state administrations and specialized organizations like the Einsatzstab were responsible for the lootings. But they were not the only ones to profit from the

grateful to the Greater Reich for the struggle it has conducted against Jewry. That is why it has no right to protest. . . . The Reich has, by a magnanimous gesture that benefits the French state, renounced the real property and other Jewish possessions in France, placing in safe keeping only the documents of scientific interest and the cultural possessions of the Jews.

worldly goods of the six million assassinated Jews, from the interminable convoys of possessions of all kinds which, day after day and year after year, took the road to Germany. "Goods stolen, concealed, and hoarded." The number of profiteers runs into the millions; through their responsibility for such minor crimes, millions of Germans directly shared in the major crime of genocide.

LIST OF OBJECTS WANTED

By the Officers of the Guard of the Ghetto of Pabianice

Order No.	Military Rank	Name	Man's Wristwatch	Woman's Wristwatch	Man's Watch	Clock	Man's Boots*	Man's Shoes*	Woman's Boots*	Woman's Shoes*	Boy's Boots*	Girl's Boots	Woman's Galoshes	Leather Suitcase	Portfolio	Shopping Bag	Woman's Handbag	Wallet	Change Purse	Raincoat (Ulster)	Woman's Coat	Blanket	Afghan	Man's Long Underwear	Sport Shirts	Woman's Umbrella	Fountain Pen	Razor	Strap	Shaving Brush	Beauty Cream	Shaving Soap	Laundry Soap	Comments
1	Zgw. d. Sch.	Mikl.	1	1	—	—	—	—	—	—	—	—	—	—	—	—	1	—	—	—	—	—	—	—	—	—	—	—	—	—	—	—	—	—
2	Obw. d. R.	Knott.	1	1	—	—	1/41	—	—	—	1/31	—	—	—	1	—	1	—	—	—	—	—	—	—	—	—	—	—	—	—	—	—	—	—
3	—	Ragg.	—	1	1	—	—	—	—	—	—	—	—	—	1	—	1	—	—	—	—	—	—	—	—	—	1	—	—	—	—	—	—	—
4	—	Rheinlander	1	1	—	—	2 4/46	—	2³/40	—	2/26	—	—	—	1	—	—	—	—	—	—	—	—	—	—	—	—	—	—	—	—	—	—	—
5	—	Wheiher.	1	1	—	—	1/42	—	—	—	—	—	—	—	1	—	—	—	—	—	—	—	—	—	—	—	—	—	—	—	—	—	—	—
6	—	Abentheim.	—	1	—	—	—	1/42	1/39	—	2/33	—	—	—	1	—	—	—	—	—	—	—	—	1	2	—	—	—	—	—	—	?	?	—
7	—	Kummerl.	1	1	—	—	1/42	—	—	—	—	—	—	—	1	—	—	—	—	—	—	—	—	—	—	—	—	—	—	—	—	—	—	—
8	—	Neumann.	1	1	—	—	—	—	—	—	—	—	—	—	1	—	—	—	—	—	—	—	—	—	—	—	1	—	—	—	—	—	—	—
9	—	Hilsner.	1	1	—	—	—	—	—	—	—	—	—	—	1	1	1	1	1	—	—	—	—	—	—	—	1	1	1	1	—	—	1	1
10	—	Warmuth.	1	1	—	—	—	—	—	—	—	—	1/40	—	1	—	1	—	—	—	—	—	—	—	—	1	1	—	—	—	—	—	—	—
11	R. d. R.	Wegner.	1	1	—	—	1/40	1/37	1/35	—	1/36	—	1/37	—	1	—	—	—	—	—	—	—	—	—	—	—	—	—	—	—	—	—	—	—
12	—	Bohacek.	—	—	—	—	—	—	—	—	1/33	—	—	—	—	—	—	—	—	—	—	—	—	—	—	1	—	—	—	—	—	—	—	—
13	—	Drecler.	1	1	—	—	1/45	1/42	—	1/38	—	—	—	—	1	—	1	1	1	1	—	1	—	—	—	—	1	1	—	1	—	—	1	1
14	—	Hillmann.	1	1	—	—	—	—	—	—	1/33	—	—	—	1	—	—	—	—	—	—	—	—	—	—	—	—	—	—	—	—	—	—	—
15	—	Klar.	—	—	—	—	1/39	1/39	—	—	—	—	—	—	—	—	—	—	—	—	—	—	—	—	—	—	—	—	—	—	—	—	—	—
16	—	Kobinger.	1	1	—	—	1/43	—	3/40	2/39	1/36	—	—	1	1	—	1	—	—	1	1	1	1	—	—	3	1	1	—	—	—	—	1	1
17	—	Kraus.	—	1	—	—	1/43	—	1/37	1/38	—	—	—	—	1	—	—	—	1	—	—	1	—	1	—	—	—	—	—	—	—	—	—	—
18	—	Kudrisch.	1	—	—	—	1/41	—	1/39	—	1/38	—	—	—	1	—	1	—	—	—	—	—	—	—	—	—	1	—	—	—	—	—	—	—
19	—	Larisch.	1	1	—	—	1/41	1/41	1/36	—	—	—	—	—	—	—	1	—	—	—	—	—	1	—	—	—	1	—	—	—	—	—	—	—
20	—	Mierscheug.	1	—	—	1	1/41	—	1/40	—	—	—	—	—	—	—	1	—	1	—	—	—	—	—	—	1	—	—	—	—	—	—	—	—
21	Obw. d. R.	Wilke.	—	1	1	—	1/40	—	1/38	1/40	—	—	—	—	—	—	1	—	—	—	—	—	1	—	—	—	—	—	—	—	—	1	1	1
22	—	Langer.	—	1	—	—	1/42	—	1/39	1/39	—	—	—	—	1	—	1	—	—	—	—	—	—	—	—	—	—	—	—	—	1	—	—	—

*The figure before the slash refers to the number of this object wanted, the figure after the slash to the size (of the shoe or boot)

CHAPTER FOUR

The Ghettos

ALTHOUGH PERSECUTED THROUGHOUT EUROPE and forced to live under ever harsher circumstances, very few Jews suspected what their ultimate fate would be. Cold-blooded extermination, so simple and so monstrous, went beyond their imagination; they expected ordeals, but firmly hoped to see them end. This is the first point to bear in mind in trying to understand what happened.

Just as the destinies of Jews had differed in different countries throughout the ages, so their reactions in the ghetto differed in accordance with the countries they came from. There was a basic difference between the Jews of the East, who constituted a well-defined national entity though of a unique kind, and those of the West, who were united by ties of a much looser and hybrid kind, half religious and half psychological. This distinction is essential. Among other things, it explains why the Germans were only able to carry out their policy of ghettoization in the East. It is the life of these artificially created collectivities which we shall study in this chapter. We stand at the last stage before genocide, the stage in which the victims, finding themselves thrust into an artificial isolation, impoverished and weakened by hunger, make attempts at organizing a life for themselves while awaiting the end of the war and the salvation they hope it would bring.

The fact that the extremely dense Jewish populations in Poland, for example, as well as in certain regions of the USSR, had always been concentrated in certain sections of the cities would sufficiently explain why ghettoization was carried out more easily in the East. The "Jewish quarter" was always the spot picked for the ghetto. The pronounced differences of the Jewish population, often including physical peculiarities, was another factor that facilitated their

84

forced isolation. Language, customs, dress—everything set off the
Jews from the surrounding population. In the course of many centuries they had created a specifically Jewish life and culture that
differed completely from those of the peoples among whom they
lived, a unique civilization that has now been obliterated forever
from the face of the earth. It had developed under the pressure of
a hostile world; in this very pressure it found the resources for its
astonishing vitality. The Jews of the East had a long experience
of persecution, so that the persecutor did not find his victims
stricken and defenseless; their psychic resistance made it easier for
them to adapt themselves to the most horrible forms of life. In
the nightmare world of the ghetto, whose mirror reflected the human condition in crazy distortion, the Jews were yet able to fashion
a life of some sort for themselves.

It may well be asked what in this astonishing experience of a
life lived in hermetical isolation was fundamentally and specifically
Jewish, and what was generally human and social. This question
can only be touched upon in these pages. One may perhaps hazard
the statement that certain intense Jewish reactions—their love of
life, their flexibility and fighting spirit, their inordinate passions
and ambitions, due precisely to the fact that their possibilities of
development had been so severely cramped and limited for centuries—were simply the universal human reflex to servitude, only
carried to its highest pitch. Such, then, would be the "universal
meaning of the Jew. . . ."

Some of the ghettos, especially in Soviet Russia, disappeared
almost without a trace; and where documents do exist, they are not
always accessible. Moreover, since each ghetto was a world in
itself, it is impossible to sketch their histories without falling into
repetition. We shall therefore limit ourselves to telling, in some
detail, the story of the largest one, the Warsaw ghetto, capital of
Polish Judaism. It is also the one whose story is best known, thanks
to its survivors, but thanks even more to the efforts of some who
did not survive. From the time the ghetto was created, a team of
historians set about creating archives and recording its life from
day to day. The diary kept by the leading spirit of the group, the
historian Emmanuel Ringelblum, is a particularly valuable source of
information.[1] When the agony of the Warsaw ghetto began in the

summer of 1942, the members of the group added their last messages to the archives and buried them deep in the ground. "What
we were not able to cry into the face of the world, we have buried
under the earth," one of them wrote.

LIFE AND STRUCTURE OF A GHETTO

As we have seen, the Warsaw ghetto was not created until October 16, 1940, after its establishment had been announced several times and then postponed. In the early summer of 1940, the
Germans erected walls in the streets isolating blocks of houses.
Little by little the walls were joined, cutting off an entire section
of the city, into which the Jews driven from the villages and provincial cities were sent. After July 1, 1940, Jews were forbidden to
reside elsewhere than in the ghetto sector. The October 16 edict
prescribed the transfer to this section of the 140,000 Warsaw Jews
living outside its limits and the evacuation of the 80,000 Poles residing there. After November 16, the Warsaw Jews were no longer
allowed to leave the ghetto without special permission.

The total number of inhabitants of the Warsaw ghetto cannot
be calculated with certainty. There were 359,827 Jews in Warsaw,
according to the census of 1939; new evacuees from the provinces
were added in 1940 and 1941—140,000 of them according to some
sources. The total ghetto population could not have been much
less than one-half million in the summer of 1941.[2] The ghetto
population embraced all ages, professions, and social classes, but
there was a marked division along the lines of culture and language: on one side the Orthodox Jew, who spoke only Yiddish; on
the other, the intellectual Polish-speaking Jew. There were also
a number of converted Jews, several thousand according to some
testimonies, who regularly attended the three churches in the
ghetto.[3] Within its original limits, the ghetto numbered nearly
1,500 buildings; after the perimeter was narrowed in accordance
with an edict of October 1941, there was an average of fourteen
inhabitants per dwelling. The overcrowding was frightful. The Germans took care to exclude any garden or open space from the
ghetto area. Fresh air became a precious commodity; the owners of
the few rare trees charged a fee for the right to sit beneath them.

This terrifying density was apparent in the crowds seething on the streets. A witness remarked that the streets looked like a cross between a madhouse and an Oriental market place.

Under such conditions, and considering the lack of medicines, it is not surprising that epidemics ran wild. The most serious, exanthematic typhus, carried off 15,749 victims during 1941. These scourges, however, were only a minor thing compared to the atrocious famine whose reign was constant in the gigantic concentration camp of the ghetto. The Germans were following a deliberate policy of extermination by famine. Food rations for the Jews were cut to a minimum; essentials such as meat, fish, fresh vegetables, and fruit, were expressly excluded from the ration. Bread, potatoes, and ersatz fat made up the ration, whose nutritive value was some 800 calories on the average. The ghetto's isolation made it easier to control all the food coming in. Starvation and its attendant sicknesses exacted their toll from the very beginning; the mortality rate rose in a dizzy spiral as a result of the lessened physical resilience and resistance of the majority of the population.[4] The refugees from the provinces, without heat or shelter, were the principal victims. Wretched people died in the streets by the dozen; passers-by hastily covered the bodies with newspapers while waiting for the hearse to come and take them away.

With certain rare exceptions, the inhabitants could leave the area only in work gangs; German and Polish sentries guarded the fourteen entrances, shooting on sight any Jews who came too close. The telephone and trolley lines leading to the ghetto were cut (a special trolley line, with the star of David on a sign, functioned inside the ghetto; this "concession" had been leased to the Kohn and Heller company, which will be discussed later). Postal communication with foreign countries was prohibited; on December 1, 1941, the receipt of food packages was forbidden under pretext of the "danger of epidemics."

In a ghetto so isolated the Germans could apply at leisure the starvation policy recommended by Frank, since they had every facility for controlling its supply of food.

German control on the whole was exercised from the outside. In fact, no German authority had an office inside the ghetto, nor were any SS or other detachments billeted there. Except on certain regularly used routes, particularly the one leading to the Pawiak political prison in the center of the ghetto, a German uniform was rarely to be seen. There were a few visits by newspaper men and a few conducted tours for soldiers on leave; the spectacle of the slow agony of the "sub-men" was offered them as a species of recreation. Visits and tours were abolished at the beginning of 1942, however, following the often unfavorable reactions they evoked among the visitors. (1) A few SS detachments, always the same ones, made occasional regular rounds. Thus the Nazis could hypocritically claim that they had granted "autonomy" to the Jews. The German administration, directed by the ghetto's commissioner, Auerswald, aimed at isolating it as completely as possible and taking away as much as it could in supplies and manpower, thus contributing to the famine that steadily enfeebled its occupants.

Like all the ghettos, Warsaw's was administered by a "Jewish council" named by Germans when the city was occupied. Much ink has already been spilled about the Jewish councils, which served as the organizations for carrying out German wishes at every stage of isolation and extermination. An indelible shame would seem to stick to these organs of collaboration. Their members enjoyed certain prerogatives and were the lords of the ghetto; they may be compared with the Quislings and the Lavals. But we should remember that the Germans were not dealing with a conquered country having its own political structure and administrative branches. The ghettos were a Nazi-created, artificial agglomeration; they had to have some way of organizing themselves internally and conducting relations with the Germans. Historically, the Jewish councils were inevitable. Different judgments may be passed depending on the specific case, on the motives of these men, and on the manner in which they exercised their functions. One judgment, however, is

(1) Emmanuel Ringelblum says in this connection:

A large number of Germans used to visit the cemetery and morgue where the corpses found in the streets or those of the wretched people who died from hunger were piled up, waiting burial in a common grave. Discussions arose among the Germans concerning the Jewish question. Some expressed pleasure at seeing the victims of the Hitler extermination policy, but others showed indignation in the name of "German culture." Since so undesirable an effect was produced, the excursions were forbidden. (Diary of E. Ringelblum, May 8, 1942.)

certain: many outright scoundrels insinuated themselves into the councils.

Whatever the motives of the council members and regardless of what can be said about their policy, in all cases they finally had to choose between martyrdom and dishonor. By a supreme irony, the choice they made had only a very restricted practical meaning for the people they administered, or for themselves. All of them died—those who hastened their death or chose suicide will undoubtedly benefit by a few extenuating circumstances in the verdict of history.

The Jewish council of Warsaw had twenty-four members, all picked by the Germans, and was headed by the engineer Adam Tcherniakov. This group was charged with the usual governmental functions. A Jewish police force consisting of more than 1,000 men was created; taxes were levied for the maintenance of a system of welfare work and public kitchens for the increasingly numerous poor. This essential branch of ghetto activity enjoyed a distinct degree of freedom. It was the duty of the Jewish council to furnish the work battalions demanded by the occupier. The training of skilled workers, as well as a small amount of teaching at the primary level, was officially permitted under the control of the council. (2) It was charged, too, with sanitary and medical responsibilities, the upkeep of hospitals, and the battle against epidemics. The council also organized a workshop where shipments of raw materials (textiles, leather, etc.) allotted by the Germans were finished by the ghetto workmen and artisans for the Wehrmacht. However, most of the work done in the ghetto was decided upon outside the council and was directed either by the Germans themselves, or by people who knew how to get into their good graces. The tragic fact of economic collaboration, like that of administrative collaboration, stares at us from the record; in the economic considerations that the ghetto represented for the Germans lay its main chance for survival. We have quoted in Chapter II a few German documents underlining the importance of the contribution of Jewish craft and industrial labor to the Wehrmacht in partic-

(2) When the ghetto was created, the Germans refused permission for schools to be opened. It was not until May 1941 that schools for 5,000 children could be opened. (*Gazeta Zydowska*), No. 34, April 29, 1941)

ular. The Warsaw ghetto's Jews were aware of this. As far back as April 1942, Emmanuel Ringelblum had noted in his diary:

> The history of man knows no similar tragedy. A nation that hates the Germans with all its soul can ransom itself from death only at the price of its contribution to the enemy's victory, a victory which means its complete extermination in Europe and perhaps in the whole world.

The major part of this work was supplied by German manufacturers such as Walter C. Többens, whose textile factories and tanneries employed thousands of workers. For the Jewish worker in the ghetto such employment meant an assured income, additional food, and exemption from forced labor. During the final period it would provide a temporary insurance against deportation and death. An astonishing solidarity of interest was established between the exploited Jew and the German overlord struggling to keep his slaves. Sometimes their work afforded them rather somber compensations. Early in 1942, for example, 200,000 bloody and torn German uniforms arrived in Warsaw for cleaning and repair in the Jewish shops. (Ringelblum relates that the pockets of some of the field coats still contained letters which the soldiers had been writing to their families from the depths of the Russian winter.)

Thus, the official economic activity was limited to the introduction of meager quantities of food and the raw materials utilized in the ghetto's shops, exported in the form of finished products. These exchanges were made principally at the *Umschlagplatz,* an immense station set up near one of the gates.

The ghetto had another sort of economic life, equally intense and sustained, but unofficial. The savings of its inhabitants, the jewels, currency, utensils, and various objects that certain Jews had succeeded in saving, formed its essential basis. Added to these were a few stocks of raw materials, rare commodities which their owners had been able to hold onto.

The ingenuity of the ghetto's manufacturers, engineers, and chemists made possible the addition of a large number of new industries to the shops and factories already established there. These included food industries (the canning of fish, horsemeat, ersatz and "synthetic" preserves of all kinds), tanneries, clandestine dyeworks, and even luxury industries (chocolate, cigarettes, watch-making). Some of these products were meant for export; Jewish traders were able during the first months of the ghetto's existence to do business with the Aryan city by telephone. Exports and imports were either smuggled out and in, or passed through with the complicity of the German officials of the *Umschlagplatz*.[5] In exchange for money and illicitly manufactured products, a regular flow of provisions reached the ghetto from which a rather thin layer of privileged people benefited. The ghetto's smugglers were the agents in this, from the big manufacturer working hand in hand with the German or Ukrainian guards right down to the Jewish children crawling through the sewers or chinks in the wall. The chief contraband commodities were flour and potatoes. Dozens of clandestine mills were set up in cellars and attics. They were turned by hand and needed a rather large number of workmen; these millers organized themselves in a clandestine union. The big smugglers were an important group in the ghetto and were treated with respect. An insurance exchange functioned at 13 Nalewki Street in order to insure the large contraband cargoes.

Such were the replies that life itself devised to the iron noose that the Germans flung around the ghetto.

To prevent these activities, the Germans established a special economic police independent of the Jewish council police and directly responsible to the Warsaw Gestapo, whose duty was to discover and confiscate smuggled merchandise. These police were directed by one Abraham Ganzweich, with headquarters at 13 Leszno Street. In the ghetto they were known as "The Thirteen," and were just such a collection of sinister figures as spring up in troubled times. People of this kind, moreover, were best suited to getting along with their SS partners and bribing them. Ganzweich's access to the Gestapo got him a number of favors, the most important among which was a limited supply of passes. These enabled him to engage in all sorts of deals which rapidly made him one of the ghetto magnates.

Ganzweich kept open house and liked to pose as a Maecanas, entertaining writers and artists at his own expense, even setting up a club for them. He also equipped his own ambulance service (the "Rapid Aid"), whose members he dressed in uniforms of his own design. The tendency for the robber barons to atone for their extravagances by a show of social and philanthropic interest was more pronounced in ghetto society than elsewhere; to justify the services they did for the Germans they assumed the role of benefactors of the people. Another reason for this may perhaps be the community of fate which bound them to the lowest wretch in the ghetto. (3)

The Thirteen were put out of the way in May 1942, sometime before the deportations and the final destruction of the ghetto, for obscure reasons, apparently by a section of the Gestapo other than the one with which they were working.

Other forces made themselves felt in the ghetto which, without having any official functions, in fact enjoyed considerable power. Such was the Kohn-Heller group, concessionnaire of the ghetto's only trolley line. Before the war they had been a trading house with numerous commercial connections with Germany. The Thirteen derived their power from the Gestapo, Kohn and Heller from Commissioner Auerswald's office. The system was much the same: gathering information and performing services for the Germans, providing bribes. Kohn-Heller's intercession was indispensable for obtaining an authorization to bring merchandise into the ghetto. They themselves were the principal importers; in particular, they enjoyed a monopoly on the import of medicines, but they also imported provisions on a large scale. (4) On occasion, they functioned

(3) In his study of the Kovno ghetto, S. Gringauz cites a similar and particularly characteristic case, that of Josef Serebrowitz:

He did not live in the ghetto but in the city proper. He had received a good Jewish education, was able and before the war had been an intellectual adventurer. He was a clear case of pathological mania, of questionable reputation and already before the war feared because he was known to be in the service of the political police and a foreign agent of the German intelligence. Although he lived outside the ghetto he was anxious to appear in the ghetto as a "benefactor" and martyr for the Jewish cause. One evening he invited to his house the intellectuals of the ghetto—the teachers, literati, lawyers, and journalists—and delivered himself of a long ideological lecture in which he presented his confused philosophy of history. He concluded with these words: "I suffer more than you do, even though I live and eat better than you do. You have at least a bare chance to survive. I will be shot much sooner than you." He, his wife and his two children were shot by the Gestapo in the beginning of 1943. (S. Gringauz, "The Ghetto as a Social Experiment," New York, *Jewish Social Studies*, January 1949.)

(4) Ringelblum gives this as an example: Twenty carloads of potatoes imported into the ghetto by Kohn and Heller and bought for 0.40 zlotys a kilo were resold at 2 zlotys a kilo.

as spies. Ringelblum blames them for the bloody actions of the night of April 18, 1942, aimed at the printers and distributors of the ghetto's undercover press, which resulted in several dozen deaths. The ostentation displayed by Kohn and Heller surpassed even that of The Thirteen, if that were possible. They organized receptions and sumptuous banquets. Heller announced the celebration of the circumcision of his first-born by bills posted in every ghetto street —it was like the announcement of the baptism of a prince royal. This astonishing fondness for regal ostentation shown by the ghetto's moguls reached its peak at Lodz; later on, we shall have something to say about its "elder," Chaim Rumkowski. In October 1941 the trolley line was done away with and replaced by a coach service. This marked the beginning of the end for Kohn and Heller; their final fate is as obscure as that of The Thirteen.

The Struggle Against Hunger

A cruel and threatening famine hung constantly over the heads of the ghetto's inhabitants; the struggle for existence became the chief aim of their lives. Under such conditions, the deepest recesses of human nature are revealed; conventional masks fall away, conflicts gain in volence, and differences are accentuated. Human society, however, continues to exist. (One can imagine what the ghetto's course of development would have been had it gone on and given birth to new generations. But it lasted barely two years.)

The situation gave rise to its own remedies: One of these was the "House Committees" that were organized in each building soon after the creation of the ghetto. Each committee was composed of from five to twelve members, elected by the inhabitants of the house. The purpose of the committee was to aid the poorest tenants secure food and clothing and to help their children; for this work, the better-off tenants were recruited. The committees were entirely outside the Jewish council's authority and remedied somewhat the terrible social injustices of the ghetto. Soon the ghetto was covered with a network of committees, which banded together to form zone committees; the latter, in turn, sent delegates to a central commission of the ghetto committees. Thus

a representative assembly was spontaneously born, enjoying no
other than a moral authority. But its scope was nevertheless broad.
A large part of the ghetto welfare work, especially the operation of
certain canteens, was under the direction of the central commission and its branches; in this way the important problem of feeding
the poor was solved. The Jewish council repeatedly tried to bring
the house committees under its authority, but without success; the
central commission succeeded in preserving its independence until
the end.

In conformity with the best traditions of Jewish solidarity, men
and women eagerly plunged into this communal work. They were
people of all ages and social classes, artisans, intellectuals, and
members of every political party. Though they also suffered from
hunger and cold, no amount of work deterred them, no difficulty
was too great to be overcome. They risked contagion in houses in-
fected with typhus, and dared the wrath of the "official" authorities. In this intensive and feverish activity, women played a role
of prime importance. Sometimes they outnumbered the men, especially toward the end. "In many of the house committees, women
are now replacing the men," noted Ringelblum on June 3, 1942.
"The latter are giving way, completely exhausted and worn out by
work. In some committees, the entire direction is in the hands of
women; in welfare work, where fresh blood is indispensable, they
furnish a reservoir of new strength."

Countless fields of activity were opened to men of good will in
the ghetto. Youth organizations, the very ones that would later
furnish the ghetto resistance units, attempted to ease the famine
by cultivating tiny patches of ground. Kitchen gardens were planted
on the sites of bombed houses; vegetables were cultivated on bal-
conies and even on roofs; a few groups of young volunteers were
authorized to cultivate fields outside the ghetto. A number of collective farms operated by young Zionists succeeded in maintaining themselves on the outskirts of Warsaw and contributed to the
ghetto's food supply.

All this activity was nevertheless only a drop in the bucket of
the ghetto's needs. In May 1942 Ringelblum noted in his diary:

> Welfare aid does not solve the problem. It prolongs existence, but
> the end is inevitable. It prolongs suffering, but does not provide a

solution; it simply lacks the necessary means. The patrons of the people's kitchens, reduced to soup and dry bread, are dying little by little. It may be asked whether it wouldn't have been more purposeful to help first those people who are valuable from the social point of view, the spiritual élite, and the like. But the situation is such that . . . even for these chosen ones, the means at our disposal are insufficient. On the other hand, it may be asked why people must be sacrificed who were workmen or productive artisans before the war, and whom war and the ghetto alone have turned into the dregs of the population and candidates for the common grave. The tragic question remains unanswered: Ought we to give everyone a spoonful so that no one will survive or to give in abundance what will suffice only for a handful?

Thus was posed the tragic problem of the useless mouths. Until the end, the policy adopted was to furnish aid to all the needy without exception, and for this reason the aid was largely insufficient. Those evacuated from the provinces were the first victims of starvation, dying by thousands, so that there was a large turnover of those depending on the people's kitchens; the Warsaw Jews replaced the provincials, only a few thousand of whom were still alive in July 1942. As Ringelblum noted in August 1941, they died without any resistance; he wondered about the reasons for this passivity, and then answered himself:

A disconcerting question is the passivity of the Jewish masses, who are dying in silence. Why are they silent? Why do complete families die, father, mother, and children without a single protest? Why haven't we carried out the threats we made a year ago, the rebellions, the pillages, the threats that aroused the house committees and moved them to collect stores of food?

There are several answers to this question. The occupiers have instituted a terror so vast that people are afraid to lift their heads. They're afraid of the mass assassinations that will be the answer to any reaction from the starving masses; this is the reason for the caution of the thinking part of the population. There is still another reason: Some of the poor people, the most active, have succeeded in getting themselves settled down in one way or another. Smuggling opens possibilities for a livelihood for thousands of porters, who receive 10 zlotys per bag transported, over and above the tariff. A large number of the workmen and artisans have found jobs in the shops working for Germans. Others became peddlers. So it is the passive people, who have no incentive, who are dying in silence. The Jewish police, which has learned to beat up people, send them to work camps, and preserve order, is another factor that keeps the masses in check. The victims of hunger are in large part refugees from the provinces who feel lost and discouraged in a strange atmosphere. Their protest is symbolized in written lamentations, energetic accosting of passers-by on the streets for alms, petty demonstrations in their own home-town groups, and pleas addressed to the house committees for a slice of bread. . . . Recently I talked with one of these refugees, who had been starving for a long time. All he thinks about is food, particularly bread: wherever he goes, whatever he does, he dreams of bread; he stops in front of every bakery, in front of every window. At the same time, he has become resigned and apathetic; nothing interests him any more. He finds it hard to wash himself and does so only because he has been accustomed to it from childhood. Perhaps this passivity, produced by hunger, was the reason why the Jewish masses starved to death quietly without strenuous protest.

There is not very much to add to these lines; they give us a glimpse of the reasons why Jewish resistance was so slow in developing in the ghettos. The begging that Ringelblum mentioned added a characteristic note to the picture of the ghetto. After spending their savings and selling the last of their old clothes, the unfortunates turned to begging as a last supplement to the meager food doled out by the people's kitchens. Adults and children, singly or in groups, held out their hands in the street, even went "to the Aryan side" at great risk to beg whatever alms they could get. Then the last stage came, the slow death agony in the streets. Mary Berg recalls in her diary "the countless children, whose parents have perished, sitting in the streets. Their poor little bodies are frightfully thin, the bones stick out of a yellow skin that looks like parchment. . . . They crawl on all fours, groaning; they have nothing human about them; they are more like monkeys than children." A few steps away, in some of the ghetto's cafes, could be found "absolutely anything one can wish, the most expensive liqueurs, cognac, pickled fish, all kinds of preserves, duck, chicken, geese; the price for a dinner, with wine, is from 100 to 200 zlotys." [6]

The experiences of 1939-45 afford many a disconcerting lesson about the way in which society functions under unimaginable pressure and about the reactions of men subjected to countless tortures. A good many concentration camp survivors have said some very disillusioning things about the sad fate of human values in death's antechambers. But when these values were maintained, it was to the point of sublimity. The ghetto was only a somewhat more autonomous and varied concentration camp, where the social contrast between luxury and beggary, as well as the moral contrast between the worst selfishness and the completest altruism, were pushed to the limit.

Did the Jewish character of the ghetto's inhabitants give its life any special qualities? It perhaps had the effect of accentuating certain traits, such as the magnificent effort at solidarity and social assistance just described. Other peculiarities, which we shall now consider, can be explained in part by the traits developed through the ages in the Jewish national character. Here again we are dealing with reactions universal in their nature, only pushed to an extreme point.

Whatever the ghetto's ordeals, the quest for artistic and intellectual recreation, as well as the spirit of disinterested research, were strengthened rather than weakened. Several theaters functioned right up to the end. Troupes of young amateurs competed with professional artists. Even the ghetto's robber barons, as we have seen, made a point of sponsoring or supporting artists, musicians, and writers. Teaching, on the other hand, though forbidden by the Germans, was secretly developed on a large scale and at all levels. Mary Berg has left a touching description of such an underground class, a school of graphic arts and industrial design with complete courses of study, final examinations, and the awarding of diplomas. Even pure science was engaged in in the ghetto. A group of doctors undertook a series of studies on the pathological aspects of starvation. The funds they needed came from private donations, and special equipment was installed in the hospitals. The results, sent to Aryan Warsaw for safe keeping as the experiments progressed, were found and used after the war.[7]

The intellectual life of the ghetto was especially intense. The Jewish fondness for reading became stronger than ever. Current affairs were obviously the chief interest, but only one slim official newspaper, controlled by the Germans, the *Gazeta Zydowska*, and a few secretly published sheets were available in the ghetto. Under such conditions, people's interest turned to literature and history, especially to those periods that offered parallels with the present.

In June 1942, Ringelblum wrote with moving clarity on this subject:

What do people read? . . . After the war they will want to know what occupied the minds of the men of the Warsaw ghetto, men who knew death was waiting for them, as it had already come to the Jewish small town settlements. Well, they can say that we did not lose our human characteristics; our minds are as busy as they were before the war.

Serious readers are much interested in the literature of war. They read memoirs like Lloyd George's, the great novels of World War I, and so forth. They especially enjoy the pages dealing with 1918 and the German defeat. They look for comparisons with present events and try to prove that the defeat of the unconquered German army is near. They enjoy the story of the reception of the German representatives at Compiègne and already see in imagination a new and more striking Compiègne taking place. For myself, I have had the occasion to read Van der Meersch's great work on the German occupation in France and Belgium. (5) At every step one sees a parallel with the present [though the situation today] is much much more terrible than in the first world war. One thing remains the same: the pillaging and the cold and pitiless oppression of the civilian population of the occupied countries. . . . The population was enslaved and forced to work for the Germans. After reading the book, I thought: What was done to prevent a new rule of the Huns in Europe?

Many readers are passionately interested in the Napoleonic era. They look for analogies between Hitler and Napoleon, always to the latter's advantage, for, though Napoleon had on his conscience the oceans of blood spilled on all the battlefields of Europe, he shook the feudal world to its foundations and ushered in a new revolutionary order; while Hitler will leave behind him only tens of thousands of victims and a desolate and ruined Europe, put back centuries by this war.

People like to read the life of Napoleon, for they see that an invincible dictator's star falls quicker than one imagines. One takes the greatest pleasure in reading about the Russian campaign that ended in so tragic a defeat, and was the beginning of the end—one hopes that history will repeat itself. . . . Tolstoy's *War and Peace* is enjoying great popularity among people who have already read it more than once, because of the way it treats the Napoleonic epic.

In short, unable to avenge themselves upon the enemy in fact, people are trying to do so in their imagination, in literature.

(5) Maxence van der Meersch. *Invasion 1914*.

Escaping in this way into books and history brought some relief to the ghetto inhabitants and helped them to go on living. But their chief comfort they found in themselves, in the vitality and optimism so characteristic of Jews. Again a distinction must be made between the Polish Jews who had kept intact the traditions and experiences of several centuries of specifically Jewish life, and the assimilated and westernized Jews. In Chapter I we have sketched the overwhelming moral tragedy that expulsion from the national community constituted for the German Jews. The great majority of Polish Jews were spared this emotional shock. We have already said something about their long tradition of persecution; from this habituation they drew the strength for their inner resistance. By a kind of mechanism of compensation it gave them a magnificent vitality and a faith in the future, formed during a thousand years of faithfulness to the Law and the prophets; this faith had helped them face every threat and survive centuries of misery and pogroms. Resistance to all calamities went hand in hand with a kind of obstinate flexibility. A special technique for dealing with the powers-that-be had been developed by the Jews over the centuries; in this they now placed a part of their hopes. They dreamed of gigantic bribes offered to the Gestapo; they banked on the Wehrmacht's economic needs. The Nazis profited from these hopes in a thousand ways, but above all through their system of fake "protection certificates" by which they were assured of a docile labor force. Above all, the Jews could not believe in such extremes of cruelty as the Nazis were prepared to go to. Everything conspired to nourish their traditional optimism: Nazi trickery and the very magnitude of the massacres which it concealed. While there was hope, there was life. An indication of the ghetto's vitality was the absence in Warsaw of any such epidemic of suicides as raged among the German Jews, with the sole exception of a group of German Jews who had been deported to Poland and who were much better off than the rest of the population. The ghetto's rage to study English (whose knowledge was to be useful for Jews who emigrated after the war) is another indication of the strong Jewish faith in the future.

The line between hope and illusion is sometimes hard to draw.

At any moment, but especially in the darkest days, the Jews in the ghetto were ready to believe that the end of the war was at hand and that life would immediately become "normal." All sorts of rumors encouraged this state of mind. Thus, a veritable industry for false radio communiqués was developed by a few unscrupulous journalists who edited and broadcast these invented bulletins. (6) Calmer minds were evidently incapable of sustaining themselves with such fake stories. Jewish humor, wry and sarcastic, gave such superior minds an outlet. Ringelblum cites a number of these striking examples of popular wit, which hide despair beneath a grin: Churchill went to consult a miracle-working Chasidic rabbi about the way to beat the Nazis. "There are two possible ways," the rabbi told him; "A natural way—a million angels armed with flaming swords can fall upon Germany and destroy it. A supernatural way —a million British soldiers can descend on Germany and destroy it."

TWILIGHT OF THE GHETTO

The Warsaw ghetto lasted scarcely two years. While its inhabitants tried to defy their fate and live, the wheels of genocide began to turn. At the beginning of 1942, mass exterminations began in Poland. The first news of the massacres in the provinces reached the ghetto in April 1942. On April 12, Ringelblum recorded in his diary rumors of the arrival in Warsaw of an extermination brigade. The massacre of 40,000 Jews in the Lublin ghetto was learned of a few days later.[8] The pogroms that took place on April 17 and during the early part of May made the atmosphere even more oppressive. On May 8, Mary Berg wrote: "The night-time murders are

(6) On May 8, 1942, Ringelblum copied the text of a few "false communiqués." An extract follows:

What is in these communiqués? First of all, Smolensk has been taken by a landing force of 60,000 soldiers, who joined up with the Red Army, on the west of Smolensk. This same bulletin also took Kharkov. It landed at Murmansk an army transported by 160 ships, not one of which was sunk. . . . In case that was not enough, Mussolini was deposed and a revolution made in Italy. Finally, [the communiqué] added an ultimatum from Roosevelt to the German people that expired on May 15.

continuing. Half the population may disappear before the end of the war. . . . It has become very dangerous to go out for any distance in the ghetto. Despite everything, life continues and the stores are open . . . the theaters are playing as usual." [9]

Detailed information about the Belzec extermination camp and about the massacres at Pabianice and Biala Podlaska were noted by Ringelblum in his diary in June 1942; these show that the men who were informed knew that the end of the ghetto was at hand—even if the illusion lasted longer among the mass of the people.

The storm broke a month later. On July 22, 1942, a notice published by the Jewish council announced to the inhabitants that they were going to be deported "to the east," regardless of age or sex. Only Jews working in German industries, or employed in council work, were exempt from this measure. The ghetto's agony had begun. While the trains were leaving for the death camps, the Jews who remained clutched tighter their chief but temporary life-saver, the employment certificates issued to them by their German masters. Systematic selections had been started by the SS in the shops to eliminate those who were over-age or poor workers; the former tried various subterfuges, such as passing themselves off as younger with false birth certificates, or dyeing their gray hair black. But the ghetto went on being emptied. Two months later, more than three-quarters of the inhabitants had been evacuated.

The internal life, once so varied, began to fade; the ghetto's structure came more and more to resemble a typical Nazi concentration camp. Cafés, theaters, and stores disappeared. Since the children and the aged had been deported first, only able-bodied men and women remained. As the protection certificates were no longer adequate, these slaves were marked by their proprietors on different parts of the body with a distinctive stamp, so that the German or Ukrainian SS would not make any more mistakes in their man hunts.[10] On Yom Kippur, at the end of September 1942, 2,000 policemen were deported with their families; only 380 Jewish policemen were left temporarily. On September 22, the ghetto's area was reduced by more than a half. Some of Mary Berg's notes show us what life in the ghetto was like during this twilight period:

The ghetto is now only an immense work camp. The streets are almost deserted during the day; there is no traffic except at six in the morning when people go to work. From our windows we can see men and women leaving home and hurrying to assembly points, where they line up to go to the factories. They march four by four, escorted by German patrols. After eight it is unusual to see a man in the streets. From noon to one there is a break for lunch. A big kettle is carried into the factory courtyard and the workers line up, mess kit in hand, for the distribution of clear soup. At night, when seven o'clock has struck, the streets are again alive, and the unfortunates rush home as fast as possible. Nobody dares go out later, for the German patrols lie in ambush everywhere. This is life in the ghetto now. The Jews continually feel the shadow of death over them, but everybody thinks he has a chance to escape, nevertheless. Without this hope, which borders on the miraculous, the survivors would commit suicide en masse. . . .

Husbands have been separated from wives and children, children from parents, and everyone sleeps where he can. People who do not know each other at all live together like close relatives. Men whose families have been deported try to escape loneliness by asking the first woman who comes along to move in with them. Life is easier with a woman; also, people feel more secure with another person in this hell.

(October 1-2, 1942)

These men and women, however, seeing at last that their fate was shortly to be sealed, began to make altogether different preparations. No longer counting on the mercy of the Germans, they fought to survive in spite of them. Some hid in bombed-out houses or barricaded themselves in their apartments. Others had themselves walled up in caves with food and water. Deep shelters, "bunkers," were dug underground. A veritable underground ghetto sprang up in the Warsaw sewer system. The Jewish resistance gradually took shape. Meanwhile the deportations continued; only 40,000 Jews remained in the ghetto at the beginning of 1943. But now the implacable SS were no longer the only masters in the ghetto; another power had appeared, the Jewish Combat Organization. A proclamation by Walter Többens, the biggest Wehrmacht contractor, throws some light on the last days of the Warsaw ghetto. It is dated March 20, 1943:

To the Armament Workers in the Jewish Quarter:

The headquarters of the Combat Organization issued a proclamation on the night of March 14-15 which I want to answer. I can state categorically that: (1) there is no question of deportation; (2) neither Mr. Schultz nor myself has received orders, at gun point, to proceed with deportations; (3) the last transport has indeed reached its destination. . . .

Jewish armament workers, don't believe those who are trying to mislead you! They want to force you into acts whose consequences would be incalculable. The bunkers offer no safety and life in them or in the Aryan quarter is not possible. Insecurity and inactivity will undermine the morale of men who are used to working. Let me ask you: Why are the rich Jews leaving the Aryan quarter and coming to me to ask for employment? They have enough money to live in the Aryan quarter, but they cannot put up with such a hunted existence. I advise you to go to Trawniki or Poniatowo. You can live there and wait for the end of the war. The leaders of the Combat Organization cannot help you; they can only make hollow promises.[11]

These astonishing appeals of the slave dealer were answered only by a minority of the Jewish workers. Those who obeyed were able to prolong their existence for a while in the Trawniki or Poniatowo *placowki* (work camps). There they lived a few months under relatively bearable conditions and then were massacred in November 1943.

Most of the ghetto's last remaining inhabitants perished in April-May 1943, during the Warsaw uprising. (*See* Chapter IX) The ghetto was bombed, set afire, and razed. A concentration camp for 2,000 Jewish and non-Jewish prisoners was then established by the SS on the site. The stories of a few survivors of this camp indicate that a sporadic and mysterious life went on for several months longer in the cellars and sewers of what had been the Warsaw ghetto.[12]

THE FATE OF THE OTHER GHETTOS

As we have seen, it was only in the east, that is, in Poland and the USSR, that ghettoization was effective. In all, more than 3,000,-000 Jews were locked up in the ghettos, of which the one in Warsaw was the biggest.

All the ghettos came to a tragic end either by deportation or extermination on the spot; however, their life-span varied. Some, like Lodz or Kovno in Lithuania, were maintained up to 1944 and liquidated on the eve of the German retreat. Others lasted only a few

months; the ghettos in the USSR, created later, generally came to
a quicker end.

The bigger the ghetto, the more perfect the isolation from the
outer world the Germans tried to achieve. The German ordinances
distinguished between "ghettos" and "Jewish quarters." (An ordinance dated October 10, 1942, listed thirteen ghettos and forty-two
Jewish quarters in the territory of the Government General.) Only
the ghettos were completely enclosed; the Jewish quarters of the
small cities were merely marked-off areas. The fact that they were
not hermetically sealed off made existence there less difficult;
famine created less havoc. Though closely guarded, their Jewish
inhabitants had more facilities for working as artisans or for engaging in barter with the surrounding population. In the spring of 1942,
a wave of deportations broke over the smaller ghettos and Jewish
quarters in the Government General, ending their existence.

Of the important ghettos, the one at Lodz, in annexed Poland,
deserves special attention. Lodz was the second city of Poland and
the country's principal industrial center. Its ghetto, established in
February 1940, numbered more than 160,000 inhabitants in its first
census; the Lodz ghetto ranked second to Warsaw's. Its different
manufacturing plants, especially its textile industries, constituted a
valuable addition to the German economy. This is why the Lodz
ghetto lasted four years, despite several partial deportations. In
August 1944 the Russian advance neared, and the Lodz ghetto's
70,000 survivors were transferred to Auschwitz, where the great
majority was immediately sent to the gas chambers.

The great economic importance of the Lodz ghetto gave the
Germans a particular interest in it. From the very first they set up
a system there that recalls the one in force in the last days of
Warsaw. Almost all the ghetto's residents were forced to work for
the German war industry and lived under communal conditions.
Extracts from a report by Hans Biebow, German administrator of
the ghetto, throw some light on its situation in April 1943:

> As the undersigned has already told you verbally, the feeding of
> the Jews has now reached the point where a drop in output detri-
> mental to the Wehrmacht threatens. In the shops and factories, where
> the twelve-hour day has just been introduced (day shift and night

shift), the workers, especially those who work standing, are collapsing at their stations.

At the time of the last evacuation in September 1942, all the Jews who were sick and crippled were evacuated. Nevertheless, between that date and March 31, 1942, the mortality has been 4,658. . . .

The food in the factory communal kitchens is intolerable. Vegetables of B and C quality, that is, of poor quality, are boiled in water; because of the lack of fat only a small quantity of oil is added. As I have said above, there are no more potatoes. It is impossible to thicken the soup with flour, which goes to the bakeries.

For months there has been no milk, neither skimmed nor whole. I have been able to make up for the lack of meat by furnishing preserves. It must be remembered that this merchandise is no longer in a state of preservation. . . . If one considers that in March 0.30 RM were spent for food per day per Jew, one can see that insufficient food was sent to the Jewish quarter. . . . The total of the orders sent to the ghetto is at least fifteen times greater than last year. I therefore beg you to intervene with the proper authorities in Posnania.[13]

As elsewhere, German wishes in the Lodz ghettos were executed by a Jewish council. Its president, Chaim Rumkowski, was all-powerful. Here again we meet up with the phenomenon of the worst trials and tribulations exacerbating personal ambitions, vanity and greed, instead of diminishing them, and producing strange pretenders to an illusory and sordid power. Rumkowski is a striking illustration of this. Every judicial power, high and low, was concentrated in his hands; he raised taxes, coined money, and surrounded himself with a coterie of courtiers and flatterers. Court poets indited cantatas to his glory; the children in the ghetto schools inscribed New Year's greetings to him. (7) For the Germans, he was only a Jew, the Jewish elder of Lodz, good enough to command other Jews, but one who also got a good beating on occasion. But in the ghetto he displayed all the pomp of a chief of state. He struck off postage stamps with his own picture on them and appeared in public in white cape and coat; he kept for him-

(7) The New Year's Album for 1942, with 14,587 children's signatures, is in the archives of the YIVO Historical Institute at New York. Here is a sample of a poem in honor of Rumkowski: "Our President Rumkowski has been blessed by the Eternal, not only with intelligence and talent, but with a strong and powerful arm as well; in office and factory, everybody works, everything functions, thanks to the strong arm of the President; troublesome elements have been eliminated, peace and order reign in the ghetto, thanks only to his powerful arm." (L. Berman, *Ghetto Zeitung*, June 1941)

self personally the right to arrest or pardon his "subjects." His aim, he proclaimed, was "peace in the ghetto"; "my workers," he called the ghetto inhabitants, "my children," and even "my Jews." Besides, he believed he had a mission: to preserve the lives of the Lodz Jews through every peril. . . . When the ghetto was evacuated in August 1944, Rumkowski was shoved into one of the last departing freight cars by the SS, just like the most anonymous of his subjects.[14]

Other important ghettos, numbering several tens of thousands of inhabitants were to be found in Cracow, (72,000[15]); Lublin, (40,000[16]); Radom, (35,000[17]); and later, after the outbreak of war against the USSR, in Lwow, (120,000[18]); Vilna, (more than 60,000, most of whom were massacred at the time of the invasion[19]); Bialystok, Kovno, and Riga. As noted, these last ghettos generally had a short life. In the summer of 1942 the ghetto population of Lwow was reduced to 20,000. It should be pointed out that, despite all German efforts, contact was always maintained among the principal ghettos. At first, the exchange of mail was allowed, and on rare occasions even visits (thus, Chaim Rumkowski paid an official visit to the Warsaw ghetto). Later, all communications had to be carried on in complete secrecy. Young couriers, generally members of Zionist or other movements, went from ghetto to ghetto disguised as Aryans, picking up information about what was happening elsewhere, spreading the news of mass deportations, warning about German intentions. This activity subsequently became a nucleus for Jewish armed resistance. A few non-Jewish Poles courageously aided this work, and, on occasion, even German soldiers. Thus, the clandestine Vilna-Bialystok liaison was assured by a Wehrmacht soldier, Sergeant Anton Schmidt.[20] A number of survivors, mostly Jews of Allied nationality who were exchanged during the war for German nationals, brought to the outside world the story of the mounting agony of the ghettos. This news was published in the press, but it was often received incredulously by Jews as well as non-Jews; to civilized minds, such things seemed perfectly unbelievable.

A ghetto of quite another kind was established by the Germans in the old city of Terezin (Theresienstadt) in Czechoslovakia. Created at the end of 1941, that is, when genocide had just begun, it was restricted to German and Czech Jews whose relations, past merit, or fortune made immediate extermination undesirable. Dutch and Danish Jews were later sent there. The inhabitants of this ghetto lived under conditions resembling those of a very harsh internment camp; but from time to time convoys would depart for some unknown destination and end up at Auschwitz. The total number of its prisoners between 1941 and 1945 was 150,000; but its average population was 30,000 and it was 17,521 at the time of liberation.[21] Theresienstadt was only a special station on the macabre route to extermination, though it performed another purpose for the Nazis: thither visiting Commissions of the International Red Cross were conducted and shown how the Jews' fate was certainly a harsh and rigorous one, but humanly acceptable.

CHAPTER FIVE

The Over-all Plan of Extermination

THE ARCHIVES OF THE THIRD REICH and the depositions and accounts of its leaders make possible a reconstruction, down to the last detail, of the origin and development of the plans for aggression, the military campaigns, and the whole array of procedures by which the Nazis intended to reshape the world to their liking. Only the campaign to exterminate the Jews, as regards its conception as well as many other essential aspects, remains shrouded in darkness. Inferences, psychological considerations, and third- or fourth-hand reports enable us to reconstruct its development with considerable accuracy. Certain details, however, must remain forever unknown. The three or four people chiefly involved in the actual drawing up of the plan for total extermination are dead and no documents have survived; perhaps none ever existed. Such is the secrecy with which the masters of the Third Reich, however boastful and cynical they may have been in other matters, surrounded their biggest crime.

THE DECISION

Undoubtedly it was the Master himself, Adolf Hitler, who signed the Jews' death warrant. Certain people might have influenced him: extremists like Josef Goebbels or the party chancellor, Martin Bormann, whose star was rising to its zenith; [1] these were just the men to press him to the decision. According to a strange piece of testimony—by Dr. Felix Kersten, (1) a Finn who was Himmler's per-

(1) Dr. Felix Kersten was a physiotherapist in Berlin. At the beginning of 1939, he was recommended to Himmler, who was suffering from violent stomach cramps. With the help of massage Kersten succeeded in eliminating the pains. Himmler made Kersten his personal physician; he became (in the phrase of the English historian, Trevor-Roper) Himmler's "confessor" and

sonal physician and confidant—the order to begin the systematic extermination of the Jews was given to Himmler by the Führer in the fall of 1940; this decision was supposed to have been extorted from him by Goebbels. However trustworthy a witness Kersten may be, his story, which refers to a conversation he had with Himmler in 1942, must be accepted with reservation. All we can

---

acquired a certain influence over him. Thus he was able to influence a great deal of humanitarian activity, a fact which was officially recognized after the war by the government of the Netherlands. He was particularly responsible for the initiation of the Himmler-Bernadotte conferences of February-April 1945.

In his memoirs entitled *Klerk en Beul; Himmler van nabij* (Amsterdam, Meulenhof, 1948), Kersten stated that Himmler confided to him in November 1942:

"I did not want to exterminate the Jews, Kersten. I had other ideas on this subject. But that miserable Goebbels did everything he could to make it turn out this way."

I looked at Himmler in astonishment.

"I fully understand your surprise," Himmler went on, "and nobody will believe me. In the beginning of 1934 the Führer ordered me to force the Jews to emigrate from Germany. We set up an organization to make this possible —to enable hundreds of thousands of Jews to create a new life for themselves abroad. Nevertheless, an infamous campaign was carried on against us, one that led to the war. Up to 1940, the Jews could still leave Germany freely; then Goebbels won out."

"Why Goebbels?" I asked.

"Goebbels thought that the Jewish problem could be settled only by the total extermination of the Jews. Every Jew still alive was an implacable enemy of German National-Socialism. That is why any consideration shown the Jews was absurd. This was not my opinion. As early as 1934, I had proposed to the Führer that all the Jews be evacuated to Madagascar and there be established as an independent state. The island was fertile, the climate excellent."

"But doesn't Madagascar belong to France?"

"We could have called an international conference, and victorious Germany would have solved the problem once and for all. But for months and years Goebbels kept exciting the Führer to exterminate the Jews by radical means. Once the war had begun, he finally gained the upper hand. In the summer of 1940, the Führer ordered that the Jews be exterminated by degrees. He gave this task to the SS and to me. That was the one and only time I contradicted the Führer. He was at his headquarters in France. I told him, 'The SS is ready to fight and die from myself down to the last man, but don't give us a mission like this.' The Führer became furious and said, 'Himmler, you are being disobedient! What is the meaning of this? This is an order; I take the responsibility for it.'

"So I had no other recourse. Understand me, Kersten, and I hope that History will understand me also." (*Klerk en Beul*, p. 197-98.)

know with certainty is that the decision to exterminate the Jews was taken by Hitler some time between the end of the western campaign in June 1940 and the attack on Russia a year later. Contrary to Kersten's account, it would seem more plausible to date the decision some months later—that is, at the beginning of 1941.

At this point we must enter the domain of psychological speculation, if we are to answer the second question: What were the factors that influenced this decision? Why was this policy adopted, whose consequences—in the words of Frank, the hangman of Poland—"could not be effaced in a thousand years," (2) and which provoked emotion even in the worst Nazi criminals? Such terms as "hatred of the Jews" and "Hitler's folly" are too general and explain nothing; Hitler could be a shrewd and calculating politician, at least so long as the fate of the Third Reich was not sealed. Besides, we have seen that extermination of the Jews did not figure among the original Nazi aims. Why, then, was this irrational decision made, and why was it made just at this particular time?

In seeking an answer to these questions it should be remembered that such deductions as we shall make are entirely speculative in the absence of any concrete evidence.

The extermination of the Jews was ordered at a moment when it had become evident that, contrary to the Nazi dreams of 1939–40, the war they had started would last a long time, whatever its outcome. A speedy victory was no longer possible. Chances for a compromise peace with England had vanished, and so the Nazis resolved to gamble everything on one big blow. The German people's efforts had to be united to the greatest possible degree. To do this, was it not advisable to involve them in an undertaking from which there was no possibility of turning back? This at least is what a passage from Goebbel's diary (dated March 2, 1943) would seem to say:

> We are so entangled in the Jewish question that henceforth it is impossible to retreat. All the better. A movement and a people that have burned their bridges behind them fight with a great deal more energy—experience shows it—than those who are still able to retreat.[2]

(2) International Military Tribunal of Nuremberg, session of April 18, 1946.

Another document, dating from a grimmer hour in German history and employing the same reasoning, gives us an insight into the workings of the Nazi mind. It is a report prepared by Jodl, chief of staff of the Wehrmacht, in February 1945.

At that time the Nazi strength was rapidly failing and a denunciation of the Geneva Convention was being considered; this would make it possible for them to murder the Allied war prisoners at their leisure. Jodl submitted a study to his master which weighed the pros and cons of the matter. And among the pros the faithful valet included the following: "Burn all bridges . . . so as to arouse the people to even stronger combativeness." (3)

Burn all bridges. . . . What proved impossible in the case of Allied prisoners-of-war at the beginning of 1945 was quite practicable for Jewish women and children from 1941 on. Burn all bridges so as to arouse the German people to even stronger combativeness. . . . At a moment when on the one hand, Germany was at the peak of her power, and so could scorn all "degenerate humanitarian" considerations, while on the other hand, confronted by an unconquered England, she had attacked Russia and gambled everything for world domination—at this juncture it quite accorded with the spirit of the "great simplifier" to make all Germans his accomplices in the perpetration of an unheard-of collective crime and so unite them to him even more strongly than before. There is no stronger bond than complicity in crime. To make retreat of any kind impossible or terribly difficult; to launch his people upon an undertaking that would banish them as a group from the ranks of humanity, into which they might be readmitted only at the price of treason to their country—such a calculation and course of reasoning are quite in keeping with what we know of Hitler. The holocaust in which such an alliance was cemented would establish for centuries to come the sanguinary myth of the thousand-year Reich and the bestial cult of blood and soil.

These calculations were made against a background of endless and unceasing hatred. The Jews had long served to excite Nazi fanaticism and discipline the faithful; now for the last time they

(3) Jodl's report to Hitler, February 21, 1945.(D 606) As we know, the Nazis did not have the time to carry out this project.

would unite master and servant in a destructive and insatiable communion. This is not to deny that the murder of the Jews represented the fulfillment of some kind of collective vow which Nazi sadism had sworn; or that its commission brought no relief to a people tormented by homicidal madness and only served as the first link in a chain of murder and destruction which would have gone on forever if the fortunes of war had not changed.

A more concrete reason was the clear and determined opposition which the Jews of the occupied countries showed to Hitlerism, and their part in the rising resistance movements; this might have been a subsidiary factor in forcing a decision. But then why kill the women, the old people, and the children? We shall see later with what cynicism the authors of these infamies, big and little, pleaded before the Nuremberg Tribunal that they were suppressing "eventual avengers."

The poisoned atmosphere of the Third Reich and the Nazi mentality made it especially easy for the decision to be taken. The preceding chapters have shown how even in their subconscious minds the Germans had been trained to consider the Jews as pariahs, the refuse of humanity. Their "elimination from the German national body" was clearly a necessity. Under the circumstances, did the method matter? What great difference is there between sending all the dogs of Constantinople to the Prinkipo Islands, and locking them up in a pound? May we be forgiven such a comparison—but it suits the character of the men and morality of the Third Reich better than any other.

THE STAGES

The decision, then, to eliminate European Judaism was made by the Führer about the end of 1940 or early in 1941. Himmler was notified of this at the very moment when the RSHA sections were busily employed on the project of the mass transfer to Madagascar. The Madagascar preparations were not discontinued immediately (such discontinuation was officially announced to the Ministry of Foreign Affairs only in February 1942).[3]

Once extermination had been decided upon, there were many stages to be gone through. First of all, there were the practical problems. Techniques had to be discovered, and these, as we shall see, proved very difficult to perfect. It was no easy matter to put to death six million people chosen arbitrarily and haphazardly from the most diverse environments, classes, and countries of the world. An industry for the slaughter of human beings had to be organized in detail. Added to the problem of exterminating so many people were the problems of deportation. The need for manpower in a Reich at war and the economic usefulness of the Jewish slaves often delayed matters; but in the end these things were never an obstacle, as we have seen, to their extermination. Finally, certain considerations which the Nazis termed "psychological," as regards their own nationals, the satellite governments and peoples, and (at least during the year 1941) American public opinion, acted more or less as a deterrent.

For all these reasons the extermination plan, known as the "final solution," (4) had to be carried out stage by stage. We can roughly distinguish three chief stages, whose crucial dates are June 1941, April 1942, and October 1942. Each stage developed out of the previous one by trial-and-error fumblings. The individual and local initiative so characteristic of the Third Reich played a considerable part, and the utter lack of precedent for such an undertaking necessitated changes and adjustments.

1. From the very beginning of the war in Russia, the Jewish population of the invaded territories was systematically exterminated by special SS detachments, the so-called "action groups" (*Einsatzgruppen*) that followed immediately behind the armies. Deep in Eastern Europe, amid the confusions and turmoil of a pitiless conflict, "psychological" and other considerations counted scarcely at all. Jews were executed on the spot. The technique employed was rudimentary, a matter of shooting people and dumping them into common graves. We can call this the stage of chaotic exterminations. In some important centers, however, the Jewish population was temporarily spared, generally for economic reasons.

(4) The expression "final solution" *(Endlösung)*, which appears from 1938 on, progressively changed in context. At the beginning it was applied to the project for total emigration. From the end of 1941 on it indicated extermination. Other Nazi terms similarly became more and more sinister in meaning as time passed; e.g., *Sonderbehandlung* ("special treatment").

Meanwhile preparations were made to extend the scope of the exterminations to include all of conquered Europe. Experience gained elsewhere, especially from the "euthanasia program" (which had just been perfected), made possible a more scientific and more discreet technique of extermination. Though the extermination program had been entrusted to Himmler, it was his rival, Goering, by virtue of his old authority, who gave Heydrich the order (on July 30, 1941), to "take all preparatory measures . . . required for the final solution of the Jewish question in the European territories under German influence." [4] Thus the head of the RSHA "became, for all practical purposes, by the terms of the mission confided to him by the Reichsmarshall, Commissioner for Jewish Questions for all Europe." [5] The actual powers of execution were concentrated in the hands of Adolf Eichmann.

The meaning of the term "final solution" began to grow clear. The anti-Semitic campaign was intensified in anticipation of the measures soon to come and out of fear of a popular reaction in Germany and the conquered countries. Goebbels gave the press instructions (5) appropriate to the "imminent political measures." While waiting for the program to begin in earnest, Heydrich authorized Eichmann to start the first deportation trains rolling. These were not the "savage deportations" of 1940, for it was no longer a question of evacuation but extermination.

2. Although the extermination system was set up during the second half of 1941, it was not until the spring of 1942 that it began to go full blast. The entry of the United States into the war did not make the Nazis reconsider; in fact, it increased the tempo of the Nazi action. After December 1941 the extermination camp at Chelmno, Poland, was used as a veritable "experimental station." Signs of what was coming multiplied; Goebbels launched a propaganda campaign, and his article of November 25, "The Jews Are the Culprits," was taken by people in the know as the signal for action.[6] Streicher, echoing Goebbels, demanded the extermination of the Jews. On December 16, Hans Frank, governor of Poland,

---

(5) Thus, for example, the *Tagesparole* (press briefing) of the Propaganda Ministry indicated on August 21, 1941: "It is in our interest to headline all Jewish attacks against Germany or other authoritarian countries. In fact, political measures of an internal order are imminent."

confided to his closest collaborators: "We must finish with the Jews.
. . . There will be big discussions on the subject in Berlin in January. . . . A huge Jewish emigration is going to start. . . . We must
exterminate the Jews wherever we find them." [7]

The discussions announced by Frank took place on January 20,
the date on which Heydrich outlined the extermination plan to a
conference of representatives of all the Reich administrative departments. The Jews would be forced to work until they died; if
death was slow in coming they would be "treated accordingly."
Here are Heydrich's own words:

> Within the framework of the final solution, the Jews must be transported under the appropriate guard and there assigned to the appropriate work service. In work gangs, the able-bodied Jews, separated
> by sex, will be brought to these territories to build roads. It goes without saying that a large part of them will be eliminated by natural
> decrease.
> The final residue will have to be treated appropriately. This residue
> will represent a natural selection, which when freed must be viewed
> as capable of forming the nucleus for a reconstructed Jewry (see the
> experience of History). [8]

What was to be understood by the term, "treated accordingly,"
was not long in being demonstrated in the months that followed.
April 1942 was a time of intensive activity. Many of the death
camps (Belzec, Treblinka, Sobibor) began to operate in Poland,
swallowing thousands of victims every day. The assassination of
Heydrich in May 1942 would seem to have been the signal for such
great holocausts as the mass deportations from Warsaw and Paris
(July 1942). Adolf Eichmann, the chief of the deportation system,
extended his network throughout all Europe. Poland, the "trashcan
of Europe" according to Nazi terminology, was the place of execution; there the gas chambers were completed and the crematories
built. At Belzec Commissioner Christian Wirth, formerly a specialist in euthanasia, completed all his arrangements; at Auschwitz,
Rudolf Hoess, Himmler's favorite, introduced new improvements
and soon surpassed his master. "Cyclone B," an insecticide with a
prussic acid base, replaced carbon monoxide.

3. In October 1942 there was a new and final intensification of
operations. At the end of September von Ribbentrop had been

charged with instructing all the German diplomatic services "to speed up as much as possible the deportation of all Jews from Europe"; [9] everywhere German diplomats lent Eichmann and his men a strong and efficient hand. Himmler ordered the setting aside of all economic considerations, and had the remaining Jewish specialists in German industries replaced by Polish Aryans.[10] Once again the propaganda trumpets were sounded; a new wave of incendiary speeches swept across the Third Reich. In its wake Bormann had a decree published which for the first time dealt publicly with what was being done, although in somewhat veiled terms.[11]

A few weeks later the Führer ordered Himmler to put the extermination program into high gear (6) and asked for a statistical report on its progress. He had the satisfaction of learning that "since 1933, i.e., during the first decade of National Socialism, European Judaism decreased by almost one half." (7)

Thereafter nothing affected the tempo of genocide, apart from such purely technical factors as the number of men Eichmann could dispose of or the availability of transport. To these factors, however, must be added the more or less shadowy and passive opposition of the European peoples. This opposition took different forms in different countries and under different governments, and even made itself felt in Germany itself. Most important, it forced the executioners, following mishaps caused by the public massacres in Russia, to adopt a highly secret technique of extermination, which complicated things a great deal. In Russia the Nazis were able to carry on their work of extermination openly, by fire and sword; in conquered and dismembered Poland they had to do it secretly; elsewhere they could not do it at all. (This perhaps throws a revealing light on what are certain of the ultimate barriers and

(6) It seems that this was in answer to the Allied landing in North Africa. Cf. Kersten, citing Himmler's words: "In answer to the landing, the Führer has ordered intensified action against the Jews still in our power." (*Op. cit.*, p. 197.)

(7) Report from Korherr, inspector of statistics in the Reich, to the SS Reichsführer. Berlin, April 19, 1943. Himmler had first asked for a report from the RSHA services. But "because of the lack of professional precision," he appealed later to the statistical services of the Reich. The compilation of the report required more than two months. It consisted of sixteen pages; an abridged extract of six pages was drawn up for the Führer.

psychological impossibilities in the world of the concentration camp.) Under these circumstances a few hundred thousand Jews were able to disguise or hide themselves, or simply be forgotten, and survive until the arrival of the liberation armies. Himmler, who had been engaging in undercover negotiations for several weeks with the representatives of American Jewry without the Führer's knowledge, thought it prudent to stop the exterminations on his own initiative in October 1944. Since June 1942 a special unit had been going about carefully destroying all traces of the Nazi holocausts.

CHAPTER SIX

Massacres on the Eastern Front, 1941-1942

IN DARKEST SECRECY the Nazi Reich made its feverish preparations for the invasion of the USSR. The vast territories to be conquered raised serious police problems; these questions were studied with the minuteness typical of the German High Command. Among these, of course, were the measures for extermination.

FORMATION AND TASKS OF THE ACTION GROUPS

As Hitler presented the matter to the Wehrmacht chiefs, the coming conflict was going to be essentially a new kind of war, "a conflict of ideologies in the broadest sense of the word." Fighting the ideological enemy called for very special measures, measures which necessarily fell under the jurisdiction of the RSHA. For this reason the details of the projected police operations were worked out toward the middle of May 1941 in negotiations between the RSHA and the Wehrmacht Oberkommando, the latter represented by SS General Müller, head of section IV (Gestapo), and the former by Quartermaster General Wagner. (1)

(1) Deposition by SS General Walter Schellenberg before the Nuremberg Tribunal (session of January 4, 1946). This high functionary of the RSHA was in charge of arranging the sometimes difficult contacts between the military and the SS.

During supplementary meetings at the beginning of July which concentrated on the problem of prisoners of war, the "moderate" generals obtained a single concession: insofar as possible, the executions would be carried out quietly, in deserted and isolated places. "It is essential to make our ideas clear to the officer corps, which behaves as though it thinks we are in the stone age, and not in the era of National Socialism," General Reinecke, chief of the administrative service of the Wehrmacht, declared. (Deposition by General Lahousen to the Nuremberg Tribunal, session of September 30, 1945.)

The agreement that they arrived at was extremely simple. It stipulated that any "representative of enemy ideology" who fell into German hands was to be done away with. This included Communist officials, political commissars—a vague but useful term—and all Jews. A special order by the Führer (whose text has not been found) gave effect to the decision.

The police detachments formed by the RSHA were joined to the Wehrmacht, on whose heels they were to follow; however, they kept their autonomy and remained administratively subordinate to the RSHA.

In May 1941 several dozen officials of the different RSHA services (Gestapo, SD, criminal police) were brought together in the village of Pretsch, in Saxony, where they underwent intensive and highly secret training. The instruction consisted of drill and target practice, and "ideological indoctrination." Heydrich himself went there to speak on the dangers of Judaism (an "intellectual reservoir of Communism") and reveal the different jobs they would have to handle in Russia. He developed these considerations at a last meeting in Berlin, a few days before the June 22 attack, insisting particularly on the necessity of including women and children in the operations—as potential avengers and sources of future corruption. The goal aimed at was "permanent security, for otherwise children whose parents had been killed, when they grew up, would constitute no less a danger than their fathers"—so General Ohlendorff explained it before the Allied Court.[1]

Thus the *Einsatzgruppen* (2) were formed, special detachments assigned to the job of exterminating Jews in Russia. These detachments, as well as the men in the Waffen-SS under their orders, were picked in the regular army way; that is, it was essentially chance that ruled in the selection of the men, who came from the different police units of the Third Reich. It is noteworthy that the personnel of the action groups were not sadists lusting for blood, but an average and representative selection from the German police corps of 1941.

Each group thus formed consisted of five to eight hundred men. There were four groups, designated as A, B, C, D; the first three

(2) Meaning approximately "action groups" or "operation groups." This is one of those numerous Nazi neologisms which it is impossible to translate.

were assigned to the three army groups (von Leeb's, von Bock's, and von Rundstadt's) covering the Russian front from north to south. The fourth, intended for the army group that was to be formed later on in the Caucasus, operated along the shores of the Black Sea and in the Crimea. The names of the different commanding officers were Stahlecker, Nebe, Thomas, and Ohlendorff; all had the rank of SS General. The groups were subdivided into commandos (*Einsatzkommandos*), which could be broken up in turn into "special commandos" or "partial commandos" (*Sonderkommandos* and *Teilkommandos*).

Two or three days after the outbreak of the war with Russia, the groups were on the move. The speed of their advance was determined by the movement of the armies in whose steps they followed. This accounts for the great speed with which they traversed the western areas of the USSR, the very regions where the Jewish population was most dense. At the rate they advanced it was impossible for them to do their job; the very density of the Jewish population, which furnished the only manpower for certain industries, made them temporarily indispensable to the economic life of the region. Thanks to this, the Jews of the Baltic countries, White Russia and the Western Ukraine—i.e., those for the most part living in the regions incorporated into the USSR in 1939—enjoyed respites of varying lengths. They were thrust into ghettos and put to different kinds of work. Besides, the conquered regions were soon handed over to the civil administration. Eastern Galicia was incorporated into the Government General; the Ukraine, White Russia, and the Baltic countries were organized as *Reichskommissariats* (*Ukraine* and *Ostland*) under the jurisdiction of Alfred Rosenberg's Ministry for Occupied Territories. Some delegates of the RSHA worked with the commissariats; new action groups were formed and placed under their orders.

Only when the German advance drove more deeply into Russia and began to slow down were the action groups able to carry out systematic and wholesale exterminations. They functioned with maximum efficiency, one might say, starting at the line of the Dnieper. And it was actually in the direction opposite to the German advance that the inexorable sword of complete genocide slowly swept, from east to west.

The first concern of the extermination squads as they went along was to excite pogroms and "spontaneous" massacres among the native populations. This had the double advantage of placing the burden of responsibility on the latter, and winning to the Germans men for their future bands of auxiliaries. This was how the nucleus of the Lithuanian, Latvian, Galician, and other auxiliary police was formed; subsequently these detachments played a very important role. Though sometimes successful, the German efforts apparently did not have the results the Nazi leaders expected. Stahlecker, chief of Group A, described the tactic as follows:

> Anti-Communist forces made up of natives have been engaged in pogroms against the Jews. . . . It was desirable that the security police not show themselves immediately, for these extremely severe measures were of a kind to arouse the emotions even of German people. It was necessary to show the world that the native population itself took the initiative in reacting against the Jews. . . .[2]

Later Stahlecker gave an account of the results achieved by these tactics. In Lithuania,

> to our astonishment, it was at first difficult to start a vast pogrom against the Jews. It was Klimatis, leader of a group of partisans, who, at our urging, launched a pogrom that showed no signs of a German order or suggestion. He had taken his directives from a small forward detachment engaged at Kovno. During the first pogrom on the night of June 25th, the Lithuanian partisans got rid of more than 1,500 Jews. . . . Nearly 2,300 Jews were made harmless during the following nights. The Kovno example was followed in other part of Lithuania, though on a smaller scale.[3]

In Latvia the Germans experienced an even greater disappointment. "It was considerably more difficult to launch similar actions and pogroms in Latvia. Nevertheless, we were able to put enough pressure on the Latvian auxiliary police to start a pogrom at Riga; this pogrom caused the destruction of all synagogues and took the lives of 400 Jews."[4] In Esthonia, complete failure. "It was impossible to set off a pogrom, since the population was not sufficiently enlightened."[5] This in spite of the fact that these regions were often backward and anti-Semitic by tradition, and would seem to have been a particularly favorable recruiting ground for the Germans. Farther south in Galicia, especially in the town of Lwow, the Nazis apparently had better success. The pogroms of June 29 and 30, followed by the "Petlura" action (3) of July 25, 26, and 27, took the lives of at least 10,000 Jews. But new mishaps awaited the Nazis in the Ukraine proper. "Our careful efforts to incite pogroms unfortunately did not have the success we expected. Only at Tarnopol and Chorostkow did we succeed in getting rid of 600 and 110 Jews respectively." [6] In the south as well as in the north the action groups had to do the job themselves.

Most of the time the extermination squads worked as follows: After going into a place, they would have the leading Jews pointed out to them, in particular the rabbi. These Jews they would charge with organizing a Jewish council. A day or so later the council would be notified that the Jewish population was to be registered for transfer to a "Jewish territory" being organized in the Ukraine or some other region. The council would then be ordered to call the Jews together; in the larger localities this was also done by posting notices. (4) Given the haste of the operation, the order was on the whole pretty well obeyed by the inhabitants, who were still ignorant of German methods. (Later, when the last ghettos in White Russia and the Baltic countries were being closed down, the victims had to be rounded up by force in indescribable manhunts.) The Jews were crowded into trucks, or freight cars, and taken a few kilometers out of town to some ravine or anti-tank ditch. There, after being stripped of their money, valuables, and often even their clothing, men, women, and children were shot on the spot.

This was the usual procedure, though every action group and

(3) So called in memory of the Ukrainian separatist *hetman*, Simon Petlura, initiator of numerous pogroms in the Ukraine during 1919–20. (S. Tenenbaum, *In Search of a Lost People*, p. 114-16.)

(4) Here is the text of one of these proclamations, posted in the town of Kislovodsk in the Caucasus:

To all Jews! In order to populate the sparsely settled regions of the Ukraine, all Jews living in Kislovodsk and those with no established residence must appear at the Kislovodsk freight station on Wednesday, February 9, 1943, at five in the morning, Berlin time (six o'clock, Moscow time). Each Jew can bring baggage not to exceed forty pounds in weight, including food for two days. Food will be provided in stations *en route* by the German authorities.

The two thousand Jews of Kislovodsk were massacred in the nearby locality of Mineralniye Vody. (Account by Col. L. Smirnov, Attorney General of the USSR, presented to the Nuremberg Tribunal, session of February 8, 1946.)

squad had its preferred methods. Certain squads forced their victims to lie face down and fired a pistol point blank into the back of their necks. Others made the Jews climb down into the ditch and lie on top of the bodies of those already shot so that the pile of corpses steadily mounted. Still others lined the victims up along the edge of the ditch and shot them in successive salvos; this way was considered the "most humane" and the "most military." (5) Sometimes only a few hours elapsed between the time the notices were posted and the execution.

The Germans preferred warmer seasons for carrying out the executions. A report from Group A complained about the difficulties of the work.

> The cold has made the executions much more difficult. Another difficulty is the fact that the Jews are scattered all over the territory. The long distances, bad roads, lack of trucks and gasoline, and inadequate number of men strain our forces to the limit.

Later the author of the report promised to finish with the Jews of that region within two months "if weather conditions permit." [7]

A new and more appalling link was thus added to the chain of massacres running through Jewish history. The victims behaved for the most part like their forefathers, whose martyrdom is movingly recorded in the medieval chronicles. They faced death with quiet and resigned courage, as the eyewitness reports which we shall read later show; the killers' own stories testify to this. "I was surprised to see how calm they were, almost too calm. The tranquillity with which these people accepted their fate seemed horrible to me," one witness testified.[8] Another wrote: "It was surprising to see how the Jews descended into the ditches while consoling one another to keep up their courage. Some prayed." [9] Ohlendorff himself told how the Russian Jews sang the *Internationale* during the massacre.[10] The speed with which things went left the moral strength of the victims intact, sparing them the slow disintegration that we find

(5) All these detailed explanations on the different proceedings used by the commandos were furnished at the trial of the *Einsatzgruppen* before the Nuremberg Tribunal. As far as the "humane and military way" is concerned, see in particular the depositions of SS Colonel Haensch and SS General Ohlendorff.

in the concentration camps; perhaps, too, the element of shock and stupefaction had a merciful effect.

Shooting was not the only method the commandos used. On the shores of the Black Sea there were mass drownings; at Bachtchissarai, that pearl of the Crimea which Pushkin sang about, the drowning of 1,029 Jews during the period July 1-15, 1942, was reported.[11] There were cases of Jews being burned alive, especially at Minsk in White Russia.[12] Finally in the spring of 1942, mobile gas chambers, designed and manufactured in Berlin and disguised as gas trucks, made their appearance all over Russia.

As we shall see, these death chambers were still very rudimentary machines which the homicide or "euthanasia" section of the Führer's chancellery had devised in Berlin. By a very simple arrangement, the exhaust gases of the Diesel motor, essentially carbon monoxide, were piped into the hermetically sealed interior of the truck instead of out into open air. Such trucks were put at the disposal of all commandos. We have a great number of documents, veritable manuals on the use of the trucks, describing their operation.

> The gas is generally not used in the right way. To get things over with as soon as possible, the driver presses the accelerator to the floor. This kills the people by suffocation instead of making them gradually doze off. My directives have proved that, with the correct adjustment of the levers, death comes quicker and the prisoners sleep peacefully. There are no more of the contorted faces or defecations there used to be.

This was written by SS Lieutenant Becker on May 16, 1942; his job was to check on the functioning of the trucks. He added,

> I had ordered the trucks of Group D to be camouflaged as houses on wheels by hanging a pair of shutters on each side, a sight that is frequently seen on our farms in the country. But these vehicles got to be so well-known that not only the authorities but the civil population called them "death trucks" as soon as they appeared. In my opinion, these vehicles, even when camouflaged, cannot long be kept a secret.[13]

The commando men stated during their trial that they disliked using these trucks. Besides, they gave mediocre results, at the most fifty to sixty people per execution. Shooting continued to be the chief mode of execution during one period of the chaotic exterminations in Russia. Here is a clear and exact description of what they were like, by the witness Hermann Graebe:

I, the undersigned, Hermann Friedrich Graebe, make the following declaration under oath:

From September 1941 to January 1944 I was director and chief engineer of the Sdolbunow branch of the Josef Jung Construction Company of Solingen. In this capacity I had, among my other duties, to visit the firm's projects. Under the terms of a contract with the army construction services, the company was to build grain warehouses on the old Dubno airfield, in the Ukraine.

On October 5, 1942, at the time of my visit to the construction offices in Dubno, my foreman, Hubert Moennikes, living at 21 Aussenmuehlenweg, Hamburg-Haarburg, told me that some Dubno Jews had been shot near the building in three huge ditches about 30 metres long and 3 metres deep. The number of people killed daily was about 1,500. The 5,000 Jews who had lived in Dubno before the pogrom were all marked for liquidation. Since the executions took place in the presence of my employee, he was painfully impressed by them.

Accompanied by Moennikes, I then went to the work area. I saw great mounds of earth about 30 metres long and 2 high. Several trucks were parked nearby. Armed Ukrainian militia were making people get out, under the surveillance of SS soldiers. The same militia men were responsible for guard duty and driving the trucks. The people in the trucks wore the regulation yellow pieces of cloth that identified them as Jews on the front and back of their clothing.

Moennikes and I went straight toward the ditches without being stopped. When we neared the mound I heard a series of rifle shots close by. The people from the trucks—men, women, and children—were forced to undress under the supervision of an SS soldier with a whip in his hand. They were obliged to put their effects in certain spots: shoes, clothing, and underwear separately. I saw a pile of shoes, about 800-1,000 pairs, great heaps of underwear and clothing. Without weeping or crying out, these people undressed and stood together in family groups, embracing each other and saying goodbye while waiting for a sign from the SS soldier, who stood on the edge of the ditch, a whip in his hand, too. During the fifteen minutes I stayed there, I did not hear a single complaint or a plea for mercy. I watched a family of about eight: a man and woman about fifty years old, surrounded by their children of about one, eight, and ten, and two big girls about twenty and twenty-four. An old lady, her hair completely white, held the baby in her arms, rocking it, and singing it a song. The infant was crying aloud with delight. The parents watched the group with tears in their eyes. The father held the ten-year-old boy by the hand, speaking softly to him: the child struggled to hold back his tears. Then the father pointed a finger to the sky and, stroking the child's head, seemed to be explaining something. At this moment, the SS near the ditch called something to his comrade. The latter counted off some twenty people and ordered them behind the mound. The family of which I have just spoken was in the group. I still remember the young girl, slender and dark, who, passing near me, pointed at herself, saying "Twenty-three." I walked around the mound and faced a frightful common grave. Tightly packed corpses were heaped so close together that only the heads showed. Most were wounded in the head and the blood flowed over their shoulders. Some still moved. Others raised their hands and turned their heads to show they were still alive. The ditch was two-thirds full. I estimate that it held a thousand bodies. I turned my eyes toward the man who had carried out the execution. He was an SS man; he was seated, legs swinging, on the narrow edge of the ditch; an automatic rifle rested on his knees and he was smoking a cigarette. The people, completely naked, climbed down a few steps cut in the clay wall and stopped at the spot indicated by the SS man. Facing the dead and wounded, they spoke softly to them. Then I heard a series of rifle shots. I looked in the ditch and saw their bodies contorting, their heads, already inert, sinking on the corpses beneath. The blood flowed from the nape of their necks. I was astonished not to be ordered away, but I noticed two or three uniformed post men nearby. A new batch of victims approached the place. They climbed down into the ditch, lined up in front of the previous victims, and were shot.

On the way back, while rounding the mound, I saw another full truck which had just arrived. This truck contained only the sick and crippled. Women already naked were undressing an old woman with an emaciated body; her legs frightfully thin. She was held up by two people and seemed paralysed. The naked people led her behind the mound. I left the place with Moennikes and went back to Dubno in a car.

The next morning, returning to the construction, I saw some thirty naked bodies lying thirty to fifty yards from the ditch. Some were still alive; they stared into space with a set look, seeming not to feel the coolness of the morning air, nor to see the workers standing all around. A young girl of about twenty spoke to me, asking me to bring her clothes and to help her escape. At that moment we heard the sound of a car approaching at top speed; I saw that it was an SS detachment. I went back to my work. Ten minutes later rifle shots sounded from the ditch. The Jews who were still alive had been ordered to throw the bodies in the ditch; then they had to lie down themselves to receive a bullet in the back of the neck.

(Signed)   Graebe

Wiesbaden, November 10, 1945 [14]

THE PSYCHOLOGY OF THE EXECUTIONERS

The action groups kept records of their massacres. Commando reports were collected at group headquarters and sent on to Berlin, where the RSHA assembled the figures in the form of a daily bulletin. Though written in the terse style of military communiqués, these reports enable us to penetrate deeper into the psychology of genocide.

The standard sentence is short and simple: "During the action against the Jews, 3,412 were shot" (Minsk, March 1942); "10,600 Jews were shot" (Riga, November 1941); "1,000 Jews and gypsies were executed" (Crimea, December 1941). More detailed reports give us a better notion of the mechanical and bureaucratic character of the Nazi officials, conscientiously doing their work and trying to increase their efficiency within the means available to them. The following lines, for example, conclude a report describing the extermination of the Jews of Pinsk.

Conclusions to be drawn:
1. The forces assigned to the rounding up [of Jews] absolutely have to be furnished with axes, hatchets, or similar instruments, since almost all the doors, etc., are bolted or locked and can only be forced.
2. Even if access to the attic cannot be discovered at first, it must be considered possible that people may be found there. Each attic must eventually be carefully searched, from the outside if necessary.
3. Even if there is no cellar, a large number of people may be found in the little space between the floor and the ground. In such places it is advisable to lift the flooring from the outside and to send in police dogs (during the Pinsk action, the police dog Oste performed wonders) or to throw in a grenade, which inevitably forces the Jews out of their holes.
4. It is advisable to explore the ground around the houses with a hard object, for many people hide away in well-camouflaged holes.
5. In order to uncover the hiding places, it is recommended that the aid of adolescents be enlisted, on the promise of their lives. This method is always effective.[15]

This is in the style of a report on the campaign against the potato bug, a detailed report on the conscientious performance of an allotted task. We even come across one of these terrible killers sending several thousand recently expelled Rumanian Jews back into Rumanian territory simply because their execution was not one of his responsibilities, his province being limited to the Jews of his jurisdiction. "We don't want to do this work for the Rumanians." [16]

Extermination of the sub-men was thus considered a routine business. The Nazi training which we described at length seems to have caught hold very well. SS General Bach-Zelewski, commander-in-chief of the anti-partisan forces, characterized this mentality in striking fashion when he was questioned about the massacres committed by the action groups:

> It's my opinion that when the doctrine that the Slavic race is inferior and the Jews not even human has been preached for years and decades, such a result is inevitable.[17]

How deeply rooted this mentality was is apparent in many private letters, of which the following is an eloquent example. A police officer is writing to a Wehrmacht general.

Kamenetz-Podolsk, May 5, 1942

My dear Lieutenant-General,

I have been here at K . . . for a month. The territory I administer, with 23 [of my own] men and 500 Ukrainian police, is as big as a German Government District. . . . As commanding officer, I am simultaneously prosecuting attorney, judge, executioner, etc.

Needless to say, we do quite a bit of clean-up work, especially among the Jews. But the population also has to be kept firmly in hand. You have to keep your eyes open. We guard the grain. Well, we shall be able to go home all the quicker. My family is very unhappy. I have been away for two years. . . .

I have a fine apartment in a former children's home. Bedroom and living room, everything that one needs; nothing lacking except of course my wife and children. You understand. My Dieter and my little Lina write often. Sometimes I want to scream. It is not good to love your children the way I do. I hope the war will soon be over. . . .

June 21, 1942

Dear Lieutenant-General Querner,

I am answering your letter of the tenth immediately. . . . Thank you for your reprimand. You are right. We men of the new Germany must be stern with ourselves, even if it means long separation from our family. Because we have to finish matters once and for all and finally settle accounts with the war criminals, so as to create a better and eternal Germany for our descendants. We are not sleeping here. Three or four actions a week. Sometimes Jews, sometimes Bohemians, partisans, and all kinds of trash. . . .

I do not know if the Lieutenant-General saw such frightful kinds of Jews in Poland. I thank my stars for having been allowed to see this bastard race close up. If destiny permits, I shall have something to tell my children. Syphilitics, cripples, and idiots were typical of the lot. One thing was plain; they were materialists to the last. Phrases like "We are good workers, you won't assassinate us," were in everybody's mouth. They weren't men, but monkeys in human form.

Oh, well, there is only a small percentage of the 24,000 Jews of Kamenetz-Podolsk left. The kikes in the surrounding country are also clients of ours. We are ruthlessly making a clean sweep and then. . . . "The waves die down and the world is at peace." (6) One request, my dear General. Write me from time to time. It is good to get news from the beloved fatherland.

Permit me to send you greetings from a distant country.

Heil Hitler!

(Signed)   Jacob
Police Officer

These letters are typical of the moral depravity of the SS. One looks in vain for any sign of moral concern or even of conscious revulsion; and yet the phrase "terrible job," applied to the extermination work, runs like a *leitmotiv* through all the documents.

The reports of the action groups show a semantic peculiarity which deserves some consideration. Besides such terms as "shot," "executed," or "liquidated," we find the most varied and ingenious circumlocutions which the exterminators coined for their operations. For example, the reports often stated that such-and-such a number of Jews had been "rendered inoffensive." Authors of other reports boasted of "having got rid" of Jews. Other expressions are much more vague: "At Nicolaiev and at Kherson respectively, 5,000 Jews were treated. . . ." Sometimes the idea was conveyed quite tacitly; thus the reports of Group A were supplemented by a map. (7) Areas were spoken of as being "liberated" or "swept clean" of their Jews, or again they were "taken care of." "Special treatment" was another frequent euphemism; but the most subtle, discreet, and definitive term was "final solution"; in such-and-such a place "the problem of the Jews has been definitively solved."

Here are the words in which Group C reported 50,000 executions:

> Executions have taken place in the following categories: political officials, active Communists, thieves and saboteurs, Jews with false pa-

(6) Line from the *Horst-Wessel Song*, the favorite of the Hitler youth.
(7) See the map at the beginning of this book.

pers, NKVD agents, denouncers of ethnic Germans, revengeful and sadistic Jews, undesirable elements, partisans, [people creating] a danger of epidemics, members of Russian bands, insurgents caught with arms in hand, suppliers of the partisans, rebels and agitators, young vagrants, and *Jews in general.*[18]

Sometimes the reports described or justified the operations: the commentaries then have a more cynical style. Thus, in White Russia a commando chief stated that "the Jewish women were particularly recalcitrant in their behavior; for this reason 28 Jewesses were shot at Krougloye and 337 at Moguilev." [19] Elsewhere, the Jews "displayed an impudent and provocative attitude," "were unwilling to work," or, "were suspected Communists and arsonists." The danger of epidemics furnished another pretext. Group B declared that an epidemic of mange had broken out in the Nevel ghetto: "In order to prevent contagion, 640 Jews were liquidated." Group C reported that at Radomychl, "it was impossible to provide food for the Jews and their children, which increased the danger of epidemics. To put an end to this situation, 1,107 adult Jews were shot by the commando and 561 children by the Ukrainian militia."

In trying to probe the depths to which Nazi indoctrination had penetrated, the degree of callousness it had produced in the officers and men of the action groups, it is well to remember that a criminal's cynicism and braggadocio are often only an expression of deep uneasiness. This cynicism, as well as uneasiness, was still more disconcertingly evident at the time the killers were being questioned before the Allied court. All the pity of which they were capable they reserved for themselves (or their subordinates). Not a word, not a thought, for their victims. "Our men taking part in the executions suffered more from nervous exhaustion than those who were to be shot." (Colonel Paul Blobel) [20] "Many men suffered terribly, and had to be sent home for all sorts of reasons, either because their nervous systems were shattered or because they were not able to stand it morally." (General Otto Ohlendorff) [21] "The Waffen-SS men said that they would have preferred fighting in the front lines to staying here. I asked why and they answered: 'We don't want to say.'" (Corporal Graf) [22]

This seems most significant. We thus learn that the exterminations were considered an unlucky assignment—and destructive—of the health of the slaughterers. A report dated July 1941, after recalling the fatigue of the first weeks of the campaign—"but the hard physical trials were overcome by all of our men"—continued as follows: "Not to be underestimated is the extreme psychic tension induced by the great number of liquidations." [23] It was made a rule not to create special squads for the actual shootings, that is to say, "the same men must not be used for one execution after another." (Lieutenant Colonel Haensch) [24] Ohlendorff criticized a certain Jeckeln, who had organized "special detachments just for executions; this clearly ruined the men spiritually and brutalized them completely." Later on he said that he himself had authorized his subordinates to return to Germany or to ask for rotation when they felt too much "internal resistance." Such cases were not too frequent. The men of the action groups sought to distinguish themselves in the service of Greater Germany; they aspired to be "hard," and competition in savagery played a considerable role. "Paper soldier" was the scornful nickname with which Commando 6 of Group C dubbed Corporal Matthias Graf, who was in charge of the intelligence section of his group and never had—and never sought—an occasion to take part in the massacres.[25] Again, it should be remembered that these were men mobilized in the regular way, that is, picked at random for the most part from the German police. Such a milieu bred complete monsters, real legendary ogres. There was, for example, the police constable who afterwards at Lwow used to kill Jewish children to amuse his own children; or another who used to bet that he could cut off the head of a ten-year-old boy with a single saber stroke.[26] Alcohol was an important ingredient in the activity of the group. Heavy drinking preceded the executions, and also followed them. We find the interpreter for the superintendent of police of the region of Slonim, one Metzner, using this terrible phrase in his testimony: "The action [at Novogrodek] was the work of a special SS commando that carried through the exterminations out of idealism, without using schnapps." [27]

We can see from this the extent of the resistance and "psychic inhibitions" which the masters of the Third Reich had to overcome. Such inhibitions were drowned in alcohol and a frantic blood lust; but by a process of displacement they would often reappear in the strangest forms, such as the self-pity we have already noted. The inner resistance against which the men of the commandos contended, however, was incapable of restraining their fury even a little bit, and only made them sneer more cynically as they went about their bloody work.

The attitude displayed by the leading members of the action groups in the course of their trial at Nuremberg several years later throws light on the astonishing confusion that reigned in the Nazi mind. Among the twenty-two accused were a university professor, eight lawyers, a dental surgeon, an architect, an art expert, and even a theologian, a former pastor. (8) All pleaded not guilty; not one expressed the least regret; at most, they mentioned the harsh necessities of war and the fact that they were acting under orders. And yet in their defense they referred to the same values of Western civilization that they had trampled under foot for years. Their witnesses and lawyers praised their honesty, their familial virtues, their Christian feelings, and even their gentleness of character.

THE ATTITUDE OF WEHRMACHT AND CIVIL AUTHORITIES

The four action groups made up a force of approximately 3,000 men. They operated over a territory of more than a million square kilometers which was administered by officials of the Ministry for Occupied Territories, or, near the front lines, by the Wehrmacht; in this area German soldiers were counted by the millions and German civilians by the hundreds of thousands. Since they were carried out openly, the exterminations were necessarily matters of public knowledge. Though the groups took their orders directly from Heydrich, the attitude of the local authorities—high officials, generals, and officers—constituted a factor of prime importance. An examination of this matter makes possible an initial analysis of the reactions of the German people as a whole to the massacres.

This is a delicate question if there ever was one. It should be borne in mind that these millions of men consisted on the one hand of ordinary soldiers of an army at war, and on the other, of very

---

(8) Biberstein-Szymanovski. We cite the incredible reply of the latter when the president of the tribunal asked him whether, as a former ecclesiastic, he did not deem it useful to speak words of consolation, as well as to hear the confessions, of the Jews who were about to be slain. "Mr. President, one does not cast pearls before swine." (Session of November 21, 1947)

carefully selected functionaries. It should also be said that some of the soldiers were shaken enough by what they saw for Bormann to mention it in a decree of October 9, 1942: "There are rumors circulating among the people of the different regions of the Reich concerning the 'very severe' measures applied to the Jews. . . . Investigations have proved that these rumors—in a distorted and exaggerated form, moreover—have been spread by soldiers on leave from the different units in the east, who were eyewitnesses to the execution of the measures." [28]

By the terms of the agreements of May 1941 the Wehrmacht Supreme Headquarters had committed itself to assisting the groups in their work. But the army commanders were in fact allowed considerable latitude in the zeal with which they might follow their instructions. Some of them seem to have shown only a perfunctory zeal; von Rundstedt, for example, forbade members of the Wehrmacht to help in the executions or to photograph them (the need for such an order is itself significant).[29] No longer, however, are there open protests based on principle, like that of Blaskowitz in February 1940. Other commanders, like von Reichenau, only added fuel to the flames; in 1941 he addressed his soldiers as follows:

> As far as the attitude of the troops is concerned . . . many vague ideas are still current. The most important goal of the war against the Jewish-Bolshevik system is the complete destruction of its means of action. . . . This is why the soldier must thoroughly understand the necessity for the harsh but just punishment we must lay on that inferior humanity which is Jewry.[30]

Commando chief Blobel has left an impressive description of his reception by von Reichenau, to whom he had come to introduce himself on June 26, 1941. This warlord had established his headquarters on a splendid Polish estate. While strutting about in a pair of bathing trunks he commented to Blobel on the "Führerorder" and recommended absolute and total ruthlessness.[31]

The vastness of Russia made it possible to find this same latitude in the lower echelons. Major Rossler, a regimental commander, in a report on the "Attitude Toward the Civilian Population in the East," after vividly describing the extermination of the Jews of Zhitomir at the end of July 1941, concluded as follows:

I saw nothing like it either in the First World War or during the Civil War in Russia or in the Western campaign; I have seen many unpleasant things, having been a member of the Free Corps in 1919, but I never saw anything like this. I cannot begin to conceive the legal decisions on whose basis these executions were carried out. Everything that is happening here seems to be absolutely incompatible with our views on education and morality. Right out in the open, as if on a stage, men murder other men. I must add that according to the accounts of the soldiers, who often see spectacles of this kind, hundreds of people are thus killed daily.[32]

This report is taken from a file entitled "Report of the Commander of the IXth Army Corp, Schirwindt, and of Major Rossler on the Mass Executions of Soviet Citizens." It is clear from this that officers with some backbone were able to protest and do something, but such cases were quite rare. It is easier to find cases of officers who granted some protection to the Jews for their own convenience; for example, at Baranovitche, the civilian superintendent of police reported that the Wehrmacht "made use of Jews right from the start; it was easier to make oneself understood [in Yiddish] to them. . . . The Wehrmacht supply services not only made use of qualified Jewish workers, but used Jews for personal services, for cleaning, and even as guards. In one typical case a Jew walked around with an armband that said 'Supply Sergeant, German Army.' . . . Even among officers in responsible posts one often encountered a complete lack of any instinctive understanding of the Jewish question." [33]

This same report protesting against the Wehrmacht's attiude goes on to point out that it was a member of the Wehrmacht, the local commandant at Mir, who had all the Jews of that town shot. On the whole, however, the following excerpt from a divisional log is much more characteristic of the attitude of the officers corps:

On the morning of August 5 [1941], one hundred Jews were shot at Rositten by the Lettish Free Corps. To forestall any false interpretation of this, the division had it confirmed by the High Command that the special action had been ordered and carried out by the SD. At a meeting of the officers of the divisional general staff, the division commander announced this fact and then warned officers and men to refrain from taking any political or personal stand on these matters.[34]

It is always dangerous to generalize. But the facts speak with enough eloquence to permit us to say the following: In the immense reaches of Russia some thousands of SS executioners, helped by an international riffraff and also by amateur murderers from the Wehrmacht, exterminated Jews with complete freedom "as if on a stage," while the Wehrmacht staff and the civil authorities turned their eyes the other way. The protests, for there were a great many, some of them strong and even violent, were limited to the criticism that it was not in this ostentatious and brutal fashion that German soldiers should solve the Jewish problem inside the limits of the New Europe, though it was well understood that any "solution" could mean but one thing—the total disappearance of the Jews.

"The mass executions have been carried out in a way which does not fit our German conceptions," complained an official attached to the army groups of the center; if we refer to the context, we get some notion of what he understood as corresponding to "German conceptions." "The sparse front line and rear occupation make it easy for civilians to escape in wagons to the Soviet lines and to keep the Soviets informed of happenings. In this way the mass executions of the Jews, some of which have been carried out in a way that does not correspond to our German conceptions, have become known to the Soviets." [35] Even more revealing is a report signed by Gauleiter Heinrich Lohse, Reich Commissioner for the East:

> We must apply the special treatment to the Jews; this needs no comment. But it seems hardly credible that there could have been such things as are indicated in the enclosed report. What is Katyn in comparison? Imagine if our enemies found out about these things and exploited them; if such propaganda proved ineffectual, it would only be because those who read it and heard it would not believe it. [36]

One begins to understand what was meant by the "German way": The extermination of the Jews, tacitly accepted by the great majority, was a matter of course and "needed no comment." But the massacres had to be carried out without offending German sensibilities; above all, it had to be done discreetly, silently, without people's knowledge. Without the knowledge of world opinion; so far as possible, without the knowledge of the Germans themselves. A technical effort of considerable scope, carried out at Auschwitz and other places, as well as a determined will not to know, would subsequently satisfy in a large measure this veritable collective wish of Hitler Germany. We shall return to this subject; it is enough to point out here the resemblance between this ostrich-like policy and a basically irrational primitive mentality. Responsible only to Heydrich, the action groups came and went at will over the Russian plains. High officials or Wehrmacht generals must sometimes have been shaken by the bloody orgies they saw. Their dismay is reflected in various reports in which protests concerning "non-German" ways of doing things are strangely mixed with economic considerations.

> As for the execution of the operation, I must say, to my regret, that it borders on sadism, [wrote the regional commissioner of Slutzk]. It went beyond an anti-Jewish operation. Rather it resembled a revolution. . . . The picture was still more sinister. In the afternoon, a great number of wagons, abandoned with their horses, were found in the streets, and I had to order the municipality to take care of these vehicles. It was later discovered that they were Jewish vehicles in which the Wehrmacht had transported ammunition. The drivers had simply been snatched off their seats and carried off, and nobody bothered in the least about the wagons.[37]

In other words, a threat to the complicated and intricate Wehrmacht system! But the Wehrmacht, while protesting, did not fail to recognize that the operations were carried out "in evident conformity with considerations of ideological principle." A highly qualified spokesman, the inspector of ordnance in the Ukraine, described the situation in a confidential report to his superiors:

> Immediately after hostilities, the Jewish population was at first left in peace. The special police squads only turned to organized shooting weeks, at times months, later. This action was essentially carried out from east to west. The Ukrainian militia participated in this completely officially, often, too, alas, with volunteer help from the Wehrmacht. The action, which included old and young men, women and children, was handled in a frightful way; up to now none in the Soviet Union has been so gigantic. The number of arrests easily reached 150,000-200,000 Jews in the area of the Ukraine, and this without so far taking economic necessities into account.
> To sum up, it can be said that the manner of resolving the Jewish problem in the Ukraine, in evident conformity with considerations of

ideological principle, has had the following consequences:

a) Removal of some of the useless mouths in the cities.

b) Removal of a section of the population that could not fail to hate us.

c) Removal of workers who are absolutely indispensable, often even to the Wehrmacht.

d) Obvious consequences for foreign policy propaganda.

e) Disadvantageous repercussions for the troops who take even an indirect part in these executions.

f) A degrading influence on the security police detailed to these executions.[38]

This, we repeat, is a confidential report addressed in December 1941 to General Thomas, the head of the Reich's military economy. Imperturbably, like the able technician he was, his representative weighed the pros and cons of the matter.

Although a small minority protested against the whole idea of the exterminations, the majority of Germans, military and civilian, demurred only against their manner or occasion; they did not dare or did not wish to attack the executions themselves. Such was the hold the Hitler myth had gained over what Blaskowitz called "the national German body."

BALANCE SHEET OF THE CHAOTIC EXTERMINATIONS

The first year of war also yielded the bloodiest harvest. In important centers, especially those farthest back, "economic needs" sometimes temporarily won out. But not for long. A combined report of Group A, dated June 1942, tells us how far the extermination had progressed during the first year. At that time, fewer than 4,000 Jews were left (out of 70,000) in Latvia; close to 35,000 (out of 150,000) in Lithuania; and 120,000 (out of 450,000) in White Russia.[39] We do not have the combined figures for Group B. Group C's reports give the figure of 75,000 victims for the period June 22-November 3—33,771 in the city of Kiev alone on September 29 and 30, 1941.[40] Ohlendorff, head of Group D, estimated at 90,000 the number of executions carried out by his group.[41] For the second half of the year 1942, a combined report submitted to the Führer by Himmler stated that during August-November (that is, at the time of the German drive toward Stalingrad and the Caucasus), 363,211 Jews were executed.[42]

These figures are incomplete and therefore have an illustrative value only, especially as they could have been inflated by particularly zealous commandos (9) or minimized by omitting the massacres carried out by the Rumanian allies in the southwest or by the auxiliary legions and Ukrainian, Balt, and other bands. However, Adolf Eichmann estimated the number of Jews exterminated in Russia at two million.[43] Estimates based on demographic data for the Jewish population of the territories in question both before and after the war are more reliable. An economist and statistician, Jacob Lestchinsky, arrived at a total of 1,500,000 victims in the USSR.[44]

The hunt for the hidden or camouflaged Jews went on continuously. Some of the bigger executions took place on the very eve of the German retreat. Commandos chosen from the most experienced groups continued their activity in Poland, where the machinery for the "final solution" had meanwhile been perfected. After May 1942, however, the RSHA was preoccupied with wiping out evidence left behind by the action groups.

This evidence consisted of thousands of graves, lightly covered with earth, scattered over the territory; they had to be destroyed. A drunken and decayed intellectual, SS Colonel Paul Blobel, had been chosen for this grisly assignment. Blobel had been an architect in civilian life. Was this why he was picked for the job of giant grave digger? Blobel does not seem to have stood too well with his chiefs:

> Your belly is bigger [Heydrich was supposed to have told him during their interview at Berlin in May 1942], you are far too flabby. You are fit only to mend crockery. But I am going to stick your nose far deeper into all of that stuff.[45]

Blobel perfected special combustibles in Berlin and left with his commando for the eastern territories. Known as "Commando 1005," it was not subordinated to any other group, but came directly under section IVb of the RSHA, that is, under Adolf Eichmann.[46] Blobel's work consisted of running all over Russia looking for common graves, digging up the bodies, sprinkling them with a special preparation, and burning them.

(9) This is what seems to stand out particularly from the trial of the *Einsatzgruppen* before the Nuremberg Tribunal.

Here is Blobel's own description of the liquidation of the cemetery at Kiev (Babiy Yar):

> I was present at the incineration of the bodies taken from a common
> grave near Kiev during my visit in the month of August (1942). The
> tomb was 55 yards long, 3 wide, and 2½ deep. After the tomb was
> opened, the bodies were sprinkled with a combustible and burned.
> The cremation took nearly two days. I was careful to see that the tomb
> turned cherry red right down to the bottom. In this way all traces
> were destroyed.[47]

Blobel became a great expert in his specialty. In Berlin he gave
lectures to Eichmann's colleagues on the process he had perfected.[48] However, his work remained unfinished. The front was
moving rapidly toward the west, and Commando 1005 had to move
west with it. Hoess, the commandant of the Auschwitz camp, reported that he put teams of Jewish workers at Blobel's disposal several times; these teams were "gradually" shot and replaced by
others.[49] He also reported that Blobel tried to work out more efficient methods, particularly with the use of dynamite, "but this
method did not yield good results." The exhumation of most of the
graves fell to the lot of the German soldiers taken prisoner by the
advancing Russian army.

CHAPTER SEVEN

Deportations to the Death Camps

THE AUTHORITY GRANTED HEYDRICH on July 31, 1941, to "solve the Jewish question in Europe," stipulated among other things that "All government organs are required to cooperate with you toward this end." An extraordinary position was thus accorded the RSHA's Bureau IVb, or Jewish Affairs Section, for this apparently innocuous sentence meant that the men charged with the "final solution" were henceforth officially invested with unlimited powers of discretion before which all administrative divisions of the Third Reich would have to yield.

THE DEPORTATION MACHINERY

Who were these men? The over-all responsibility for the task was entrusted to Reinhard Heydrich, the ruthless head of the RSHA who was always in the forefront of the moves against the Jews. Himmler, who seems to have shown less initiative, backed him with all the authority he possessed as chief of the SS. Several months before, as we have seen, Himmler had been orally charged by Hitler with certain general responsibilities. "It is a very difficult task that the Führer gave me," he wrote to his friend, Gottlieb Berger, some weeks after Heydrich's death. "Anyway, I am the only one to shoulder the burden of this responsibility." [1] Acting under their orders was Adolf Eichmann, head of Bureau IVb and the actual technician of the "final solution," at least so far as its first stages were concerned: that is, the census, arrest, and transportation of the Jews to the places of execution. To be exact, Eichmann was given a double function, for he was also required, in his capacity as chief informant in all Jewish matters, with maintaining liaison, over the

140

heads of his immediate superiors, between Himmler and his representatives in the occupied territories, the "supreme chiefs of the SS and the police." In addition, he was well informed about the exterminations and actively assisted in carrying them out. As head of Bureau IVb, he was entrusted in particular with the organization of the deportations and all the negotiations that this entailed. His jurisdiction extended to all the European countries, with the exception of the Reich and Poland, which were directly under Himmler and Heydrich.

Bureau IVb had been considerably enlarged since the days of Vienna and Prague. Eichmann now had a well-organized team at his disposal. His lieutenants—most of them like himself of Austrian descent (1)—ranged up and down Europe; everywhere IVb sections, officially attached to the "supreme chief of the SS and the police" in each occupied territory, enjoyed enormous powers, taking their orders only from Eichmann. Among his associates were the brothers Rolf and Hans Günther, who, if we are to believe Dieter Wisliceny,[2] were the sons of the redoubtable theorist on racial questions, the anthropologist Hans K. Günther. Rolf was Eichmann's second in command, while Hans, installed in Prague, was IVb's plenipotentiary for Bohemia and Moravia. Commandant Franz Novak conducted all the laborious negotiations necessary to obtain deportation trains.[3] Théo Dannecker (France, Bulgaria, Italy), Dieter Wisliceny (Slovakia, Greece, Hungary), Alois Brunner (Greece, France), Franz Abromeit (Croatia, Hungary)—these are the names, which still ring with a sinister sound today, of some of Adolf Eichmann's special envoys, *missi dominici* with the power of life and death over the Jews of Europe.

The complexities of Eichmann's task may be seen from a series

(1) In particular Franz Novak, Alois Brunner, Franz Abromeit, as well as almost all the members of Eichmann's personal staff. Eichmann tended to surround himself with compatriots; moreover, (as Eugen Kogon, the historian of the concentration camps, recalls) during the years of the growth of the SS, 1933–38, the Austrian recruits, from the "Austrian Legion" formed in Bavaria, were particularly numerous. (*Der SS-Staat,* Düsseldorff, 1946, p. 288.)

At any event, the part taken by the Austrians in the "final solution" was singularly important. Kaltenbrunner, Heydrich's successor to the command of the RSHA, as well as Odilo Globocnik, in charge of the exterminations of the Jews in Poland, were also compatriots of Adolf Hitler.

of consultations held at RSHA headquarters, in which delegates from the "interested departments" participated. The first of these, held on January 20, 1942, was presided over by Heydrich, those which followed either by Eichmann or Rolf Günther.

What was the total number of Jews to be deported? In his speech of January 20, Heydrich estimated the number of European Jews at more than eleven million, of whom 95 per cent lived in territories "in the German sphere." (2) Certain countries in this sphere were completely enslaved; others enjoyed a greater or lesser degree of freedom. Also, Jews of foreign nationality, neutral or enemy nationals, resided everywhere; their consulates and governments were likely to intervene in their behalf, so that their deportation could sometimes lead to diplomatic complications. For this reason the experts in the Ministry of Foreign Affairs were required to play an important part in these matters.

Two categories of Jews were exempt from deportation right off. It is not the least of the paradoxes of the mournful history of the exterminations that the ones who escaped were just those one would have thought would have been the first victims. Jews who were nationals of enemy countries (English or America) were not deported, nor were Jewish war prisoners of French, Belgian, Dutch, and Polish nationality. In both cases the Nazis feared retaliation. The prisoners of war were protected by the Geneva convention and their camps inspected by the Red Cross. Young men of fighting age were thus spared, while their wives, children, or parents shared the common fate, as did also the liberated prisoners, who were some-

(2) Here are the figures given by Heydrich, country by country: "Old Reich," 131,800; Austria, 43,700; Eastern Territories, 420,000; Government General of Poland, 2,284,000; Protectorate of Bohemia and Moravia, 74,200; Bialystok, 400,000; Estonia, purged of all its Jews; Latvia, 3,500; Lithuania, 34,000; Belgium, 43,000; Denmark, 5,600; France (Occupied Zone), 165,000, (Free Zone) 700,000; Greece, 69,500; The Netherlands, 160,800; Norway, 1,300; Bulgaria, 48,000; England, 330,000; Finland, 2,300; Ireland, 4,000; Italy, 58,000; Albania, 200; Croatia, 40,000; Portugal, 3,000; Rumania (incl. Bessarabia), 342,000; Sweden, 8,000; Switzerland, 18,000; Serbia, 10,000; Slovakia, 88,000; Spain, 6,000; European Turkey, 55,500; Hungary, 742,800; USSR, 5,000,000 (of whom 2,994,684 were in the Ukraine); White Russia, 446,484. The total was more than 11,000,000. In general accurate enough, these figures are greatly exaggerated for the USSR and for France. (Subsequently, section IVb in France gave much more precise figures.)

times arrested the day after their return to their native country. On the other hand, the neutral countries were invited to repatriate their Jewish nationals, which they generally hastened to do.

Even more complex was the problem of the satellite and autonomous countries. At the January 20 meeting, Heydrich proposed that "in every single case experts from Foreign Affairs should confer with the proper RSHA specialists." But the Foreign Affairs representative, Under Secretary of State Luther, had already prepared a memorandum which expressed "the desires and views of the Ministry of Foreign Affairs on the final solution contemplated for the Jewish question in Europe." (3) This memorandum consisted of eight paragraphs, three of which stated: "3. Deportation of all Serbian Jews. 4. Deportation of Jews turned over to us by the Hungarian government. 5. Declaration of our good intentions toward the Rumanian, Slovak, Croatian, Bulgarian, and Hungarian governments regarding the deportation to the east of Jews living in those countries."

Under these conditions, it was easy to reach an understanding. The Ministry of Foreign Affairs had "Attachés for the Jewish Question" accredited to the satellite governments; their mission was to obtain the agreement of these countries to the deportation of the Jews as well as to the "coordination of anti-Jewish legislation." Working hand in hand with the emissaries of IVb they showed themselves everywhere to be zealous functionaries. Officially, it is true, they were being asked to cooperate only in what was described as deportations to the east, a "transfer of populations." The young men, party members, threw themselves into the task with complete fervor, while the diplomats, with Secretary of State Weizsäcker at their head, acted as indifferent technicians; their watchword seems to have been: Know Nothing. "The Ministry of Foreign Affairs lacks the information and the necessary elements for giving con-

---

(3) Berlin, December 8, 1941. The signature on the memorandum is illegible. It was certainly drawn up by Rademacher. The meeting called by Heydrich on January 20, 1942, had been called the first time for December 9, 1941 (which explains the date on the Foreign Affairs memorandum). It was called off at the very last moment, however, "because of unexpected events," that is, the attack on Pearl Harbor and the subsequent entry of the United States into the war.

crete judgments on the measures contemplated," wrote the legal expert of the ministry when consulted on a particular point of the "final solution." [4] Not to know, to close one's eyes; the attitude of the German diplomatic corps on the whole markedly recalls that of the military.

Another big problem which confronted IVb was transportation. The deportations were carried out by rail and required thousands of trains during a period when the German communications system was strained to the limit. The priorities of the "final solution" conflicted with military priorities. Sometimes the deportations were suspended, for IVb everywhere tried to adapt its requirements to the existing situation. Thus, when the Ministry of Transportation announced in the summer of 1942 that "military reasons prevent the transfer of Jews in Germany to the zone of eastern operations," the order was given "to transfer a greater number of Jews from southeast Europe and from the occupied western region." [5] On the other hand, when Eichmann was notified that in the west, particularly in France, "the Reichsbahn was probably not going to have the necessary transportation in November and December 1942, and January 1943," he gave orders "to speed up the tempo of the deportations beginning on September 15, so that a thousand Jews a day may be deported from this date on." [6] According to Dieter Wisliceny, "transportation required for the final solution, since it came immediately after military transportation, had priority over all other freight movements." [7] Nevertheless, despite all the energy Eichmann and Novak showed, despite all the good will of the Ministry of Transportation, in certain sectors the lack of rolling stock delayed deportations for months on end.

The available transportation thus had a great bearing on the choice of destination for the deportees and on the general schedule of deportations. In this sphere the Himmler-Heydrich-Eichmann trio had no preconceived plan, and made the most of their opportunities, whether transportational or political, as they arose. The essential thing, according to Himmler's expression, was "to send as many Jews to the east as is humanly possible." [8] Since it was natural to begin with the Jews of Germany, their deportation started long before the first exterminations took place. Just as logically, the

Polish Jews took second place. In this regard, Undersecretary of State Buehler, who represented Hans Frank and the Government General at the meeting of January 28, spoke up as follows:

> The Government General would be happy if, when the final solution of the question is undertaken, it might be begun in the Government General, as the transportation problem there is only a secondary one and no manpower problems would militate against the action. Of the 2,500,000 Jews affected by this measure, the majority are unfit for work in any case. . . . I ask only one thing: that the Jewish question in this country be settled as soon as possible.

Buehler's wishes were completely satisfied.

For the most part the convoys of Jews from the Government General were sent to one of the three extermination camps in eastern Poland (Belzec, Sobibor, Treblinka), while Auschwitz was reserved for Jews of other nationalities. But thousands of Polish Jews were also exterminated at Auschwitz, and numerous convoys from western Europe, especially from the Netherlands, ended up in the Government General. There must, of course, have been a section at IVb that parceled out the convoys according to the capacity of the camps and the conditions of the moment; but no trace of it has yet been found. If the number of trains requested from the Ministry of Transportation was in principle determined by the number of Jews to be deported, in practice the rate of deportations was often fixed by the number of convoys available, with special round-ups sometimes being organized to fulfill the quota.

As in all other phases of the planned exterminations, the deportation procedures were enveloped in secrecy. The destination of the convoys was elaborately concealed; officially, it was said that the Jews were being readied for "colonization in the east." We have seen the intentionally vague terminology used by Heydrich at the meeting of January 20: "Formed into labor columns . . . the Jews will be taken to these territories; part of them . . . will be eliminated by natural decrease . . . The rest must consequently be accorded [special] treatment. . . ." Characteristically, the Nazis disliked dotting their "i's." Eichmann, who had been in possession of a more explicit written order since April 1942, did not reveal its exact contents to his closest collaborators until November, that is, seven months later. (4) And Himmler's secretary wrote in April 1943, in reference to the statistical report ordered by Hitler: "The Reichsführer desires that no mention be made of the 'special treatment of the Jews.' It must be called 'transportation of the Jews toward the Russian east.'" [9] Sometimes even this last term seemed too crude. A directive from the Army headquarters of the Supreme Command forbade use of the expression "'dispatch to the east,' since this term is still associated with the Czarist deportations to Siberia. . . . It will therefore be necessary to use the expression, 'assignment to forced labor.'" [10] This fiction was carefully maintained. A note from Undersecretary of State Luther, dated August 21, 1942, stated: "Transportation to the Government General is a temporary measure. The Jews will be transferred to the remotest eastern occupied territories as soon as technical conditions permit." [11] Needless to say, these circumlocutions deceived no one. A report sent to Luther at this time by his collaborator Rintelen contains this sentence: "The plan is for the transfer of Rumanian Jews toward the region of Lublin to take place in successive waves; there those able to work will be given appropriate assignments, while the rest will undergo special treatment." [12] There are many more examples of such "slips." Despite every effort, knowledge of the real destination of the convoys became more and more widespread. For this reason the precautions were partly dropped later on, and Eichmann himself spoke openly in 1944 of his Auschwitz "mills." [13]

DEPORTATIONS FROM GREATER GERMANY

In Greater Germany (Germany, Austria, Bohemia, and Moravia), which for our purposes constitute a single area, the deportations were carried out by the regular German police, under the supervision of IVb.

Mass deportations from Germany began on October 15, 1941. They started before procedures for the "final solution" had been settled by the RSHA, even before the technical plans for exter-

(4) According to Dieter Wisliceny, who is the only member of the Eichmann team to make full revelations before Allied justice. The information he furnished is substantiated by other sources, such as the German archives and depositions of witnesses.

mination had been completed. But Heydrich and Eichmann, as we have seen, had been eagerly looking forward to the moment when they could make the Jews disappear from the Third Reich. After July 31, they were given *carte blanche* to realize their wishes.

Between October 15 and October 31 close to 20,000 Jews, for the most part old people, were deported to the Lodz ghetto, despite the protests of the German authorities in that ghetto, including its commissioner, Hans Biebow. Later, during November 1941, 50,000 German and Czech Jews were deported to occupied Russia, principally Riga and Minsk. The first group was exterminated some weeks later, the second survived for several months. The Jews picked for deportation were notified individually, sometimes one or two weeks in advance. The possibilities of taking flight or going into hiding were nonexistent; almost nobody escaped. On the other hand, suicides were frequent. Carefully organized, the convoy departures aroused little emotion in the German population. The reports sent to the RSHA by convoy escorts mention hardly any incidents. Indifference mixed with hostility generally accompanied them on their interminable trips. "The Union of Jews of the Reich" took an active part in organizing the transports, and its branches were sometimes also charged with selecting the deportees.

We thus see emerging here the customary Nazi procedure of making their victims assist in the different stages leading up to their own extermination. Doubtless arising out of a desire to simplify things, since self-governing Jewish organizations were already available, this procedure everywhere furnished ample occasion to the Nazis for giving vent to their hatred. The Jewish leaders, who paid with their lives or those of their families in case of defection or escape, were asked to become accomplices in the search; one can easily feel the anguish of their dilemma. In the end the entire personnel of the Union was obliged to lend a hand in the deportations. The naive account of a young Jewess, a social worker in Berlin, is an example.

> At eight o'clock in the evening we were summoned to the headquarters of the community. The Gestapo told us that a convoy of orphans was to leave, and that since the necessary quota would not be supplied by children's homes, we had to find orphans living with

private families and bring them to the transit camp. We young Jewish girls were to go out and look for Jewish children. Even today I do not understand how I found the courage and strength to do it. I was twenty at the time. We received a pass for the night, a list of four or five addresses. They gave us until four in the morning.

We set out in pairs, looking for the houses in the dark. Since doors were locked at nine o'clock in Berlin, we had to wake up the porter and show our pass. The Jewish apartments opened only after we rang the bell a great many times, for this was the frightening hour of the night when the arrests were made, when a family turned pale at every ring of the doorbell and the wife went to look for bags while the husband opened the door.

Seeing us with our [yellow] stars, the people began to breathe again, but what terrible scenes we witnessed after they learned the reason for our coming.[14]

The rate of deportation fell off considerably at the beginning of 1942, picking up again in the fall with added vigor. The statistical report already cited estimates at 217,748 the total number of Jews deported up to December 31, 1942 (in Germany proper: 100,516; Austria, 47,555; Bohemia-Moravia, 66,677). The few tens of thousands of skilled workers that remained were deported during the first months of 1943 (in Berlin the "clean sweep of the factories" of February 27 and March 3, 1943, affected 12,000 Jews). All these convoys went directly to Auschwitz, with the exception of a few "privileged" transports sent to Theresientstadt.

A few words need to be added about the fate of those deported in the fall of 1941. As we have said, they were granted a respite of several months. Those sent to Minsk profited in addition from the unexpected intercession of the Commissioner General of White Russia, Gauleiter Wilhelm Kube, a veteran of the Hitler movement. "I beg you to send me instructions," he wrote to his chief, Reich Commissioner Heinrich Lohse. "These Jews include war veterans, holders of the Iron Cross, those wounded in war, half-Aryans, and even three-quarter Aryans. . . . I do not lack hardness and I am ready to contribute to the solution of the Jewish problem, but people who come from the same cultural circles as ourselves are different from the bestial, aboriginal hordes."[15] A long report by the SD of White Russia enumerated the many failings of the old Gauleiter: he had shaken hands with a Jew who had rescued his car from a burning garage; he had confessed to appreciating the music of Mendelssohn and Offenbach, adding that "beyond a doubt there were artists among the Jews"; he had promised safety to 5,000 German Jews deported to Minsk.[16] But on July 31, 1942, a report from the same Kube reported to Lohse: "At Minsk approximately 10,000 Jews were liquidated on July 28 and 29. . . . Most of them had been deported to Minsk last November from Vienna, Brunn, Bremen, and Berlin by order of the Führer." [17]

THE POLISH DEPORTATIONS

In the Government General of Poland, the "final solution" was entrusted to a personal friend of Eichmann, SS General Odilo Globocnik, "Supreme Commander of the SS and police" for the Lublin region. The deportations of Jews to the extermination camps began in March 1942. As everywhere else, these were represented as "transfers" and "expulsions" (*Aussiedlungen*). From the end of 1943 on, Globocnik took care to destroy all documents bearing on these operations, still known by the popular term of "actions." [18] In the special circumstances of the Government General the "actions" changed on the spot into massacres in broad daylight—extermination began right in the ghetto. A deathly silence shrouded the true destination of the convoys, which were supposed to be leaving for Russia but in fact were headed for the Belzec extermination camp, set up 100 kilometres from Lublin on the eastern frontier of the Government General.

SS Captain Höffle, who led the first commando in charge of the "actions," seems to have hesitated at first as to what technique to employ. Should he pick out the men still capable of working right in the ghetto itself, or wait until their arrival at the extermination camp? (5) No precise rule was followed. Sometimes the inhabi-

(5) Note kept in the archives of the German Administration at Lublin dated March 17, 1942, signature illegible. The author of the note had conferred with Höffle on the matter of the deportations:
During the conversation, Hauptsturmführer Höffle declared: 1. It would be well to divide the convoys for the Lublin region at the departure points into Jews fit to work and those not suited for work. If this was not feasible, it would eventually be necessary to make a selection at Lublin with this in

tants were taken away indiscriminately; more often a careless selection was made before the embarkation. In the majority of cases the "action" took place as follows: The commando would break into a ghetto and round up a contingent of Jews for the extermination camp. The local Jewish council would then be informed. Helped by special police auxiliaries, Polish or Ukrainian, and sometimes even by members of the Jewish police, the SS would smash down doors, machine-gun people, set houses afire, and herd and drive the Jews toward the assembly point. At the least sign of resistance, at the slightest hesitation, Jews were knocked down on the spot, the sick and the lagging among them. Here is a brief description of one of the first "actions," that at Zamosc.

> On August 11, 1942, a Saturday, the SS, the SD, and the mounted police, fell like a pack of savages on the Zamosc Jewish quarter. It was a complete surprise. The brutes on horseback, particularly, created a panic; they raced through the streets shouting insults, slashing on all sides with their whips. Our community then numbered 10,000 people. In a twinkling, without their even realizing what was happening, a crowd of 3,000 men, women, and children, picked up haphazardly in the streets and in the houses, was driven to the station and deported to an unknown destination. . . . The spectacle which the ghetto presented after the attack literally drove the survivors mad. Bodies everywhere, in the streets, in the courtyards, inside the houses; babies thrown from the third or fourth floors lay crushed on the sidewalks. The Jews themselves had to pick up and bury the dead.[19]

It was a bloody orgy, but carried out with a concern for efficiency: the complete panic made it possible to assemble and fill the convoys with the smallest delay. The proportion of Jews killed on the spot was considerable, 5 or even 10 per cent.

From March until July 1942, the ghettos within a 200 kilometer radius of Belzec were raked through in this way. (6) The deportations took several weeks in the large ghettos of Lublin (March 17

---

mind; 2. Jews not fit to work are all to be sent to Belzec, the last station in the Zamosc district; 3. Hauptsturmführer Höffle foresees the establishment of a huge work camp for Jews who are fit for work.

(6) Although it is difficult to get a precise idea of the plan adopted for the successive "actions" we can perceive that Globocnik envisaged an immense concentric sweep, with its center at Belzec. In fact the ghettos farthest from Belzec, like Lublin, Mielec, and Lwow, were attacked in March and April, while the nearest ghettos, such as those of Bilgoraj, Tomaszow, and Hrubieszow were not attacked until May and June.

to April 20) and Lwow (March 10 to April 1). The size of the contingents were calculated according to the capacity of Belzec; most of the ghettos were evacuated in several "actions," occurring sometimes at intervals of several months. Meanwhile, farther north, the Sobibor and Treblinka extermination camps were set up in May and July, respectively. On July 19 Himmler, after having personally checked the progress of the "final solution" in Poland, had the area of operations extended to the whole of the Government General. From Lublin he ordered SS General Krüger, "Supreme Commander of the SS and Police for the East," to "carry out and finish the evacuation of the whole Jewish population of the Government General before December 31, 1942 . . . except for those that are in an assembly camp (Warsaw, Cracow, Czestochow, Radom, Lublin.)" [20] Three days later, on July 22, 1942, Captain Höffle's commandos appeared at the Warsaw ghetto.

In this immense ghetto, with its 400,000 inhabitants and a police corps of more than 2,000 Jewish agents, the "action" began in a somewhat different manner. At first, the SS demanded from the Jewish council a daily contingent of 5,000 Jews for evacuation, picked from the non-workers; the Jewish police were put in charge of the selection. Convoys left for the Treblinka camp from the selection center. A few days later the quota for the daily contingent was raised to 7,000. Tcherniakov, president of the Jewish council, committed suicide the next day. A system of food premiums (seven pounds of bread, two of marmalade) was introduced for those volunteering for "evacuation"; for two or three days the influx of volunteers, starving and desperate wrecks, surpassed the required number, which had been raised to 10,000. But later on the number of people deported daily dropped—the Jewish police were not up to the job. Therefore on August 7 Höffle's commandos descended upon the ghetto and conducted direct manhunts, thus bringing their methods into conformity with the general practice. With brief interruptions, the great Warsaw action continued for more than ten weeks, until October 3, 1942. According to the German figures, 310,322 Jews were evacuated from Warsaw during the summer of 1942. (7)

(7) Report by SS General Stroop on the destruction of the Warsaw ghetto. Warsaw, May 16, 1943. (PS 1061)

In all parts of "Old Poland" deportation actions were being carried out in the same way and under the same conditions, occasionally with some innovations. Thus at Radom, where the action began on the night of September 4-5, 1942, floodlights were used to illuminate the Jewish quarter.[21] As the population of the ghettos decreased, the tenacious struggle carried out by the slave traders to safeguard what Jewish manpower remained took a new form. They tried to assemble their workers into labor commandos working outside the ghetto, the *placowki*. But this was useless—the SS made their "selections" from these groups on the spot. During this same summer of 1942, the "actions" were extended to the last ghettos in the "annexed territories" (Sosnowice, Dabrowa, Czestochow, Bielsko); the neighboring Auschwitz camp had been considerably enlarged. As for the big Lodz ghetto, its "useless mouths" had been sent in small groups to the Chelmno extermination camp since the beginning of the year; all the children and old people were deported there at a single stroke in September 1942.

Thus, almost five-sixths of the Polish Jews were deported during 1942. The schedule set by Himmler, however, was not kept to. By the deadline date of December 31 there still remained close to 300,-000 Jews in the Government General, according to German statistics. On February 16, 1943, the Reichsführer sent Krüger one of those long-winded instructions so characteristic of his pedantic hangman's manner.

> For security reasons I order the demolition of the Warsaw ghetto [to take place] after the reestablishment of the concentration camp elsewhere, all parts of buildings and salvageable materials to be reutilized judiciously. The demolition of the ghetto and the reestablishment of the concentration camp are necessary, for otherwise we shall probably never be able to pacify Warsaw and exterminate the criminal hordes.[22]

These lines show a fear of a growing resistance. A long report by General Katzmann, Supreme Commander of the SS and police in the province of Galicia, also notes the existence of organized resistance.

> The Jews tried every means to escape evacuation. . . . As their numbers diminished, their resistance became more desperate. They used all kinds of weapons in their defense, among them Italian weapons

bought at a very high price from Italian soldiers quartered in the country. . . .[23]

The winds of revolt had finally risen in the ghettos. The last great evacuations, at Warsaw in April 1943 and Bialystok in August 1943, were accompanied by desperate fighting.

SPECIAL CHARACTERISTICS OF THE POLISH DEPORTATIONS

The density of the Jewish population in Poland is explanation enough why the Nazis set up the great death camps in that country. This proximity, as well as the gigantic scale of operations, gave a special character to the Polish tragedy. At the time of the ghetto "actions," there was no discontinuity between the deportations proper and the exterminations. Extermination started right in the ghetto; Belzec and Treblinka, within easy reach, were merely technical simplifications. However, the death camps made it possible to spread a veil over the mass butchery which satisfied the demands of the "German way." A fiction was created that took no one in, but which made it easier to feign ignorance and cut short complaints. These complaints consisted, in the German manner, of a lot of bureaucratic forms and papers which the deportations gave rise to, such as the file on a claim by the Cracow Public Welfare Service demanding arrears of 2,260 zlotys for "hospitalization expenses" from the Mielec Jewish council. After having made the rounds of several offices, this file returned from Lublin to Cracow three months later with the notation: "In answer to your claim I am notifying you that the Mielec Jewish council has been evacuated to Russia. It is unfortunately impossible to give you precise information as to its address, as it is unknown." [24]

The Polish Jews themselves, unlike their brothers in other countries, were scarcely to be duped. Their first cries of alarm resounded from the time the extermination station was installed at Chelmno near Lodz. One of these tragic messages has been preserved, a letter sent by the rabbi of the small place of Grabow to his friends in Lodz on January 19, 1942:

My very dear friends,
    I did not answer you until now, because I knew nothing very definite about all the things I've been told. Alas, to our great misfortune,

we now know everything! I had here at my home an eyewitness who
was saved by the grace of heaven. . . . I found out everything from
him. The place where they are exterminated is called Chelmno, near
Dabia, and they are buried in the neighboring forest of Lachow. The
men are killed in two ways: shooting or gas. . . . For several days
they have been taking thousands of Jews from Lodz and have done
the same to them. Don't imagine that all this is written by a madman. Alas, it is the terrible tragic truth. . . . Horror! Horror! "Man,
rend thy clothing, put on sackcloth with ashes, and go out into the
midst of the city, and cry out with a loud and bitter cry." I am so
tired that my pen can write no more. Creator of the universe, help us!

Jacob Szulman [25]

This letter was written in January 1942, when the Chelmno
camp's operations were on a small scale. Information and proof
later began coming in in large quantities. For a long time, however,
the mass of Jews in the ghetto refused to believe it. Their will to
live fed on blind optimism. But this only anticipated German
wishes; a silent connivance linked victims and executioners.

Many factors contributed to maintaining the Polish Jews' attitude of passive resignation, until the hour of the "actions" struck.
A number of things, as we have seen, are explained by the simple
physical debility of the majority. A lack of all military tradition, as
well as a want of arms, are other elements, to which we shall return. The Germans were careful to keep Jewish illusions alive by
all sorts of stratagems and crude ruses.

News and signs of life from the few deportees permitted to survive, fantastic rumors about an exchange of Jews for Germans interned by the Allies, were some of their devices. The work certificates played a very important role. These were constantly being
checked, modified, revoked, or revalidated; this very confusion stimulated a lively faith in their magic virtues. In this way the Jews
were ensnared for long months in the illusion that their ghetto
would be saved, or that they personally would be spared, even if
the worst befell the community.

The fate of the Warsaw ghetto was the principal event that
brought home the reality and dispelled all doubt. People's imag-
inations now began to work in new directions, seeking out subterfuges by which to escape their fate: hiding places, shelters, bunk-

ers, deep excavations, false papers, escape abroad. Nothing of this sort went unnoticed by the Germans.

Not only did they try to escape, they hid in every corner imaginable: in tunnels, chimneys, even in manure pits. They barricaded themselves in the passages of catacombs, in caves transformed into forts, in holes in the ground; they prepared ingenious hiding places in attics, sheds, and even in the furniture. . . . They tried desperately to escape abroad. . . . They used every means to gain their ends and often appealed to German and allied members of the Wehrmacht, begging them for transport to the frontier, or over it, in a military vehicle. They offered considerable sums to have themselves smuggled out.[26]

Except in rare cases, these devices were quite as useless as all those attempts to escape death by cooperating with the Nazis which cast a dull, cruel light over the last days of the ghettos: enlistment in the Jewish police, the activities of the Jewish councils, and the part taken by certain Jews in the deportations so as to escape deportation themselves. And so we come back to the matter of the Jewish councils, which the Nazis set up or planned to set up in all countries, and in Poland brought to the peak of their development. The following testimony, taken from a diary kept by the Jew Jacob Littner in the small town of Zbaraz in Galicia, gives some idea of how they functioned:

(November, 1943): The number of the Jewish militia has risen from 80 to 130 men. An "action" must be imminent. Grunfeld (8) knows what he wants. He is feared by the Jews quite as much as any of the SS butchers. He is convinced that he can save himself and his family by betraying his brother Jews. The militia men also think their job is an assurance of safety. The young people pay large sums, up to 10,000 zlotys, to get into the militia. . . . Life is cruel, and man also becomes so: what guards we have over us! The Jewish militia, the Ukrainian militia, the regular SS, the special SS commandos, the German gendarmerie—all patrol our miserable ghetto. . . .

(A few days later): Whiskey has been issued to the Jewish militia by the Jewish council. The news flashed through the ghetto. We know what that means—a great manhunt—and I had to go down into our bunker shaking with fever, sick.

Unfortunately, two visitors were in our hut when the starting signal was given. There was not enough room in the bunker. At our insist-

(8) The president of the Jewish council.

ence, the visitors, who thus found out it was our hiding place, climbed out and tried to escape. Some time later we heard footsteps above; we recognized various militiamen by their voices. After minutes that seemed like centuries, they left the house. We wrongly thought the worst had passed.

About five o'clock in the morning other militiamen entered and went to our shelter without hesitation, took the camouflage off the entrance, and knocked. Our hiding place had been betrayed. We had to open the trap door and my companions climbed out; trembling with fear and fever, I remained below all alone. Mietek was led away by the police. Cursing, they left me where I was. They could not take me away; they would have had to carry me. Alone, abandoned, and desperate, I stayed in my hole. I shook. . . . Five other militiamen suddenly appeared. They dragged me through the narrow opening and threw me on the ground. I finally roused their pity. They left me where I was and sent for a doctor. Then a second miracle happened: the Jewish council set Mietek free. . . .

(Some weeks later): I was awakened this morning by a savage burst of firing. I jumped to my feet and looked out the window. In the morning dusk, men in uniform were pursuing other men. . . . I woke everybody up. We dressed hurriedly and went down into the bunker. . . . Little by little the shooting stopped; the cries and the shots faded.

When daylight came, Mietek decided to leave the bunker. He went to the Jewish council. . . . An hour later he returned and told us to be calm; a major action was in process; 900 Jews had already been captured, among them his fiancée. At noon Mietek came back again. He was desperate. His own position was terrible, but he wanted to free his fiancée. During preceding actions militiamen had been able to free a relative if their work had proved satisfactory. They could go see the SS who directed the action and say, "I have been a good worker." Kohanek, one of the most efficient militiamen, was able to free his parents in this way, but he had to hand over twenty-four other Jews. He wanted to liberate his sister in the same way, but was only able to have twelve more people arrested. . . . Hours passed. Mietek did not come back. We opened the trap door to breathe a little fresh air, but did not dare leave our shelter. . . .

Night came. It was a long night. In the morning I ventured cautiously out into the street. Bodies were lying on the ground. . . . Curious peasants on their way to market stood around them, but without any emotion, it seemed to me. There were few Jews alive in the street. We looked at each other hesitantly, like hunted animals. . . . We learned that Sternberg, commander of the militia, had been shot along with forty-eight of his men. The militiamen had shot 1,050 Jews. They had been buried by the remaining militiamen. These were then shot in their turn. Mietek had been shot, too. . . .[27]

Such were the situations that the Nazi "actions" gave rise to in the ghettos progressively being "liquidated"; these situations were incommensurable with all human experience, they defy all moral criteria, so it would seem that we should be extremely cautious in passing judgment on them—here we are unmistakably in the world of the concentration camp. During the same months, however, the Jews of the last remaining ghettos summoned up all their moral resources, as we shall see later, and ended the thousand-year history of Polish Judaism with an act of resistance that they knew was doomed to defeat.

THE DEPORTATIONS IN SOUTHEASTERN EUROPE

The fate of more than one and one-half million Jews in southeastern Europe differed according to the degree of vassalage of their countries to the Nazis and the distance separating them from Germany. One feature was everywhere apparent: the states whose frontiers had recently been revised seized on the Jews of their "annexed territories" and sacrificed them first to the Nazis; they took care themselves to see that the death sentences, raids, and measures of internment were carried out.

Serbia, a country under direct German military administration, was chronologically the first to be affected by the "final solution." In September 1942 the Berlin press announced to its readers that "Serbia is the first region of Europe to be cleared of its Jews." (9) In fact, there were no deportations in Serbia; with the exception of those who found shelter with the partisans, the Serbian Jews were exterminated on the spot. Characteristically, the Ministry of Foreign Affairs played a decisive part in this massacre. In September 1941 General von Weichs, Commander-in-Chief in Serbia, and his political counselor, Minister Benzler, demanded the deportation of 8,000 Jews.[28] But this was to stand too much on ceremony: "As I see it, the Commander-in-Chief must himself take care of the elimination of these 8,000 Jews. In other regions, military commanders have got rid of a much greater number of Jews without even mentioning it"—such was Undersecretary of State

(9) The Berlin *Boersenzeitung*, September 9, 1942. The same phrase recurs in a report by the State Counselor Turner on the political situation in Serbia sent to the "Southeast Military Commander" on August 29, 1942.

Luther's comment on the matter.[29] With Ribbentrop's authorization, Luther made contact with Heydrich; Rademacher, the Ministry's principal expert, was sent to Serbia to "settle the Jewish question" with the cooperation of the local SS authorities. The result was that the Jewish men were shot on the spot beginning in November 1941. The Jewish women and children, interned in the gypsy quarter of Belgrade, were exterminated in the summer of 1942.

From 1941 to 1945 a separate Croatian state figured on the map of Europe. Massacres of Serbs and Jews, totaling close to 200,000 victims according to certain statistics, marked its birth. Kasche, the German Ambassador to Croatia, had no trouble reaching an agreement on the deportations with the *Poglavnik* (Führer), Ante Pavelitch. Croatia, however, was divided into "spheres of influence," German in the north, Italian in the south. In their zone, the Italian authorities opposed the deportations. This was the first evidence of the sharp conflict over treatment of the Jews which divided Germans and Italians. While the German diplomats strove unsuccessfully in Rome to bring Italian policy "into line" with their own, Croatian Jews were taking refuge in the Italian zone or joining Tito's guerrillas. Because of this only a few thousand of the 25,000-30,000 Jews were deported in 1943 and 1944 (3,000, according to certain sources).[30]

Like Yugoslavia, Greece was divided into German and Italian zones under military administration. But unfortunately the great majority of the 75,000 Greek Jews lived in Macedonia, in the German zone; more than 55,000 in the city of Salonika. Because of this concentration they were an especially easy prey; only their great distance from Poland and perhaps the German desire to couple their deportation with that of the Bulgarian Jews, postponed their fate somewhat. After a rapid inspection trip by Rolf Günther in January 1943, Eichmann appointed Brunner and Wisliceny to carry out the deportation of the Greek Jews.

The operation was efficiently carried out in the period March-May 1943. The more than 1,500 kilometres separating Salonika from Auschwitz made it easier to hide the true meaning of these "population transfers." The experts from Germany contributed some special refinements. The Jews were invited to exchange their

drachmas for zlotys and were given special receipts; they were assured that these novel traveler's checks would permit them to buy
land near Cracow.[31] The trick worked so well that when a number
of unmarried Jews were assigned to the Todt organization in
Greece itself, many of them contracted fictitious marriages so as to
be included in the deportation convoys.[32]

Between March 15 and May 9, 43,000 Jews were deported to
Auschwitz in sixteen consecutive convoys. The trip lasted ten
days on the average; the weak condition of the newcomers was
perhaps the reason why the Greek Jews, "poor human material"
according to Rudolf Hoess, were sometimes exterminated *en masse*
upon their arrival, without the customary selection.[33]

The rest of the Macedonian Jews were deported in three supplementary convoys in July-August 1943. As for the Jews of the
southern zone, particularly those of Athens, who had been long
protected by the Italians, they were deported only on the eve of
the German retreat in July 1944.(10)

The Jews of the Greek islands felt confident that the sea stood
as a barrier between them and deportation; but several hundreds
of them, particularly from Rhodes, were crowded into antiquated
boats and sunk in the Aegean Sea.[34]

The "final solution" in Slovakia was also entrusted to the Wis-
liceny-Brunner team. Situated at the very door of Germany, Monseigneur Tiso's Slovakia had been the first satellite country
(March 1939). In August 1940, Dieter Wisliceny had been sent
there in his role as an expert on Jewish matters; the 90,000 Slovakian Jews were steadily driven from their homes and concentrated in camps and ghettos. In February 1942 the German government requested through its diplomats the shipment of 20,000
"strong young" Jewish workers; the Slovakian government took up
this suggestion with "enthusiasm." [35] Two months later came the
offer "to deport in the same way the rest of the Slovakian Jews and
thus rid Slovakia of its Jews," an offer to which the Bratislava
authorities agreed "without any German pressure." In two successive groups, a total of 52,000 Jews were deported in March-April

(10) Wisliceny reported the number of Jews deported in the "action" as
8,000-10,000. (Affidavit by Wisliceny, Bratislava, June 27, 1947)

and May-June 1942. The arrests and organization of the convoys were carried out by the Slovakian authorities. The deportations from Slovakia were, after those in Germany and Poland, the first in Europe.

These deportations came to a sudden halt in the summer of 1942, when information about the fate of the deportees began to filter back. First the Slovakian episcopate, then the Vatican, made strong protests to the government of this Catholic country. Alarmed, the Slovakian rulers asked Wisliceny for authorization to have the deportee camps inspected by a government mission. Eichmann obviously could not agree, but the Germans did not insist on resumption of the deportations: "The instructions [of Secretary of State von Weizsäcker] have clearly emphasized that under no circumstances must internal political complications be created by the evacuation of the Slovakian Jews." [36] The rest of the Slovakian Jews were allowed to live on in relative security for more than two years. At the beginning of September 1944 the Slovakian popular insurrection, which the Germans immediately suppressed, furnished Eichmann with a pretext for sending Brunner to Bratislava. Hardened by experience, most of the Jews were able to escape; only a few thousand were caught and deported.[37]

Slovakia occupies a special place on the map of Nazi genocide. It was the first satellite country, completely subjugated though it was, where the Germans encountered a strong enough resistance to force them to interrupt their plans for the "final solution." Bordering on Poland, it was also the passageway by which a few escapees from the death camps were able to reach Hungary and so inform the outside world on the progress of the exterminations. Finally, it was in Slovakia that the fantastic project for a general ransoming of the surviving European Jews took shape; despite the almost complete failure of this scheme, it had, as we shall see, some influence on the fate of the Jews.

South of Slovakia, the agony of Hungarian Jewry blazed out with sudden intensity in the spring of 1944. Hungary was a haven where over 800,000 oppressed and harried Jews had yet been spared from falling into the clutches of the Germans. Except in certain annexed territories (17,000 Jews from Subcarpathian Russia were deported to Poland in August 1941; 1,500 Jews from the

Yugoslavian Banat were massacred in January 1942), they enjoyed a temporary safety. The pressures which the Germans brought to bear had no result, since the attitude of the vassal state was independent enough in this matter for it to refuse to permit any German "expert" to take charge of its anti-Jewish measures; [38] throughout the war this Hungarian attitude remained firm.

At the beginning of March 1944 Regent Horthy gave indications of intending to recall the Hungarian troops from the Russian front. Immediately the Germans sent in troops to occupy the country, and a government chosen by Berlin was imposed on the old Regent. Eichmann could now take his long-awaited revenge. Though he very seldom traveled, he came to Budapest on March 21 with a full team and took personal charge of operations. The drama unfolded at a dizzy speed. The new ministers punctually carried out Eichmann's instructions. According to Wisliceny, "The only purpose of the new cabinet was to solve the Jewish question." [39] Extraordinary demands were made on the Ministry of Transportation, which guaranteed Eichmann four convoys a day. The country was divided into five zones: north, east, south, west and the city of Budapest. The 450,000 Jews of the first four zones were interned during April and deported within six weeks, from May 15 to June 30. The beginning of the action against the Budapest Jews was set for June 30.[40]

However, as the police of the capital were completely loyal to him, the Regent Horthy was able to intervene and block the deportation of the Budapest Jews; he even succeeded in recalling the first convoy, which had already departed. Against a background of intrigue and palace revolution, a confused struggle took place around the lives of the Budapest Jews. Eichmann pressed on with all his strength; but he got only weak support from Himmler, who was kept in a state of uncertainty by the ransom negotiations, which had been resumed with new vigor. The neutral countries, churches, and great international organizations pressed the Regent to stand firm, and he threw the last fragments of his power into the balance. The Red Cross and foreign legations worked feverishly to save Jews in the city from arrest and internment. More or less official visas, the "protection papers," were issued by the thousands; blocks of houses displaying the Red Cross emblem were placed un-

der that organization's protection. The names of Raoul Wallenberg, (11) a special envoy of the King of Sweden, and the Swiss
consul, Victor Lutz, will forever be enshrined in the memory of the
people of Israel. It might be said that the conscience of the world,
which had been so long apathetic, tried with a sudden, tardy leap
to come to the aid of the Budapest Jews. The situation hung in the
balance until October 15, when, following an abortive attempt at a
separate peace, Horthy's regime was swept away by the Nazis. Its
successor, Szalassy's "Arrow Cross," at once organized bloody massacres which took a toll of several thousand. But Himmler had already given the order to stop the exterminations and dismantle the
Auschwitz crematories. Deportation was no longer possible. Eichmann's last revenge was to evacuate 30,000 Jews on foot from
Budapest to Vienna by forced marches; regimented into "workers'
companies," many of them died on the way. More than 100,000
Budapest Jews were thus miraculously spared and freed by Russian
troops in January 1945.

The second favored target in southeastern Europe was the 700,000
Rumanian Jews, with whose case the Jewish Sections in Berlin had
been preoccupied throughout the war. At the very last moment,
when the German High Command planned to occupy Rumania
after that country's defection in August 1944, Eichmann once again
prepared to follow the German troops and got as far as the Wehrmacht jumping-off point in south Hungary.[41] But, as we know, this
invasion never took place; the era of *Blitzkrieg* was at an end. The
prey which lay so close at hand in the end escaped the strategists
of the "final solution," though it is true that Rumania's *Conducator,*
Antonescu, and the men of the Iron Guard were able to wreak
enough destruction on their own.

Rumanian Jews were massacred by the tens of thousands in the
pogroms at Budapest, Jassy, Constanza, and Ploesti at the beginning
of 1941. At the end of 1941 those in the "annexed regions" of Bessarabia and Bucovina were deported wholesale to "Transnistria"—
that is, to say, to that part of the USSR between the Dniester and
the Bug Rivers which had been occupied by the Rumanian army.

(11) When the Russians took Budapest, Raoul Wallenberg was arrested by
the Soviet military police. For over a decade, nothing was known about his
fate. In 1957 the Soviet government informed the government of Sweden that
he had died of a heart attack in a Moscow prison in 1947.

These deportations were not carried out at the insistence of Berlin—
on the contrary, they were protested against by German departments concerned with Jewish matters, chiefly IVb, as upsetting the
over-all plans; in general, their disordered execution offended the
methodical German mind. At the very beginning of the Russian
campaign, Berlin was informed that

> The Rumanians are acting against the Jews without any over-all
> plan. There would be no objection to the many executions of Jews if
> the preparations and technique of execution had not been so shoddy.
> In general, the Rumanians leave the bodies on the spot without bury-
> ing them.

It is in such terms that the head of "Action Group D" remon-
strated against the Rumanians.[42] Eichmann tried to take things into
his own hands, awaiting an opportunity to establish German "security measures" on the spot. At his request, the German Ambassador von Killinger intervened with the Rumanian government and
it was agreed that no deportations should take place from then on
"unless first cleared with Germany through regular channels and
through the intermediary of the Minister of Foreign Affairs." [43]

Of about 300,000 Jews deported, only 55,000 were still alive two
years later, even though the Rumanian authorities conducted no
systematic extermination campaign in the Nazi style.[44] Starvation,
cold, epidemics—there was, we are tempted to say, also a "Rumanian way." The interventions of the German "action groups" completed the work of extermination.

In the "Old Kingdom" (Moldavia and Walachia), the "Rumanian
way" at least had the advantage that the Rumanian administration
could be easily bribed from the top down. At the end of 1942 it
would seem Antonescu had conceived his own ransom scheme; he
proposed to let the Jews under his control leave for Palestine in
return for a substantial payment. "In my opinion, Marshal Antonescu wants to kill two birds with one stone; he wants to collect
sixteen billion lei, which would be very useful to him, and he wants
to get rid of a large number of Jews in an easy way," von Killinger
wrote to his government in December 1942.[45] The Germans categorically vetoed this project. But Antonescu, on his side, going back
on his promises, refused to permit deportations to Poland of Jews

from the "Old Kingdom." The Reich and its satellite thus effec-
tively blocked each other; no deportations took place to the very end.
But these only just missed being carried out. After November 1941
a IVb expert, Captain Richter, came to Budapest; and in August
1942, as we have seen, Rintelen announced that the deportations
were shortly to begin. (Cf. p. 146) However, we do not know all
the influences acting on Antonescu. Other considerations might
have influenced him; in any event the "Rumanian way" made possible the survival of 250,000 Rumanian Jews by a last-minute
reprieve.

In Bulgaria the situation began to develop in almost the same
way. After the summer of 1942 King Boris's government consented
in principle to the deportation of the Bulgarian Jews and wel-
comed in a German expert, Théo Dannecker, sent from Paris by
Eichmann for this purpose. An actual contract was drawn up in
proper form and signed on February 23, 1942, by Dannecker and
Belev, the Bulgarian Commissioner for Jewish Questions; the Bulgarian government committed itself to the deportation of a first
group of 20,000 Jews, and promised "in no case to demand their
return." [46]

As elsewhere, the deportations began in the annexed regions,
Thrace and Macedonia, where 13,000 Jews were deported at the
end of March, 1943, along with the Greek Jews of Salonika. As a
prelude to the deportation of 50,000 Jews from Bulgaria proper,
25,000 were expelled from Sofia to the provinces in May. But things
went no further because of the direct pressure of Bulgarian public
opinion. This made itself felt in all sorts of ways: questions in the
Chamber, clerical intervention, protests from associations of pro-
fessionals and others, and popular demonstrations in Sofia, turning
into riots, that took place to the accompaniment of cries of "We
want the Jews to stay." The Bulgarian government thought it wise
to yield. According to Beckerle, the German ambassador to Sofia,
the Bulgarians did "not find sufficient fault with the Jews to justify
the particular measures taken against them"; certainly they were,
to conclude with the words of this same diplomat, "especially lacking in the ideological enlightenment that exists among Germans." [47]

ITALY AND THE ITALIAN ZONE OF INFLUENCE AS "CENTERS OF REFUGE"

If the pro-Fascist governments of enslaved Europe on the whole offered only feeble opposition to the deportations, a very different attitude was taken to the matter in the Fascist homeland itself. Wherever Italian troops set foot, a protective screen was thrown around the Jews shielding them from the clutches of the IVb, as well as from massacres and persecutions by local Quislings. An open conflict finally broke out between Rome and Berlin over the Jewish question. This Italian policy, however, owed nothing at all to Mussolini; Il Duce, resigning himself to the inevitable, only gave it his reluctant assent. There was a deep logic in this, for in the last analysis such a crucial question can nowhere be solved by a stroke of the pen, but must be decided by the national collectivity according to its wisdom and degree of civilization.

The paradox of the Fascist regime's setting up as protector of the Jews deepens when one remembers that Italy was only too eager after 1938 to coordinate its legislation with that of the Nazis, copying the German anti-Jewish measures. Rome inveighed against the Jews with a ferocity only slightly inferior to that of Berlin. Profane or sacred measures can be taken at the whim of the Prince in a dictatorial country; but genocide, because it affects the deepest levels of a nation's spirit, cannot be carried out without the concurrence of all the people.

It is significant that in Italy proper the Germans never raised the Jewish question. Undoubtedly they were afraid of offending Italian feelings, and planned to bring the matter up after the war. It was over the treatment of the Jews in Croatia and France that the argument broke out. (After November 1942 the Italian army occupied the region of Nice and the Alps in France.) In these regions, the theoretical sovereignty of the satellite governments of Pavelitch and Pétain furnished the Germans with a convenient pretext for taking action. In both areas the developments were almost the same. From the moment they arrived in their zones of occupation, the Italian military authorities set aside the measures enacted at Zagreb or Vichy. The Jews of the other regions of the country then came streaming in by the thousands to place themselves under Italian protection. This jeopardized the "final solution" for the whole country. The German answer to this was a two-pronged application of pressure, carried out with energy and tenacity on Eichmann's insistence; [48] here is an example of the astonishing influence enjoyed by this simple SS commander. While Ribbentrop and his ambassadors intervened through diplomatic channels, Vichy government departments and Pavelitch's ministers protested to the Italian commander against the infringement of their national sovereignty. Himmler on his side sent emissaries to Rome to intervene with the Italian administration and police. All these efforts failed. Although Mussolini had promised the German negotiators at least twice to rouse his generals out of their "stupid sentimental notions," (12) the situation continued unchanged right up to the Italian débâcle. Thus in the middle of a tormented Europe there were these two zones of refuge where Jews were protected not only against the Germans, but also against part of the internal measures of discrimination, despite the protests of Pavelitch and—to its eternal shame—the efforts of the Vichy government. (13) In this curious situation all a Jew had to do to be able to breathe freely was to make a one-hour trip from Lyon to Grenoble or from Marseille to Nice, without having to cross a frontier or demarcation line. We have no exact figures on the number of Jewish refugees in the Italian zone of Croatia; in France it reached at least 30,000. The existence of these zones also encouraged resistance to the German "actions" all over the country. Knochen, the head of the SD in France, pointed out that "the French government, which only reluctantly concerns it-

(12) Mussolini used this expression during his conference with German Ambassador von Mackensen on March 18, 1943. (Report from von Mackensen to his government, Rome, March 18, 1943): "Il Duce has agreed to a solution in conformity with our proposition no. 1," concluded von Mackensen. The question had already been discussed previously, during von Ribbentrop's visit: "Il Duce . . . agrees that the military do not have a correct conception of the Jewish question. He attributes this, above all, to their different intellectual background. . . ." (Report of the conference between von Ribbentrop and Mussolini, February 25, 1943.)

(13) In France the Italian authorities opposed sending Jews into "forced residence," constituting workers' units, and stamping their identification papers. (Report from the prefect of the Maritime Alps to the head of the government, Nice, January 14, 1943.) In Crotia, according to German ambassador Kasche, "The Italians oppose any interference by the Croats, and their participation in any measure contemplated, including the inventory of Jewish property." (Kasche's report to his government, Zagreb, November 20, 1942.)

self with the solution of the Jewish question, shows a stronger opposition because of the Italian measures." [49] To use the words of an Italian diplomat, "Events created a paradoxical situation in which the Italian Ministry of Foreign Affairs was obliged to fight against Laval's collaborationist government in order to defend the life and property of French citizens within France itself." [50]

How could such a state of affairs come about? The initiative for it came from the Italian Ministry of Foreign Affairs.[51] Encouraged by Count Ciano, according to some informants,[52] this policy received the full cooperation of the Italian military. Against such unanimity, the efforts of Il Duce himself could not prevail. (14) Diplomats and generals skillfully coordinated their measures, avoiding any head-on clash with German demands. In Croatia they insisted upon a general inquiry into the situation before any steps were taken. This inquiry was, "by its very nature and consequences, extremely complex and laborious." [53] Actually, it was never finished. In France the pretext was the security of the territory: "For reasons of military security, the occupation authorities must reserve to themselves all decisions relative to the Jews, without distinction of nationality," the military commandant notified the Vichy government.[54] It is beyond the scope of this book to detail the innumerable subtleties and tricks by which the Italians procrastinated and prolonged matters for many months. (15) The appeal to "the elementary requirements of Italian prestige," to which Mussolini's ears evidently could not remain insensible, furnished the most important argument.[55] It is clear from this, by the way, that the chancelleries and high commands of the German allies did not misunderstand the real meaning of the "final solution." "We must keep the Italian army from dirtying its hands with this business," wrote a member of the Italian High Command in Croatia. "If the Croats really want to hand over the Jews, let them do so, but let them do

(14) In his communication of March 18, cited above, von Mackensen reported with satisfaction that Il Duce had decided in favor of "solution no. 1", i. e., to hand over the Jews to the French police. Some days later Undersecretary of State Bastianini informed Mackensen that "solution no. 2," reserving the question to the competency of the Italian services, had finally been decided upon. (Report by von Mackensen, March 22, 1943)

(15) We refer the reader to our work: *La Condition des Juifs en France sous l'occupation italienne,* Paris, Editions du Centre, 1946.

it themselves, and let them deliver them directly to the Germans without our playing the part of middleman. It is already painful enough for the army of a great country to permit crimes of this sort, not to speak of taking part in them." [56] And a detailed file on what the Germans were doing in Poland, submitted by the Italian Undersecretary of State Bastianini to Il Duce at an opportune moment between two visits of Ambassador von Mackensen, served to temper his pro-German zeal in the matter of the Jews. [57]

After the downfall of Mussolini, Badoglio's ephemeral government tried to continue and broaden the policy of Italian protection. But the débâcle following the Italian armistice of September 1943 made all these efforts futile. The Italian occupation was replaced by that of the Wehrmacht, and Italy itself was occupied. Eichmann dispatched his best lieutenants into the hunting ground now open to him. Abromeit returned to Croatia, Dannecker was transferred from Sofia to Rome, while Alois Brunner was sent to Nice. But the solidarity of the populations, the mounting resistance they offered to the Germans, and the attitude of the Jews themselves, now aware of the fate awaiting them, prevented the IVb men from making up lost time. Some 10,000 of the 45,000 Italian Jews were arrested and deported through Dannecker's efforts. [58] Despite measures unmatched in ferocity in Western Europe and resembling the Polish "actions," Brunner could lay hands only on a fraction of the Jews in the former Italian zone of France. (16) The results in Croatia were even less successful. Though it failed in the end, the protective action undertaken by Italy gained precious months for the hunted quarry of the Nazis.

THE WESTERN DEPORTATIONS

On June 22, 1942, Eichmann notified the Ministry of Foreign Affairs that large-scale deportations of Jews from the occupied territories of the west were being considered by the RSHA. To begin with, they contemplated deporting during July and August "40,000 Jews from the occupied French territories, 40,000 from the Low Countries, and 10,000 from Belgium, to work in the Auschwitz

(16) Cf. our aforementioned work.

camp." As always, there was the preface "for the time being, this refers only to able-bodied Jews." [59] In this way the "final solution" would be extended to the western countries, where there had already been a few isolated deportations after March 1941. (17) The deportation machinery was immediately set in motion; the methods employed varied according to the country. In the Netherlands, at first, men from sixteen to forty years of age only were asked to appear individually in order to "participate in the reconstruction of the devastated east"; a few thousand fell into this crude trap.[60] Huge raids were organized in France and Belgium against men and women of foreign nationality; in the beginning French Jews were deported only as individuals. (18) The age limits, first set in France at from sixteen to sixty years, were extended in the second half of August to all Jews from two to seventy, and were finally abolished entirely.[61] Thus, the situation was fluid from the outset, the results of the special conditions which the "final solution" met in the west.

We have already explained why anti-Jewish measures progressed at a slower pace in the western territories held by the German army. It was feared that too shocking a show of brutality would stimulate anti-German tendencies and resistance propaganda. Civilian or military occupation authorities had strong reasons for putting on the brakes from time to time. In the period of the "final solution," which began with a very considerable round-up, a technical factor increased this caution. Since the Germans nowhere had at their disposal effective police forces, they were forced to rely on the local authorities; this circumstance permitted their propagandists to declare that the countries in question were purging the Jews with their own hands. (19) But this made it necessary to take

(17) Deportation of 400 Jews from Amsterdam to the Mauthausen camp in March 1941; deportation of 550 French Jews interned in the Compiègne camp to Auschwitz in March 1942. Made under the pretext of reprisals, these deportations involved only able-bodied men.

(18) The majority of the French Jews deported during the summer of 1942 had been arrested in December 1941 in the course of a round-up of a thousand "notable" Jews of Paris, interned at first in the Compiègne camp.

(19) Among the comments in the German or pro-German press that dealt with the deportation of Jews, the following article from the *Hamburger Fremdenblatt*, published on July 24, 1942, is significant:

Our correspondent in Amsterdam informs us that Dutch citizens are show-

into account the local administrative state of mind. In France, especially, antagonizing the Vichy government had to be avoided. Finally, as the last special point regarding the western countries, Wilhelmstrasse diplomats had decided

> to refrain temporarily from the deportation of about 30,000 Dutch, Belgian, French, Norwegian and Soviet Russian Jews . . . in order to hold these people ready for an eventual exchange; those concerned are Jews with family ties or economic, political, or friendly relations with the citizens of the enemy states.[62]

For all these reasons, many exceptions to the "final solution" were made in the western countries. But above all, it was the completely different atmosphere, the great cooperation and support given them by their fellow citizens, from which the Jews benefited and which deprived the anti-Jewish action in the west of the overwhelmingly tragic character that marked it in the east. One finds nothing like the Polish "actions," or like the lightning deportation of the Hungarian Jews. Sufficiently daring and enterprising people had a good chance to escape. On the other hand, the numerous exceptions entailed thousands of selection procedures, each stranger than the last, which illustrate the grotesque side of the deportations. The limits of the absurd were extended; the prophetic imaginings of a Jarry or a Kafka were surpassed by reality.

The initial program of IVb was only partially carried out. In the Netherlands, the Jews (to use the words of Bene, the observer assigned by the Ministry of Affairs) "understood quickly what was involved from the moment deportations to the east began," [63] they ceased answering the deportation calls. The number of deportees was only 12,000 up to August 31.[64] In France the great Parisian raid of July 16-17, aimed at rounding up 25,000 people, got together only half that number "as a result of numerous indiscretions committed by the administration and the police." [65] Yet the number of deportees, according to German statistics compiled on

---

ing a lively animosity toward the Jews. The Jews have appealed to the Wehrmacht for protection. Despite the eternal Jewish enmity, the Wehrmacht has taken the Jews under its protection, and, at their request, has transferred them to Germany, where they will be employed according to their ability. To show their gratitude for this generosity, the Jews have put their furniture and apartments at the disposal of the German victims of the English bombings.

September 3, was 18,069, to which was added a contingent of 9,000 handed over by Vichy [66] from the Free Zone. (Among these were the German Jewish survivors of the "Burckel Action" of October 1940.) [66] On the same date, 2,630 Jews in Belgium were also deported.[67] Everywhere the IVb representatives were anxious to fill the trains at their disposal with a minimum of fuss. "It has been difficult to fill the last two trains and no one knows how they are going to be filled in the future," Bene wrote from the Netherlands.[68] When a convoy was canceled in France at the last moment because there were only 150 Jews in Bordeaux, Eichmann flared up and even threatened "to drop France as a deportation country" (*Abschubland*).[69] In the following months, as a result of numerous raids, extension of the age limits, combing of asylums, hospitals, prisons, and children's homes, the number of deportees was slowly raised. Everywhere informers went to work, spurred by rewards and paid by the head: from 5 to 75 florins in the Netherlands, from 100 to 500 francs and more in France.[70] Using a method employed from the very beginning, the arrested Jews were taken to "assembly camps" (*Auffangsläger*), the most important of which were Drancy in France, Westerbork in the Netherlands, and Malines in Belgium. There a selection was made to exclude numerous categories of "non-deportables," some of whom were freed and others kept in the camp: "A convoy a week can leave every camp; this solution has been reached since each convoy requires serious preparation," forecast Dannecker on the eve of the big July raid.[71]

These categories were not exactly the same in every country. In Belgium and France the principal category of exempted persons was the native Jews, these being exempt because of a bargain made by Laval. The Belgian Jews were protected by Commander-in-Chief von Falkenhausen, whom Queen Elizabeth and Cardinal van Roey had appealed to.[72] These exceptions were not scrupulously observed in both cases, and during the last months of the occupation the Germans disregarded them entirely. In the Netherlands there was no such general category. The names of privileged Jews were entered on special rosters called "blocked lists" (*Sperrlisten*), some of which were permanent, others temporary. The lists of prominent people were broken down one after another into: important Dutch industrialists, converted Jews, Sephardic Jews, Jews exchanged with Palestine, those from the Barnevelde camp, the Callmeyer, Puttkammer, and Weinreb lists. . . .[73] In the case of half-Jews, the "spouses of Aryans" in Holland, where "sacral" measures were in force, this list was subdivided into two main categories and four subcategories: (20) Jews of neutral and of certain satellite countries; "disputed cases" under investigation (i.e., internees who denied being Jewish); "economically useful persons," like the fur workers in Paris or the diamond workers in Amsterdam; the members and functionaries of the Jewish councils as well as their families (the Joodsche Rad in the Netherlands; the Association des Juifs de Belgique [AIB] in Belgium; and the Union Générale des Israélites en France [UGIF] were everywhere exempted from deportation. To these were added other categories, whose definition caused the Berlin experts many a headache: the Georgian Jews and the "Djougoutes," (21) because they did not belong to the Jewish race; the Karaites, a sect whose founder, Ananias, had clashed around 800 A.D. with the masters of the Talmud in Babylonia. . . . On the other hand, the Sephardic Jews, after mature consideration, were considered Jews,[74] though the Sephardic Jews of the Netherlands, listed as "Portuguese," benefited from certain secondary privileges (for example, they could ride in street cars without special permission). These favors were extended to certain other categories, such as "spouses of Aryans" who, if they volunteered for sterilization, were exempt from wearing the yellow star.[75] But how was a Jew to be tracked down in a modern city, if he did not "declare" himself and refused to recognize himself as such? Circumcision itself no longer offered a valid criterion, for it was a question of race, not religion. An appeal was made to the specialists, and

(20) First category: a) marriages between Jews and Aryans or one-quarter Jews; b) marriages between half-Jews and Aryans, or one-quarter Jews; c) marriages between half-Jews; d) marriages between quarter Jews.

Half-Jews in category b) were considered as Jews. New marriages between Aryans and one-quarter Jews were authorized. Those between one-quarter Jews and one-half Jews needed a special authorization; later these were regularly refused. New marriages between Aryans and one-half Jews were forbidden, as were marriages between one-quarter Jews. Such were the problems in the year of grace 1943 in the Holland of Erasmus and Spinoza. (H. Wielek, *de Oorlog die Hitler won*, p. 299-300)

(21) A Judaizing sect of Central Asia (Afghanistan, Russian Turkestan, etc.), related, it seems, to the ethnic group of the Tadjiks.

an anthropologist in Paris, Professor Montandon, gravely offered his expert opinion along these lines:

> Blood AB. Feet poorly arched. Septum slightly depressed at extremity. Lips very prominent. Something Jewish about the total facial cast. Gestures not Jewish. Circumcision: very short mucous sheath, but with the fraenum intact. Presents, therefore, rather the character of the Mohammedan operation than that of the Jewish ritual.[76]

(In this particular case the person concerned was "more than 80 per cent Jewish.")

Since these surveys were paid for by fee, it is useless to add that the arch of the foot or the prominence of the lips could vary in proportion to the tact or the financial means of the candidate for "Aryanism." We can only guess at the extent of the business that was transmitted at the time these surveys, lists, and categories were compiled. In the Netherlands, moreover, the most important deals of this sort were officially sanctioned by Himmler himself. By paying in foreign currency the sum of 50,000 Swiss francs per person, several dozen Dutch Jews were able to leave the Netherlands during the year 1942, in the very midst of the war.[77] It should be noted in conclusion that the complex classifications were constantly modified and revised, usually, but not always, unfavorably.

The final selection took place in the camps, Drancy or Westerbork, where the internees were divided into "permanent" and "transient" categories, vaguely defined. On the eve of the departure of the convoys, depending on the condition of those available and the whim of the camp commander, the permanent category was frequently dipped into. The "permanents" were therefore never sure of their fate. The mixing together of all these categories of more and less unfortunate people, which acted to destroy any feeling of solidarity and equality in misfortune, stimulated endless troubles and tension in the camps and placed an additional premium on shrewdness and unscrupulousness. As elsewhere, the Germans were interested in creating a situation that made the recruiting of "collaborators" easy. After Brunner arrived in France in July 1943, he even tried, with no great success, to set up a special team of Jewish agents at Drancy in charge of home arrests.[78]

The loopholes in the deportation system in the west made many attempts at escape possible. One had a choice of going into hiding, or "Aryanizing" oneself with the help of false papers, or fleeing to unoccupied France, and farther, if possible. The *camouflés* in France, and the *onderduikers* in the Netherlands ran into the tens of thousands. Little by little, numerous clandestine organizations sprang up in all the countries to help and supply funds to the *"camouflés."* Jews and non-Jews cooperated in this effort. Veritable factories for manufacturing false papers operated in the large cities. Aiding the Jews became a subsidiary activity of the numerous resistance movements. Across the Alps and the Pyrenees, along hazardous routes, Dutch, Belgian, and French Jews were convoyed by the thousands to Switzerland or to Spain.

Inevitably, one asks: Why did the Jews let themselves be taken in such large numbers at the first cast of the net? First of all, it took a certain amount of time to prepare the roads to freedom. Also, the Germans tried to keep their actions secret and unexpected. The foreign Jews were the first to be arrested and they lacked the necessary connections and contacts; their accent increased the danger of their being detected. Moreover, for the average person to use false papers, besides its intrinsic dangers (some 50 per cent of the *onderduikers* in Holland were denounced or tracked down), meant violating a rather deeply rooted taboo against illegality. Finally, the real meaning of the deportations was often unknown to the victims to the very end. One might also say that the Jews underestimated the extent of German insanity; the existence of a veritable industry of death seemed scarcely credible. For these reasons, the great majority disregarded such warnings as there were. Though hard and cruel, the trials of deportation seemed surmountable to the deportees. "Pitchipoi"—such was the name at Drancy for the mysterious place whither the convoys went. . . .[79] As Georges Weller, the historian of this camp, says,

> To the very end, people in the camp were almost completely unaware of the fate awaiting the deportees. It was known that the London radio was broadcasting reports about the horrors of the gas chambers and the other ways in which the Jews were being exterminated, but nobody could believe it. Such tales were considered the

exaggerations of English propaganda; nobody paid them much attention.[80]

One needed an extraordinary power of intuition to glimpse, through all the orders and instructions and established categories of things, the future lying in wait for the deportees. These rare Cassandra-like natures could in truth say, with Tertullian, *credo quia absurdum*. For the majority, the ultimate revelation came only in the gas chambers. . . . Needless to say, the Germans fostered this state of mind by all their customary methods: false news and propaganda articles, (22) sending postcards signed by deportees, exchanging (at Drancy) francs for receipts in zlotys, and so forth. Which is why, during their first throes of indecision at Drancy, mothers could be seen finally deciding to take along children whom they might have left behind in France.[81]

The rate at which convoys were sent off varied. At this particular time, it would seem that rolling stock was more available in the summer. (23) The deportations, after an almost total interruption during the winter of 1942–1943, were resumed in the spring. The beginning of the summer of 1943 was a period of intense activity. A counterpart to the big June raids in the Netherlands was planned for France, but it failed to take place as a result of Vichy's antagonism. Eichmann sent Brunner to Paris to speed up the deportations. His arrival signaled the end of all distinctions between French and foreign Jews; the Germans extended their operations to the Vichy area (which the German army occupied after the Allied landing in North Africa), and, at the beginning of September 1943, to the former "Italian zone." But Vichy obstructionism became more and more evident; reduced to relying on their own police, the Nazis disposed of insufficient forces in France. In the Netherlands, on the contrary, where the "blocked lists" were canceled one after the other, the Germans were able to carry out the "final solution" to a considerable degree.

The final figures for the deportations are as follows: France,

(22) Articles which appeared in Paris in July 1942, particularly in the German-language *Pariser Zeitung*, painted life on the "Jewish reservations" to the east in the rosiest colors.
(23) Cf. above, p. 144.

90,000 Jews; Belgium, 25,000; the Netherlands, 110,000. (24) If we estimate the number of Jews living in these countries at the time of the invasion at 300,000, 45,000, and 140,000 respectively, the approximate percentage of Jews deported was 30, 55, and 79. (25)

The difference between the percentage of Jews deported from France and Holland is certainly astonishing. There are various factors to explain this. First of all, if we glance at the map, it is apparent that France, with an area sixteen times larger than that of Holland, and with great mountainous regions, offered excellent opportunities for hiding out. Little Holland, in the firm grip of the Nazis, had been subjected for five years to a particularly intensive police surveillance. In addition, a line of demarcation, which it was easy to cross, divided France in two, with Marshal Pétain's regime installed on the other side at Vichy. Which brings us to the part that Vichy played in the Jewish question, particularly in the matter of the deportations.

THE SPECIAL CASE OF VICHY FRANCE

Vichy was the chief factor accounting for the relatively more lenient fate of the French Jews. First of all, it was, for a time, a Free Zone in which thousands of French, Dutch, and Belgian Jews took refuge after the invasion of 1940; afterwards, those same "rights of sovereignty" which its high officials insisted on so detestably with the Italians, when required from the Germans sometimes had salutary consequences. In the matter of the "final solution," Vichy's position was essentially determined by Pierre Laval. His policy seems to have been to get rid of the foreign Jews, but to protect French Jews in the two zones as much as possible, though ready to abandon them in return for substantial concessions. (26)

(24) Of whom 4,000 were deported to Theresienstadt, and 4,500 to Bergen-Belsen (Wielek, *op. cit.* p. 335-36).

(25) H. Wielek, *op. cit.*, Roger Berg, *La Persécution raciale en France*, Paris, O. F. E., 1947. Jacob Lestchinsky, *Crisis, Catastrophe and Survival*, New York, 1948. These figures are only approximations. Though the German statistics give us a precise minimum for the number of deportees, the number of the Jews in each country can be estimated only very approximately, because of the vast population movements in May 1940. Thus, it is estimated that out of the 90,000 Belgian Jews close to half had left the country at this time, going in part to increase the number of Jews in France.

(26) We refer the reader to Knochen's evaluation of the situation: "Laval himself will approve the measures against the Jews, if, in return, he can ob-

Pétain's attitude seems to have been more rigid. Such, at least, was the opinion of Dannecker and his successors. Thus, in setting up his campaign plan for the summer of 1943, Röthke, the new head of the IVb in France, wrote: "It will be necessary, in order to carry out the above program, to force the French government to put its police at our disposal; in view of the attitude of the Marshal and certain members of his cabinet, coercion may be the only means to accomplish this." [82] Laval eagerly complied with the German request to hand over the foreign Jews in the Free Zone; not only were 9,000 Jews sent to Drancy after August 1942, but at Laval's suggestion, so as to "reunite families," children under sixteen were included in the convoys. (27) As for the naturalized French Jews, the following compromise was arrived at by Röthke and Laval after a characteristic bit of bargaining: All Jews naturalized after a certain date (Vichy proposed 1932; IVb demanded 1927) were to be handed over to the Germans. After having been deprived of their nationality by a general decree, tens of thousands of Jews (50,000 according to Röthke's estimate) [83] were to be arrested as stateless persons on the date of issuance of the decree by the French police. In this way France could not be convicted of having handed over French Jews.

But this plan, though the subject of long discussions, and far along in its preparations, was never carried out. As the German doings in Poland became better known, raising universal shudders of horror, and undoubtedly too as the fortunes of war changed, the attitude of Vichy stiffened. At the last moment Laval, entrenching himself now behind Pétain and now behind the Italians, refused to publish the text of the law prepared by the Commissariat for Jewish

---

tain political promises. . . . He will direct the anti-Jewish measures if he obtains a political guarantee, whatever form it may take." (Report from Knochen to the RSHA, Paris, February 12, 1943.) On the decision reached regarding the French Jews, Röthke wrote in his aforementioned report to Dannecker: "By the terms of a new agreement with the French government, only stateless Jews must be arrested." (July 15, 1942)

(27) A report from Dannecker to IVb in Berlin, Paris, July 6, 1942. "President Laval has proposed (*hat vorgeschlagen*) the inclusion of children under sixteen at the time of the deportation of Jewish families from the non-occupied zone. The question of the Jewish children remaining in the occupied zone does not concern him." *See also* the study by Georges Wellers "Les Rafles des 16 et 17 juillet 1942 dans la région parisienne," *Le Monde Juif*, no. 21, July, 1949.

Questions. (28) For this reason the mass raid scheduled for June–
July 1943 did not take place; under these circumstances, the Germans were reduced to carrying on for the most part with their own

(28) A last attempt was made to publish the Laval law in August 1943.
We reprint below Röthke's report on his talk with Laval. It is quite characteristic. The marginal notes are in Knochen's hand (designated in the document as BdS—*Befehlshaber der Sicherheitspolizei* [Commander of the Security
Police]).

As for the other names in the document, Bousquet was the Undersecretary
of State of the Vichy police; Guerard, chief of the Laval cabinet; Gabolde, the
Keeper of the Seals; Darquier de Pellepoix, the Commissioner for Jewish Questions.

IVb BdS SA 225a
Rö/Ne

Paris, August 15, 1943.

Re: Law on the cancellation of naturalization for Jews naturalized after 1927.
Conversations with Laval and Bousquet at Vichy, August 14, 1943.

1. *Note*—Hauptsturmführer Geissler and the undersigned on the morning
of August 14, 1943, went to see Bousquet, and then Laval, to confer with
both on the details of the proclamation of the proposed law.

Conversation with Bousquet.—Bousquet, who was to leave Vichy that very
day, and who will return to Paris on August 16, declared that Laval had recently violently reproached him because he had had a second proposed law
signed (the Darquier project). Bousquet had then answered the President
that he was completely unaware of a second project. He knew, it is true, of
the first one, signed by Laval and Gabolde, which is in his possession. He
could say nothing about its proclamation, since it was entirely in Laval's jurisdiction. (Bousquet had also noted that Vichy had insisted on rearming the
foresters and harvest guards. A proposal to this effect had been made by
General von Neubronn[?]. Bousquet, himself, considered this measure to be
very dangerous, since there had recently been a number of cases of sabotage
of harvest machinery and fires in silos.)

2. *Conversation with Laval.*—Hauptsturmführer Geissler and the undersigned conferred with Laval from 12:30 to 1:30 P. M. Guerard and Bousquet,
administrative chief, were also present. On being questioned about the situation, Laval answered as follows:

Pétain had heard of the proposed laws. He had been very irritated to learn
that, according to the terms of one of them, women and children would also
be denaturalized. Now, Pètain wanted to see the originals of the two projects.
(Project Bousquet had been taken to him by his administrative chief. Project
Darquier, which Laval pretended to have searched for at Paris and Vichy for
three days, was finally "found" by one of Laval's secretaries during our conference, after Laval had three times demanded that an intensive search be
made for it.)

We told Laval that we wanted the Bousquet proposal published immediately
and that I was to report to the BdS, who had sent me to Vichy for this purpose.

Laval answered as follows:

a. On signing the proposal he had not dreamt that we would arrest Jews

forces, helped by finger men, informers, the "anti-Jewish police" of the commissariat, and Joseph Darnand's militia. The grand projects of Röthke and Brunner, carefully calculated and drafted several months in advance, collapsed one after the other. The French

---

affected by the law *en masse*. Now, the BdS had recently told him exactly that. [(*Manuscript note*): *This is typical. The fox has long known that this is the purpose of the law.*]

I answered Laval that the Führer's orders on the final solution of the Jewish question in Europe were unequivocal. To my knowledge, a year ago it had been agreed that the Jewish question in France would be solved in stages. A year ago, it had also been understood that there was to be a denaturalization of Jews recently naturalized, for the purpose of their arrest and deportation.

b. Laval claimed that the proposal was still to be discussed before the Council of Ministers that would meet on August 17, 1943. Several ministers would certainly question him in order to know why such a law was going to be promulgated. He would then have to answer that the Jews affected were going to be interned and deported.

c. Finally, the law had such wide implications, because of its contents, that it had to be signed by the Marshal, who alone, as Chief of State, could order naturalization or denaturalization. Furthermore, the Marshal was already interested in these laws; it was therefore urgently necessary for him to confer with the Marshal.

Hauptsturmführer Geissler replied to Laval that the latter had himself signed the two proposals and that he had already had the Bousquet proposal officially forwarded.

At this, Laval remarked that he had many files to sign every day; in this case, in signing the Darquier proposal, he had not thought of anything, believing everything to be in order.

d. For Laval, the principal obstacle to any action against the Jews was the attitude of the Italians. He had always thought that we could influence the Italians to change their attitude toward the Jewish question. Nothing had been done up to now. It was necessary to understand that as head of the government his position in regard to the laws against the Jews was delicate. In France four different regulations affecting the Jews were in force; the old occupation zone had its French and German laws, the southern zone occupied by the Germans had exclusively French regulations; the zone of Italian influence had French laws and special Italian ordinances; and the *départements* of the north were under the jurisdiction of the Commander-in-Chief of Belgium and northern France.

Laval was told that the settling of the Jewish question did not concern France alone. As for the attitude of the Italians, he could certainly count on a change, but that, nevertheless, this was not a reason to block completely the solution of the Jewish question in France.

e. Laval then declared that the law should only be applied in such a way as to allow the Jews in question a three months' delay (*see* article 3), to allow them to ask for exceptions as provided in the text [*Insolence becomes a method!*]. Consequently, the police measures against the Jews mentioned in the law were to be applied only three months after its proclamation. In the

administration and the regular police collaborated less and less, following the example of the higher-ups. "Only the following solution is left," Röthke wrote in July, 1943: "The arrest *en masse* of all the Jews we can find, through a general operation by the security police (commandos and special commandos) with the help of German troops." [84] But for reasons unknown, Wehrmacht aid was refused the IVb. During the numerous killings and massacres

---

southern zone he could not authorize the French police to apply any other procedure.

If we acted otherwise in the old occupation zone, as head of the government he would be obliged to protest. He knew, without doubt, what we thought of his interventions. . . . (Laval was obviously and correctly thinking of the waste basket.) For that reason he could no longer put the police in the former occupation zone at our disposal; if we wanted to operate with our own men, he could not oppose us.

I answered Laval that we could not agree to a three months' delay. Besides, in my experience, all Jews affected by the law would ask for exemptions during this period, whose investigation would cause still further delay. Besides, it must be easy for the French administration to decide which Jews were exceptions under the terms of the law of June 2, 1941.

Laval thought that it was only a question of thirty Jews at the most. As head of the government, he will be held to the exact application of the law.

In conclusion, it must be stated that the French government no longer wishes to follow us in the Jewish question.

We can even suppose that at the next Council of Ministers there will be so much opposition to the Bousquet proposal that it will be rejected.

Furthermore, we have the impression that Pétain wants to prevent the adoption of this law, since a great many Jews have attacked the proposal.

(A few minutes before our reception by Laval, the latter had received the Jew Lambert, President of the UGIF of the southern zone. The Jew Lambert declared to Darquier's representative that Laval had also received him some minutes before and that "he had complained" to the President about the arrest of Jews in the southern zone by detachments of the *Sicherheitspolizei* [SD]. An order for Lambert's arrest has been telegraphed.)

Moreover, we have the impression in the case in point that Laval does not consider Pétain's intervention undesirable. It is handy for him to hide behind Pétain, although he declared during our conversation that while he was not anti-Semitic, he was not pro-Semitic, either.

The same is true of his pretended need first to submit the proposed law to the Council of Ministers. [*The old parliamentarian!*] It has never happened before. It is our impression that Laval is using every means to prevent promulgation of the law and to delay it in every possible way.

Laval will inform us through Ambassador Brinon, Tuesday or Wednesday at the latest, of the decision of the Council of Ministers.

We propose to ask *immediately* for a company of *Schutzpolizei*, since, with or without publication of the law on the cancellation of French nationality, it is no longer possible to count on any large-scale help from the French police

which marked the last period of the occupation, the Jews were evidently marked out as the first victims; the number of those who perished in this way in France is estimated at several thousand.

THE SCANDINAVIAN COUNTRIES

The small Jewish communities of the Scandinavian countries hoped that their very insignificance would enable them to escape the German grasp.

Among the occupied countries of Europe, Denmark enjoyed a special and almost privileged position. For a long time, indeed, the Germans hesitated to extend the deportation system to this peaceful little country, believing, not without reason, that this would bring a quick reaction from the population and cause considerable difficulties. The state of emergency proclaimed in Denmark in September 1943, following internal troubles, finally furnished them with the needed excuse. Under cover of the state of siege, mass raids were organized all over the country. In this case, however, the "final solution" was almost completely thwarted. Informed in time, the 7,500 Danish Jews scattered and hid; the great majority was able to slip away into Sweden. Only about 500 Danish Jews were taken and deported to Theresienstadt.

Danish solidarity was particularly effective. The yellow star was never introduced into the country; King Christian himself threatened the Germans that he would be the first to wear it.

Conquered by force and administered by Gauleiter Terboven, Norway's losses were proportionately higher. Of its 2,000 Jews, about 750 were arrested and deported; the others hid or escaped into Sweden. Finally, it should be pointed out that far-off Finland, allied to Germany and bound, it would seem, to its fate, refused to have its Jewish citizens deported despite all Himmler's efforts, particularly during a visit he paid Finland in July, 1942.

---

for the arrest of Jews, unless, a few days or weeks from now, the military situation in Germany changes radically in our favor.

2. To be submitted to Knochen, SS Standartenführer, with the request for him to acknowledge it and make a final decision.

3. To be returned to IVb BdS.

By order of:
Röthke
SS—Obersturmführer

CHAPTER EIGHT

The Industry of Death

GERMAN TECHNICAL GENIUS made it possible to set up an efficient and rationalized industry of death within a few months. Like other industries, it had its departments of research, improvement, administrative services, a business office, and archives. Many aspects of these activities remain unknown because they were cloaked in greater secrecy than any of the other German war industries. The technicians who made the German fuses and torpedoes, the planners of the Reich's economy, have survived and delivered up their plans and procedures to the conquerors; almost all of the technicians of death perished or disappeared, after destroying their records.

The first extermination camps had primitive installations; the later ones were much improved. Who perfected them? A real mastery of mass psychology was required to secure the complete docility of the doomed. Who were these masters? These are questions which we can only answer now in a partial and hypothetical way. Having perhaps learned from their mishaps in Russia, the technicians of genocide left no stone unturned to work out an efficient system. Only once did the usually verbose Himmler unseal his lips about the "final solution": "We have written a glorious page of our history," he said in October 1943 to a small group of followers, "but it shall never appear on paper."

In the following pages we shall only consider the chief establishments where extermination was systematically carried out, and pass by those other murder methods which were used almost everywhere, of which mass shooting was always the leading one. The morbid ingenuity of the Nazis devised dozens of different individual and collective techniques: the quicklime method, used particularly in Poland; [1] injections of carbolic acid into the heart, used in most concentration camps; or the one which made the Mauthausen camp infamous, which consisted of throwing the victims from the top of a quarry. But these represented an exercise of local initiative, the refinements of individual sadism. What concerns us here is the more or less official method commanded from Berlin by the officials charged with the job of genocide. This method, employed in specially prepared places, resulted in the death of the overwhelming majority of the victims of Nazism; the exact figures can never be finally established. The method chosen was asphyxiation; by carbon monoxide in the four large Polish camps (Chelmno, Belzec, Sobibor, Treblinka), and by prussic acid fumes at Maidanek and in the huge Auschwitz installations in Upper Silesia. We shall review these camps successively, studying Auschwitz especially closely as we have far more information about it. But we must first consider another death campaign, launched in Germany itself at the end of 1939, and embracing those categories of Germans considered "useless mouths": "euthanasia" for the feeble-minded and mentally ill.

EUTHANASIA

The technique of an effective and discreet extermination, conforming to what the Nazis considered the "German way," was first perfected in the laboratory by German doctors and scientists before being applied on a large industrial scale by Himmler's SS. Here the German mentally ill served as guinea pigs for determining the most efficient way to exterminate the European Jews. The "euthanasia" program, however, was not undertaken for this express purpose; it had an independent genesis. But though the connection between "euthanasia" and "final solution" seems fortuitous, they were linked by a deep inner logic.

Everybody knows what euthanasia is—a merciful death inflicted on the incurably ill. As the subject of many a dramatic trial, it has been passionately discussed in numerous countries. Nowhere, however, has it been given official sanction; in the contemporary world it has met with a refusal that finds its clearest expression in the principled stand taken on the matter by the churches. For the "humanitarian" considerations that might argue in favor of a mercy killing are more than outweighed by the possibility of many other motives, so difficult to identify, influencing the decision to take another being's life. Are we sure it is a matter of pity, pure and simple, or are there entirely different considerations behind the decision to do away with a sick person whose unproductive existence is only a burden on his family or society?

Its planned and rationalized aspect, behind which one might see so many morbid possibilities, undoubtedly constituted euthanasia's appeal to the Nazi mind. The formula, "suppression of lives unworthy of being lived," was a large one and permitted of a broad interpretation. Hitler, however, hesitated for a long time before carrying euthanasia into practice. It is significant that the decree activating the program is dated September 1, 1939, that is, the day on which war was declared.[2] Certainly, in time of war the opposition to euthanasia would be less vigorous; at such a time, moreover, one needed all the hospital space, physicians, and medical personnel one could find, and the fewer "useless mouths" the better. For this reason, from the very beginning, the measure aimed less at those on the point of dying than at the feeble-minded and incurably insane.

Hitler took the precaution of keeping the euthanasia decree a strict secret, and it was never officially promulgated. Philip Bouhler, head of the Führer's personal chancellery, assisted by Kurt Brandt, Hitler's personal physician, was entrusted with its execution; he was to have the cooperation of the services of the Ministry of the Interior. The organization created for this purpose, and established in Berlin at 4 Tiergartenstrasse, was designated by the code figures "T-4"; its head, Viktor Brack, assistant to Bouhler, gave it the cover name of "Jennerwein."[3] Inoffensive names were coined to disguise euthanasia establishments and their associated services. (1) Several well-known German psychiatrists, such as Professors Heyde,

---

(1) The organization of doctors in charge of administering euthanasia was called "Reichsarbeitsgemeinschaft Heil-und Pflegeanstalten" (National Coordinating Agency for Therapeutic and Medical Establishments). The financing of euthanasia was provided by the "Gemeinnützige Stiftung für Anstaltspflege" (Foundation for Hospitalization). The association "Allgemeine Kranken-Transport-Gesellschaft" (General Ambulance Service) was, as its name indicates, responsible for the transporting of the victims. (Written deposition by Viktor Brack, Nuremberg, October 14, 1946)

Nietzsche, and Pfannmüller, gave T-4 their active and enthusiastic cooperation. Another prominent scientist, Professor Kranz, estimated at one million the number of Germans whose "removal" he deemed desirable.[4]

The offices of T-4 prepared a questionnaire which was sent to all mental hospitals and psychiatric clinics in Germany. On the basis of the completed questionnaire, which generally listed only the patient's name, age, etc., and the disease from which he suffered, a committee of three experts, chosen from among the doctors connected with T-4, made a decision. If this long-distance diagnosis was unfavorable, the patient was sent to an "observation station." There he stayed a few weeks, after which, unless there was a contrary diagnosis by the director of the "observation station," he was transferred to a euthanasia establishment proper. (According to Brandt's testimony only 4 to 6 per cent of the cases were not transferred.)[5] Because euthanasia was considered a state matter, decisions were made without consulting either the victims or their families. The successive transfers blotted out all traces of the patients and facilitated their quiet disappearance.

The first euthanasia station was established in an abandoned prison at Brandenburg, in Prussia, at the end of 1939; its administration was entrusted to Police Commissioner Christian Wirth. Five more stations were created in different regions of Germany during 1940. (2) They were set up in abandoned properties, or in asylums whose occupants were transferred elsewhere. At first Wirth deemed it sufficient to kill his patients by shooting them in the neck;[6] when doctors were placed at the head of these establishments, more efficient methods were introduced by the T-4 experts with the assistance of a chemist, Dr. Kallmeyer, assigned to them by Jennerwein-Brack. The method they devised was asphyxiation by carbon monoxide gas. The installations this required were simple— the euthanasia stations had a relatively insignificant "production." In each institution, there was a hermetically sealed room camouflaged as a shower into which pipes passed that were connected to

---

(2) In the order of their founding: Grafeneck, in Wurtemberg; Sonnenstein, in Saxony; Hartheim, in Austria; Bernburg, in Thuringia; and Hadamar, in Hesse. (Viktor Brack's deposition before the Nuremberg Tribunal, session of May 15, 1947.)

cylinders of carbon monoxide gas. Patients were generally rendered somnolent by being given morphine, scopolamine injections, or narcotic tablets before being taken, in groups of ten,[7] to this gas chamber. The euthanasia stations also included a small crematory where the cadavers were incinerated. Families were advised of the patient's death by form letters which stated that the patient had succumbed to "heart failure" or "pneumonia."

From January 1940 to August 1941, when the euthanasia program was stopped, 70,273 mental patients were so "treated." (3)

A section of T-4, the "Reich Committee for Research on Hereditary Diseases," was in charge of euthanasia for feeble-minded children or children suffering from serious hereditary ailments. This program was begun at the same time as the main euthanasia program and was carried out in the same way.

How a physician of National-Socialist Germany might avoid participating in euthanasia activities can be gathered from the following letter, addressed by Dr. Holzel, director of an institution for mentally deficient children, to Professor Pfannmüller:

August 20, 1940

My dear Director,

I am very grateful for your kindness in giving me time to think things over. The new measures are so convincing that I had hoped to be able to discard all personal considerations. But it is one thing to approve state measures with conviction, and another to carry them out yourself down to their last consequences. I am thinking of the difference between a judge and an executioner. For this reason, despite my intellectual understanding and good will, I cannot help stating that I am temperamentally not fitted for this work. As eager as I often am to correct the natural course of events, it is just as repugnant to me to do so systematically, after cold-blooded consideration,

(3) 35,224 in 1940, and 35,049 in 1941. These figures come from a German document published by the Commission for War Crimes in Poland (*German Crimes in Poland,* vol. 9, pp. 152-53).

This document, unknown to the prosecution, was not presented at the time of the arguments on euthanasia before the Nuremberg Tribunal. During the trial, Viktor Brack mentioned a figure of the same size (50,000-60,000) (session of May 15, 1947). The document in question states in another connection that T-4 estimated very exactly at 885,439,800 marks the savings realized by the Reich from the suppression of "useless mouths."

The figure of 275,000 victims accepted by the International Tribunal of Nuremberg seems exaggerated.

according to the objective principles of science, without being affected
by a doctor's feeling for his patient. It has not been scientific interest
that has made work in a children's home worthwhile for me, but a
doctor's hope to aid and bring about some improvement. . . . I feel
emotionally tied to the children as their medical guardian, and I think
that this emotional contact is not necessarily a weakness from the
point of view of a National-Socialist doctor. It prevents me, however,
from adding this new task to the one I have performed up to today.

If this leads you to put the children's home in other hands, it would
mean a painful loss for me. However, I prefer to see clearly and to
recognize that I am too gentle for this work than to disappoint you
later. I know that your offer is a mark of special confidence and can
honor it only by absolute honesty and frankness.

Heil Hitler!

Your devoted,
F. Hölzel [8]

OPERATION 14 F. 13

In its operations, the euthanasia program came directly under
the Führer's personal chancellery, and had nothing to do with
Himmler's and Heydrich's RSHA. Was it an accident then that
most of the euthanasia stations were established near large concentration camps? (4) The fact is that from the summer of 1940 on,
the superintendence of the concentration camps kept in contact
with T-4 and "commissions of experts" began making periodic selections of candidates for euthanasia from among the camp prisoners.

The code designation "14 f. 13" appearing on the files for these
operations remains associated with this extension of the "euthanasia program." [9] In accordance with an agreement between
Himmler and Jennerwein-Brack, T-4 experts visited the concentration camps and, with the cooperation of the camp physician, picked
out the men who seemed to them mentally or physically defective.
In fact, however, the reasons for the prisoner's arrest was a decisive
element, particularly in the case of Jews, who according to the
"expert," Mennecke, "were picked out not on the basis of their
health but according to the reasons for which they were orginally
arrested." [10] In a letter that he sent to his wife from Buchenwald,
Mennecke described the commission's work as follows:

(4) Brandenburg was not far from the Oranienburg camp; Bernburg was
near Buchenwald; Hartheim in the immediate vicinity of Mauthausen, etc.

We continued our examinations until four o'clock; I examined 105 patients, Müller 78, so that 183 questionnaires were filled out. Our second batch consisted of 1,200 Jews who do not have to be "examined"; for them it was enough to pull from their files (very voluminous!) the reason for their arrest, and write them down on the questionnaires. So purely technical labor kept us busy until Monday. I copied out 17 cases from this second group, Müller 15, after which "we downed pick and shovel" and went to dinner. . . .

We shall continue with the same program and the same work. After the Jews will come 300 Aryans who have to be "examined." We shall be busy up to the end of next week. Then we shall go home.[11]

In the Dachau camp, "operation 14 f. 13" was started in the fall of 1941 by Professor Heyde himself. According to the camp doctor's story,

The commission of four members was headed by Professor Heyde. We four doctors sat at four tables placed between two huts, and several hundred prisoners had to file in front of us. The prisoners were divided according to their fitness for work and their political record. Since this commission stayed at Dachau only a few days, it was impossible for it to examine so many prisoners in so short a time. The examinations consisted solely of a rapid study of the documents in the prisoner's presence.[12]

This seems to have been the way in which the method of the future "selections" at Auschwitz and elsewhere was perfected with the cooperation of German physicians and professors.

THE END OF EUTHANASIA

Despite all the secrecy in which the euthanasia program was enveloped, its existence soon became known. Families that began to suspect something when they received death notices told their friends. The collective transfers of patients from asylums to "observation stations" and thence to the euthanasia establishments could not go unobserved, and stirred up popular feeling. Various reports tell of uneasiness even in the party ranks. The party delegate in the town of Ansbach reported that "the transfer of a part of the pensioners from the Bruckberg home caused a great deal of disquiet among the people of Bruckberg, the more so as some of those transferred—those who, in popular opinion, 'are still in possession of their wits'—insisted on saying goodbye personally to the village people. . . . The disquiet will persist," concluded the official, "because it is supported by the churches. Matters will quiet down sooner if the Party doesn't respond to these attacks." [13] The Nazi "Kreisleiter" in Lauf, Franconia, reported the case of an epileptic young peasant who had been sent to an asylum to be sterilized; a few days later an urn containing his ashes was returned to his mother. "Since young Koch was well known in the neighborhood for his industriousness, the case of his 'violent' death naturally aroused great indignation. . . . The local physician tells me that families refuse to send their ailing people to the asylums, not knowing whether they would ever see them alive again. . . . Two murder complaints have been made at Nuremberg by the relatives of such patients." [14] "Ortsgruppenleiter" Langhof sent the following report from Langlau:

> On last Friday, February 21, 1941, 57 inmates of the Alsberg Asylum were sent to Erlangen in two groups for a so-called examination at the clinic. When they climbed into buses, a large crowd of spectators collected because the loading was done in the street and not in the asylum courtyard. Some wild scenes took place, for some of the inmates did not get in willingly and the male nurses had to use force.
>
> I found out that some people went so far as to criticize the National-Socialist State. Unfortunately, I could not identify them, as no one would say very much during my investigation. These incidents must be considered all the more serious as even some party members wept and cried out along with the other onlookers. Some of the spectators even shouted the following: "Our State must be very badly off if it has to send these poor people to their death so as to use the money saved to wage war."
>
> It seems that these poor victims—at least that is what the church and the people of Alsberg call them—were even taken to the Catholic church for confession and communion. It is really a ridiculous thing for them to try to absolve from their sins people some of whom are completely insane.[15]

The feeling excited by the euthanasia program spread all over Germany. The popular outcry made it easy for the Catholic and Protestant churches to take a firm stand. Such Catholic and Protestant clergymen as Bishops Wurm and Gaalen protested more and more openly in their pastoral letters. One of the leaders of the Lutheran Church, Pastor Braune, undertook to warn ministers and

high officials, and sent a memorandum to the Reich Chancellery in
which he summed up his arguments.

> How far can one go in destroying unworthy lives? The wholesale
> actions taken so far have shown that many persons clearly of sound
> mind have been included. . . . Are they directed only at the hopeless
> cases, the idiots and the imbeciles? The questionnaire also lists the dis-
> eases of senility. The newest regulation calls for the elimination of
> children with illnesses resulting from birth trauma, as well. What
> serious misapprehensions must come to mind! Will they stop at the
> tubercular? The euthanasia program has already begun to be applied
> to prisoners. Where is the limit? Who is abnormal, asocial, hopelessly
> sick? How will the soldiers fare who acquire incurable ailments fighting
> for their country? Such questions have already been raised in the army
> circles.[16]

A few days after sending his memorandum, Pastor Braune was
arrested by the Gestapo for "irresponsible sabotage of government
measures." He was freed after three months of imprisonment.
Brandt and Bouhler tried indirect conversations to change the
churches' attitude, to no avail. Popular opposition grew. In the summer of 1941 the Bishop of Limburg informed the Minister of Justice
that "the children, when they quarrel, say to each other: 'You are
insane, you will be sent to the Hadamar ovens!' Young people who
do not wish to marry say: 'Get married? Never! Bring children into
the world so they can go through the racks?' Old people beg not to
be sent to old age homes because they think it will soon be their
turn." [17]

In the light of all this, Hitler decided to order the euthanasia
program discontinued in August 1941. He assured Bouhler and
Brandt that it was only a suspension, and that the program would
be resumed at the end of the war.[18] So the T-4 machinery was kept
intact and questionnaires continued to go out. Not until the winter
of 1944–45 did Brack give orders to destroy the euthanasia installations. T-4 personnel were used for sanitary missions on the Russian front during the winter of 1941–42; but before this their skill
and technical abilities were employed on another task: the total,
methodical, and secret extermination, "German style," of the Polish
Jews.

Such, in brief, was the history of the euthanasia program, which
was certainly in perfect accord with the most intimate ideas of the

master of the Third Reich. The course its development took was quite significant. It shows the limits which were set to Hitler's power. By whipping up popular emotions Hitler could lead his people down all sorts of new and dangerous paths. But in this particular case, the people's spontaneous opposition forced him to retreat. Yet it needed a unanimous refusal on the people's part, a veritable reflex of horror that shook them to the bottom of their being.

THE POLISH EXTERMINATION CAMPS

Fragmentary information gives us a glimpse into the part played by the euthanasia technicians in the extermination of the Polish Jews. But many things still remain obscure. In general, our knowledge of the history of the Polish camps is incomplete. It seems certain, however, that according to the original RSHA plan, the Jews of Europe were to be exterminated, at least in part, in the occupied territories of the USSR, that "Reichskommissariat Ostland" to which the first convoys of German Jews were sent at the end of 1941. A few letters that passed between the "Reichskommissariat" administration in Riga and the "Ministry for the Occupied Regions of the East" in Berlin give us some exact information on the matter. We learn from them that after preliminary contacts between Eichmann and the high officials of this Ministry, the cooperation of the euthanasia experts was solicited for the establishment on the spot of the necessary installations. A report by Wetzel, whose specialty was "demographic planning" in the East, dated October 25, 1941, pointed out that "Oberdienstleiter Brack, of the Führer's Chancellery, has agreed to help us build the necessary buildings and gas machines."

> The machines in question are not at present available in Germany in sufficient quantity and must be specially built. Brack thinks that their manufacture in Germany itself would create more difficulties than if they were made locally. For this reason he prefers to send his men directly to Riga, particularly his chemist, Kallmeyer, who will take care of what is needed. I should like to point out that SS Major Eichmann, a specialist on Jewish questions in the RSHA, agrees with this procedure.[19]

For unknown reasons, probably because of a shortage of rolling stock, the project was not carried out in the USSR but in Poland, for the most part in the territories annexed to the Reich, but also in the Government General, and always with the capable cooperation of Viktor Brack's "people."

The first camp, Chelmno, near Lodz, began operations in the annexed territory in December 1941; it had a maximum rate of a thousand executions a day. Chelmno as yet had no permanent gas chambers; only a large garage on an isolated piece of property containing several "gas trucks" similar to those going up and down the roads of invaded Russia. In March 1942 the completion of the Belzec camp, with a daily rate of several thousand executions, made a real start on the "final solution" possible; with the completion of Sobibor and Treblinka in May and July 1942, respectively, "production" speeded up still more. All these camps were under the supreme authority of Odilo Globocnik, who had the help of a team of euthanasia technicians directed by Christian Wirth.[20] They had been "loaned" to Globocnik by Bouhler and Brack, on the express condition that these indispensable specialists would be returned when the euthanasia campaign started again in the Reich.[21] It should be noted that the Maidanek camp, near Lublin, was not an extermination camp proper, but a work camp—that is to say, a delayed extermination camp where according to the conclusions of the commission of investigation of the Polish Government, over 200,000 Jews, as well as non-Jews, died during 1943 and 1944.[22] (Auschwitz, as we shall see, combined these two methods.)

The victims are no longer here to testify; the butchers, too, have either died or gone underground. Among the very few statements that we have on the operations of these camps is one from Kurt Gerstein, a chemical engineer who was a tragic hero in the German anti-Nazi resistance. His account was written down directly in an uncertain French; we have basically retained its original style. (5)

(5) An active member of the anti-Nazi *Bekenntniskirche* ("Confessional Church"), Gerstein had been at odds with the Gestapo since 1935 because of his anti-Hitler propaganda activities. In 1938 he was interned for a time at the Welzheim concentration camp. In 1941, after learning that one of his relatives has been put to death as "incurably ill" at the Hadamar euthanasia

In January, 1942 I was named chief of the Waffen-SS technical disinfection services, including a section for extremely toxic gases.

On June 8, 1942, SS *Sturmführer* Günther of the RSHA came to see me. He was dressed in civilian clothing. I had never met him before. He ordered me to get for him immediately 100 kilograms of prussic acid and to bring it to a place known only to the truck driver. He said he needed the acid for a top secret mission.

Several weeks later, we left for Prague. I had a vague idea of the purpose for which the prussic acid was going to be used, and what sort of an order I had been given, but I agreed to do it, because this was my long-awaited chance to see for myself what was going on. Besides, as an expert on prussic acid, my authority and competence were such that it would be easy for me, under some pretext, to say that the prussic acid was unusable, that it was spoiled, or something' to that order, and so to prevent it being used for extermination purposes. We took along, pretty much by chance, Professor Pfannenstiel, a doctor of medicine with the rank of SS *Obersturmbannführer*, who was professor of hygiene at the University of Marburg on the Lahn.

As soon as the truck was loaded, we left for Lublin (Poland). There, SS *Gruppenführer* Globocnik was waiting for us. At the Collin plant, I expressly let it be understood that the acid was intended for use in killing human beings. That afternoon, one man showed a great deal of interest in our truck. As soon as he realized that he

---

station, he made the audacious decision to join the SS, in the hope that he might be able to sabotage the extermination operations from within. Thanks to his technical abilities he managed to get himself placed into the "hygiene section" of the health department of the Waffen-SS, the section which worked at developing poisonous gases under the pretext that they would be used for fumigation. As an expert, he was asked in the summer of 1942 to visit the Belzec camp, which is described in the account quoted above. He then attemped to let the world know what he had seen and, in fact, succeeded in making contact with a Swedish diplomat, Baron von Otter. According to von Otter, Gerstein believed "that when the great masses of the German people would learn about this extermination, and the facts would be confirmed to them by unprejudiced foreigners, they would not tolerate the Nazis for even one more day." He also tried to obtain an audience with the Papal nuncio in Berlin, but he was put off. It seems that the Swedish government also treated his report with caution, because a note in this matter was communicated to the British government only after the war. Gerstein was captured in May, 1945 by French troops and interned at the Cherche-Midi military prison where, lonely and disheartened, he took his own life in July of that year. (Cf. M. H. Krausnick's study, *Dokumentation zur Massenvergasung*, Bonn, 1956.)

In 1962 Gerstein's memory was recalled from oblivion by Rolf Hochhuth's famous play, *The Deputy* (an attack on Pope Pius XII), in which Gerstein figures as one of the principal characters. See Saul Friedländer, *Kurt Gerstein ou l'ambiguité du bien*, Paris, 1967.)

was being watched, he made a quick getaway. Globocnik said to us,
"This is one of the most secret matters there are, even the most secret. Anyone who talks about it will be shot immediately. Only yesterday two who talked were shot." Then he explained to us: "At the
present time—it was August 17, 1942—there are three installations:

1) Belzec, on the Lublin-Lwow road. A maximum of 15,000 people per day.
2) Sobibor (I don't know exactly where it is), 20,000 people a
   day.
3) Treblinka, 120 kilometers NNE of Warsaw.
4) Maidanek, near Lublin (under construction).

Globocnik said: "You will have to disinfect large piles of clothing
coming from Jews, Poles, Czechs, etc. Your other duty will be to im-
prove the workings of our gas chambers, which operate on the exhaust
from a Diesel engine. We need a more toxic and faster working gas,
something like prussic acid. The Führer and Himmler—they were
here the day before yesterday, August 15—ordered me to accompany
anybody who has to see the installation." Professor Pfannenstiel asked
him: "But what does the Führer say?" Globocnick answered: "The
Führer has ordered more speed. Dr. Herbert Lindner, who was here
yesterday, asked me, 'Wouldn't it be more prudent to burn the bodies
instead of burying them? Another generation might take a different
view of these things.' I answered: 'Gentlemen, if there is ever a generation after us so cowardly, so soft, that it would not understand our
work as good and necessary, then, gentlemen, National Socialism will
have been for nothing. On the contrary, we should bury bronze tablets
saying that it was we, we who had the courage to carry out this gigantic task!' Then the Führer said: 'Yes, my brave Globocnick, you are
quite right.'"

The next day we left for Belzec. Globocnik introduced me to SS
[Wirth?] who took me around the plant. We saw no dead bodies that
day, but a pestilential odor hung over the whole area. Alongside the
station there was a "dressing" hut with a window for "valuables."
Further on, a room with a hundred chairs, [designated as] "the barber." Then a corridor 150 meters long in the open air, barbed wire
on both sides, with signs: "To the baths and inhalants." In front of
us a building like a bath house; to the left and right, large concrete
pots of geraniums or other flowers. On the roof, the Star of David.
On the building a sign: "Heckenholt Foundation."

The following morning, a little before seven there was an announcement: "The first train will arrive in ten minutes!" A few minutes later
a train arrived from Lemberg: 45 cars with more than 6,000 people.
Two hundred Ukrainians assigned to this work flung open the doors
and drove the Jews out of the cars with leather whips. A loud speaker
gave instructions: "Strip, even artificial limbs and glasses. Hand all
money and valuables in at the 'valuables window.' Women and young
girls are to have their hair cut in the 'barber's hut.'" (An SS Unter-

führer told me: "From that they make something special for submarine crews.")

Then the march began. Barbed wire on both sides, in the rear two dozen Ukrainians with rifles. They drew near. Wirth and I found ourselves in front of the death chambers. Stark naked men, women, children, and cripples passed by. A tall SS man in the corner called to the unfortunates in a loud minister's voice: "Nothing is going to hurt you! Just breathe deep and it will strengthen your lungs. It's a way to prevent contagious diseases. It's a good disinfectant!" They asked him what was going to happen and he answered: "The men will have to work, build houses and streets. The women won't have to do that, they will be busy with the housework and the kitchen." This was the last hope for some of these poor people, enough to make them march toward the death chambers without resistance. The majority knew everything; the smell betrayed it! They climbed a little wooden stairs and entered the death chambers, most of them silently, pushed by those behind them. A Jewess of about forty with eyes like fire cursed the murderers; she disappeared into the gas chambers after being struck several times by Captain Wirth's whip. Many prayed; others asked: "Who will give us the water before we die?" [A Jewish rite] SS men pushed the men into the chambers. "Fill it up," Wirth ordered; 700-800 people in 93 square meters. The doors closed. Then I understood the reason for the "Heckenholt" sign. Heckenholt was the driver of the Diesel, whose exhaust was to kill these poor unfortunates. SS Unterscharführer Heckenholt tried to start the motor. It wouldn't start! Captain Wirth came up. You could see he was afraid because I was there to see the disaster. Yes, I saw everything and waited. My stopwatch clocked it all: 50 minutes, 70 minutes, and the Diesel still would not start! The men were waiting in the gas chambers. You could hear them weeping "as though in a synagogue," said Professor Pfannenstiel, his eyes glued to the window in the wooden door. Captain Wirth, furious, struck with his whip the Ukrainian who helped Heckenholt. The Diesel started up after 2 hours and 49 minutes, by my stopwatch. Twenty-five minutes passed. You could see through the window that many were already dead, for an electric light illuminated the interior of the room. All were dead after thirty-two minutes! Jewish workers on the other side opened the wooden doors. They had been promised their lives in return for doing this horrible work, plus a small percentage of the money and valuables collected. The men were still standing, like columns of stone, with no room to fall or lean. Even in death you could tell the families, all holding hands. It was difficult to separate them while emptying the rooms for the next batch. The bodies were tossed out, blue, wet with sweat and urine, the legs smeared with excrement and menstrual blood. Two dozen workers were busy checking mouths which they opened with iron hooks. "Gold to the left, no gold to the right." Others checked anus and genitals, looking for money, diamonds, gold, etc. Dentists knocked out gold teeth, bridges, and crowns, with hammers.

Captain Wirth stood in the middle of them. He was in his element, and, showing me a big jam box filled with teeth, said, "See the weight of the gold! Just from yesterday and the day before! You can't imagine what we find every day, dollars, diamonds, gold! You'll see!" He took me over to a jeweler who was responsible for all the valuables. They also pointed out to me one of the heads of the big Berlin store Kaufhaus des Westens, and a little man whom they forced to play the violin, the chiefs of the Jewish workers' commandos. "He is a captain of the Imperial Austrian Army, Chevalier of the German Iron Cross," Wirth told me.

Then the bodies were thrown into big ditches near the gas chambers, about 100 by 20 by 12 meters. After a few days the bodies swelled and the whole mass rose up 2-3 yards because of the gas in the bodies. When the swelling went down several days later, the bodies matted down again. They told me that later they poured Diesel oil over the bodies and burned them on railroad ties to make them disappear.[23]

There is little to add to this description, which holds good for Treblinka and Sobibor as well as for the Belzec camp. The latter installations were constructed in almost the very same way, and also used the exhaust carbon monoxide gases from Diesel motors as the death agent. At Maidanek, which was built later and lasted until the last days of the German occupation, the method of asphyxiation by prussic acid fumes (Cyclone B) was introduced after the example of Auschwitz, although, as we have pointed out, Maidanek was not an extermination camp proper.

The inquiries of the Polish Commission for War Crimes have established that the total number of victims at Belzec was close to 600,000, 250,000 at Sobibor, more than 700,000 at Treblinka, and more than 300,000 at Chelmno.[24] More than 90 per cent were Polish Jews. However, there was not a European nationality unrepresented in the remaining 8 to 10 per cent. Of the 110,000 Jews deported from the Netherlands, at least 34,000 were exterminated at Sobibor.[25]

The Belzec camp ceased functioning in December 1942 after nine months of activity. In the fall of 1943 Sobibor and Treblinka were also shut down, once the "final solution" was practically completed in Poland, and their remains concealed as far as possible, the buildings dismantled or destroyed, and the terrain reforested. Only the first one, the Chelmno camp, functioned continuously until October 1944, being shut down only in January 1945.

Every Jew sent to one of these four camps was doomed to immediate extermination. There were few exceptions to this rule. In a small number of cases quick "selections" were made when the convoy arrived. Thus, in 1943, after the revolt of the Warsaw ghetto, when the last convoys were reaching Treblinka, the Germans took away men who seemed able-bodied, in order to send them to Maidanek.[26] Some of these have survived. At Sobibor, too, as a survivor reports, appeals were made on the arrival of certain convoys for "volunteers for hard work." [27] In any case, however, the number of these survivors was scarcely more than a few dozen. Of the 34,313 Dutch Jews deported to Sobibor from March to July 1943, 19 people (16 women and 3 men), who were included in these rapid selections, lived to return to the Netherlands. According to them, the selections involved only 35 to 40 persons in each convoy.[28] On the other hand, we know of only one survivor of Belzec.[29]

Within the extermination camps there was a category of Jews not doomed to immediate death. These were members of the commandos assigned to clean out the installations: to pull the bodies from the gas chambers, search them, bury or burn them. The imagination finds it hard to conceive a matter in which physical and moral horror are so intimately blended; we shall have to come back again to this terrible subject. The members of these "Sonderkommandos," or special commandos, who were themselves exterminated at regular intervals and replaced with new teams, rebelled at various times. Thus, on August 2, 1943, an armed revolt broke out at Treblinka. Part of the plant was set afire and more than ten SS men and Ukrainian guards were killed. The camp was closed down a few weeks after this revolt. The last surviving members of the Jewish Sonderkommando of Chelmno, forty-seven of them, also rebelled on January 18, 1944, on the eve of their execution; two of them, Srebrnik and Surawski, succeeded in escaping and are at present its only survivors.[30]

The History of Auschwitz

Rudolf-Franz-Ferdinand Hoess, the son of a Baden-Baden tradesman, Franz-Xavier Hoess, member of the party from 1922, and a member of the SS "Death's Head Division" from 1934, went rapidly up the ladder of the SS administration of the concentration camps. He enjoyed the general esteem of the SS; had he not been one of the executioners in 1923 of Walter Kalow, the teacher who denounced Leo Schlageter, the Nazi national hero? After May 1, 1940, Hoess became head of the new camp built four kilometers from the little town of Auschwitz (in Polish, Oswiecim) in Upper Silesia, an area which Poland and Germany had fought over so bitterly and which was finally incorporated into the Third Reich. Like most sites picked for concentration camps, this sparsely inhabited region was unhealthy and swampy. A few huts left over from an old Polish artillery barracks served to house the first prisoners, a few dozen common German criminals, who were joined, after June 1940, by an ever growing number of Poles. This abundance of manpower attracted industries to the site, in accordance with the laws governing the concentration camp world; I. G. Farben and the Hermann Goering Works began building factories near the camps in the spring of 1941.[31]

Of the prime movers in the program of extermination, Rudolf Hoess was the only one to be captured and tried by Allied justice. In the course of his trial he made lengthy depositions; their sum and substance was: Himmler had called him to Berlin in June 1941, and said that the Führer had given orders to proceed with the "solution of the Jewish question in Europe." Since Auschwitz was situated in a sparsely populated region near the junction of four railroads, it lent itself well to the work of wholesale extermination; for this reason he had picked Auschwitz. Whereupon Himmler ordered him to start making his preparations immediately.[32]

Hoess's statements, as well as the rest of his testimony, have been substantiated by the findings of the Inquiry Commission set up by the Polish government after the war. Hoess added that Himmler had made it clear to him that he would be the sole head of the undertaking. "He thought it inadvisable for two officers to be in charge of this work at the same time."[33] We have seen that, in addition to the Hoess group, the SS group proper, there was a group of specialists from Hitler's chancellery working in the Polish camps. Himmler, characteristically, tried to stimulate the zeal of his underlings by getting them to compete with one another. A spirit of professional rivalry did in fact develop; Wirth treated Hoess like an "awkward disciple,"[34] while Hoess believed that he had surpassed his master. In his testimony before the Nuremberg Tribunal, Hoess complaisantly enumerated the improvements introduced at Auschwitz for which he took credit.[35] Other SS chiefs at this time were also assigned to developing mass murder methods. FranzZiereis, the Mauthausen commander, has left a description of a demonstration meeting for concentration camp commanders which took place at Sachsenhausen in 1941, during which an experimental automatic weapon invented by SS Oberführer Loritz was shown to the audience.[36] It fell to Hoess to devise the most efficient method of extermination. The idea, really, was simple enough. All kinds of vermin, bedbugs, etc., infested the old Auschwitz barracks, and the regular methods of disinfection were used to fight them. The Testa company, which worked for the Wehrmacht, supplied a gas with a prussic-acid base patented as "Cyclone B"; a stock of it was on hand. Under the circumstances, hitting on the idea of using this gas on condemned human beings probably required little imagination. It somehow followed naturally; from Hitler's curses in *Mein Kampf* to the threats uttered by Goebbels, just this kind of death and no other was wished for the Jews. (6)

If the idea came easily, developing it was more complicated. We still know very little about the first Auschwitz experiments, undertaken in the fall of 1941. Kurt Gerstein, the sinister and tragic "expert," played some part in the business, as we shall see later. Apparently Russian prisoners of war were used as the first guinea-pigs. According to the Polish Commission on War Crimes:

> Mass killing was tried on 250 patients from the hospital and about 600 prisoners of war in the underground shelters of Block 11. The windows of the shelter were covered with dirt. An SS man wearing a gas mask threw the contents of cans of Cyclone B through the open door, which was then closed. The next afternoon SS man Palitsch, again wearing his mask, opened the door and noted that many of the prisoners were still alive. More Cyclone was added and the door shut until the following evening. This time all the prisoners were asphyxiated.[37]

(6) Hitler in *Mein Kampf*: "If at the beginning of, or during, the war 12,000 or 15,000 of these Jewish corrupters of the people had been plunged into an asphyxiating gas . . . the sacrifice of millions of soldiers would not have been in vain." (462nd edition of 1939, p. 772).
Goebbels: "It is true that the Jew is human, but the flea is also a living

According to the historian Philip Friedman, this first large-scale experiment was made on September 15, 1941,[38] near the hamlet of Birkenau (Brzezinka), which thereafter served as the extermination site. Later in the year, according to Hoess, "the two farm-buildings on one side of the road, near Birkenau, were made airtight and equipped with solid wooden doors."[39] These were the first permanent installations. Their capacity was small, and they did not have a crematory; the bodies were burned in the open. Nevertheless, these installations were used to the end, and, unlike the better ones built later, were not destroyed in October 1944. It is impossible to indicate even approximately the number of victims exterminated at Auschwitz during this first period. For the most part they seem to have been Russian prisoners of war, whose number Hoess estimated at 70,000.[40] (Later, "Aryan" prisoners were assassinated individually, generally on orders from Berlin; only occasionally were they sent to the gas chamber. Such prisoners were generally dispatched by an injection of potassium cyanide in the region of the heart.)

It was not until the beginning of the summer of 1942—according to certain estimates, June 20, 1942—that the mass extermination of Jews began. (7) Auschwitz had meanwhile undergone major alterations. It was now a veritable concentration city with a population of at least 150,000, guarded by more than 3,000 SS men[41]— one of the most important centers of that underground world of deported slaves which burgeoned so extensively during the last years of Nazi Germany. Divided into three main camps (Auschwitz I, Auschwitz II-Birkenau, and Auschwitz III-Monowitz) and dozens of branch camps or "outside commandos," the city of Auschwitz embraced an intense and varied life, in which the exterminations were a relatively secondary matter, though the red glow of the crematories and the pestilential smell of the incinerated

---

being, not too pleasant a one. . . . Our duty towards ourselves and our conscience consists in making the flea harmless. The same is true of the Jews." (Goebbels, *Questions and Answers for the National-Socialist*, 1932, p. 12.)

(7) *Het doedenboek van Auschwitz*, 's Gravenhage, Dutch Red Cross edition, 1947. The estimate of the author of this remarkable pamphlet is based on the discovery of fascicle no. 22 of the Auschwitz death record. This fascicle contains 1,500 names, entered at the rate of 300 names a day, numbered 31,500-33,000, and runs from September 28 to October 2, 1942. A rapid calculation shows that at this rate, fascicle no. 1 must have been started on June

corpses did not allow them to be forgotten. The periodic selections of all kinds were the principal link between the Auschwitz of the crematories, the Jewish Auschwitz proper, and the international Auschwitz of slave laborers. Tens of thousands of prisoners, Jews and non-Jews alike, worked in the I. G. Farben factories making artificial rubber and synthetic gasoline; others toiled in the Krupp armament works, in the coal mines of the Upper Silesian basin, in the various secondary factories, or on the many farms and SS experimental stations. Some rose to envied positions of affluence in the camp administration or in the "Canadas," which were immense warehouses for the baggage and personal effects of the victims. The first and most important of the selections took place on the arrival of the convoy, and then and there the majority were sent to an anonymous death; whereas the survivors joined the ranks of the slaves and were assigned civil status and tattooed with a number, though they had what the statisticians call a "normal life expectancy" of no more than three months. (Nevertheless, the prisoner was a legal person from then on, duly registered in the camp books. His rapid and practically inevitable death was attributed in the records of the Bureau of Vital Statistics to such imaginary causes as "heart attack" and "pneumonia.") [42]

From the summer of 1942 a continuous stream of convoys, sometimes at the rate of four trains a day, brought to Auschwitz the victims rounded up by IVb from the four corners of Europe, Eichmann's offices notifying Hoess when the transports departed.[43] When the two original gas chambers proved inadequate, four new installations were built. The contractors awarded the work, Topf and Son of Erfurt, wished to bring under the same roof the two essential phases of the operation, asphyxiation and incineration.[44] At the beginning of 1943 crematories II and III, veritable masterpieces embodying an absolutely new technique, were solemnly dedicated in the presence of important visitors from Berlin. According to certain testimonies, 8,000 Jews from Cracow, the capital of the Government General and the residence of Hans Frank, were the first and symbolic victims.[45] Two more crematories were finished six months later. A spur track was lengthened by a kilometer so that the convoys might be unloaded in the immediate vicinity of the crematories.[46] The four crematories contained forty-six ovens

20, 1942. Let it be clearly understood that only the deaths of deportees "selected for labor" were entered in these records.

in all, with a total capacity of close to 12,000 bodies every twenty-four hours.[47] In general, the rate of arrival of the convoys varied according to the efficiency of the deportation machinery. In certain periods, deliveries were such that entire convoys were gassed without any selections, because of lack of space.[48] The maximum of 12,000 to 15,000 a day was reached in May–June 1944 during the deportation of the Hungarian Jews. "In June 1944 they set a record of 22,000 incinerations in twenty-four hours," a witness wrote.[49] As with criminals, it was not so much the murdering itself as the getting rid of the bodies which continually worried Hoess and his associates. The four crematories were no longer adequate, and besides, the ovens were deteriorating, so enormous funeral pyres in the open made up the deficiency. During this last period, on a night in August 1944, 4,000 gypsies were gassed, the last survivors of Auschwitz's gypsy population; this is the only example of a complete and mass extermination of non-Jews.[50]

History, however, followed its course. As a result of a combination of factors, which we shall analyse later, Himmler ordered the exterminations put a stop to in October 1944. One of the last selections, the biggest and cruelest according to the survivors, took place on October 1, 1944.[51] There were no new convoys or selections after November.

After some thirty months of intense activity, the Auschwitz balance sheet showed close to two million immediate exterminations (this figure can never be fixed exactly), (8) to which one must add the deaths of some 300,000 registered prisoners—Jews for the most part, but not entirely—for whom the gas chamber was only one of any number of ways by which they might have perished. The crematories were dismantled at the beginning of November

(8) In his affidavits, Hoess spoke of two and a half million, "a figure set officially," he wrote, under the signature of Lieutenant Colonel Eichmann, in a report to Himmler. This figure has been accepted by several authors, and it appears in the verdict at the trial of the major war criminals. However, there is no reason for accepting without question the statistics attributed to Eichmann, which may err on either side. Adding the number of victims to those deported from different countries gives a lower figure, although we have little data, for example, on the number of Polish Jews sent to Auschwitz.

An approximate figure in the neighborhood of two million seems closer to the truth.

1944,[52] though the camp was kept up without any great change for two months more. Evacuation of Auschwitz's principal industries began at the end of the year. The Russian winter offensive of January 1945 hastened the evacuation. Nearly 5,000 untransportable sick prisoners were freed on January 27 by the Red Army. Nearly 60,000 prisoners considered physically fit, Jews for the most part, were evacuated to the interior of the country, especially to Buchenwald in central Germany.[53] Though there was no systematic extermination of this group, the conditions under which the evacuation took place and the life in the "small camp" at Buchenwald were such that only a few thousand were able to live through the three months until the Americans arrived.

Today, only the crematory I and some huts and dismantled factory sheds are left at Auschwitz-Birkenau, now turned into a museum by the Polish government. For months after the liberation of the region, Polish peasants came to dig in the heaps of ashes or at the site of the latrines, looking for bits of gold or other valuables left over from the incineration of the thousands of bodies.[54]

THE SELECTIONS—"CYCLONE B"

A secret order from Himmler dated April 1942, issued at the very moment when the extermination program went into high gear, expressly stated that Jews able to work were not to be exterminated right off, but were to be used as a labor force. (This order was mentioned at the Nuremberg Tribunal, but it has not been located.) [55] Thus the selections were established in principle.

At Auschwitz they were carried out on the station platforms immediately after the trains arrived. The cars would be unsealed; the deportees driven out onto the platform with blows and curses, stripped of their baggage, and subjected to a rapid selection. Here is how one witness, Professor Robert Waitz, describes it:

> The deportees move little by little toward the end of the platform. Two SS men stand in the center of the platform, one of them a medical officer. The deportees pass in front of him. With his thumb or a cane the officer sends them to the right or left. In this way two columns collect at both ends of the platform. The one on the left includes men between twenty and forty-five who have a more or less healthy appearance. These age limits are flexible and sometimes men from six-

teen or eighteen to fifty are chosen. The prisoner's appearance and bearing, the fact that he is more or less well-shaven, influences the choice. A few young women are also put into this column.

The column on the right includes the older men, the aged, most of the women, children, and the sick. Families try to get back together again. Sometimes the SS officer then picks out those who are young and physically fit from the family. More rarely these are allowed to stay with their family in the right-hand column.

The women in the column on the left are marched off to the neighboring camp; the men are piled one on the other into trucks and trailers, which then drive off. The prisoners in the right-hand column are loaded on trucks.

In my convoy, a very large proportion of the 1,200 deportees (about 330) was kept, along with a few women. This figure is unusual. Rarely are more than 150 to 200 men selected per convoy.[56]

A remarkable statistical analysis made by the Dutch Red Cross [57] confirms the accuracy of this description insofar as the age and sex of those selected are concerned. The number of those selected, however, seems to have varied; on the average, the percentage of deportees temporarily spared seems to have been slightly higher than that indicated by Professor Waitz. Hoess spoke of 25 per cent in his depositions; this figure is substantiated by documents in which the RSHA set forth its manpower requirements, estimated, in one case, for example, at 10,000-15,000 out of a total of 45,000 deportees. (9) All this is of course of no great importance when one remembers that the normal life expectancy at Auschwitz was three months, survival for even six months being considered excep-

(9) This refers to a telegram sent to Himmler by the RSHA, and signed SS General Müller.
Berlin, December 16, 1942.
In view of the increased shipment of labor to the concentration camps ordered for January 30, 1943, the following details can be given for the Jewish section:

1. Total number: 45,000 Jews.
2. Beginning of transportation: January 11, 1943.
3. End of transportation: January 31, 1943.

These 45,000 Jews include 30,000 from the Bialystok region and 10,000 from the Theresienstadt ghetto. . . . As before, only Jews with no particular connections or without special decorations have been picked for deportation. Finally, 3,000 Dutch Jews, 2,000 from Berlin, which makes [a total of] 45,000. These 45,000 include the sick, the aged, and children. When the selection has been made, at least 10,000-15,000 workers will be available after the assignment of the Jews at Auschwitz.

tional. We should add that selections were made in a quite superficial way; often, to give an example cited by Hoess, women standing in the left-hand column were able to hide their infants under
their skirts or in their bundles.

But let us return to the right-hand column. The men and women
who could walk went to the crematories on foot, the old and sick
in trucks. There, either right away or after a few hours, they were
told by an interpreter or by the SS man on duty that they were
going to take a shower and be disinfected. Then they were led to
the "dressing rooms," where numbered hooks lined the walls; the
guide advised them not to forget their numbers. Bars of gritty soap
were distributed to complete the deception. The trick worked in the
great majority of cases. The gas chambers proper, into which they
were brought undressed, even had simulated shower heads in the
ceiling. An SS man wearing a gas mask (this must have been the
only instance of the gas mask being put to any real use in World
War II) dropped the necessary quantity of cans of Cyclone B gas
(from five to seven kilos for every 1,500 persons) through several
small windows which had been installed in the roof for this purpose. In accordance with Wehrmacht regulations on the use of
asphyxiating gas, a camp doctor was required to be present at each
extermination.[58] The asphyxiation process lasted three to ten minutes, depending on resistance, and also on "atmospheric conditions"
(Hoess)—that is, the gas acted more rapidly when the weather was
warm and dry. The reader has perhaps had enough horror documents set before him; we shall spare him another. A half hour later,
members of the "Sonderkommando" opened the doors and carried
off the bodies to the ovens, after first cutting off the women's hair
and removing all gold teeth, rings, and earrings. Crematories 1 and
II used electric hoists. Incineration took half an hour, with four or
five bodies at a time in each oven. The ashes were at first dumped
into ditches; but later on they were loaded onto trucks and emptied
into the nearby Vistula.[59]

Since the fake showers and cakes of soap generally served their
purpose, the victims remained unaware of their fate until the last
moment. Hoess, who complacently discussed all this in his depositions, insisted on "this advance" which had been made over Treblinka. "The Treblinka victims almost always knew they were going

to be exterminated, while at Auschwitz we joked with them, made them believe that they were going to have a delousing treatment." [60] "Naturally, they sometimes discovered our real intentions," he added, "especially in the convoys from the east, in which case we strengthened our security measures; the convoy would be split up into small sections which were then sent separately to the different crematories in order to avoid any disturbance [sic!]. The SS formed a chain and dragged along the ones who balked by force. But this happened very seldom." [61]

The Sonderkommando was kept strictly isolated. The SS chose its members from the prisoners as needed. "It was completely isolated from the rest of the camp; it lived entirely inside the crematory buildings, was not allowed to leave the area which was enclosed by a double row of barbed wire, was supplied with its provisions in a special way, had its own doctors who worked on the spot and were under the direct authority of the *Politische Abteilung*, that is, the camp Gestapo." [62] The Sonderkommando ended up with 900 members, divided into three teams working eight hours apiece. Its members were themselves exterminated and replaced with others about every three months. (10) Since they were better fed, these men were not so debilitated; it was among them that the only organized uprising in the history of Auschwitz broke out, in August 1944. A last-minute betrayal wrecked a carefully worked out plan to blow up the crematories; one month later, at the beginning of October 1944, another attempted uprising took place, during which Crematory III was burned and two German "Kapos" killed on the spot. Needless to say, all the rebels were shot.[63]

Along with the main "selection on arrival," partial selections were constantly taking place at Auschwitz among the Jewish prisoners whose age and physical condition had spared them immediate extermination, so as to eliminate those whose work output was no longer sufficient. These partial and unexpected selections took place either at the camp infirmary once or twice a month, or in the barracks or huts every three or four months.[64] Like the main selec-

(10) According to the confession of Ziereis, commander of the Mauthausen camp, secret instructions provided for the extermination of the Sonderkommandos every three weeks.

tion, they were made by an SS camp doctor. At Auschwitz they were one of the chief features differentiating the fate of the Jewish prisoners from that of the "Aryans." "The few 'Aryans' could die of natural causes," Georges Weller wrote, and he added a brief description of a "partial selection":

> Cell block by cell block the Germans made the people file stark naked in front of them, and a glance at their buttocks decided their fate, for no part of the human body so faithfully reveals a person's loss of flesh. . . . The skeletons and half-skeletons made an heroic effort for the minute to put on a brave and gay front before the Germans, puffing out their fleshless thoraxes. But the pitiless buttocks allowed no cheating! [65]

Other witnesses point out that there were doctors who swore by other criteria: swollen legs, pimples on the face, etc.[66] The condemned were brought together and locked in a separate barracks to wait their turn; this might often take as long as three days.[67] Apparently these partial selections took place on orders from Berlin. For the camp administration, they were a way of adjusting the size of their effective labor force. The manpower needs of the moment, as well as the arrival rate of new convoys, determined the frequency and the severity of the selections.

A few words remain to be said about Auschwitz' most remarkable innovation: Cyclone B. Here is disclosed one of those instances of enterprising business men and hard-working German technicians taking their place alongside the Nazi murder experts. In the foreground, however, looms the sinister shadow of I. G. Farben, the huge trust symbolizing German industrial power whose name will forever be linked to the Buna factories of Auschwitz III-Monowitz.

Gerhard Peters,[68] director of production of Cyclone B, stated before the Allied court that it "is an invention of Dr. Heerdt's. It is highly concentrated prussic acid absorbed into various porous retainers and combined with an irritant that serves as a warning." Cyclone B had been developed around 1924 by the Degesch Company of Frankfort on the Main. In 1941 Peters became one of the directors of this company, which about this time was absorbed by I. G. Farben, becoming one of its branches. A third company came on the scene as the product's distributor. East of the Elba, Degesch had given exclusive distribution rights to the Testa company (Tesch and Stabenow) of Hamburg, which supplied the Wehrmacht with disinfectants and insecticides and, as was customary, gave instructions in its use and put on the necessary demonstrations. According to the account given by E. Sehm, the accountant for the Testa company, Bruno Tesch, the head of the company, had suggested Cyclone B when consulted at the beginning of 1942 by the SS administration on the question of using prussic acid to get rid of the "useless existences." [69] Tesch, who was condemned to death by the British tribunal, denied this during his trial. Be that as it may, the Testa company's books show the delivery of more than 27,000 kilos of Cyclone B to the SS camp administration during the years 1942 and 1943, of which more than 20 tons were for the Auschwitz camp alone; they made a gross profit of 32,000 Reichsmarks in 1942 and 128,000 Reichsmarks in 1943 on this one item.[70] The SS administration, on the other hand, was inclined to eliminate a middleman whom it probably considered useless. On orders from Professor Mrugowski, "supreme hygienist" and physician of the SS, Peters went to Berlin at the beginning of 1944 to deal directly with Kurt Gerstein. During this last year, most of the deliveries to Auschwitz were made directly by Degesch without going through Testa. Deliveries were made by rail or the camps sent a small truck to pick up the stuff. According to Peters, Gerstein asked him to "humanize" Cyclone B by eliminating the irritant factor, which apparently increased the suffering a great deal. Peters stated that he had a lot of trouble carrying out Gerstein's request, since he was not able, he said, to find suitable reasons to give to his colleagues for the modification. This was so, even though he considered Gerstein's request perfectly "legal," as he considered "legal" "a great many other things that are to be explained by the distortion of all the moral concepts of the time." [71] A German tribunal condemned Peters to five years in prison in the spring of 1949.

THE HANGMEN: THEIR METHODS AND PSYCHOLOGY

In Rudolf Hoess's personal file, under the heading "branch of service," the word "cavalry" was originally noted; this was crossed

out and over it was entered "concentration camps." And indeed the
units assigned to guard the camps constituted a veritable special
branch of service inside the SS; they were "Death's Head" formations (SS *Totenkopf*) trained since 1933 to guard, degrade, and
torture the "sub-humans" and enemies of the regime. The essential
function of these specialized troops was to crush the slightest
tendency to resistance in the prisoners, and to surround their bleed-
ing expiations with horror and mystery, "darkness and mist"; to
this there had originally been added the task of "re-educating" and
reforming the German prisoners. They had only one method: the
infliction of a varied, cruel, and refined suffering. The Death's
Heads benefited, then, from a long tradition. To the attitude of professional insensibility engendered in these men by long habituation
was added the uneasy pleasure some of them got from sufferings
inflicted on order and, what was more important, in the service of
a higher and ideologically consecrated purpose.

Thanks to the methods used at Auschwitz as well as in the other
extermination camps, only a few dozen officials actually saw and
lent a hand to the extermination process proper. The Sonderkommandos, composed of prisoners, served the crematories; a handful
of SS men and a few doctors constituted the German personnel. It
was indeed a factory working with great efficiency on the assembly-
line principle. "I have never personally killed or struck anybody,"
Hoess could state.

Perhaps the reader will be interested in glancing into the consciences of these technicians. Here is an abstract from the diary of
one of them, a professional man, Dr. Kremer:

1. IX. 1942. I wrote to Berlin for a leather belt and suspenders.
During the afternoon I was present at the disinfection of a cell block
with Cyclone B, to kill the lice.
2. IX. 1942. This morning at three o'clock I attended a special
action for the first time. Dante's hell seemed like a comedy in comparison. Not for nothing is Auschwitz called an extermination camp.
5. IX. 1942. I was present this afternoon at a special action applied to prisoners in the female camp (Moslems), (11) the worst I
have ever seen. Dr. Thilo was right this morning in telling me that
we are in the *anus mundi*. Tonight, about eight, I was present at a

(11) At Auschwitz the prisoners who had reached the limits of physical
endurance were called "Moslems."

special action on the Dutch. All the men are anxious to take part in these actions because of the special rations they get on such occasions, consisting of ⅕ of a liter of schnapps, 5 cigarettes, 100 grams of sausage and bread.

6-7. IX. 1942. Today, Sunday, an excellent lunch: tomato soup, half a chicken with potatoes and red cabbage, *petits fours*, a marvelous vanilla ice cream. After lunch I was introduced to . . . [illegible word]. Left at eight in the evening for a special action, for the fourth time.

23. IX. 1942. Present last night at the sixth and seventh special actions. In the morning, Obergruppenführer Pohl arrived with his staff at the Waffen SS house. The sentinel at the door was the first to salute me. In the evening, at eight o'clock, dinner in the commanding officer's house, with General Pohl, a real banquet. We had apple pie, as much as we wanted, good coffee, excellent beer, and cakes.

7. X. 1942. Present at the ninth special action. Foreigners and women.

11. X. 1942. Today, Sunday, rabbit, a good leg, for lunch, with red cabbage and pudding, all for 1.25 RM.

12. X. 1942. Inoculation for typhus. Following this, feverish in the evening; still, went to a special action that night (1,600 Dutch). Terrible scenes near the last bunker. The tenth special action.[72]

Dr. Kremer's diary goes on in this way to the end of the year, alternating between noting the menus he particularly enjoyed and the carefully numbered special actions he attended, on which he commented with growing indifference. Professional habituation? For that a particular mentality was undoubtedly needed. Rudolf Hoess furnishes a typical example. "One gets the general impression of a man who is intellectually normal but with the schizoid apathy, insensitivity and lack of empathy that could hardly be more extreme in a frank psychotic," according to the diagnosis of Dr. Gilbert, the Nuremberg prison psychiatrist. Dr. Gilbert questioned Hoess several times in his cell while in search of some emotional reaction, and could only get the following out of him: "You can be sure that it was not always a pleasure to see those mountains of corpses and smell the continual burning.—But Himmler had ordered it and had even explained the necessity and I really never gave much thought to whether it was wrong. It just seemed a necessity."[73] Tranquil and apathetic, Hoess did not show the slightest sign of remorse: "Even the prospect of being hanged does not seem to bother him too much." When pressed by questions, Hoess tried to explain: "The thought of refusing an order just didn't enter one's head, regardless of what kind of order it was. . . . Guess you cannot understand our world.—I naturally had to obey orders and I must now stand to take the consequences." [74] To illustrate the professional attitude of the great hangmen with a different example, let us quote from a document about Eichmann, Auschwitz's great provider. A report by Röthke, his representative at Paris, describes a telephone conversation with Eichmann on the subject of a convoy that was to leave Bordeaux in July 1942, but which had been called off at the last moment. Röthke tried to explain the reasons for this over the telephone, but Eichmann flared up angrily.

> Major Eichmann reminded me that our prestige was at stake. There had been laborious negotiations with the Ministry of Transportation. These had been successful and now we are canceling a train from Paris. It's the first time such a thing has happened to him. What a shame! He did not want to tell SS General Müller about it for fear of making himself a laughing stock.

And how does the great organizer of the deportation of the European Jews conclude? By threatening this punishment: "He said that he was forced to consider whether there were grounds for having France dropped as an evacuation country." [75]

If a few dozen Germans, some hundreds at the most, actually observed the last agony of the Jews in the gas chambers, those who witnessed their long Calvary were numbered in the hundreds of thousands. The SS formations stationed in the camps; the German workers, Army units, and officials at the numerous yards and factories where the Jewish slaves were used, whom they passed by daily; the railway men handling the innumerable transports of deportees all over Germany, which they saw coming back empty, if they were not loaded with the used clothing which was distributed to the needy by all the welfare offices in the country. This is a very incomplete list of those who can properly be called eyewitnesses. As for the rest of the Germans, the press and radio of the Reich undertook to inform them more and more openly of what was going on. The time for vague and prophetic imprecations by Hitler had passed. The language now sharpens and it is the past tense that is employed. "The Jewish population of Poland has been neutralized, and the same may be said right now for Hungary. By this action five million Jews have been eliminated in these two countries," a

Danzig newspaper wrote in May 1944.[76] And the next day Goebbels' *Der Angriff* published under the byline of Ley: "Judea must perish that mankind may be saved." [77] The fate of the Jews was an example and a warning: "Whosoever imitates the Jew deserves the same end: extermination, death," threatened *Der Stürmer*. The extermination policy thus became a matter of common knowledge and enough information filtered through a thousand channels for the location of the murder camps and the methods of execution to become notorious. A witness states that in the trains passing near Auschwitz (where, we will recall, four rail lines crossed) "the passengers stood up and leaned out the window to see as much as they could." [78] Another witness, none other than Rudolf Diels, the first director of the Prussian Gestapo in 1933–34, later police prefect of Cologne and administrator of the Hermann Goering Works during the war, stated that as far as he knew, the expression, "You will go up the chimney," had become proverbial in Germany toward the end of the war.[79] Only those who did not wish to know might continue to pretend ignorance. During a dramatic session at one of the Nuremberg trials, a highly qualified witness, SS General Bach-Zelewsky, who was "head of the anti-partisan campaign" of the German armies during the war, insisted on clarifying the matter.

> For me it is a question of principle. Though imprisoned for years, I see that people are still saying: Who knew? Nobody wants to be in the position of having known anything. I want to establish the truth here, regardless of whether it hurts or helps me. . . . Of all the German generals, I am perhaps the one who traveled most all over Europe during the war, since it was my job to manage the entire fight against the guerrillas. I talked to hundreds of generals and thousands of officers of all categories, and it is a fact that exterminations began on the first day of the war. This is the truth; anything else is a lie and a euphemism. . . . And anyone who traveled knew from the beginning that the Jews were being exterminated in a way that at first was not systematic. Later, when the Russian campaign began, the extermination of Judaism was an explicit part of the aim.[80]

A veil of absolute secrecy, however, hung over the actual work of extermination action, and the participants were sworn to silence on pain of death. In addition, propaganda aimed at the neutral and Allied countries, and especially meant for the foreign press, strove to picture the lot of the "Jewish workers" in the rosiest colors.

"Jews unfit for work are transferred to family ghettos, all the others are used according to their professional background, the principle being that couples stay together. Food and lodging are the same as for other workers." (Press conference held by Sündermann, "Deputy Press Chief of the Reich," on April 19, 1944) This sort of thing might be reported in Rumanian or Hungarian newspapers, but was rarely published in Germany itself. The fate of the Jews, and all the police operations and administrative steps connected with it, fell into the category of *Geheime Reichssache*, state secrets, with which it was better not to get involved. Those fearless Germans who dared publicly bring this matter up, or even, like Protestant Bishop Wurm, to protest in writing to the Führer—("I must state . . . that as Christians we feel that the policy of exterminating the Jews is a very grave iniquity and fatal for the German people." —These brave sentences were dated December 18, 1943.) (12)— could be counted on the fingers of one hand. In the continual concern for secrecy, one may see something else than just the desire not to noise abroad a state of affairs which under other circumstances the Nazis allowed to become known. Around the holocaust they wished to draw a veil of sacred horror, to transform it into a sanctifying and purifying mystery. We have already cited some of the Nazi feats of circumlocution; one cannot insist too much on the significance of this constant perversion of ordinary ideas and words by the SS. Thus, Hoess's work is commented upon in his administrative file as follows: "H. is not only a good camp commander, he has been a real pioneer (*bahnbrechend gewirkt*) in this field thanks to [his] new ideas and new methods of education." [81] Mind, this is not a propaganda statement, but confidential service notes. Apart from the question of secrecy, why dwell on Hoess's qualities as an "educator," and what is the true meaning of this verbal mumbo-jumbo? One is inclined to see it as a real exercise

(12) Letter from Bishop Wurm to the Chief of the Reich Chancellery. In a preceding letter, dated July 16, 1943, and addressed directly to the Führer, the bishop made a similar protest.

It is interesting to note that, at the time of the debate in the German post-Hitler press which accompanied or followed the Nuremberg trials Bishop Wurm showed his disapproval of Allied justice in scarcely less vehement language.

in magic, an attempt to influence things (to make the obscene innocuous and even noble) by manipulating words. Genocide was no small matter even for Himmler's unleashed pack. Despite their professional habituation, the hangmen, big and small, felt a vague uneasiness; their fear of punishment, which sharpened as the war progressed, found an echo in some deeper disquiet, so true was it perhaps that even amid the worst excesses of these bestial natures certain mental barriers still remained. (Let no one be misled as to our meaning. We do not mean that the SS men were tormented by pangs of conscience. Not all, however, attained the attitude of sovereign indifference that was held before them as an ideal.) Himmler, otherwise so talkative, never mentioned extermination in his numerous speeches with but one exception, when he was addressing a small group of faithful SS chiefs:

> I should also like to talk very frankly to you about a very important subject. We can discuss it quite frankly among ourselves, though we must no more speak about it in public than we do about June 30, 1934. . . . Not to have discussed it was a question of tact for us. Everybody was dismayed by it and yet everybody knows that he will do it again on the next occasion if he is given the order and it is necessary.
>
> I should like to talk about the evacuation of the Jews, about the extermination of the Jewish people. This is something that is easy enough to talk about. "The Jewish people will be exterminated," every party member says. "That's clear enough, it's in our program: elimination of the Jews, extermination." Well, we set about doing that, and eighty million brave Germans turn up and each has his "good" Jew. Obviously, the rest are pigs, but this one is a first-rate Jew. Not one of those who talk like this has seen the corpses, not one of them has been there. Most of you know what it is to see a pile of 100 corpses, or 500, or 1,000. To have gone through that, and to have remained an honest man just the same, save for the exceptions due to human nature, that is what has made you tough and strong.
>
> This is a glorious page in our history, never before, never again to be written.[82]

Let us return now to the Death's Head units of the SS who guarded Auschwitz and its constantly replenished force of 100,000 slaves. Their extreme cruelty, their sadistic jokes, their ingenuity in evil have been repeatedly described, and were only the inevitable result of factors we have already considered. Because of one feature of the system progressively introduced at Auschwitz and the other camps, the SS took less and less of a hand in directing the internal life of the camps, leaving matters to be run by a complicated hierarchy of authority established by the prisoners themselves. Even Jews could sometimes aspire to certain positions in this hierarchy. Thus, once inside the camp, the rigidly religious kind of anti-Jewish discrimination was softened.

Just being alive was a kind of defiance in a Jew, as one can gather from the innumerable SS sayings, such as: "You leave here only through the chimney," "An honest prisoner dies before three months," and the like. A Jew who lasted two or three years found himself wearing a kind of halo in the eyes of the SS, and they allowed him numerous tacit privileges; he ran practically no risk of being selected. But prolonged living in a concentration camp, as we shall see, necessarily worked deep changes in the prisoner himself.

Another feature of the concentration camp system, even more astonishing, perhaps, than the general sadism, was its pervasive didacticism and moralizing. "Work is freedom" (*Arbeit macht frei*) was inscribed on scrolls above the camp entrances. "On the road to freedom there are four milestones: work, justice, discipline, and patriotism," was another maxim, carved on stone plaques posted up everywhere. Dressed in rags, the slaves had to march at parade step and with a martial air when going off to work, while other slaves played military marches. Crippled by disease, their feet running with sores, the prisoners were forced to make their beds with geometric precision. Some of the new cell blocks, like those of Auschwitz I, were model barracks from the architectural point of view. The concern for decoration extended even to the crematories: "In accordance with an order from Lieutenant Colonel Hoess, camp commander, Crematories I and II shall be provided with a green strip of decorative shrubs, to serve as a natural boundary for the camp." [83]

The sadistic punishments, beatings, and executions took place with elaborate pomp, in the presence of thousands of prisoners specially mustered for the occasion according to a carefully prepared ceremony. While prisoners were being murdered by the thousands, some few murders, because they were "committed without orders," or an individual case like that of the "bad treatment inflicted on the prisoner Eleonore Hodys" [84] would arouse the ire of a special SS department, which sent its men to Auschwitz, Buchenwald, and Dachau to investigate. All this rigmarole, this drilling, bureaucratic pedantry, and bloody buffoonery, was calculated to strengthen the blind and mechanical obedience of the SS and of the prisoners who were the foundation of the system. At the same time, wasn't this another aspect of that huge magical rite which we have already described, a deliberate effort to call white black, and black white? In short, was it not the elaborate ritual of a demoniacal cult? "They call evil good, and good evil. And they put darkness for light and light for darkness."

We may conclude these few fragmentary observations by pointing out that even in the world of concentration camps human differences sometimes exercised their claim; even in the SS one found a few less ferocious guards, a few physicians moved by pity, like Dr. Munch, at Auschwitz I, whom Professor Marc Klein described as a "very rare, but not unique, example of an SS doctor who had remained a man beneath his uniform"; [85] or SS Lieutenant Schottel, adjutant to the commandant of Auschwitz III, who adopted an almost benevolent manner toward "his prisoners." . . . Such examples, however, are more characteristic of the last years of war, when the Death's Head division's rigorously selective system of recruiting of the first years began to be replaced with mass drafts. There was even—five hundred kilometers from Auschwitz, it is true—the unusual case of a handful of Jewish prisoners who had been forgotten in the small Osterode camp, in Lower Saxony; when a Jewish prisoner died, he was buried in the town's Jewish cemetery, while the physician at the camp had to attend the funeral service.[86]

The Agony of the Slaves

All over Europe there are men and women today, numbering no more than a few tens of thousands, who are united in a close fraternity. These are the people who survived the German concentration camps. Of all nationalities, backgrounds, and social classes, some of them "political deportees," others "racial deportees," they are joined together by the memory of the unparalleled ordeals they underwent, and which mark them out from all other mortals. What they endured throws a new and disquieting light on certain human tendencies and possibilities. In the world of the concentration camps we can distinguish three principal types, according to their degree of cruelty. There were also different phases in the over-all development of the concentration camps; the first camps and the last ones were the most terrible. In short, there were successive circles in this inferno, the last being reserved for the Jews; and at the dead center of this world stood Auschwitz and its crematories.

It should be remembered that in the majority of the cases, deportees arriving at Auschwitz were completely unaware of what lay in store for them; they imagined, perhaps, that they were being sent to some kind of "reservation," a Jewish colony in the heart of Poland. Once the barrier of the selection on arrival had been surmounted, the prisoners thus granted a few months' reprieve were initiated into their new life by a series of ordeals that soon undermined their capacity for physical and moral resistance. Stripped of their belongings, deprived of even the smallest object or personal souvenir, they were forced to undress in the open, whatever the weather and season, and carefully searched, in this way losing every vestige of their previous life. Then they were sent to the showers, sometimes after a long wait in the rain or snow; finally they were issued the cast-off clothing of convicts, blue-and-white striped pyjamas that were tossed to them haphazardly. The next step was to be inscribed in the camp books, to have a serial number tattooed on one's forearm, all this to the accompaniment of a storm of insults and blows; after which the deportees were marched to their huts or tents. Some older prisoner would then tell them about the crematories, whose glare reddened the night sky. The fate of their wives or children became clear to them, at the same time as their own situation. Two or three days later they were assigned to a work commando, and were now definitely a part of the life of their new world.

In very rare cases they could find easier jobs, sometimes even in their former occupations; this was the case, for instance, with a few doctors, draftsmen, and musicians. Chances for survival in these few cases were better. But the immense majority who worked in the mines, factories, or open yards, subjected to every hardship and difficulty, found themselves launched almost inevitably upon that terrible path of physical and moral decline which began with the first shock of the "reception." The fate of any prisoner in the camps was bad enough; but in three specific regards Jews were at a disadvantage in comparison with their "Aryan" fellow prisoners: they could not receive packages from the outside; they had much less chance of getting a privileged position; and they were subject to periodic selections. Because of the selections, their average life expectancy in the camps could be estimated at approximately three months. (This period varied according to circumstances; it was the shortest at the beginning of the mass exterminations in 1942—for the first Dutch Jewish convoys it was only six weeks.) [87] It was customary at Auschwitz to consider the Jews of some nationalities as being more resistant than others. The Polish, Slovakian, and German Jews were thought to be more tenacious of life; these were followed by the Hungarians and French; the Dutch, Greek, and Italian Jews came last.[88] However, it should be noted that most of the Poles and Germans benefited from a certain training in concentration-camp life. Other factors, such as the time of one's arrival at the camp or the language one spoke, also made a difference. It is doubtful how much importance should be assigned to such judgments, or to others based on social class.[89] For the decisive factor was a purely personal one—the physical, and above all, moral resistance, vitality, will to live, and general adaptability of each individual.

Out of almost 115,000 French political deportees, nearly 40,000 returned from the different German camps; out of the 110,000 Jews deported from France to Auschwitz, hardly 2,800 survived. The mere juxtaposition of these figures shows how precarious the life of the Jews was in the concentration camps. Each case of survival was unusual and needed the assistance of special circumstances. Here we shall mention only one of these: rising up the ladder of the internal camp hierarchy to some sort of post as head of a cell block, a "Kapo" or commando head, or a *Stubendienst* or barracks guard. In order to survive in such position, one needed a great fund of brutality and very few scruples.

The prisoner thus became more or less of a cog in the SS machine, and even began to think and feel in the manner of the SS. Apart from all other considerations, the yellow triangle marking the striped pyjamas of the Jews was a major, though not always an insurmountable obstacle to their adaptation. In any case, only the lower or middle positions in the hierarchy were open to them. The luxurious privileges enjoyed by a small class of prisoners belonging to the camp "aristocracy," such as recreation, sports, and private quarters, were forbidden them.

Another way Jews might survive, especially members of certain professions, was by finding work in their field in one of the numerous SS institutes or laboratories, in the research departments of factories, in the camp hospital, or even in the camp orchestra. Such jobs did not force their holders to make moral compromises; these men, the doctors especially, could render innumerable services to their less fortunate comrades. Most of the Auschwitz survivors owe their existence to having had such privileged posts. In order to survive, a certain amount of luck was necessary: running into a friend already "established" in something, or a job becoming open, etc. But in addition, to stay alive one needed a strong will to live and also a faculty for not feeling things. Life in the concentration camp worked very strange changes on body and soul.

First of all, one needed an insensibility to physical hardships: Underfed men with hardly any clothes on had to endure the interminably prolonged roll calls, sometimes standing eight or twelve hours exposed to the rigors of the Polish winter; later came the evacuation marches, the terrible trip from Auschwitz to Buchenwald in January 1944, seventy kilometers on foot in one night, then three days and three nights in open cars in 20 degrees below Centigrade temperature. At the same time, one needed a moral insensibility: a callousness to the disappearance daily of friends and relatives. The glow from the crematories could never be escaped, and yet "with the calmness of a citizen reading his newspaper," the deportees told each other in the morning how many convoys had arrived, how many people had been gassed—the day's news. Thus by an apprenticeship, the prisoners learned how to be hard and unfeeling, qualities on which the whole concentration camp system was based and which were so carefully cultivated in the guards.

It would be difficult and even presumptuous to try to describe all changes worked in people by the Auschwitz environment, especially when one considers the inevitable diversity of individual reactions. The martyrdom of the Jewish people in the camps, the cruelest ordeal to which a human collectivity has ever been subjected, gave certain exceptional natures an opportunity to elevate their moral qualities to the heights of sublimity; they preserved their individual humanity in spite of and against everything. The circumstances were such, however, that their heroism could most of the time be expressed only in a stoic and resigned acceptance of a fate worse than death (inevitably followed in a short time by death itself). For the value of moral example, the crystallizing virtue that it possesses in human societies, was reduced to nothing in the camps. A Gandhi there would have been the object of general laughter. (13)

When one tries to define the dominant reaction of the prisoners, it is the general passivity which is most striking. The consequence of this, regardless of what group the prisoner belonged to, was apparently an absolute obedience, a perfect submission to the orders of the SS, their henchmen, block leaders, or Kapos. This obedience actually reached the point of automatism. Even if an order meant grave and sometimes directly fatal consequences for the prisoner, it was nonetheless carried out. This kind of behavior can best be understood with the help of a few examples. The "beret trick," an SS amusement in vogue at certain periods, consisted of snatching off a prisoner's cap and throwing it beyond the line of sentries into the zone where they had orders to fire on sight. He was then ordered to go and pick it up; prisoners regularly committed suicide in this way, such cases being listed as "killed while trying to escape." There were also the Kapos who would hand a prisoner a rope and order him to hang himself. It was normal at Auschwitz for such an order to be carried out. The writer M. Rusinek, in his book *Listy spod Morwy*, describes the case of a block leader one night ordering a poor unfortunate "to hang himself at midnight."

(13) The Jewish historian Wulff, who was himself a survivor of Auschwitz, relates how during a discussion he had in the camp with his fellow prisoner, B. Kautsky, the question had been raised: What would have become of Gandhi in the camp? The speakers agreed that, after having been the object of some of the coarse jokes and pranks in which the SS and the Kapos shared, he would have passed into the category of the "Moslems" in a few days, and would have succumbed at the first selection. . . .

When the time arrived, the victim, who slept next to his tyrant, got up and went slowly on tiptoe, so as not to waken his persecutor, and hanged himself. Other such cases are reported in numerous authentic testimonies.

Thus an act of disobedience became impossible, not because a healthy and rational prudence forbade it, or because one instinctively recoiled from it, but as the result of a flagrant violation of the laws of self-preservation. Between the imperatives of self-preservation and obedience, the latter proved the stronger. It was as if, under the terrible pressure of life in the camps, by a kind of psychic osmosis, the utter obedience that had been so consciously inculcated in the SS was communicated to their victims.

It may seem incredible that men could have been turned into such robots. But if we study other examples of prison life and organized suffering, we may perhaps discover indications of similar tendencies, less marked and developed only because they were produced by a system that was not so extremely cruel and all-embracing as the Nazi one.

Is it possible to give a psychological explanation of such behavior? An attempt has been made by Professor Bruno Bettelheim, a Viennese psychiatrist who spent a year as a prisoner in the Dachau and Buchenwald camps before the war. His interpretation is a psychoanalytic one and is specially relevant to the prisoners in the German camps in the years 1938–39; but it furnishes us, perhaps, with the beginning of an explanation for the behavior at Auschwitz. The shocks to which the prisoners were subjected, he says in substance, were so strange and terrible that they could not be assimilated by the normal psychic mechanisms, and their own existence seemed to the prisoners to be tinged with unreality. New psychic mechanisms had to be developed to enable them to adjust to the reality of the camp, their development being preceded by a regression to, a taking refuge in, purely infantile behavior. (Perhaps here we have put our finger on the methodology of the "re-education" so dear to the hearts of the SS.) This evolution, which was almost inevitable, according to the author, was favored by the camp environment. The system of collective punishment, by which an individual's least slip was harshly expiated by his entire block, if not by the camp itself, forced the prisoners to spy on one another and thus espouse the interests of the SS. "All the changes brought about by camp life seemed to cause the prisoner to regress to infantile attitudes and behavior, making him a more or less conscious instrument of the Gestapo." [90] The only possible way of finally adapting oneself to life in this infernal world was by an imperceptible but progressive acceptance of the SS universe and values. The author cites many examples of this; imitation of the SS embraced not only their brutality of feeling and cruel behavior, but also such details as vocabulary, general bearing, and dress, choice of amusements, and, insensibly, even the very ideas and sentiments that dominated in the dreadfully mutilated souls of the SS. This transformation required one to five years, according to Professor Bettelheim.

The survivors of Auschwitz who came in contact with the small group of veteran German prisoners at that camp confirm Professor Bettelheim's descriptions, and the kind of psychic evolution he analyzes would explain many of the things reported in this chapter. Such a transformation could only begin to take place in the few Jewish prisoners who managed to keep alive; the immense majority quickly traveled the steep road whose inevitable last stage was known in the camp as "Moslemization." This was the term used to describe the state of total debility which preceded death. Most prisoners arrived at this stage of incredible emaciation and utter mental languor after two months in the camp:

> When they could still walk, they moved like automatons; once stopped, they were capable of no further movement. They fell prostrate on the ground; nothing mattered any more to them. Their bodies blocked the passageway. You could step right on them and they wouldn't draw back their arms or legs an inch. No protest, no cry of pain came from their half-open mouths. And yet they were still alive. The Kapos, even the SS men, could beat and push them, but they would not budge; they had become insensible to everything. They were men without thoughts, without reactions, without souls, one might say. Sometimes, under the blows, they would suddenly start moving, like cattle, jostling against each other. Impossible to get them to tell their names, much less the date of their birth. Even gentleness was not enough to make them talk; they would only give you an expressionless stare. And when they tried to answer, their tongues could not touch their dessicated palates to produce sounds. You smelled

only a poisonous breath, as though it issued from entrails already in a state of decomposition.[91]

Such was the description that a former Buchenwald prisoner gave of the "Moslemized" prisoners transferred from Auschwitz to Buchenwald.

Although an average of 25 per cent of all Jewish deportees survived the first selection, scarcely 2 or 3 per cent of these returned to their homes; in general these were men with less than twelve or eighteen months of concentration camp life; 2,800 of the 110,000 Jews deported from France survived; 600 of the 90,000 deported from the Netherlands; 1,800 of the 60,000 deported from Greece, and so on. Among the different extermination methods perfected by the Nazi technicians of mass murder, that of immediate death in the gas chambers was by no means the cruelest.

CHAPTER NINE

The Jewish Resistance

THE PRECEDING PAGES have perhaps enabled the reader to understand how it was that the concentration camp slaves, under the pitiless compulsion which only modern techniques made possible, submitted passively to their fate, each playing the part and doing the particular jobs required for the functioning of the whole enterprise. Auschwitz and Treblinka, however, were only the last stages in a whole process. Before ending up there, the Jews of Europe, wherever Hitler's legions set foot, first went through a period of oppression and progressive debasement. In every occupied country they tried to defend themselves in all sorts of ways; despite their own weakness and the enemy's great strength, time and again they answered violence with violence and died defying their executioners. We shall now depict a few sides of that desperate struggle. But first it would seem necessary to answer a question that immediately comes to mind. How is it that the deeds of the Jewish Resistance, numerous and brilliant though they were, seem to be only the exceptions that prove the rule? How was it that several million men let themselves be led to the slaughterhouse without joining together in a final furious battle with their oppressors?—since their death warrant had been sealed, why did they not choose to die fighting?

This is certainly a rankling question for the Jewish people, who are ready either to overestimate and generalize legendary but isolated feats of arms, or to point resignedly to the impotence of the disarmed ghetto population. However, the wars in Israel have since shown the world what military virtues slumbered in the people of the dispersion; they sprang to life as soon as the Jews were allowed to establish a proper national life of their own. Perhaps we can agree to this, that traditional Judaism, the Judaism of the ghettos, allowed only a limited development of the military virtues and of the capacity for resisting force with force, assigning them a secondary place in its scale of values, and that this bitter but incontestable fact was an inevitable sociological result of the traditional Jewish position.

When one considers the Jewish history of the past thousand years, with its procession of humiliations and expulsions, funeral pyres and pogroms, it is possible to see in it a faint likeness to the world of concentration camps. In the latter case, however, a martyred group of people, rendered helpless by a scientific and unimaginably extreme persecution, was forced to bow and conform to the demands of their oppressors; this was no simple medieval persecution, nor were these the medieval Jews who created their own Jewish values and sublimated their checked and bounded passions by retiring within themselves behind the ghetto walls. Though they abstained from answering blows with blows, and lacked all military tradition, the Jewish people, by their fidelity to the Law and their refusal to accept conversions imposed with fire and sword, reached the summit of human heroism. There are pages of Jewish history unknown to Christians and unappreciated by the Jews, in which one reads about the voluntary burning of the Rhenish ghettos by its inhabitants, who preferred death to forswearing their faith when attacked by the Crusaders; about the sublime obstinacy of the Spanish Jews during the Inquisition, echoed two centuries later by the Polish Jews martyred by Bogdan Chmielnicki. Such martyrdom was a kind of ethical choice, for there was always the alternative of baptism; this ethical quality gave it its historical meaning and exemplary value, cementing and consolidating the faith of an uprooted and scattered people.

The biological exterminators of the twentieth century allowed the Jews no such alternative. They struck, moreover, during a transitional period of Jewish history, when the bonds of the traditional faith had already slackened and the ghetto walls were crumbling; when for decades ever increasing numbers of people had taken the path of assimilation to the surrounding society, the Zionist movement, in which the Jewish national glories found renewed expression, being a corollary and reaction to the movement of assimilation. But if the ancestral faith and practices lost hold more and more, traditional national characteristics still endured; and among these was the tendency, which is no special trait of the Jews but manifests itself in all oppressed minorities, to rely on compromise, patient waiting, diplomacy and guile, rather than open, armed resistance. The heroic memory of the Maccabees, solemnly celebrated every year, burned in vain in the hearts of young Jews; real life, with its long series of insults and malicious humiliations, soon taught them that hitting back openly was not for them. For this reason the Jews only rarely put up an organized defense to the pogroms let loose against them in Tsarist Russia at the turn of the century. With anguish Bialik, the Jewish national poet, apostrophized the sons of his humiliated people:

> Do not pity them! the whip has burned them,
> But they are used to sorrow and intimate with shame.
> Too unfortunate to be blamed,
> Fallen too low to be pitied. (1)

Even in the Western, "assimilated" Jews, who, it would seem, had merged completely with the society around them, certain residues of the past might persist in their own fashion. As for the Eastern Jews, the Jews of the ghetto, they had neither a military tradition nor a military psychology, still less, therefore, those techniques, cadre groups, and hidden stores of submachine guns and revolvers with which the partisans of the forests and the maquis were provided. Many German documents reflect this impotence of the Jews, which to the Nazis seemed complete. "I had warned my men to load their guns, since we were not dealing with Jews," were the words with which an SS lieutenant tried to deny that he was the person responsible for the outbreak of a group of Russian prisoners who, risking everything at the moment of their execution, tore the weapons out of the hands of their executioners and fled into the fields.[1] The contract between General Globocnick and Toebbens, the clothing contractor, for the hiring out of Jewish slaves from the Warsaw ghetto and also a number of Polish prisoners, stipulated in paragraph 9: "The Poles are to be quartered separately and placed under much stricter SS guard."[2]

(1) "The City of Slaughter," 1905.

Physical courage is a more complex notion than one would think. During these years Jewish solidarity could manifest itself in certain social and humanitarian activities that did not require open resistance, but which ran exactly the same risks. This was what is generally called "passive resistance": the fabrication of false papers, seeking out of hiding places, rescuing of children, laying out of escape routes, etc. Many Jews who showed prodigious heroism in this field refused more or less consciously to take the last step into open rebellion, often enough out of crippling fear of the terrible reprisals that would be visited on all the Jews collectively.

If further explanation were needed for the passivity of the Jews, we find it in the way the Nazis managed things. For not only was there a huge disproportion between the strength of the Jews and that of their oppressors, but the former generally did not realize what this "final solution" was that the Nazis were getting ready for them. Proof of this is to be found in the fact that a resistance worthy of the name arose amongst the Jews only when a knowledge of the death camps became widespread. There was resistance in Poland, but not in Hungary, where the Jews remained ignorant of the fate awaiting them at Auschwitz. Most often, too, those who fought back were a minority of survivors whose eyes had been opened by the tragic end of the majority. We have seen how the Germans taxed their ingenuity to keep their victims in the dark until the last hour in the gas chambers. The alternative in the minds of the Jews was not between succumbing passively or dying in a last outburst of resistance; it was between dying—or keeping alive by adapting themselves to the circumstances. And the latter course, as we have seen, accorded best with habits and tendencies imposed by the historic defenselessness of the Jewish position that went back a thousand years. Who has the right to pass judgment on them? In conclusion, we should remind ourselves of the terrible practical difficulties that faced any attempt at organized resistance within the amorphous masses of the ghetto: the hunger, physical debility, the general hostility of the surrounding population, especially the Poles, and the fantastic overcrowding of the ghettos, which represented a well-nigh insuperable obstacle to the conduct of conspiratorial activities.

Considering all this, it is to the eternal glory of European Jewry that it could produce, in the hour of its agony, men and groups who knew how to fight and die with weapons in their hands.

It is significant that it was the Zionist circles which most often gave rise to the various Jewish resistance movements that sprang up almost everywhere in Europe. The Germans made no mistake about this. General Stroop, commander of the German troops during the battle of the Warsaw ghetto, constantly mentioned in his reports "the Chalutz movement," [3] and Eichmann himself, at the time of the Hungarian deportations,[4] raged against the Zionists, "human material of great biological value." Not that the Zionists acted according to over-all instructions coming to them from a center; their initiative was always scattered, spontaneous, and local. The leaders could hardly keep up their few and infrequent contacts, via Constantinople or Geneva, with the Jewish authorities in Palestine. At most, it can be said in explanation that the closed groups, cells, and training centers, or *kibbutzim*, in which these Jews had chosen to live before the war made them better fitted for concerted and conspiratorial action. More important, however, was the concrete and definite Jewish national ideal which shaped their actions beyond all personal, family, or even humanitarian considerations and cut short all hesitation. This ideal directed and animated their actions and gave them their deeper meaning. And has not the experience of the last war shown once again that whatever the slogans, policies, or ideologies, the people fight and die only for a national ideal?

The European resistance movements pose many difficult problems for future historians. Their secrecy, for one thing, their dispersed and scattered organization, for another, were essential conditions for their success. The whole story is composed of many threads which must be reconstituted and traced back one by one, principally with the aid of memoirs and retrospective narratives. The same difficulties, only more of them, confront any chronicler of the Jewish Resistance, which varied so according to the country and region, and of which few, if any, survivors remain. The most we can do in the following pages is to recall a few of the most striking episodes, or those that lend themselves best to exact reconstruction.

The Battle of the Warsaw Ghetto

Ever since the First World War, Poland had been the principal training ground for the young pioneers, or *chalutzim*, who created Jewish Palestine by draining the swamps and reclaiming the desert. But if many were called, few were chosen. While waiting for their turn to enter the Promised Land, tens of thousands of young men and women, living in agricultural or artisan groups, did preparatory work in their countries of origin. When the Jews were herded into the ghettos, these *kibbutzim* struggled to keep together. In some special cases, the German authorities approved the keeping together of certain groups, because of the amount of work they could turn out. Among other matters, the idea of armed resistance was sometimes discussed by these ardent young people. But before the program for the "final solution" was set in motion, dominant Jewish opinion held that it was necessary to conserve Jewish blood and strength for the reconquest of Palestine.

The most effective Jewish-organized resistance came from these cells. It is important to note that they were not alone. In the Warsaw ghetto, with which the following pages are concerned, other movements and parties also led a secret existence: the Bund, (2) for example, or the Communist Party, which published clandestine newspapers and plotted armed resistance. Old political rivalries continued to make themselves felt, but no group had weapons. When the Warsaw leaders of the *chalutzim* proposed to the other political groups in the ghetto that they unite for the supreme resistance after the start of deportations in June 1942, the majority thought the time had not yet come, that they had to await "the development of events." The *chalutzim* then tried to organize their own combat organization, whose arms, at the time of the establishment, consisted of a single revolver. Some weeks later other clandestine movements joined the Zionists. A coordinating committee was established, including representatives of all the political parties, and having contact with the Polish Resistance—an essential condition for obtaining arms and ammunition. Mordecai Anielewicz, a twenty-four-year-old Zionist, was put at the head of the Jewish

(2) Jewish Socialist Party of Eastern Europe, especially important at the beginning of the century. The Bund's program was opposed to Zionism.

combat organization, which was thus finally unified. At the time, the ghetto population, reduced by nine-tenths, numbered only about 50,000 men. But it included a large proportion of young, able-bodied workers. The well-organized chalutz units, who had been provided with false papers and money, had been relatively spared.

In the fall of 1942—that fall in which the German "actions" ravaged, one after another, the last Polish ghettos—feverish and se-cret activities went on in the Warsaw ghetto. The German adminis-tration had ordered anti-aircraft shelters to be set up in the city, and the ghetto population profited from this decision to dig a net-work of camouflaged hiding places with false entrances deep under the earth; certain of these were quite elaborate, with baths, toilets, arrangements for lodging entire families, ammunition depots, and food supplies for supporting a long siege. This underground later served as the main base for the Jewish combat group. For the mo-ment the latter's principal task consisted of procuring arms, and these could only come from the "Aryan" part of Warsaw. After 1942 a few revolvers and grenades were forthcoming from the Polish Communist Party, but the "Armia Krajowa," the principal organization of Polish resistance, was reluctant, if not hostile, and additional revolvers, a few rifles, and several pounds of dynamite, had to be bought with gold from traffickers and German or Italian deserters. Endless obstacles had to be overcome to smuggle in even a single weapon into a ghetto that was closely guarded and swarm-ing with spies. For this young girls of "Aryan" appearance—blond hair and blue eyes—were used. Several hundred Jewish fighters trained secretly in the shelters. When the resistance group executed several spies, the zeal of the agents of the Germans in the ghetto was moderated somewhat. On August 22, Joseph Szerynski, an apostate Jew who commanded the ghetto's Jewish police, was mor-tally wounded by Israel Kanal, a young fighter. Despite its small numbers and few weapons, the Jewish combat group soon became a power in the ghetto. The rich Jews—there were still some of them left—no longer refused funds for arms and food. "I no longer have any authority in the ghetto; the Jewish combat group rules here," Mark Lichtenbaum, successor to Tcherniakov as head of the Jewish council, admitted to the Nazis. We have already quoted Toebbens' astonishing appeal to the ghetto workers when he was trying to discredit the Jewish Resistance in the eyes of his workers. (Vichy talked the same way about the Free French.) Thus the Germans could hardly have been ignorant of the preparations the Jews were making.

Toebbens and the other German contractors had only an economic interest in the ghetto, whereas the essential question for the SS was a security one. Warsaw was a way station of prime importance for the eastern front; serious trouble in the ghetto, if it spread to other parts of the city, might have threatened the Wehrmacht's supplies.[5] We have already seen in what terms Himmler spoke about the "pacification" of Warsaw. However, especially at the beginning, the SS scarcely imagined that the Jews would put up a serious fight. So they used a simple police operation in the "action" style to try and empty the ghetto in January 1943.

The opposition they met was strong enough to force them to call a halt. For the first time, German detachments entering the ghetto were met by salvos of shots. A laconic remark by the SS General Stroop, who completed the operation three months later, in his detailed report indicates that hidden pressures were exerted by the German ghetto contractors to stop the evacuation. "Carrying out the order proved difficult," Stroop wrote, "for the company heads as well as the Jews opposed the evacuation by every means." [6] These slave traders must certainly have been frightened by the disaster that threatened their industries. The operation was postponed. Only 6,500 Jews, deceived by the usual promises, let themselves be evacuated voluntarily.

Though of little intrinsic importance, this first clash had a considerable moral effect. It fired the zeal of the Jewish fighters; it also impelled the "Armia Krajowa" to provide the ghetto with less contemptible assistance. Fifty revolvers, 50 grenades, and 5 kilos of explosives were received from the "A. K." on February 2, 1943. WRN, a clandestine Socialist organization, made possible the purchase of 2,000 liters of gasoline, a stock of potassium chloride, and other material necessary for making primitive explosives. The chemist Klepfisz, a Bundist, after a period of instruction in the ranks of the WRN, taught the defenders how to manufacture rudimentary grenades.

Thus this last delay gained by the ghetto permitted its defenders to carry further their final preparations. The fighters were organized in twenty-two combat groups, of thirty men each. Each group was assigned to a certain sector or block. (3) Because of the lack of weapons, however, the number of armed men was no more than a few hundred. The other fighting group (Jewish Military Union, ZZW) was better armed and numbered also several hundred men.

Certainly the Jewish leaders had no illusion about the outcome. None of that hope which encouraged the other resistance fighters was permitted them: neither dreams of victory nor the expectation of saving their own lives. They were animated solely by a lucid resolve to preserve their human dignity, to die fighting, and to save their Jewish honor. Some lines from a farewell letter which one of them, Mordecai Tenenbaum, was able to send his sister in Palestine, show the clear-eyed way in which they advanced to meet· their fate.

> The second "action" began on January 19. . . . The block of our kibbutz in Zamenhof Street defended itself for two days. It was destroyed by explosion. All letters and telegrams addressed to Wanda's friends remained unanswered. (4) Absolute silence. This meant that she was no longer alive.
>
> In a few days (or weeks) I shall be with her. Her death was that of all of us. Will anybody ever know the story of our heroic struggle? Will they understand how we lived under the Hitlerite oppression?
>
> . . . We shall all disappear without a trace. Itzhak is gone. Zywia and Franka, too. Also all the Shomers. (5) (I think that your Rosh Hagdud (6) was called Schmuel—we had burned the house in Leszno Street together—he was shot a month later. Yes. The last. Our men look at me a little beseechingly and with a little shame: "Not yet— next time, perhaps. . . ." How men want to live!) That is all.
>
> A pleasant conversation, isn't it? I am leaving you, then, keep well. Each of you must really replace a hundred others. The devil alone knows what will happen. But that is no longer our business.
>
> Wait, wait, that's not all. Another one has gone. If only at least he had remained, Itzhak Katzenelson. (7) You have certainly heard

(3) Of the twenty-two groups, fourteen were made up of members from the different Zionist and chalutz movements; four groups belonged to the Bund, four to the Communist PPR.

(4) Wanda was another sister of Tenenbaum's, also a member of the resistance organization.

(5) Members of the Shomer Hatzair ("Young Watchman") chalutz group.

(6) "Troop leader"—the head of a chalutz unit.

(7) One of the best poets writing in the Yiddish language, who disappeared at Auschwitz.

of him. His work before the war doesn't count. He did not interest me then. But the Katzenelson of the Warsaw ghetto, the one who worked and created with us, the one who cursed and called for vengeance, he became our brother. . . . All that we thought, felt, or imagined, he wrote about. He cursed, prophesied, hated better than Bialik. We furnished him with the debris of our misery, and he made it eternal, sang of it, it was our common property. He is no longer alive. I hid his verses at Warsaw; God knows if you will ever read them.

Now it is really all. Tomorrow the deportation begins. (8) If I really saw the necessity for it, we could—at the cost of my dignity—see each other again. But I do not want to. It must not be so.

Let come what may!

And you won't cry, will you? That won't help at all. I know what it's like.

Mordecai

On April 19, 1943, General Jürgen Stroop launched the final operation against the ghetto. This time the Germans attacked in force; Stroop commanded more than 2,000 elite troops, a detachment of engineers, tanks, and a battery of light artillery. Opposing him were several hundred men armed with revolvers and grenades; as his report says, he counted on finishing the action in three days at most.

It was a strange battle. The defenders were hermetically sealed off from the outside world behind the ghetto wall. No weapons were parachuted to them. No army advanced to liberate them. The Russian lines (this was just after Stalingrad) were still more than a thousand kilometers away. No "hinterland," no countryside, no forest into which they could retreat. Indifferent or hostile populations surrounded them; outside the ghetto, Polish holiday crowds celebrated Easter 1943. The cellars, shelters, and sewers were the only places to which they could fall back.

Stroop's detachments entered the ghetto at dawn. (9) A sustained fusillade greeted them. Some German soldiers fell and two tanks were set on fire. The SS set about taking the Jewish strong

(8) This letter was written from Bialystok, where Tenenbaum had been sent by his organization to instruct the resistance group that had been formed there. As we shall later see, Tenenbaum died at Bialystok in August 1943.

(9) The following data are based essentially on the daily telegrams Stroop sent to his superior, General Katzmann, copies of which were attached to his report: "The Warsaw Ghetto Is No More!"

points one by one. A few house blocks were captured by assault, but the defenders escaped over the roofs or through the cellars and joined the other strong points. In many places, the Germans were forced to retreat. From the very first day they had to use artillery and flame-throwers.

This first day had scarcely any results for the Germans, nor the next either. On the evening of the second day, Anielewicz sent this short note to his adjutant: "What we have lived through in two days of defense cannot be described in words. The reality has surpassed our wildest dreams. The Germans have retreated twice. One of our sectors held out for forty minutes; another, six hours. . . . I feel that big things have been done and that what we have attempted was of great importance." [7]

Not until two days later, after having succeeded in clearing out a section of the ghetto, was Stroop able to "evacuate" 5,000 unarmed inhabitants. When no noticeable result had been attained in the allotted period of time, Stroop was roundly reprimanded by Himmler, and two days later he ordered the "complete destruction by fire of the blocks of Jewish houses, including those attached to the armament factories." (10) In other words, all the factories and houses in the ghetto were systematically set afire without regard to the complaints of the slave traders, who now saw a definite end being put to the source of their extraordinary profits. "We noticed again that although the fire was much more dangerous, the Jews preferred to go back into it, rather than fall into our hands," Stroop observed the next day.[8] In another place, he noted that "during the battle, the women in the combat groups were armed just like the men and some of them belonged to the chalutz movement. It was not rare to see these women pulling the triggers of revolvers with both hands. Often they hid revolvers and grenades in their bloomers until the last minute and then used them against the Waffen SS or the Wehrmacht." [9] However, the new tactics facilitated the evacuation of the unarmed workers. Two days later more than 20,000 were sent to Trawniki, where they were exterminated the following November.

(10) This quotation, as well as those that follow, is taken from the report: "The Warsaw Ghetto Is No More!"

The battle changed its character and went completely underground. Down in their shelters, jammed in with women and children, harassed and suffocating, the defenders continued, in a Dantesque atmosphere, to offer savage resistance. On the German side, mechanical drills, dynamite, and gas shells replaced the artillery and tanks. The sewers were flooded. Police dogs were unleashed. Skillful torture was applied to prisoners to make them reveal the principal shelters. These were demolished one by one under conditions whose horror we can glimpse from Stroop's report. "No one would have expected to find living people there. Nevertheless, we found a series of casemates in which the heat is furnace-hot." (May 6) "The best and only way to wipe out the Jews is by fire," he commented the next day, adding: "These creatures understand that they have only two possibilities: to hide as long as they can, or to come out trying to kill or wound the largest possible number of soldiers and Waffen SS men." On May 8 the headquarters shelter of the Jewish combat group was captured and most of the defenders, including Anielewicz, took their own lives.

Little by little the organized Jewish resistance was extinguished, a resistance improvised under conditions that defy description and of which there is no other example in history. On May 16 Stroop declared major operations over and, after dynamiting the big synagogue (one of the few remaining buildings), he withdrew his troops from what had been the ghetto. The battle had lasted four weeks, during which more than two thousand picked German soldiers had been tied up; the German war industry lost one of its most important supply centers in the east. The figures of the German losses will never be known exactly. (11) An echo of the con-

(11) In his report, Stroop gave the following figures: fourteen SS officers and men killed, sixty-seven wounded; two Polish police auxiliaries killed, fifteen wounded. At the time, considerably higher figures, running to hundreds of dead Germans, were given out by a clandestine Jewish source. Can Stroop have minimized his losses? When questioned after his capture, he stated: "I no longer remember the number of German losses. . . . The Polish police losses were higher than officially admitted." (*Bleter far Geszichte*, nos. 3-4, August-December, 1948, p. 183)

However, the reasoning by which certain Jewish historians attempt to prove that German losses were much greater than Stroop's figures seems inconclusive. Whatever the understandable passion of the chroniclers, some of whom were

cern that the ghetto revolt caused in the highest Nazi circles may
be found in Goebbels' personal diary, May 1, 1943:

> The extremely bitter fighting at Warsaw between our police forces,
> and the Wehrmacht itself, and the rebellious Jews should be noted.
> The Jews have succeeded in making the ghetto a kind of fortified
> position.
> Fierce fighting is in progress and the Jewish high command even
> publishes daily communiqués. This joke isn't going to last long. But
> one sees what the Jews can do when they are armed.[10]

The diary came back to this subject several times. Only on May
22 did Goebbels write: "The Warsaw ghetto battle continues; the
Jews are still fighting. But it can now be said that on the whole
this resistance is no longer dangerous and is virtually broken."

The great majority of the ghetto defenders died during the battle.
A few dozen at most succeeded in escaping through the sewers and
joining partisan groups. A few other groups continued for weeks
and months to lead a ghost-like life in the ghetto ruins, hunted by
German patrols, continually changing their hiding places and sup-
plying themselves from caches that had survived the dynamite and
fire. Some of these men held out, apparently, until the fall of 1943;
a few isolated cases by miraculous luck after numberless adventures
finally found refuge on the "Aryan" side and lived through the war.
As for the ghetto ruins, they were carefully razed to the ground by
teams of Jewish prisoners brought from Auschwitz especially for
the purpose.

THE RESISTANCE IN THE OTHER POLISH GHETTOS
THE JEWISH PARTISANS

Jewish resistance in the other ghettos followed the main outlines
of the epic of the Warsaw ghetto. Everywhere the idea of active
resistance had been passionately embraced by a few minds from
the moment the ghettos were created; but the idea died stillborn,
because of the general passivity, the opposition of the Jewish councils, and lack of arms and means of action, not to be revived again

---

eyewitnesses, the question is basically of secondary importance. The epic of
the Warsaw ghetto will not live in the memory of man just because of the
number of German losses.

until 1942 when the extermination campaign began. "Combat organizations" were then set up, and were directed and coordinated by former Zionist, Communist, or Bundist political leaders. The power of the councils was broken, and stocks of weapons were accumulated in the face of a thousand difficulties. Communication among the ghettos was maintained as far as was possible. But the very excess of German savagery often had the effect of putting off or even paralysing entirely the outbreak of revolt; situations arose in which just the most determined ghetto fighters were deterred by the most high-minded scruples. One example of such a situation comes to us from the Vilna ghetto, where a united Jewish resistance organization existed from the beginning of 1942. Under the leadership of an energetic chief, Itzik Vitenberg, a few hundred armed Jewish youths got ready to fight just as soon as the deportations began. During 1942, however, the Germans learned from an informer of the existence of the organization and also the name of its leader. They demanded the latter's surrender; if not, they threatened to have the ghetto bombarded by a squadron of planes. Panicky and despairing, even some of the members of the combat group thought that Vitenberg should surrender. Torn by scruples, though apparently convinced of the futility of the gesture, Vitenberg agreed; he surrendered and was executed the next day. The organization was now leaderless; instead of making a last stand in the ghetto, as Vitenberg had planned, its members escaped in little groups and formed a band of partisans under the direction of a new chief, the poet Abba Kovner.[11]

Because of the innumerable difficulties of raising the banner of revolt within the ghetto, Jewish rebels in other ghettos from the first tried to carry the battle to the outside. This was the case with a group formed in Cracow, seat of the Government General; it organized a series of attempts against the German troops stationed in the city at the end of 1942. Here again the active core was a group of young Zionists, led by an admirable couple, Szymszon and Justyna Draenger, members of the "Akiba" movement. For several weeks the bombings and individual attacks planned by the group created havoc among the Germans in Cracow. In February 1943 the Gestapo succeeded in getting its agents into the organization and its members were almost all captured. Szymszon and Justyna

Draenger, who were captured and escaped from prison, were recaptured in November 1943.[12]

Bialystok is another example of an attempt at concerted resistance in the ghetto itself. This big industrial city in eastern Poland
served the Wehrmacht as an important supply center after its capture in July 1941. Whereas the Jews of the region were exterminated at the end of the year, the ghetto, with nearly 40,000 inhabitants, lasted almost two years more. An "Anti-Fascist Committee"
sprang up in February 1942 within the Jewish working population,
out of which came a combat organization. The arms that it succeeded in collecting, though plainly quite rudimentary, were apparently somewhat more formidable than elsewhere. In December
1942 the Warsaw Coordinating Committee sent Mordecai Tenenbaum, Anielewicz's former aide, to Bialystok to lead the resistance.

In February 1943 a big "action" aimed at the children, the sick,
and the aged was begun at Bialystok by the Germans. The combat
group was unsuccessful in setting off a general ghetto uprising; only
a few skirmishes took place. The minutes of a meeting held by the
ghetto *chalutzim* a few days later have been preserved. Here are
extracts that reveal the tragic dilemma that confronted these young
Jews:

> *Mordecai* (Mordecai Tenenbaum): "It is good that at least the
> general morale has not deteriorated, though unfortunately today's
> meeting will not be a joyful one. You may consider it a historical
> occurrence, a tragic episode. We who are gathered here are the last
> *chalutzim* of Poland, all about us are corpses. Have you heard of
> the fate of Warsaw? None remained alive. The same in Bedzin,
> Czestochowa, and probably everywhere else. We are the last. This is
> not a very pleasant feeling. This puts upon us a special responsibility.
> We must decide today what to do tomorrow. To sit in an atmosphere
> of regret makes no sense. Simply awaiting death without resistance
> is also not sensible. What, then, are we to do?
>
> "We face two possibilities. We may decide that the assault on the
> first Jew in Bialystok shall be the spark to counteraction, that from to-
> morrow on, nobody should go to work in the shops; we may even
> forbid the seeking of shelter during the action. All would be mobilized.
> We can manage it so that no Germans should leave the ghetto alive,
> that no factory should remain intact. It is not entirely improbable
> that after such accomplishments some of us might by chance remain
> alive. Whatever the outcome, we could fight to the end.
>
> "On the other hand, we can flee to the forest. Let us weigh the

possibilities realistically. Today, two people went there to examine the terrain. But whatever our decision, after today's meeting, military discipline will be introduced. We alone must decide on all matters. Our fathers will not worry about us. We are orphaned. If anybody imagines that there are real possibilities of remaining alive and he wishes to make use of these possibilities, let him suit himself. We will help him as far as possible. Let everyone decide for himself about his own personal fate, but our cause is a common one. We must act collectively. I do not want to coerce anybody into accepting my point of view. That is why I abstain at present from declaring myself one way or the other."

Henoch: "Let us have no illusions. Complete liquidation will be our share. We have the choice of but two kinds of death, for neither resistance in the ghetto nor in the forest will preserve our lives. All that remains is to die with dignity. . . . It is clear that in the forest there are greater chances for revenge. To go to the forest means not to live off the peasants, but to organize there an active partisan war."

Yocheved: "Why speak so much of death? A soldier on the front, a partisan in the forest thinks of life not of death. It is necessary to join the attack from the forest."

Dorka: "In the forest there are greater possibilities of revenge but we wish to die with dignity. We must not scatter in the woods like stray beggars, but remain there as active partisans. . . ."

Etl: "In the next few days, if there should be a German 'action,' then there is but one conclusion—counteraction. If on the other hand there should remain at our disposal a longer span of time, then we ought to make preparations for going to the forests."

Mordecai in conclusion: "The stand taken by the assembled comrades is clear. We will do everything possible to enable as many as can be mobilized for this purpose to join the partisan war in the forest. Everyone else from our midst who remains in the ghetto will have to react with the first attack on a Jew. There is no desire in us to bargain for life, but it is necessary to face objective conditions. The most important thing is to preserve to the last the dignity of the members of our Movement. . . ." [13]

In the woods the "objective conditions" Tenenbaum spoke of proved to be unfavorable, and most of the fighters stayed on in the ghetto. The final "action" was undertaken by the Germans six months later on August 17, 1943. Begun without warning during the night, it took the Jews by surprise and, despite the zeal of the defenders, here too the majority of the inhabitants let themselves be driven along by the SS whips. Concentrating at a few "strategic points," the combat group fought a last battle that lasted several hours, and then tried a sortie that crumpled under machine-gun fire. The defenders then withdrew to their underground shelters, where they were able to hold out for a few more days. As at Warsaw, a few finally escaped into the neighboring woods.

The formation of partisan groups outside the ghettos was terribly difficult for the Jews. Imbued with an ineradicable anti-Semitism, the Polish partisan bands did not welcome Jews into their ranks. But to set up independent Jewish partisan groups that would be lacking in those local connections which everywhere helped and supported the maquis was almost always a desperate undertaking for these city-dwellers. They not only had to hide their activities, but also their very existence. The country swarmed with informers; the hunt for Jews was made the more appealing for a large part of the population by the rewards offered by the Germans. Detailed and painfully elaborated preparations would fail at the last minute. A German report recalls one of these attempts, which occurred in the Lwow area; about twenty Jews were getting ready to escape from the Lwow ghetto and join a partisan group; they were furnished with false papers and had eight pistols and an automatic rifle. But they fell into the hands of the SS when their truck driver, an Italian, denounced them. A close interrogation of the arrested Jews revealed that a man named Horowitz, who was hiding in the woods near Brody with a large group of Jews, had organized the flight. "Following the interrogation, we were able to locate the spot, and on the same day the gendarmerie, the Ukrainian police, and two companies of the Wehrmacht were sent to surround and clean out the region." At a very small cost, the report states (one Polish game warden killed, one SS wounded), the operation was quickly carried out.[14]

However, some groups were able to act with effect, like the "Vilna Avengers," the survivors of the Vitenberg organization, who kept to the woods with about 400 men and women until the Russians arrived, dynamiting trains and attacking isolated patrols; or the Tobias Belski "division," which operated farther south in the Lida region. It had only six armed men at the end of 1941, more than 100 the following spring, and finally included more than 1,000 Jews, 600 of them fighters. A veritable free Jewish city had sprung up near the end of the war in the forests of White Russia, a refuge for escaped Jews, which the local peasants called "Jerusalem." These, too, held out until the Red Army arrived. Because of this we have been able to learn the story of their exploits.

How many other individual or group epics, cut short or carried to a rough consummation, have remained unknown? A witness has related that on the day of the final "action," the Jews of the city of Tulczin set their ghetto afire and perished in the flames, recalling the medieval example of the Rhenish ghettos at the time of the Crusades. It was the same story, apparently, at Dvinsk in Latvia where, as a German report reveals, "the Jews started so many fires that a large part of the city was destroyed." [15] Astonishing accounts of isolated feats can be found, or veiled references to "camouflaged" Jews who slipped into the German administrations or even into the army to spy and sabotage until the day of inevitable denunciation. It was perhaps in circumstances like these, where skillful dissembling was called for, that the Polish Jews acted with most effect. Sometimes the German reports throw some light on these obscure figures: "The inquest on the fire that broke out in the Reich fur factory at Kovno has shown that sabotage and theft were committed one after the other. . . . It has also been established that the factory superintendent, supposedly a German, was a pure-blooded Jew." [16] Other episodes we know about from Jewish survivors, such as the odyssey of young Szmuel Rufhajzen, hired as an interpreter for the Kommandantur of the Polish city of Mir, then promoted to gendarme, who not only warned his brothers in the ghetto of imminent "actions," but even gave them weapons until the very day he was caught.[17]

Belski, like the "Vilna Avengers," operated in the eastern part of old Poland, that is, the section annexed by the USSR in the 1939 partition. Beyond the Polish area proper, the obstacles in the way of Jewish partisan action were no longer insurmountable. The White Russians, in particular, were not contaminated with anti-Semitism to the same degree as the Poles. Still farther east, in the USSR proper, where twenty-five years of Soviet rule had partly wiped out traditional differences and race hatreds, and where assimilation had made large advances, the Jews played a major role in the partisan battles. German documents and reports underline this fact with sadistic cheerfulness and a pertinacity that the aims and necessities of propaganda cannot explain. "The sabotage and fires that began shortly after the entry of German troops into Latvia were for the most part caused or carried out by Jews." [18] "Two hours after the Jews in Ushomir had been shot, four Jews entered the city and burned forty-eight houses. At Zhitomir, the Ukrainian militia was fired upon by Jewish partisans." [19] "At Nikolaiev, too, the Jews led the resistance after the entry of German troops." [20] And Goebbels exclaimed, when mentioning the Russian situation in his diary: "Everywhere the Jews fan the flames and cause revolts." [21] But we lack all details about these Jewish guerrillas; moreover, Soviet historiography tries to conceal the "ethnic allegiance" of its partisans and guerrillas.

THE JEWISH RESISTANCE IN WESTERN EUROPE

A report by the Reich prosecutor for the "People's Tribunal" reveals that "on May 18, 1942, Jewish malefactors placed an incendiary bomb in the Soviet Paradise exhibit in Berlin."

> The Jews who took part in this attempt have been tried and condemned to death. The Gestapo investigation established that those condemned after the attempt belonged to two organized Jewish groups which, during 1941 and 1942, collected contributions, spread Communist teachings, distributed and exchanged agitational tracts, and were preparing to print and distribute other such works. Moreover, these groups secured *Ausweise* from French workers to facilitate the clandestine stay of their members in Berlin.
>
> Thirteen Jews between the ages of nineteen and twenty-three are still under preventive arrest. Seven of the accused took flight. The members of the second group will be tried soon.[22]

This report gives the only information we have about the affair. How did they fight and what kind of hopes did they cherish, these anonymous fighters out of the very depths of the Hitlerian night? Were there other such organizations? We are completely in the dark and probably shall always be. Only small clandestine organizations could arise among the scattered Jews of Central Europe, with very limited possibilities for action. Generally no trace of them has survived.

In the occupied countries of the west, conditions were certainly more favorable for a Jewish resistance of some scope. But the situation was such that a specifically Jewish resistance was not called for. For stout-hearted fellows, there were a thousand opportunities to fight the invader side by side with and in the same way as their non-Jewish comrades. Exact statistics are unavailable, but an accounting like David Knout's, in his book, *La Résistance juive*, shows that in France, for example, the proportion of Jews in all echelons of the resistance organizations varied between 15 and 30 per cent. (12) Among them we find many figures of the first rank, whose deeds are already a part of history—men like José Aboulker, a young Algerian Jewish medical student, who at the age of twenty-two organized the resistance in Algiers which made the American landing possible, or André Manuel, one of the leaders of the B.C.R.A. in London, the right hand of the famous Colonel de Wavrin-Passy. Others who are less well-known are just as deserving of honor, as for instance the Russian Jew Albert Kohan, co-founder of the "Liberation" movement, who won a parachutist's rating at the age of sixty-four and died shortly afterwards in a stupid flying accident; or the French Jew Jacques Bingen, General de Gaulle's representative in the Occupied Zone, who committed suicide when captured in May 1944 rather than betray his comrades. But to cite them all would be to write a history of the French resistance.

Another aspect of Jewish Resistance in France concerns the more specifically Jewish organizations founded by recent and as yet imperfectly assimilated immigrants. One of these Jews was the first victim of the German courts in France: on August 27, 1940, Israel Leizer Karp was shot at Bordeaux. He was an isolated individual who committed an apparently absurd and yet most symbolic act—armed only with a club, he attacked a detachment of German soldiers marching along in goose step.[23] A few months later, well-organized movements arose in both the occupied and free zones. In Paris, Jewish guerrillas and partisans carried out a number of attacks, some of them among the most important of the Resistance, in particular the execution in September, 1943, of Ritter, Gauleiter Sauckel's representative in France. This was the work of a nineteen-year-old partisan, Marcel Rayman. In the Southern Zone, the Jewish

(12) David Knout, *Contribution à l'histoire de la résistance juive en France*, Paris, Publications of the C.D.J.C., 1947.

Union for Resistance and Mutual Aid spread a network from Lyon to Toulouse and from Limoges to Nice; it had sections for sabotage, propaganda, false papers, etc. "Jewish maquis" sprang up, the best known of which is the Jewish Scouts, a Zionist group. All these organizations were busy at the same time with setting up escape routes, undercover work, and fabricating false papers—in a word with that passive resistance of which we have already spoken.

Just as in France, and wherever circumstances elsewhere made it possible, in Holland, Belgium, and in Italy, the Jews played an essential and sometimes preponderant role in the resistance movements. And yet was there a Jewish resistance, properly speaking? Though the Hitler persecutions gave the outlawed and hunted Jews their own special reasons for joining the resistance ranks, they fought for the common cause on terms of perfect equality with their brothers-in-arms. In the last analysis, one must look to Jewish Palestine for examples of an integrally national Jewish resistance. In this connection, perhaps no feat of arms will ever equal the extraordinary action of a handful of young Palestinians who parachuted into Hungary and Rumania in 1944 in order to establish contact and bring some words of comfort and hope to a European Jewry in its last death throes. This exploit, though without great practical significance, had a high symbolic value. Many of these Palestinians, including the young poetess Hanna Senesch and the Jewish national hero Enzo Sereni, were captured by the Germans and executed.[24]

CHAPTER TEN

"More Rational Exploitation"

WITH A CONCERN FOR DETAIL that may seem tedious to many, we have tried to reconstitute the birth and development of the idea of systematic and complete genocide. Many of its aspects are still inadequately explained; we know for certain, however, that the plan was originated and decided upon by the very small group of Nazi leaders—Hitler, Goebbels, Heydrich, and certainly Bormann—who best understood the deep meaning of the hellish cataclysm that was let loose. They found zealous, ardent, and enthusiastic workers at every level, from Eichmann down to the lowest SS man. But other Nazi chiefs, no less eager and quite as ferocious and sadistic, tended to regard the operations against the Jews from a point of view they believed more rational. Doubtless they misunderstood the true meaning of the operations, their invocation of destruction and death, and the tragic twilight of a Wagnerian night. Let us suppress the Jew, they argued, let us kill him; but wherever he can be of any use, let us look for German profit rather than the Jew's death. Can't the Jew be made to work in such a way that at the same time, thanks to modern techniques, the extinction of the race would be assured? Can't he also be sold for cash? This attitude, too, was apparent in every phase of the tragedy. We have seen that it was impossible to impose such an attitude (this is perhaps one of the best ways of gaining an insight into the basic meaning of Hitlerism) in the face of Hitler's will and the logic of his system. Not always, however; the struggles that were waged around the lives of the Jews of Europe, and the repercussions these had even in the chancelleries of the Allies, have much to tell us, though they constitute one of the least known aspects of the history of World War II.

245

Many Jewish prisoners in the Nazi inferno tried to escape and leave Europe by bribing their jailers. The latter were scarcely incorruptible. But the punishment for such an offense was severe; one can cite many cases of members of the SS or Wehrmacht being executed for taking money from Jews. Other attempts at ransoming individuals succeeded; there is of course hardly a trace of these in the German archives. There are also some examples of successful political interventions, especially during the initial phase of the Nazi program in 1939 and 1940. One of these involved the famous rabbi of Lubawicz, who was able to leave occupied Poland and go to the United States, via Berlin, in 1940, thanks to diplomatic intervention and with the concurrence of the Abwehr counterintelligence.[1] In some cases, because of the confusion of powers in the Third Reich and the multiplicity of individual satrapies, it is difficult to say whether the exceptions made by the Nazis were due to individual corruption or to political motives. Among these satrapies, the SS, a state within a state, was the most powerful, and its Grand Master, SS Reichsführer Heinrich Himmler, early tried to turn the proceeds of such dealings to his exclusive profit. Here is as good a place as any to pause a little while we consider the man whom the Führer charged with the work of extermination, but who was at the same time the foremost proponent of a more "rational" genocide.

HEINRICH HIMMLER, MODEL INQUISITOR

All sorts of tendencies to hatred and violence slumber in the human breast; under the best circumstances education and morality have difficulty restraining them. But of what destructiveness are these elemental forces not capable the moment they are justified and abetted, instead of opposed, by morality and ideology! Men, moreover, have always known how to invert their loftiest gospels in the most disconcerting way and make them serve their destructive passions; we can find many examples of this in the history of all societies and civilizations. German National Socialism was admirably suited to this destructive aim, which was almost the essence of its meaning. The mystique of the leader, on whom all responsibility was placed, was an excellent way of silencing the slightest doubts; the last scruples were swept away by saying that "It is the Führer's orders." Why the Germans lent themselves so readily to these destructive purposes, and to what degree this is peculiarly German, are troublesome questions that cannot be gone into here. However this may be, an indissoluble bond of complicity was woven between leaders and subordinates; this is no doubt one of the chief factors in explaining the indisputable faithfulness shown by the Nazi henchmen to Hitler. The most varied kinds of men—subtle intellectuals like Goebbels, primitive brutes like Sauckel, fortune hunters like Goering, and technicians of genius like Speer—were bound to the Führer by bonds of personal devotion that sometimes lasted even beyond the grave. The basis of the SS system was this bond of complicity, and Himmler's attachment, in turn, to his Führer was just as absolute as that of the SS to him. But what is most striking about the master executioner of the Third Reich, especially when he is compared with the other leading Nazis, is the peculiar disproportion between the demoniacal role he played in history and his human insignificance.

Absolutely nothing seemed to mark out Heinrich Himmler for the dizzy rise he was to make in the Third Reich—neither exceptional dynamism, a striking appearance, the gift of speech or writing, or any other quality to distinguish him from ordinary mortals. The man was dull, diffident, often hesitant and irresolute, and intellectually mediocre to the point of stupidity. Flabby-cheeked, with his hair brushed straight back and his pince-nez drooping, he seemed to personify so perfectly the type of the pedantic school master that the profession has come to be associated with his name, although he was never in fact a teacher. (1) Doubtless this very diffidence, joined together with his earnestness, helped and distinguished him among all the unstable and the neurotic Nazi rank-and-filers in his early days. In addition to possessing an absolute faith and a certain sense of realities, which later helped him in his skillful handling of subordinates, he had a considerable capacity for methodical work—this was his trump card. Moreover, his diligence, simple and frugal life, and absence of any ostentation,

(1) Himmler was graduated from an agricultural school and had been a farmer. On the other hand, his father had been tutor to Prince Rupert of Bavaria. Cf. Count Bernadotte, *La Fin*.

the responsibility, and even concern, he showed for the lowest subordinates, earned the "Reichsheini" (for so he was nicknamed) a sincere popularity in the SS, and even a great deal of devotion and affection, of which there are a thousand proofs. Perhaps all this only helped him to play his particular part all the better.

It seems to be a pretty constant thing, at all times and under all regimes, for the grand inquisitors to possess all the bucolic and familial virtues, often to an excessive degree. A direct and profoundly logical though apparently contradictory line runs from Thomas Torquemada and Robert Bellarmin through the incorruptible Jacobin tribunes of the French Revolution to the modern totalitarian inquisitors. Their affability serves to counterbalance the very excess of their fury; the purity of their habits is a kind of supplementary self-justification, and arms them against the least sentimentality. And if such an impulse does threaten to weaken their resolution, they disembarrass themselves of it by lavishing affection on innocent children or, like the benevolent Bellarmin, on flies; it would be a mistake to doubt their sincerity. This was also true of Himmler, who was a good father and very fond of German children and animals of all sorts. A conflict in his private life that arose in his later years (a married man, he became involved with one of his secretaries around 1940 and two children were born of this liaison during the war) so troubled him that at times he would seem to have seriously considered suicide.[2] Yet during these years he contemplated the streams of innocent blood that gushed out from under the wheels of the SS Juggernaut with a placid and ingenuous equanimity that no other high dignitary of the regime seems to have been able to equal. Considering this, and considering the Nazi reticence on all matters of genocide, the abovementioned speech which he gave in Posnania must be regarded as his frankest confession. (2)

(2) Here is a characteristic passage:
    The fate of a Russian or a Czech does not interest me in the least. . . . I am completely indifferent as to whether these nations prosper or starve. This interests me only insofar as these nations are needed by us as slaves of our culture. Whether or not 10,000 Russian women drop exhausted from digging an anti-tank ditch is completely meaningless to me provided the ditch is dug. Obviously, this does not mean being harsh and pitiless. We Germans, who are the only people to treat animals properly, also treat

Strange manias are easily associated with such characteristics. Even when we take into consideration the superstitions and aberrations that proliferated among the Nazi madmen, certain of Himmler's fantasies seem to border on feeble-mindedness and leave one stupefied and wondering. The cult of the German past was one of his most serious concerns; in the middle of the war, the information services of the RSHA were asked to study problems as serious as the Rosicrucian brotherhood, the symbolism of the suppression of the harp in Ulster, and the occult meaning of Gothic towers and Eton top hats.[3] The day after the Stalingrad defeat, he ordered his collaborator, Sievers, to find an old Danish woman in Jutland, the only person, he had been told, who still knew the knitting methods used by the old Vikings.[4] He spared neither time nor money for such matters; costly expeditions were sent into every corner of Europe, into the flaming ruins of Russia, even to distant Tibet, to discover traces of the passage of Germanic tribes.[5] Hair and eye color seemed to him a particularly convincing indication, among others, of this; one story has it that Himmler complimented the Grand Mufti of Jerusalem on his blue eyes, formal proof of Nordic descent. It was at their first meeting, during the tea given on this occasion to a few SS leaders, that the guests unanimously deplored the fact that blind history had set back the final crushing of Judaized Christianity by allowing the Holy Roman Empire to defeat the Turks in the seventeenth century.[6]

As his power increased (he became Minister of the Interior in August 1943 and, towards the end, Commander-in-Chief of the Eastern front), and new functions came under his hand, Himmler found new scope for his whims. In March 1944 he informed the meteorological services of the Third Reich that "the roots or bulbs of the meadow-saffron plants reach into the earth to depths that vary annually. The deeper they go, the harsher the winter; the closer to the surface, the milder the winter." And to dispel any doubt in the prosaic minds of the technicians to whom he was writ-

---

human animals properly. But it would be a crime against our own blood to trouble ourselves about them and to ascribe any ideal to them. (October 4, 1943)

ing, he hastened to add: "This observation was sent me by the Führer." [7]

All in all, there is good reason to believe that it was Himmler's intellectual mediocrity, his simple incomprehension of the meaning of the work of destruction to which his name will always remain attached, that chiefly accounts for the vacillation he showed on the question of the "final solution." This most faithful of the faithful was in effect led to work out a policy of his own, diametrically opposed to the Führer's. Probably, too, his mundane realism rebelled against the investment of funds and energy in an industry devoted purely to death, without any economic purpose. Did naive expectations of ensuring his personal safety enter into this at the end? Did he anticipate gaining the mercy of the conquerors, a softening of his fate; did he believe he had a role to play in the future? Was this model inquisitor really tempted to break his word? Some of his biographers have thought so, and some of his efforts support this belief. His activity during the last months was baffling. His entourage openly plotted against Hitler; Walter Schellenberg, his right arm, urged him to seize power. Harassed on all sides, he went along with this scheme, and even made contact with Count Bernadotte—but he was incapable of coming to a real decision. What was in his mind? Human complexity can also go hand in hand with stupidity—and, like stupidity, be unfathomable.

X-Rays and Caladium Senguinum

A "more rational exploitation" might be managed in any number of ways. To work the Jews to death, to exterminate them by hard labor pure and simple, was the first official attempt along these lines, since it was approved personally by the Führer—and we know that Heydrich, who was perhaps the most conscientious exterminator among the Nazi leaders, recommended such a policy. But it was Himmler's idea to give certain Jews with special capacities privileged treatment, thus postponing their death. In line with this, a concentration camp for Jewish mathematicians was set up, or, to use the Reichsführer's own words, "a center for scientific studies, where the special knowledge of these people will be used for calculations that take time and demand brains." [8] In the Sachsenhausen camp a few dozen Jewish mathematicians, in striped uniforms as required, but abundantly provided with calculators and logarithm tables, reckoned ballistic trajectories or drew up long-range meteorological forecasts. Jewish draftsmen were used at Oranienburg and Schlier, in Austria, along with engravers and lithographers, to manufacture counterfeit English and American bills or false documents and passports. This large-scale project occupied more than one thousand prisoners; according to one witness, nearly 750,000,000 false notes of pounds sterling alone were printed there.[9] However, the evidence indicates that only a limited number of Jews was temporarily spared death in this way.

A much more far-reaching project looked to bring about the "final solution" not by direct and bloody physical suppression, but by mass sterilization and castration. Castration, the worst injury one man can do to another, was a solution that appealed deeply to many a Hitlerian soul; the method itself, with its surgical aspect, answered the objection raised by many witnesses to the massacres that they were not "in accordance with our German conceptions." Finally, castrated Jews would furnish an army of several million inoffensive and impotent workers. It is no surprise that this project appealed to the most different kinds of people; physicians and functionaries, men involved in the extermination work, and others who had nothing to do with it.

Himmler was the first to whom sterilization appealed, even before the start of the "final solution" proper. In January 1941 he decided to have its practical possibilities investigated.[10] For this purpose he turned to none other than Viktor Brack, the high official in the Führer's Chancellery who had so brilliantly solved the problems of the "euthanasia program." An old friendship united the two men: Brack's father had been the Himmler family doctor, and young Brack, when he first joined the SS in 1931, had been Himmler's private chauffeur. Two months later, Brack submitted the following report:

Top Secret

It will be necessary to use X-ray treatment on people who are to be definitively sterilized, so as to bring about castration with all its consequences. . . . The dose can be administered in various ways, and the treatment carried out without the subject's knowledge. For men, the source of radiation must have a strength of 500-600 r, for women, 300-350 r. There is a practical way of doing this: We could, for example, call the people to be treated to stand before a little window and make them fill out a questionnaire, or ask them questions, so as to hold them there for two or three minutes. The person behind the window can regulate the apparatus by turning a knob controlling both tubes at the same time (radiation must be bilateral). Thus a device with two tubes could sterilize 150-200 people per day, and with twenty such devices, 3,000-4,000 per day. The expense of such a contrivance would come to approximately 20,000-30,000 marks per two-tube system. However, the cost of remodeling a building must be counted in, since it would be necessary to provide rather considerable protective devices for the men on duty.

In conclusion, I can state that, thanks to this method, present techniques and knowledge of X-rays permit our beginning mass sterilization without delay. However, it would seem impossible to expose the people concerned to this treatment without their knowing sooner or later that they had been sterilized or castrated by X-rays.

Signed: Brack [11]

This report was commonly called the "window document" at the Nuremberg trial. Let no one think that the author of this bureaucratic Grand-Guignol would submit to being considered an anti-Semite. During his trial, Viktor Brack stated that he was a moderate and feeling man, easily affected by the suffering of others (hence his enthusiasm for euthanasia), and that the document in question only went to prove this; that he was, in short, a friend of the human race in general and of the Jews in particular. His lawyers as well as a large number of witnesses—one of them a former Nobel prize winner, Professor Warburg—outdid one another in confirming this. Was it not a question here, "not of exterminating Jews, but, on the contrary, of protecting and saving them from a terrible fate"? [12] Had not Viktor Brack acted "like a commander-in-chief who sacrifices a few thousand soldiers to save hundreds of thousands"? The author of the "window document" protested: "All my life I have only helped the Jews; I never hated them." If we have expatiated somewhat on Brack's case, it is because it is instructive, after reviewing the interminable exterminations, to see what a so-called defender of the Jews among the Nazis was like.

Thenceforward, the experiments with X-ray castration were no longer interrupted in the concentration camps. A few months later, a minor military doctor, Pokorny, no doubt anxious to get ahead, submitted another suggestion to the Reichsführer, "motivated by the thought that the enemy must not only be beaten but destroyed." This proposal involved making úse of the peculiar properties of a Brazilian plant, *Caladium senguinum*, whose juice could sterilize the male reproductive organs.[13] This suggestion was likewise received with favor, and after the beginning of 1942, when the exterminations began, experiments were conducted on an increasingly larger scale. At Auschwitz and Ravensbruck, Professor Clauberg worked on an experimental study of the sterilization of women. Brack's "window" method was tested at Auschwitz, while the SS hothouses were used for the intensive culture of *Caladium senguinum*. From Vienna, through the mediation of the local Gauleiter, a group of doctors called attention to the admirable properties of *Caladium*, as well as to "the perspectives opened by the possibility of sterilizing an unlimited number of people in the shortest conceivable time and in the simplest conceivable manner." [14] Himmler ordered the Viennese doctors to get in touch with the SS experimenters at Auschwitz and work with them. The interest he showed in all these different ideas was tireless, and he even ventured to make technical suggestions. Thus, he wrote to Professor Clauberg that "thorough experiments should be made to assure the efficacy of sterilization, eventually by radiography, with the aim of establishing what modifications have occurred. In any event, it will also be necessary to carry out a practical experiment and lock up a Jew and Jewess for a given time, and then see the result." [15] It should also be pointed out that these ambitious projects were not aimed at the Jews alone, but looked to the immediate sterilization of all the so-called inferior races. Dr. Pokorny, for instance, suggested administering *Caladium* to 3,000,000 prisoners of war, while the Vienna group noted that "stopping the proliferation of inferior races is one of the most urgent tasks of German racial policy." Mixing a few ounces of a drug in the food of subjugated populations was obviously not an impossible task, but the drug had to be an effective one. Fortunately for many European peoples, the three years from which the SS scientific pioneers benefited to carry on their experiments were insufficient to obtain conclusive results. The "window system," so appealing on paper, proved useless in practice: "It has been proved that the castration of a man by this process is virtually excluded or requires so large an expenditure that it is not worth the trouble," one of Brack's assistants wrote to Himmler in April 1944.[16] As for *Caladium senguinum*—if we may believe an expert—though it was infallible in principle, the SS horticulturists failed to recreate inside their hothouses the conditions that were required for the perfect flowering of this formidable tropical bush.[17] The "final solution" was carried out according to the original plan, before a method for cheap, simple, and effective mass sterilization could be discovered. Only a few human guinea pigs, some of whom made heart-rending anonymous depositions before the war crimes tribunals, preserve in their flesh the marks of one of Reichsführer Heinrich Himmler's grandiose ideas.

THE EUROPA PLAN

Another project for the more rational exploitation of the Jews, one that engaged the attentions of a number of highly placed SS men and strongly tempted the Reichsführer himself, contemplated a gigantic ransoming of all the Jews still alive in German hands. This project, unlike the preceding one, was actually begun.

As we have said, Himmler very early in the war permitted certain SS bureaus to make individual arrangements to allow very rich Jews to emigrate in exchange for payment in hard currency, dollars or Swiss francs, which in principle were earmarked for the equipping of the Waffen-SS. This was done especially in the Netherlands, and the ransom was considerable: $5,000-$10,000 per person. However, only about fifty Dutch Jews were able to ransom themselves in this way.[18] At the end of 1942, Himmler's staff thought of extending the ransoming to other countries, especially Slovakia, where the deportations had just been suspended.[19] The ground was thus gradually prepared for a more comprehensive transaction.

It turned out that the permanent IVb representative in Slovakia, Dieter Wisliceny, although one of Adolf Eichmann's oldest friends, deviated somewhat from the classic type of the Nazi executioner. This former journalist had a certain cultivation, even some refinement. He tended to carry out his functions like a dilettante, and showed an exemplary correctness toward his victims; he pursued his own interests rather than trying scrupulously to carry out his task, for which, all told, he seems to have had only a limited enthusiasm. Such a person was just the kind of intermediary needed for extending the scope of the ransoming from individual rich Jews to the entire Jewish collectivity, so that many, not merely a few, might be saved. But the idea first occurred to a Bratislava Jewess, Gisi Fleischmann, a woman with a great heart and devouring energy.

Since individual Jews could escape the fate lying in wait for them by paying a ransom, why not try to ransom all the Jews at a single stroke, even if the sum ran into the millions? Gisi Fleischmann made contact with Wisliceny, and at the same time sent couriers to alert the American Jewish Joint Distribution Committee (JDC), the powerful Jewish philanthropic organization. Collected on the spot, a first payment of $25,000 was handed to Wisliceny; the latter tried hard to obtain the Reischsführer's approval of what the negotiators called by the code name "Europa Plan." These conversations and negotiations were of course carried on in complete secrecy, since the slightest indiscretion entailed serious consequences. No trace of it has remained in the SS archives, but the flaming appeals that Gisi Fleischmann sent abroad have been preserved. Here are a few extracts that recall the hopes that filled the hearts of this little group:

(March 24, 1943) Our chances are unfortunately limited. But a tenacious and inflexible determination to attain our ends gives us the strength and courage to continue along this way. We must strive with all our strength to reach our sacred goal.

(June 18, 1943) I am finishing this report at perhaps a historic moment, for your acceptance of the project opens possibilities for stopping the terrible work of extermination. If this great labor of human love succeeds, we can say that we shall not have lived in vain.[20]

Characteristically, Himmler hesitated a long time before giving Wisliceny exact instructions. His first reaction apparently was favorable; it would seem that a mass emigration of children figured among the first measures under consideration. But Eichmann, solidly entrenched in a key position, tried his best to wreck the agreement. He found an unexpected and influential ally in the Grand Mufti of Jerusalem, a refugee in Germany since the summer of 1941, who jealously watched to see that no Jew left the European continent alive.[21] Other high-ranking SS men, especially Walter Schellenberg, chief of the SS information service, tried to influence Himmler in the opposite direction; a definite answer was forthcoming only after many months.

Deportations meanwhile continued, and the gas chambers continued their work. The Bratislava plan, however, did not go through in its original form, and in 1944 Eichmann took his revenge by maneuvering successfully to have Gisi Fleischmann deported and executed. The project was taken up again in Budapest when the complete IVb team appeared there in March 1944 following in the wake of the German armies. With catastrophe imminent, the journalist Rudolf Kästner, who had been kept informed of the Slovakian negotiations, tried to have them resumed again. The presence of Wisliceny among the people Eichmann had brought to Budapest made Kästner's task easier.

The fortunes of war had meanwhile changed sufficiently for Himmler to take a serious interest in these overtures. He selected a special agent to continue these negotiations—Kurt Becher, a Waffen SS administrative officer who had already come to his attention by negotiating the release of the Jewish owners of the Manfred Weiss Hungarian industrial trust, in exchange for substantial economic advantages. Parleys were finally begun during the spring of 1944. Having succeeded in making contact with Jewish organizations abroad, Rudolf Kästner tried by every means to put Hitler's emissary in direct contact with their representatives. An interview in Lisbon was contemplated, with the SS proposing an exchange of Jewish lives for trucks and medicines. The affair was to be handled on a strictly economic basis, without any humanitarian considerations, since the latter might very well ruin the whole thing. A daring chance, but Kästner and his friends showed themselves good psychologists, and the arguments they advanced were admirably conceived to impress the Nazis. Here they are, as summed up in a memorandum submitted to Himmler in July 1944:

> We believe that the cessation of the deportations in Hungary represents an indispensable premise for the Lisbon conversations; once

agreement is reached, this would be followed by a regular emigration of the remaining Hungarian Jews.

We again insist most urgently that the Jews already deported from Hungary be spared from total or partial destruction; people able to work by this very fact constitute an actual value for the German economy, while those unable to work, who will be the first ones to be exchanged, constitute a potential and quickly realizable value.

In this regard, we recall that it was agreed at our last meetings that the meaning of our agreements is not solely financial. The security to be put up by us, especially the trucks, means in fact a saving of German blood. In this way, as a counterpart to the Jewish lives, you will indirectly be saving German lives. Any deterioration of the Jewish substance in your hands would, it seems to us, be unwise under these conditions and a blow to your own national substance.[22]

It is certain that Himmler for his part was now completely for the "Europa Plan." But he took care not to tell the Führer, and maneuvered with extreme caution. One of Kästner's aides, Joel Brandt, was able to go to Constantinople, and then to Cairo, to expedite the negotiations. The deportation of the Jews of Budapest was postponed, and, in fact, never took place. Small groups of Hungarian Jews, 3,000 in November 1944, 1,200 in February 1945, were convoyed to the Swiss border and set free as a "gesture of good will."

In fact, it was on the Allied side that obstacles were raised. Joel Brandt was interned by the British authorities without having had a chance to accomplish his mission, and the United States Department of State forbade Joseph Schwartz, director of the JDC, to negotiate with enemy subjects. Only after great difficulty, thanks to the intervention of various Swiss and Swedish intermediaries, did these excessively complicated negotiations manage to continue; but this was enough for the SS Reichsführer, especially as the German military situation was rapidly deteriorating, to grant new concessions. The success of the Allied landing in Europe seems to have caused Himmler really to change his course. From then on, he not only acted without Hitler's knowledge, he no longer paid any attention to Hitler's express wishes. In October 1944, still unbeknownst to Hitler, he stopped the exterminations, and at the end of 1944 he agreed to continue negotiations not only on an economic but also on a "humanitarian" basis. The transfigured Himmler of 1945 now emerged, a man so unselfconscious that when preparing to surrender he wondered whether he should or should not shake General Eisenhower's hand,[23] and in March asked for a meeting with a representative of the World Jewish Congress, mentioning in this connection his pre-war "benevolent efforts" in favor of Jewish emigration, efforts which "war and human folly" had terminated.[24] A few days before this, he ordered General Pohl, supreme head of all the concentration camps, to drop everything and go to the principal camps and see to it that preferential treatment was given to the Jews still alive.[25] On April 5 he named Kurt Becher special Reich commissioner for concentration camps; Becher was authorized to stop the evacuation of the camps, or, as the case might be, turn them over to the Allied authorities.[26] These missions by Pohl and Becher, although impeded by the anarchy into which the Third Reich was already collapsing, stopped many a last-minute massacre, and the tireless Kästner was even able to save several hundred lives by donning an SS uniform and making a mad race through the chaos of Nazi Germany's last hour.

Such were the results of the desperate efforts of a handful of Jews and neutral missionaries to come to terms with Himmler and slow down the exterminations. It should be pointed out that the above lines concentrate on the main theme of the "Europa Plan," an excessively complex negotiation shot through with a thousand intrigues and participated in by many other important actors, of whom we need mention only Count Bernadotte and Carl Burckhardt, president of the International Red Cross. But a direct line leads from the initiative taken by Gisi Fleischmann in 1943 to the events of April–May, 1945. In the last analysis, the "great work of human love" begun by the unknown Jewess of Bratislava saved the lives of thousands of deportees of all categories and nationalities and prevented the worst from happening during the collapse of the German concentration camps.

Just as no one will ever know the exact number of the victims of Nazi genocide, so it is impossible to tell the number of lives saved by the "Europa Plan." A few thousand Jews were allowed to go to Switzerland and Portugal; some tens of thousands of Jews were spared deportation from Budapest; and finally, the surviving remnant in the concentration camps, Jews and non-Jews, were saved from being exterminated while the last act of the Hitler *Götterdämmerung* was being played in Berlin—such is the balance sheet. The problem that next presents itself is what part the negative attitude of the Allied chancelleries and High Command played in the partial failure of "Europa Plan." This question deserves a rapid examination.

Certainly the reasoning of the Allied authorities would at first glance seem to have been perfectly valid and logical. It is a fixed principle that in time of war nothing must be done that might increase the enemy's war potential. The delivery of trucks and medicines to the Nazi enemy and the unblocking of funds in territory under his control would doubtless have been of help to the enemy. Simply to negotiate with the Nazis, even indirectly, would have meant to violate the principles proclaimed at Casablanca and Teheran. And did not one of the conditions suggested by the SS negotiators—"that these trucks would not be used on the Western front"—apparently aim at sowing discord among the Allies? It can also be said that the total depravity of the Nazis and their system, which showed up most clearly just in this matter of genocide, disqualified them from participating even in limited negotiations, since their actions had placed them outside the bounds of humanity.

But other negotiations of this sort did take place, and were carried to a successful conclusion. There were, for example, the negotiations over the seriously wounded prisoners, whom Great Britain and the Third Reich exchanged several times. Civil internees were also exchanged. However savage the conflict, a number of important international agreements, such as the Geneva Convention on the treatment of war prisoners, remained effective all during the hostilities. But the Jews of the occupied countries were not protected by these covenants; as noted, only citizens of belligerent or neutral countries escaped deportation. The Germans could thus base "on legal grounds" their reasons for refusing permission to the delegates of the International Red Cross and the neutral missions to inspect the concentration camps. In this connection, it should be recalled that when the Red Cross Committee proposed, after the declaration of war in 1939, that the belligerents extend the benefits of the Geneva Convention to the civil populations, "without distinction of race, religion or politics," it was—by a cruel paradox—Great Britain that showed the most reluctance, while the Third Reich "declared itself ready to discuss the project." (3) (Even if it had been accepted, nothing would have kept the Nazis from disregarding it. But the question would then have had a different basis, and the Red Cross, the neutrals, and the Allies would have been in a better position to do something. The fact that the Jewish prisoners of war were never touched by the Nazis is very significant here.)

Nothing, in short, was done, or what was done proved to be too little and too late. A special board created by President Roosevelt for this purpose, the War Refugees Board, came into being only in 1944; its activity was hampered from beginning to end by shabby bureaucratic obstacles. The British government pursued its Palestine policy, based on the 1939 White Paper, with implacable obstinacy, systematically sending back to sea the few ships transporting refugees who had escaped from the Hitler hell. Sharp accusations, sometimes from authoritative sources, were leveled against the Allied chancelleries; Henry Morgenthau, the American Secretary of the Treasury, spoke of the "satanic combination of British chill and diplomatic double talk, cold and correct, and adding up to a sentence of death." [27] In a public document Morgenthau also charged that certain officials of the State Department

(3) In a circular letter dated September 4, 1939, the International Committee of the Red Cross proposed to the belligerents, among other measures, "the anticipated and at least provisional adoption, only for the present conflict and for its duration, of the provisions of the above-mentioned proposed convention." (This referred to the so-called Tokyo project, which extended to civilians the benefits of the Geneva Convention.)

In a letter dated November 30, 1939, the Reich Ministry of Foreign Affairs confirmed that "on the German side, it is believed that the Tokyo project can serve as the basis for concluding an international agreement on the treatment and protection of civilians in enemy or occupied territory."

On November 23, 1939, the government of the Third Republic wrote: "The French government fully recognizes the interest . . . of the so-called Tokyo project. It believes, however, that the text in question requires careful study . . . that might entail a fairly long delay and postpone the solution of the problems."

As for the British government, only on April 30, 1940, did it answer the circular letter, indicating that it preferred to make a bilateral agreement with the government of the Third Reich. (Cf. International Committee of the Red Cross, documents relative to the activity of the Committee in behalf of civilians detained in German concentration camps. Geneva, 1946.)

1. Utterly failed to "prevent the extermination of Jews in German-controlled Europe."

2. Hid their "gross procrastination" behind such window dressing as "intergovernmental organizations to survey the whole refugee problem."

3. Suppressed, for two months, reports to the State Department on German atrocities after publication of similar reports had "intensified" public pressure for action.[28]

More impressive means of action, like the vast reprisals which Allied supremacy in the air made possible, were never considered. The bombardment of the death factories, which was an easy operation to carry out and would have thrown the entire extermination machinery into confusion, as well as yielding great psychological returns, was never permitted, although the Jewish organizations many times requested that it be done.

A number of authors, especially Jewish historians, after listing all these failures, speak openly of anti-Semitism. A dreadful remark has been quoted as having been made by an Allied statesman in the spring of 1944, when German diplomats had spread the rumor of a coming mass expulsion of the Jews into Allied or neutral territory: (4) "But where are we going to put them?" (5) Doubtless anti-Semitism explains many of these failures to do anything; but it is perhaps unnecessary to attribute the almost total quiescence of

(4) Apparently it was Ribbentrop's idea, born at a time when, on the eve of the Allied landing in Normandy, German propaganda tried various psychological maneuvers.

Cf: the report of Veesenmayer, German ambassador in Budapest, to his government on April 3, 1944.

The reaction of the Budapest population to the two aerial attacks was an increase of anti-Semitism in numerous quarters. Today tracts were distributed that demanded the life of a hundred Jews for every Hungarian killed. . . . I would not have any scruples about shooting ten carefully chosen Jews for every Hungarian killed. . . . Moreover, I have the impression that the (Hungarian) government is ready to execute a similar measure on its own initiative. On the other hand, such an action, if taken, must be carried out without faltering. In order to take into account the proposals made to the Führer by the Minister of Foreign Affairs on the possibility of offering all the Jews as a gift to Churchill and Roosevelt, I beg you to tell me if this idea is still under consideration or if I can begin with the said reprisals before the next attack.

(5) There is no reason whatsoever to doubt the authenticity of this remark, which was quoted to us by a very reliable source. The remark was made by Lord Moyne, who was then the British Minister of State in the Near East.

the world in the face of the Jewish martyrdom to conscious hostility. This quiescent attitude toward the plight of the Jews was after all a customary and established thing; and the absence of any formal convention protecting the Jews of the modern world only increased their age-old weakness. If their suffering found no echo, it was because the world had resigned itself to their complaints. And they had nothing else to throw into the balance. The situation of a stateless people, whose very impotence had been a standing invitation to massacre down the centuries, was in truth the chief reason for the impunity that the Nazis felt so confidently they possessed. In a German report on the so-called "inferior races" by Wetzel, he spoke of the future of Poland and let drop these significant words: "Evidently the Polish question cannot be resolved simply by the liquidation of the Poles, as is the case with the Jews. Such a solution of the Polish question would burden the German people far into the future, would obliterate all sympathy for it, at the same time causing other peoples to wonder whether they might not have to undergo the same fate in due time." [29] And at a time when the exterminations were going full blast, Goebbels with good reason could pour forth this sarcasm on the Jewish agony:

> What will be the solution of the Jewish question? Whether a Jewish state will one day be created in some territory remains to be seen. But it is curious to note that the countries where public opinion is rising in favor of the Jews refuse to accept them from us. They call them the pioneers of a new civilization, geniuses of philosophy and artistic creation, but when anybody wants them to accept these geniuses, they close their borders: "No, no. We don't want them!" It seems to me to be the only case in world history where people have refused to accept geniuses. (May 1943.) [30]

CHAPTER ELEVEN

Nazi Plans for the "Inferior Peoples"

WE NOW PASS OUT of the crazy world of the death industries, with its atmosphere of pure malevolence and its devotion to destruction as an end in itself, and enter into a domain where the deeds and designs of the Nazi leaders, however ferocious and implacable, at first glance seem less disconcerting. The plans the Nazis entertained for the conquered peoples, or so-called "inferior races," were not so utterly unprecedented as their attempt to exterminate out of hand the entire Jewish people; what they intended for the peoples under their yoke more or less resembled what the great conquerors in all ages have always tried to do with their slaves, only carried to the furthest extreme. These Nazi projects, though they were not meant to be carried out completely until after final victory, were put into operation with feverish haste in proportion as German hegemony was extended over Europe.

If the Jew occupied Satan's place in Nazi eschatology, the non-German or "sub-human" lacking any sacred attribute was for the most part classified among the animals; at best, he was considered, according to a contemporary definition, as a "transitional form between the animal and Nordic man." In the case of the Poles, Czechs, and French, however, the Nazis do not seem to have regarded them with the same burning hatred—this would have led to their extermination and Hitler's loss of a useful beast of burden with a part to play in building the thousand-year Reich. Nazi persecution of the "inferior men" was part of an imperialist plan; it was based on economic and demographic considerations and aimed at assuring the permanent supremacy of the German race. What was involved here was not a "final solution," but birth rates, reproduction indices, the menacing proliferation of the Slavs, and the loss of

263

German blood as a result of the war. Nevertheless, though this kind of persecution had a more rational point of departure and resorted to more subtle techniques, in the final analysis it led to the same goal: the physical suppression of other peoples. The same word "genocide" applies to the persecution of the "inferior peoples," even if this was sometimes a "delayed" genocide. Behind the nuances of terminology and method one sees the brute fact plain enough in the end; behind the rationalizations and ideological structures are the same homicidal outbursts and rivers of blood. As soon as one surveys the whole ensemble of Nazi racial policy and practice, one perceives the true significance of the extermination of the Jews: as a warning sign of greater and more general holocausts to come. Once the "final solution" had been launched out on, all mental barriers were smashed and the necessary psychological precedent created; it also enabled the Nazis to test their technical processes of collective murder. It was easy enough to see, moreover, by simple induction that so insane a scheme could not stop half-way; if the fortunes of war had given the Nazis enough time, the force of the logic of genocide would have inexorably driven other peoples and races into the gas chambers. For "racism is like the rabies: no one knows in advance on whom the worshipper of his own blood will vent the rage that torments him." (1)

Nothing is more useless than to forecast events that have not, in fact, taken place: the German rule of Europe was too short-lived for this threat of universal genocide to materialize. But in five years of war Nazi racial policy provided us with sufficient evidence to foresee, without resorting to pure speculation, what would have been the fate of the "sub-men" who were not Jews. The Germans followed two simultaneous courses with respect to these "inferior races," more or less vigorously according to the time and place. One course was that of the direct, if partial, extermination characteristic in Russian areas; the other, more circumspect and cautious, aimed at eventual, not immediate, extermination of "inferior peoples."

(1) J. Billig, *L'Allemagne et le génocide*, Paris, Editions du Centre, 1949.

DIRECT EXTERMINATION

THE GYPSIES

With the astonishing obsession so characteristic of Nazi aggressiveness, the Germans passed a second death sentence on an entire people even before having finished with the first. These were the Gypsies, who, like the Jews, were also a scattered and wandering people, but numbering no more than a few hundred thousand.

Before the war, the Gauleiter of the province of Styria in Austria demanded "a National Socialist solution for the Gypsy question," justifying this demand as follows:

> For reasons of public health, and especially as the Gypsies have a notoriously foul heredity, are habitual criminals and parasites within the body of our people, causing immense damage and imperiling the purity of the borderland peasant's blood and way of life, it is proper that in the first place they should be prevented from reproducing themselves, then made to do forced labor in the work camps, though they should not be prevented at the same time from choosing voluntary emigration abroad.[1]

Some of the arguments advanced, as well as solutions proposed, differ very little from those used in connection with the Jews. Nevertheless, it was impossible to elevate the Gypsy into a myth; the excuse for condemning them to death was that they were an "asocial people."

The documents that might permit us to reconstruct the story of the extermination of the Gypsies are few and far between. A text dated March 10, 1944, states that all the Reich Gypsies (as well as Jews) had been evacuated by that time—this was a circular from Himmler ordering the taking down of all the warnings, signs, and bans posted against them as being henceforth unnecessary.[2] Moreover, we lack statistics to show even approximately the number of Gypsies that were scattered over Europe on the eve of the war (around 1900, it had been estimated at 1,000,000).[3] They were particularly numerous in Hungary, the Balkans, and the USSR. Thus we cannot estimate the total number of victims or the proportion of survivors. The Gypsies in Germany proper, about 30,000, were mostly deported to Auschwitz, where they were exterminated during 1944, as we have noted above. In the invaded areas of the

USSR the "action groups" were ordered to exterminate the Gypsies at the same time and in the same way as the Jews. In the Crimea, for example, in the region of Simferopol alone more than 800 Gypsies were killed in the suburbs of the city on December 24, Christmas Eve, 1941.[4] In Croatia, Pavelitch's Ustachis were the principal initiators of the Gypsy massacres; the Inquiry Commission of the Yugoslav government set the number of victims at 28,000.[5]

Probably at least 200,000 in all died in the Nazi massacres. The Nuremberg Tribunal, after trying the members of the "action groups," devoted a few sentences of its verdict, full of melancholy wisdom, to this little wandering people, the inspiration of so many poets and musicians:

> In addition, the "action groups" received orders to shoot the Gypsies. No explanation was given as to why this inoffensive people, who for centuries contributed their share of music and songs to the world, was to be hunted down like so much game. With their picturesque dress and customs, they amused and diverted society, though they sometimes also annoyed people with their indolent ways. But no one ever condemned them as a mortal menace to organized society, no one, that is, except National Socialism, which by the voice of Hitler, Himmler, and Heydrich decreed their extermination.

THE RUSSIANS

We must now consider a more complex matter, which involves projects only just begun and never definitively formed. These plans were drawn up by experts, grave university professors who sometimes differed in their opinions. Thus Professor Abel (a former assistant to the anthropologist Eugen Fischer), the expert picked by the Wehrmacht to study the racial composition of the Russian people, recommended their total extermination. Wetzel, an expert attached to the Ministry for the Occupied Territories of the East, found this solution somewhat impractical and voiced his objection in a memorandum:

> Abel's proposal, which aims at the complete liquidation of the Russians, can not be considered acceptable for political and economic reasons, to say nothing of the impossibility of carrying it out in practice. A complete biological annihilation of the Russian substance is not in our interest, so long as we are not in a position to fill the void [thus created] with our own people. Under these circumstances it is neces-

sary to use other means to arrive at the solution of the Russian problem. We shall try to indicate them here.[6]

The purely empirical solution that was provisionally adopted came from the Führer himself when he stated in connection with the guerrilla warfare that had broken out in the USSR: "This guerrilla warfare has its advantages, since it makes it possible for us to exterminate anybody who opposes us!"[7] It was under the guise of anti-partisan warfare that the innumerable systematic massacres behind the front were perpetrated. A report by Reichskommissar Lohse on these massacres contains the following reflection: "Burning men, women, and children in barns does not seem to me a proper method for combatting the partisans, even if we want to exterminate the population. The method is unworthy of the German cause and lowers our prestige considerably."[8] (Here again we have the kind of reasoning encountered so often in connection with the Jews.) Keitel's orders on the fight against the partisans stated that "in this struggle, the troops have the right and duty to use any means, even against women and children. . . . No German engaged in the military operations must be subject to disciplinary or legal action because of his conduct in combat."[9] This applied to the whole Wehrmacht, as did the following admonishment to the soldiers: "Bear in mind that in this country human life has no value whatsoever."[10]

The systematic extermination of the prisoners of war contributed to the same end. In a personal letter to Keitel, Alfred Rosenberg complained of the Wehrmacht's "lack of political comprehension" in this matter; the document, full of a macabre humor, gives details on the manner in which the mass executions of prisoners were carried out:

> Mention finally should be made of the shooting of prisoners of war; these are sometimes carried out according to principles that lack all political understanding. For example, "Asiatics" have been shot in certain camps although they were natives of the Transcaucasus and Turkestan, Asiatic territories where the peoples of the Soviet Union most violently opposed to Russian oppression and Bolshevism reside. The Ministry of the Occupied Territories of the East has many times called attention to this deplorable situation. Nevertheless, last November a commando showed up in a prison camp near Nicolayev and wanted to liquidate the "Asiatics."

The treatment of prisoners of war seems to be based on totally erroneous conceptions concerning the peoples of the Soviet Union. One comes across the misconception that the populations become less and less civilized the farther east one goes. So, if the Poles are treated severely, runs the argument, the Ukrainians, the White Russians, the Russians, and finally the "Asiatics," must be treated much more severely.[11]

SS men were the principal organizers of these massacres. That they represented the application of a systematic and preconceived plan for mass blood-lettings of the population is clear from one of Himmler's speeches: On the eve of the attack on the USSR, he stated before a group of SS generals that one of the goals of the campaign was to reduce the Slav population by 30,000,000.[12] In another speech, given in the fall of 1943, he formulated his ideas in somewhat different and clearer terms.

> Here is the alternative: Either we win over to our side the precious blood we can use and make part of our own, or—gentlemen, you may find this cruel, but nature is cruel—we wipe it out. We shall have to answer to our sons or to our ancestors for having overlooked blood belonging to the other side, thus giving the enemy talented leaders and chiefs.[13]

In effect, this theory implied that all the ruling classes of the European countries must necessarily have some German ancestry, since Nordic man was the only one with leadership ability. In this same speech, Himmler tried his best to show that only those generals in the Polish Army of 1939 who possessed some German blood had known how to put up a fight. (2)

THE POLES AND THE CZECHS

Thus, the direct extermination of inferior races was aimed first of all at the elite. "Either we win this precious blood over to our side, or we wipe it out." Only Quislings were spared by the second half of Himmler's formulation. In Poland this policy was systematically pursued. Governor General Frank, in the spring of 1940, told his collaborators of instructions he had received from Hitler.

(2) Himmler laid particular stress on General Rommel, one of the defenders of Warsaw, and Admiral Unruh, commander of the Hela base. He also included General Thome, the defender of Modlin, "of Huguenot descent."

The Führer told me: "What we have now recognized in Poland to be the elite must be liquidated; we must watch out for seeds that begin to sprout again, so as to stamp them out again in good time." [And Frank went on in the same cynical style and with the same care for the well-being of the German executioners.] We don't have to start dragging these elements into the Reich concentration camps, for then we would only have a lot of trouble and useless correspondence with the families. We will liquidate the business in the country itself. And we will do it in the simplest way. Gentlemen, we are not assassins. The task is a terrible one for any policeman and member of the SS obliged by duty to carry out the executions. We can easily sign hundreds of death warrants, but by burdening German men with their execution, disciplined German soldiers, our comrades, we are imposing a heavy burden on them. . . . Thus, every policeman, every SS Führer obliged to carry out a sentence, must be 100 per cent sure that he is carrying out a verdict of the German nation. That is why a summary form of court martial must take place.[14]

Thus began the mass executions of intellectuals and Polish officers, called by the code name "A-B Action"; thirty-five thousand victims of the "A-B Action" were identified among the bodies in the common graves alone after the war.[15] The Polish government estimated at nearly 3,000,000 the total loss suffered by Poland's non-Jewish population between 1939–45.

The essentials of the instructions given by the Führer to "resolve the Czech question" are found in a document dated October 1940:

Germanization of Bohemia-Moravia by the Germanizing of the Czechs, that is, by their assimilation. This last would be possible for most of the Czech people. Exception must be made of Czechs against whom there would be racial objections, or who might have an anti-German attitude. This category must be exterminated.[16]

We see reappearing here the distinction between the "assimilable" or "Germanizable" elements of a people, and those destined for execution. From the example of the foreign workers imported by the millions into Germany, we can see very clearly how such a distinction was drawn in practice.

THE "WORKERS FROM THE EAST"

The lot of the more than 5,000,000 "foreign workers" concentrated in the Reich varied markedly according to their country of origin. Those from the East, the *Ostarbeiter*, were the most numerous and worst treated. The Russians and the Poles were under the sole authority of the SS, since the Reich Ministry of Justice had disclaimed any jurisdiction over them. (In a letter to Bormann, Minister of Justice Thierack gave the following reasons for this decision: "I base this act on the ground that justice can contribute very little to the extermination of these peoples. To be sure, justice passes some very severe sentences on them, but that is not enough.") [17]

The least offense by an Eastern worker resulted in his immediate internment in a concentration camp. As the slave laborers lived under conditions of forced celibacy, it is not astonishing that the most common transgression was cohabitation with a German woman —that is, "race defilement." At this point a department of the SS's Commissariat for Strengthening Germanism, the Office for Race and Colonization (3) (RuSHA), with its fearsome "racial inspectors," took a hand in matters.

Of all the phantasies that issued from the skulls of Heinrich Himmler and his henchmen, the RuSHA, which among other things had the job of judging people's race, was surely the most delirious. All across conquered Europe, so-called anthropologists examined the shape and angle of skulls, measured the spread of ears and studied the expressions of eyes. Hair color was a very important index, and a human life might hang on it. When an Eastern worker was caught with a German woman, he was examined by one of these dangerous maniacs. If the man looked sufficiently German, he was pardoned, naturalized on the spot, and eventually even authorized to marry his partner. If not, he was promptly hanged, since race defilement was considered the worst crime. Blond hair or an extra inch of height could thus decide a man's life. Any reader who might feel some doubts about this need only consult the involved and detailed regulations drawn up by the RuSHA on this subject, including about fifteen successive ordinances passed between 1940–45. Of all the slave laborers from the East caught having sexual relations with German women, only the Czechs, the Poles, and the Lithuanians had a chance of saving their lives by

(3) *Rasse und Siedlungshauptamt.*

Germanization followed by marriage. As the RuSHA circular III/2B, dated February 26, 1942, states, the expert's opinion was required to be based on "conscientious" examination and to include, in addition to the "racial evaluation" (height, shape of skull, cheekbones, eye aperture, color and texture of hair, hair distribution over body, skin color), a section marked "general impression" which considered such things as: "(a) gives an impression of frankness, openness, shows firmness of bearing and presence; (b) is uncommunicative, timid, and of a character hard to make out; or (c) gives the impression of being crafty and underhand, etc."[18]

At the beginning of 1945, a final circular from the RuSHA (4) stated that the alternative offered to "Germanizable" Poles or Czechs was henceforth abolished by order of Himmler. (The reason for the decision was not given; probably it was connected with the general collapse of the Third Reich.) Russian or Serbian slave laborers had never benefited from this provision; in any case of "race defilement" in which they were involved they were automatically and immediately accorded "special treatment," the kinds and modes of which were also carefully outlined in official circulars. "The method for administering special treatment is hanging. It must not take place in the immediate neighborhood of the camp."[19] "The aim of application of special treatment is above all the intimidation (Abschreckung) of foreign labor working in the Reich area. This can only be fully accomplished if the punishment follows immediately after the crime. . . . The execution must take place on the scene of the crime in cases where such is deemed necessary for the purpose of intimidation."[20]

DELAYED EXTERMINATION

While the Nazi practitioners went on with their massacres, the Nazi theorists revised and completed the anthropological systems meant to serve the former as directives. There is no great need to study them in detail, as there were so many and often they flatly contradicted one another. The one most favored, on which the codification of the Nuremberg laws was partly based, rejected any simple distinction between "Aryans" and "non-Aryans," and distin-

(4) Circular 3/45, January 5, 1945.

guished between races of "German" and "kindred blood" and races of "foreign" blood. (5) But the SS bothered little with such subtleties; for a primitive like Himmler, there were only Germanic men and sub-humans. (As we shall see, it was the black sheep of Germanism that turned his disappointed solicitude into implacable hate.)

As for the Führer, he was the last person to keep within the boundaries of an established doctrine. At once opportunistic and inflexible, he took the most direct route that offered to the realization of his visions of conquest and domination.

Though little attention was paid to the innumerable professional lucubrations, the result was the creation in the conquered countries, even while the war was on, of a coherent system of measures aiming at the establishment for centuries to come of German racial predominance. The most varied measures were employed, but they all pointed toward this one end.

GENOCIDE BY "LOWERING THE FERTILITY OF THE PEOPLE"

Next to pure and simple homicide, this was the most direct method. Instead of physically suppressing the present generation, it was seen to it that there would be no future generations. The mass sterilization plans which have already been mentioned never got beyond the planning stage, but other large-scale measures did. The minutes of a meeting of experts charged with drawing up these plans lists the following measures:

a) Raising the marriage age to twenty-five (after completion of labor service or some such required service for a period of three or four years).

b) Authorization of marriage only in cases where the economic position [of the people concerned] is assured.

c) Requiring financial restitution to the public welfare funds in every case of illegitimate birth. If the mother is without funds, she will have to furnish her labor.

d) If the same mother has burdened the public welfare funds with several illegitimate children, her sterilization can be ordered.

e) Deliberate lowering of the standard of living of large families (no monetary relief, no allocations for children, no premium during the nursing period, etc.).

(5) The former were *Artverwandt:* Nordic races, Faliscan, Ostic; the latter were *Artfremd:* Orientoid, Armenoid, and Indoid (sic!).

f) Official authorization for abortion at the mother's request (when desirable from the social point of view).[21]

These measures were prepared by the experts of the Reich Ministry of the Interior and primarily had the Polish population in mind. They were introduced into the Government General by a decree of October 19, 1941. One year later, the Führer ordered their extension to all populations under the control of the "Ministry of the Occupied Territories of the East." Bormann sent the following instructions to Rosenberg:

July 23, 1942

My dear Party Comrade Rosenberg:
The Führer wishes you to see to it that the following principles are applied and observed in the Occupied Territories of the East, and I am entrusting you with this task.

1) When girls and women in the Occupied Territories of the East have abortions, we can only be in favor of it; in any case, German jurists should not oppose it. The Führer believes that we should authorize the development of a thriving trade in contraceptives. We are not interested in seeing the non-German population multiply.

2) The danger that the non-German population in the Eastern territories may increase more than before is very great. Their living conditions have improved considerably. For this very reason we must take the necessary precautionary measures to prevent an expansion of the non-German population.

3) German medical relief must therefore not be set up for the non-German population in the Eastern territories in any way. Vaccination, for example, and other such health measures, are out of the question.

4) The population must in no way benefit from higher education. If we let ourselves be pushed into committing this error, we shall ourselves be cultivating the elements of a future resistance against us. According to the Führer, then, it will be enough for the non-German populations—even the so-called Ukrainians—to learn to read and write.

5) We must on no condition by any measure whatsoever cultivate any sort of feeling of superiority in the population! The contrary is necessary! [22]

In the recommendations in his memorandum for the practical execution of these measures, Wetzel gave proof of a fertile imagination.

Every propaganda means, especially the press, radio, and movies, as well as pamphlets, booklets, and lectures, must be used to instill in the Russian population the idea that it is harmful to have several children. We must emphasize the expenses that children cause, the good things people could have had with the money spent on them. We could also hint at the dangerous effect of child-bearing on a woman's health. Paralleling such propaganda, a large-scale campaign should be launched in favor of contraceptive devices. A contraceptive industry must be established. Neither the circulation and sale of contraceptives nor abortions must be prosecuted. It will even be necessary to open special institutions for abortion, and to train midwives and nurses for this purpose. The population will practise abortion all the more willingly if these institutions are competently operated. The doctors must be able to help out without there being any question of this being a breach of their professional ethics. Voluntary sterilization must also be recommended by propaganda. Infant mortality must not be combatted. Mothers must be kept in ignorance of child care and of everything that has to do with children's diseases. We must try to reduce as much as possible the training and knowledge of Russian doctors in this field. Such institutions as day nurseries and children's homes must be abolished as far as it is possible.[23]

THE KIDNAPPING OF CHILDREN

This method was generally applied after intervention by a "racial inspector." It was mostly the children of foreign workers who were affected. As future janissaries of the Third Reich, children of recognized Nordic descent were placed in nurseries for SS children, while a network of homes was provided for children and babies of foreigners who did not pass the "racial test." A few establishments of this kind were already functioning in 1944. An inspector's report sent to Himmler gives a few details on their functioning:

During my visit, I noticed that all the babies in that home were undernourished. As the director of the home, SS Oberführer Langoth, told me, the home receives only a pint of milk and a piece and a half of sugar per day per baby. With these rations the babies are sure to die of malnutrition in a few months.

I asked SS Oberführer Langoth to inform Gauleiter Eigruber of this state of affairs, and to ask him to assure sufficient supplies for these babies while waiting for your opinion on the subject. I consider the manner in which this business is now being managed to be impossible. There are only two solutions. Either we do not want these children alive, in which case we should not let them die slowly of hunger while they use up so much milk from the general supply; there are ways to achieve this without torture or pain. Or, on the other hand, we intend to bring up these children for later use as labor.

In this case they must be nourished in such a way that it will be possible to make full use of them as workers.[24]

Kidnappings of children from the occupied territories were particularly frequent during the time of the German retreat in the East. The Wehrmacht services were the principal perpetrators. A memorandum from the Political Section at headquarters in June 1944 envisaged the following huge operation under the characteristic code name of "Operation Hay" (*Heuaktion*):

1. The Center Army group intends to assemble and send to the Reich 40,000 to 50,000 children between ten and fourteen from the territories now under its control. This measure is taken at the suggestion of the 9th Army. It will have to be strongly backed up by propaganda and have as its slogan: Reich Aid to White Russian Children, Protection Against the Partisans. This operation has already been commenced in a five-kilometer zone. . . . The operation is planned not only to reduce the direct growth of enemy strength, but also to impair its biological strength in the distant future. This point of view has been expressed by both the SS Reichsführer and the Führer. Appropriate orders to this effect were consequently given in the Southern Sector at the time of last year's retreat.

2. A similar action is now under way in the region controlled by the North Ukraine Army group (General Field Marshal Model). In the Galician sector, which enjoys special privileges from the political point of view, measures have been taken to collect 135,000 workers in labor battalions, while young men over seventeen will be incorporated into SS divisions and youngsters under seventeen will be placed in the charge of the SS Aid. This operation, which was begun a few weeks ago, has led to no political unrest up to now.[25]

We lack even the slightest information on the ultimate fate of tens or even hundreds of thousands of Russian children who were thus taken from their families and dragged along in the more or less chaotic retreat of the German armies. On the other hand, a large-scale project to trace and return home the Czech children, most of whom, as we have seen, the Nazi experts considered Germanizable, and the thousands of Polish children, was begun after the war. A search organized in 1946 by the United Nations Relief and Rehabilitation Administration (UNRRA) found more than 60,000 cases of child abductions. Despite tireless inquiries, however, scarcely 10,000 children, or one-sixth of the abductions known to have taken place, could be located.[26]

GENOCIDE BY MENTAL DEGRADATION

As we have seen, it was the Führer's opinion that the non-German populations should be allowed only the barest minimum of education: "It is enough that the non-German populations—and even the so-called Ukrainians—learn to read and write." Wetzel was more explicit about the goals the Nazis sought and their methods for attaining them.

It is of prime importance to keep in the Russian territory only a population composed for the most part of a mass of primitive European types. They will not offer any appreciable resistance to German domination. This dull and obtuse mass has to be energetically commanded, as the history of these areas in past centuries has shown. If the German ruling classes are able in the future to keep the necessary distance between them and this population, if German blood does not penetrate this mass via illegitimate births, German dominance could be maintained in the area in question for a long time to come. On condition, of course, that we dam up the biological forces that work ceaselessly to increase the numerical strength of this primitive mass. . . .[27]

In regard to the treatment of the population, especially the Poles, our starting point must always be the principle that all administrative and legislative measures aim only at Germanizing the non-German population as rapidly as possible and by every means. This is the reason why maintaining an autonomous popular cultural life in Poland, for example, must absolutely be prevented. . . . Corporations, associations, and Polish clubs must cease to exist. Similarly, Polish cultural organizations will have to be dissolved. Polish cafés and restaurants, all centers of Polish national life, must be closed down. The Poles will not be allowed to go to theaters, music halls, or German movies. Polish theaters and movies will be closed. There will be no Polish newspapers; no Polish book will be published, nor any Polish magazine. For the same reason, the Poles will have no right to own either a radio or a phonograph.[28]

In this way the desired result was to be attained—the exaltation of the German race against a dim background of peoples degraded in body and mind, strong working cattle without faces or individualities, whom the Masters would allow to exist so long as they were useful.

Despite everything, some of the Masters occasionally happened to utter strangely heretical opinions on the basic racial dogmas. One evidence for this is a semiprivate correspondence found in the archives of the Ministry of Occupied Territories. The writers, two high functionaries (Dargel, Director General of the Reich Commissariat for the Ukraine, and von Homeyer, one of the adjutants of the Commissioner General for the Crimea) both agreed on the necessity of treating the slaves like cattle "in order to facilitate victory." Nevertheless, von Homeyer allowed the following reflections to slip out:

> Permit me, my dear party comrade, to return to the Slav question. The thesis that all Slavs are inferior to us is debatable for various reasons, not to mention the fact that this overgeneralized formula should be avoided out of deference to certain of our allies. I give you the reasons in question:
>   1. The Prussians, from our point of view the most efficient of the Germans, are the product of a Germano-Slavic blood alliance.
>   2. The Slavic world is as little uniform as the German world. We do not admit that the Swedes and ourselves can be considered alike, for example; the Russians feel the same way about the Poles, and the Poles about the Ukrainians.
>   3. In certain areas the Slav is our superior. Let me remind you of the healthy virtue of the women in that country (the USSR) after a quarter of a century of Bolshevik demoralization—I dare not think of what would happen to us after such events.
>   I am convinced [so this curious Hitlerian Hamlet concluded] that our aspirations can be realized only by our moral superiority, rather than by a dominance based on material power.[29]

GENOCIDE BY DEPORTATION

The mass deportation of peoples was the keystone of the Nazi plans for the non-German peoples. The turning topsy-turvy of the ethnographic map of Europe, of which the Nazis dreamed, would best assure the suppression of ethnic or national entities and with the least amount of bloodshed. Shrewdly dispersed across Siberia, South America, or Africa, these peoples could quickly lose all feeling for their former national allegiance. At least this is the way the Nazi theorists figured. How practicable would have been the forced migrations of tens not to say hundreds of millions of persons, what would have been the immediate loss in human life, are questions which the course of events has fortunately left unanswered. Characteristically, these deportations, though enthusiastically undertaken after the conquest of Poland and started in Alsace after the 1940 armistice, were soon stopped (with the exception, of course, of the convoys of foreign workers and of deported Jews) in the face of the more pressing requirements of the military operations.

The organization charged with the mass deportations was Himmler's Commissariat for the Strengthening of Germanism. In the fall of 1939 more than 200,000 Poles were evacuated from territories annexed to the Reich and deported to the Government General, while an almost equivalent number of "ethnic Germans" from Volhynia and the Baltic countries replaced them in their houses and on their farms. But the operation, whose total scope embraced the 6,000,000 Poles of this area, was interrupted at the insistence of the Wehrmacht, which sent a memorandum to Goering outlining these dangers:

> The contemplated transfer, which has already been partially undertaken, of 6.75 million Poles and Jews threatens to disorganize and paralyze economic life, all the more as it is being done without any regard for military, civil, and economic necessities. Here are some possible consequences:
> *In the annexed German regions.*—Loss of irreplaceable labor for agriculture, industry, and business; decline in production, imperiling of the civilian food supply, and disorganization of economic life.
> *In the Government General.*—Tremendous overpopulation of the territory, whose density would rise from 98 to 158 inhabitants per square kilometer (Germany: 135 inhabitants per square kilometer). The population would no longer have an adequate supply of food in these overpopulated agricultural regions with their small yield. Serious political dangers are to be feared. The starved population would be a prey to Communist propaganda from neighboring Russia. Mass sabotage is to be feared.[30]

From then on, the practical execution of the program (except for certain strictly localized deportations, such as the expulsion of 140,000 Poles from the region of Zamisz, renamed Himmlerstadt, in the winter of 1942–43) was postponed until after the war.[31]

In Alsace-Lorraine, the small size of the area of experimentation made it possible to carry the enterprise a little further. We know that Frenchmen living in the region since 1918 were expelled after the armistice of 1940; as for the rest, an essential role fell to the "racial inspectors." Under the circumstances it would seem that it was far more preferable for people to be recognized as "racially inferior" than to become the object of Germanic solicitude. For, in the latter case, they were selected for "colonization of the East," and if they refused German nationality, or showed ill will in any other way, they were sent to a concentration camp; whereas "racially inferior" Frenchmen were simply returned to France.[32] As for the elite of the country, or what one of the Nazi reports called the "intellectual strata," they were to be "calmly eliminated" (*ruhig ausgemerzt*), to quote the Führer.[33] The Alsatians gave many a disappointment to the prophets of Germanism. Two weeks after the Allied landing in France, SS General Berger, Himmler's chief of staff, sent his chief these peremptory lines:

> The Alsatians are—with all due respect to you—a nation of pigs. They had figured the French and English were going to return. Which is why they were especially hostile and vicious when the reprisals began. My Reichsführer, I think we should send half of them away, no matter where. Stalin would certainly accept them.[34]

The Nazis, however, experienced their greatest disappointments in the Netherlands. Opinion was unanimous on this. Goering exclaimed: "The Dutch are unique as the nation of traitors to our cause." But then he added: "I don't hold it against them; I perhaps wouldn't have acted differently myself." [35] In a fit of anger, however, Hitler in April 1941 ordered the deportation of all Dutchmen to the Government General, with the sole exception of members of the Dutch National-Socialist Party (NSB) and their families. Here, again, the imminence of the Russian campaign (apparently along with certain hesitations on the part of Himmler, who had been entrusted with organizing the deportation) saved these people, who perhaps in all of Europe resisted the Germans the most, from horrible trials.[36]

Many other orders, decisions, and projects lay dormant in the Nazi files, ready to be applied when the situation called for them, but events did not permit their being carried out. In the event that the Germans landed in Great Britain, the Wehrmacht's plans provided for the deportation to the Continent of the entire male population between sixteen and forty-five.[37] It was probably intended that these Englishmen should occupy the depopulated areas in the East. In fact, according to the main outlines of the projects prepared by Himmler's and Rosenberg's departments, the Russians, as well as the non-Germanizable Czechs and part of the Poles, were to be thrust beyond the Urals, while the remaining Poles were to be sent to the Guianas or Brazil. The Balts, and a large part of the White Russians, were to enjoy the privilege of being deported to the Reich itself, as agricultural workers. The Russian areas were destined to be colonized in part by the Germans, in part by "kindred peoples." In Western Europe, where the population transfers were to be rather smaller, the protectorates of Burgundy and Brittany were to be set up, cut away from France proper, so as to reduce that country, renamed "Gaul," to its minimum area. (6) At no time did the Nazis' hatred for France slacken, though for opportunistic reasons, or because they were hypnotized by the threat of the "biological potential" of the Eastern peoples, the "French question" was only of secondary importance in their eyes.

Projects scrupulously drawn up, crammed with statistics, and providing for the slightest detail—it is not so much their enormity that overwhelms one, as the thought that their authors were quite capable (they have given the proof) of keeping their wildest promises and breathing life into their most delirious dreams.

(6) Wetzel's memo, which has been quoted several times, gives details for these projects, and is corroborated, among others, by Kersten.

CHAPTER TWELVE

Conclusion: Genocide and the Peoples of Europe

"AND ABRAHAM SAID, 'Wilt thou also destroy the righteous with the wicked? Peradventure there be fifty righteous within the city. Wilt thou then destroy . . . the place?' "

GERMANY: INDIVIDUAL REACTIONS AND COLLECTIVE GUILT

Like Sodom and Gomorrah, Hitler's Germany too had its fifty righteous men. They could be found in every social circle and in every social class. For these people, silent disapproval or a chance service secretly rendered to a Jew was not enough; recoiling in horror and dismay, they committed their entire lives to a revolt against Nazism. There was the dean of the Church of Saint Hedwige in Berlin, Canon Lichtenberg, who was jailed in October 1941 for his pro-Jewish sermons and public protests; he asked the Gestapo to be transferred to the Lodz ghetto and died at Dachau in 1943.[1] There was the anonymous German doctor who voluntarily followed his Jewish wife to the Warsaw ghetto and was killed during the insurrection of April 1943.[2] Examples of this kind (most of which will never be known) must certainly be numbered in the hundreds, perhaps in the thousands, when one remembers that there were several thousand German Jews with false papers who were able to find a secret shelter in Hitler Germany. These acts of resistance by courageous Germans make part of the general German resistance to Hitler which, however sporadic and ineffectual it was, and inhibited at every step by false scruples against betraying the fatherland at war, was nonetheless a reality. When one turns one's attention from heroic isolated deeds to instances of silent and timid disapproval, the first thing to remember is that in March 1933, in the last Reichstag elections, 55 per cent of the German

281

people voted against Hitler.[3] However, it should be remembered that anti-Semitism was not limited only to the followers of Hitler; there were anti-Semites to be found elsewhere than in the Nazi Party. We have almost nothing in the way of exact statistics on this matter of popular attitudes. After analysing his compatriots' conduct with respect to the anti-Jewish persecutions in 1942, when the deportation of the Jews was going full blast, a German democrat of the old school came to the following conclusions: [4] 5 per cent gave enthusiastic approval to the Nazi Jewish policies; 69 per cent were totally indifferent; 21 per cent were uncertain and confused; 5 per cent categorically disapproved. These observations can be relied on, for the observer, Müller-Claudius, possessed good faith and objectivity combined with intellectual caution.

What is there to say?—90 per cent of the German population was indifferent for a variety of reasons. This was a passive majority, ready to change with the wind, the kind of people you find in every group, just as much inclined to yield to temptation as to be daunted by terror. As for the active minority (especially the fanatical youth), we know only too well what their choice was. Although there were many Germans, even in the very bosom of the Party, who, as individuals, did not approve of the massacres, they always acceded in silence to what their leaders called "the will of the people." Another German author, Enno Kind, wrote that

> The year 1941 was marked by the beginning of the extermination of the German Jews; all adversaries of the regime, as well as all those who were neutral, were henceforth compelled to give proof of their personal courage by refusing to abandon friends persecuted by Hitler. And it must be said that most of the indifferent elements at this time dropped their last pretenses to any sort of resistance and passed over into the Fascist camp. Henceforth, there was scarcely any place in Germany for human feelings.[5]

Here again we must understand what is meant by "human feelings." The instructive example of the "euthanasia program" indicates clearly enough how the "will of the people," German public opinion, was able to be an active and effective factor on other occasions. We have seen how this other extermination project, much smaller in scope but kept just as secret and easier to conceal, as its victims had already been withdrawn from the world and put away in asylums, had to be stopped because of the outcry against it of a population whose "human feelings" it had outraged. (1) Also, the extermination of the so-called "useless mouths" concerned German lives that were flesh of their flesh. Despite the Führer, most of these were spared. The eloquent example of Fascist Italy has shown us how many Jewish lives might have been saved in spite of a dictator's wishes.

And so we come back to an ensemble of specifically German modes of thinking and living, national characteristics which influenced historical developments, or were influenced by them, and prepared the way for Hitler and Nazism. It was a strange mixture of morbid rationalism and nationalistic exaltation. One recalls that such matters as the recovery of gold teeth from corpses were already being discussed in the German press in 1925, in the Germany of the Weimar Republic.[6] At this same time, euthanasia was already being advocated and defended warmly with the same specious arguments. (2) Returning to our subject, we find that "anti-Semitism

(1) These lines had already been written when the author found much the same thing being said in the text of a judgment of the German Supreme Court (British Zone) quashing the verdict in the case of Veit Harlan, the producer of the Nazi film *Jew Süss*. After a judicious appraisal of the effect of anti-Semitic propaganda on anaesthetizing the collective conscience, the judgment made this observation: "If large groups had openly or secretly opposed the persecution of the Jews as, principally because of the efforts of the churches of the two Christian denominations, they had opposed the murder of the mentally ill, the development of the terror would have been impossible *in the long run,* or at least it would have been retarded and made very difficult." (Annulment of the verdict in the case of Veit Harlan, German Supreme Court for the British Zone, December 12, 1949, p. 14.)

(2) In 1931 the famous German psychiatrist Oswald Bumke addressed these prophetic words to the many advocates of euthanasia:

For the love of God, keep financial considerations out of these questions. This is a problem that concerns the future of all our people, and, indeed of the human race. . . . The logical consequence of the idea that economic reasons justify the extermination of all useless human beings is monstrous; it would be necessary to kill not only the mentally ill and the insane, but all the cripples, including crippled veterans, unemployed spinsters, people living off invested funds, and the retired. We would save a great deal of money in this way; but probably we would never go quite so far. Moreover, there is reason for being cautious, at least until the political atmosphere of the country clears up. For if we continue these discussions, it will no longer be a question of the mentally ill, but of Aryans and non-Aryans, of the blond Germanic race as against the inferior round-headed peoples.

(Quoted from the indictment by General Telford Taylor, Nuremberg Tribunal, session of December 9, 1946.)

came from across the Rhine, from the old Germany always ready for religious quarrels and imbued with the spirit of caste; and from the new Germany puffed with race pride and scornful of everything not Teutonic." [7] These lines, by the French historian Leroy-Beaulieu, a conservative of the old school, were written in 1893, at about the same time that the great Mommsen was judging his country clear-sightedly and noting the following in his spiritual testament:

> I have never had and have never sought political position and political influence; but in my innermost being, I believe, with the best part of me I have always been a political animal and have wished to be a citizen. That is impossible in our nation, where the individual, even the best, cannot rise superior to the body of our political fetichism. This inner estrangement of mine from the people to whom I belong has convinced me that, with my personality, I ought insofar as possible to avoid making any public appearance before the German people, whom I lack respect for completely.[8]

All this was so well known and yet so easily forgotten! When Mommsen was writing these lines, the Pan-Germanist agitation had reached its peak in Germany. For decades, innumerable philosophers, journalists, and teachers had exalted the Prussian ideal of inflexible hardness and blind obedience—while the solemn Hegel himself deified the state. For a century the Jahns, the Arndts, the Lists, the Treitschkes, and the von Bernhardis had proclaimed the superiority of the German race and urged Germany on to new and joyous wars. Nietzsche's message, with its dangerous subtlety, carried away the German crowds, who interpreted and deformed it to please themselves, keeping only what they liked, principally the glorification of the "blond beast." (3) The ground for the Nazi catastrophe had been prepared long in advance; when the Führer, before marching the Nazi legions off to conquer the world, care-

(3) Here let us cite the well-known passage in which Nietzsche gives his views about the Jews:
Every people and person has his unpleasant, yes even dangerous traits; it is cruel to demand that the Jews be an exception. Perhaps these traits are particularly unpleasant and dangerous in them; and perhaps the young Jewish petty speculator is the most repellent invention of humanity. But I should like to know what the final balance sheet would be for this people that, not without the guilt of all of us, has had the most unhappy history of all peoples, and to whom we owe the most noble of men (Christ), the purest sage (Spinoza), the most powerful book and the most effective moral law in the world. (*Complete Works*, Musarion edition, VIII, 337.)

fully trained them to be hard, cruel, and violent men, to stamp all pity from their hearts, to silence their conscience—that "Jewish invention"—he merely gave life and form to a vague ancestral dream. It still remains to be seen how far the collective conscience of any group, even one as receptive and pliable as the German, can be bent and turned so as to make it conform to the worlds built, with the aid of every modern technique. Was the grandiose plan of the SS realizable? Could a society of "violent, hard, and cruel wild animals" such as Hitler dreamed of be created? Could certain conditioning processes, employed on children taken from the cradle, progressively dehumanize people?

Perhaps we can glimpse an answer to this question in the different reactions of the Nazi executioners as we have observed them. Was not the self-pity and persistant uneasiness of the murderers an indication of a secret inner protest, of a confused realization that they were destroying something of themselves in the death and destruction that they spread (4). This leads one back to what seems to us to be the deep essence of Hitlerism: the fact that it was an explosion of hatred and blind fury which, in venting itself on others, in the last analysis turned against itself. From this, one may conclude that over and beyond the revolt which he led against the Judeo-Christian spirit and morality, the German Führer also sought to attack and destroy an essential component of all human society. It is inherent in man's nature to recognize himself in others and to revere in them his own image and essence (the double meaning of the word "humanity," which we find in all languages, can have only this significance). Mass slaughters of human beings are perpetrated on the battlefield, but by soldiers running the same risks in accordance with the rules of warfare—when one group of men slaughters another, not as adversaries and men, but as noxious insects, the price it pays for this is its own humanity.

(4) We have already quoted many personal accounts. Let us quote still another, the fact that it is not of SS provenance, and is uttered so casually, lends it a particular significance. It is dated October 23, 1941. Its author was a Wehrmacht officer, reporting his observations during a trip to the "Eastern zone of operations." Notice the similar construction of the two paragraphs quoted, both of which end on the same note of self-solicitude. The first paragraph concerns Russian prisoners of war:

"The columns of prisoners marching along the roads resemble a senseless flock of sheep. . . . Because of the physical exertion of the marches, the poor food and the bad conditions in the camps, the prisoners often collapse and

VON DER EINSATZGRUPPE A DURCHGEFÜHRTE
JUDENEXEKUTIONEN (1)

PETERSBURG

KRASNOGWARDEISK

REVAL

963

JUDENFREI (2)

3600

DABÖ

LOSEL

ARENSBURG

OSTSEE

RIGAER
BUCHT

GHETTO 2500 RIGA

35.238

GHETTO 4500
OSCHAULEN

DUNABURG
GHETTO 950

136.421

KAUEN
GHETTO 15.000

41.828

O MINSK

GESCHÄTZTE ZAHL DER NOCH VORHANDENEN JUDEN 128.000 (3)

EXTERMINATION MAP FOR THE BALTIC COUNTRIES

Map illustrated with coffins attached to the comprehensive report of "Action Group
A" for the year 1941. (PS 2273)

(1) Execution of Jews successfully carried out by Action Group A.
(2) Free of Jews.
(3) The number of Jews still alive is estimated at 128,000.

We should perhaps add that the history of the human race teaches us this same lesson, as do also the investigations of anthropologists. We are wrong if we think that savage or half-civilized peoples feel no restraints or inhibitions on the cruelty they show to their foes. In all civilizations and races, not excepting the most primitive, the murder of a man or the killing of an enemy has always been a very serious matter, fraught with all sorts of consequences and subject to numberless restrictions, expiatory rituals, and taboos.[9] Whatever the complex psychic reasons for this may be, the rule itself is absolute and universal.

However boundless, therefore, may seem the powers of the modern demiurges, we shall find that there will always be certain limits to the perversion and robotization of even the most docile crowds. But incapable in the end though they may be of creating "a new man," modern totalitarian leaders nevertheless dispose of almost unlimited means for wreaking destruction pure and simple. Only in a society of men dedicated and given over to death have completely new forms of human behavior been able to develop. By a sordid irony, the complete extirpation of the moral sense which the Führer dreamed of for the "new Nazi man" was able to be carried out only among his victims in the inferno of the concentration camp. But the shadow of the concentration camps still lowers over the world; and Adolf Hitler's last message continues to re-

---

have to be dragged along by their comrades or left where they are. The 6th Army ordered all stragglers shot. This was done on the road and even in the villages, with the unfortunate result that German employees returning home at night had to pass by the bodies of prisoners who were shot."

The second paragraph of the report concerns Jews: "In accordance with orders, the Jews are transferred. This is done in the following way: They receive an order to report the next night, in their best clothes and with all their jewels or valuables, at a designated assembly point. . . . They are then taken to a place, already got ready for them, outside the particular locality. Under the pretext of fulfilling certain formalities, they are required to deposit all their clothing, jewels, and ornaments. They are then led off the road and liquidated. The resulting situations are so agonizing that they cannot be described. The consequences this has for the German Kommandos are inevitable. In general, the executions can be carried out only in an alcoholic stupor. According to what an SD officer who had been detailed for this duty told me, he had to endure (durchstehen) the most terrifying nightmares the next night." (NOKW 3147)

verberate across the ravaged continent of Europe, echoing the sullen mutterings in the hate-filled minds of men.

POPULAR ATTITUDES IN THE OCCUPIED COUNTRIES

In Germany, a primitive and ill-comprehended patriotism intensified the indifference and hostility shown to the Jews; whereas in the countries under the heel of the Third Reich, attachment to a national ideal, it would seem, could only result in acts and manifestations in their favor. Any aid given the Jews was a challenge to the invader; they could escape the fate prepared for them only by a series of deeds that fitted quite naturally into a larger context of insubordination and open rebellion against the conqueror.

But up to the organization of the resistance, this was far from being the case in the countries of Eastern Europe. We have already spoken of the reserved attitude the clandestine Polish organizations showed even toward those Jews who tried to fight with weapons in their hands. As for the mass of the people, their attitude was primarily one of indifference—while active minorities assiduously gathered in the countless fruits of pillage and denunciation. This ran contrary to General Blaskowitz's prophecy in 1940: "Very rapidly . . . the Poles and the Jews, helped by the Catholic Church, will join in their hate against their executioners." There were of course a number of acts of devotion and individual heroism; but the dominant feeling was one of complete apathy, the result of fear as well as unavowed satisfaction. This apathy, which only echoed the traditional anti-Semitism of the Poles, was negatively expressed by the complete absence of any collective protests or manifestations, such as the episcopates of very Catholic Poland repeatedly sent to Governor General Frank on other subjects. (When the author of one of these documents mentioned the fate of the Jews it was only to grow indignant at the moral debasement suffered by *the perpetrators of the massacres:* "I am not going to write at length on a fact so terrible as the use of drunken young men of labor battalions for the extermination of the Jews." This horribly ambiguous phrase is taken from a protest sent to Frank by Adam Sapieha, Prince Archbishop of Cracow.[10]) Whatever the deep historical reasons for this, whatever the character and number of the individual exceptions, the overwhelming weight of the evidence (8) leads inescapably to the bitter conclusion that the attitude of the Polish people toward the agony of the Jews differed little from that of the Germans. Farther east, especially in the Ukraine, in areas for which we have scarcely any direct testimony, popular feeling seems to have been much the same, if we are to believe the complacent observations and splenetic sarcasms that fill the Nazi archives:

The native population, which is completely aware of the liquidation process, regards it calmly, with some satisfaction; the Ukrainian militia participates in it.[11] The population of the Crimea is anti-Jewish and in individual cases hands over Jews to the commandos for liquidation. The *starostas* (mayors) ask to be authorized to liquidate Jews themselves.[12]

It is perhaps possible to pass a more discriminating judgment on other countries of Eastern and Southeastern Europe. This is not to say that the Hungarian people, for example, showed any great emotion at the time of the lightning deportations of the Hungarian Jews. (9) And we have already mentioned the monstrous pogroms,

(8) Dozens of published works and hundreds of depositions and stories by survivors are almost unanimous on this score. To avoid repetition and because of lack of space, we give no details or quotations.

(9) In a report submitted to Washington by the Office of Strategic Services, dated October 19, 1944, there is an interesting analysis of Hungarian reactions to the deportations of the Jews.

"The general reaction of the Hungarian population to the anti-Semitic measures of the government is difficult to characterize. On the one hand, there is evidence that large sections of the Hungarian intelligentsia and especially of the lower middle class supported the anti-Jewish propaganda. Numerous stories in the Hungarian press report the institution of proceedings against many elements in the population who tried to get rich by outdoing the government in their zeal to expropriate the Jews. Likewise, reports from authoritative sources show that the Hungarian police tend to treat the Jews worse than the Gestapo.

"On the other hand, a number of reports mention Hungarian aid to Jewish compatriots. In the city of Nagyvarad alone, 2,004 Christians have been prosecuted for possessing goods entrusted to them by Jews before their departure. (It must be remembered, however, that this was not always done for altruistic reasons.)

"It can be said that there is no active resistance to the government's anti-Semitic measures. A certain amount of passive resistance is evident from the cases of people being arrested for helping Jews secure false identity papers or baptismal certificates, hiding Jewish goods to avoid their confiscation, and other similar stratagems."

taking tens of thousands of victims, that drenched with blood the cities of Rumania at the beginning of 1941. The density of the Jewish population in each country doubtless had something to do with this. For decades Jewish sociologists have been tempted to set up a "coefficient of saturation," or percentage of Jews in a population above which endemic and virulent anti-Semitism becomes inevitable. This might explain why the Jews more easily found help in Bulgaria or Yugoslavia, for example, than in Hungary and in Rumania. Added to this was the factor of the degree of assimiliation and integration of the Jewish masses (the fact that Jews in the eastern countries for the most part still formed a class apart cannot be discussed here), which in turn was essentially dependent on the general cultural level and economic development of the country. We must also take into account the different policies pursued by the satellite countries, and the different courses followed by their clergies. All these different factors, which are sometimes obscured by the darkness of the times, are difficult to evaluate. Whatever may have been their relative importance, they resulted in a popular attitude of indifference, sometimes mixed with secret satisfaction, toward the agony of the Jews of Eastern Europe.

It has already been said that popular reactions in Western Europe were quite different. In the centers of ancient European civilization, compassion for the Jews was general and the rejection of the bestial Hitlerian variant of anti-Semitism was almost unanimous. Active aid was given the Jews by ordinary citizens as well as by many officials and still more clerics. Veritable networks for rescuing Jews were progressively set up; there is scarcely a survivor today who does not owe his life and liberty to an act by some non-Jewish compatriot. In the last analysis, it was this attitude which was the real reason for Western Europe's considerably higher proportion of survivors.

And yet these survivors emerged from the years of trial with mixed feelings. For the memory of their forced and artificial segregation remained, reviving old fears that the Jews had thought long dead, fears as impossible to efface now as the memory of the scalp dances engaged in by traitors and collaborators of every shade, who though their number was small, made up for this by their violence. Did not complete galaxies of illustrious names, as well as the national glories made to serve the new regimes, seem to lend their support to the actions of the conquerors? Were not the raids and arrests the work of the local police, the complacent servant of the law and the nation? Once the first emotion had passed, did not the population tend to lose interest in the fate of the Jews, tacitly accept matters as they were, and give themselves up entirely to their own worries? (10) Exacerbated Jewish sensibilities are quick to ask such questions. And it still remains a question whether the sympathy shown would not have been more active and positive if some other minority had been the arbitrarily selected victim.

In Western Europe, the "Jewish question" is essentially a psychological one, since it no longer corresponds to material antagonisms and conflicts of interest. The persecutions had all the qualities needed to envenom this psychological complex. By an inexorable mechanism, they drove deeper and deeper the wedge between a majority which, happy at being spared, gradually accepted the accomplished fact, and a bitter and mistrustful minority. Troubling memories from the past associated with the idea of the Jew came to the surface again, evoked by Israel's new misfortune, which extended through four interminable years. For the ordinary man's pity and commiseration is excited by sudden disaster, but the contemplation of prolonged suffering tires and finally irritates him. Imperceptibly, people tend to draw ? ay from the outcast marked with the obvious signs of punishme ↓ and misfortune. Ancestral hostilities revive in an atmosphere where defamation is relentless, omnipresent, and insinuating, stimulating doubts even in milieus traditionally removed from and indifferent to the "Jewish question." (11)

(10) "The Dutch population has got used to the deportations. They no longer cause any trouble," Bene, Ribbentrop's representative in the Netherlands, noted on November 16, 1942. Earlier, on July 31, 1942—that is, when the deportations began—he had notified his chief of "the popular excitement that can be observed, especially in Amsterdam." And on April 30, 1943, Bene again noted: "People are no longer interested in the deportations, from which they have benefited, except where their half-Jewish friends are involved. Sometimes formerly pro-Jewish people go to great lengths to obtain the apartments of evacuated Jews." (NG 2631)

(11) Here is one of many documents that is particularly characteristic in this respect. It is a petition addressed to Marshal Pétain in 1941 by the popu-

On returning home after the liberation, impatient to resume their
old ways, to find their homes again, and to collect their goods, the

---

lation of Tournon-d'Agenais, a remote village in the Lot-et-Garonne region
whose inhabitants had probably never in their life laid eyes on a Jew. The petition has 195 signatures:

"We the undersigned, inhabitants of the principal township of the canton of
Tournon-d'Agenais (Lot-et-Garonne), have the honor to inform you of the
following facts:

"The total population of our little place is 275 people and we have been
told that we shall shortly receive 150 undesirable Jews who must live among
us. Everything leads us to believe that this information is correct, for bedding
and some straw have already been deposited in our public buildings.

"We are all, Monsieur le Maréchal, very much upset at this prospect. The
invasion by 150 undesirable Jews of the homes of 275 entirely peaceful French
people is tantamount to a colonisation, and we are afraid of seeing ourselves
outrageously supplanted by the sheer force of the strangers' numbers.

"We are told that we are going to get undesirables. But by the same token
they are that for all Frenchmen; they cannot be less undesirable to us than
they are to the places that are getting rid of them.

"One hundred fifty undesirables, if need be, can go almost unnoticed
among several thousand people. But their presence is intolerable and becomes
a ridiculous harassment for a population less than twice their number and
forced by this fact into a promiscuity, if not a cohabitation, that is revolting.

"Faithful to our tradition of hospitality, we did our best to welcome people
from the Saar, Spaniards, then unfortunate Frenchmen from the invaded
regions and the Lorraines driven from their homes, but we can only protest
with the utmost energy against the unjustified occupation of our buildings by
a lot of undesirables pitilessly driven out of other cities and villages.

"Besides we have no water or public conveniences at Tournon. Nor do we
have a market for supplies; right now the three little restaurants here have a
hard time feeding the few travelers who occasionally pass through.

"Questions of hygiene and food supply must certainly be among the chief
concerns of your administration; here they are allied in the closest possible
way with the truly French moral-ethnic question.

"Knowing your paternal solicitude for all our interests, we are sure, Monsieur le Maréchal, that it will be enough for you to be informed of the painful
and unjust prospect by which we are menaced to give orders to spare us its
unhappy realization.

"However, we realize that the Jews are human like ourselves and must find
a shelter somewhere. If in your wisdom you believe that the higher good of
the State demands that we make the sacrifice of tolerating them among us, we
resign ourselves to it, though not without great bitterness; we ask only if it
would not be possible to reduce this painful association by quartering them
apart in a camp near a spring or a little stream (there is one in our commune)
where all questions of surveillance, hygiene, and food supply could be solved
to the advantage of the guests whom ill-fortune imposes on us, as well as to
our own.

"In this hope, we beg you, Monsieur le Maréchal, to accept the expression
of our sincere gratitude, and the assurance of our respectful devotion."

Jews encountered the fierce organized opposition of those who had succeeded to their places (as the Machiavellian calculations of the Nazis had foreseen). (12) Thus, although many marks of good will and solidarity had been shown them during the years of misfortune, their fate as the eternal outlaw was harshly recalled to the people of Israel.

Was the popular reaction the same in all the Western countries from Italy to Norway? Evaluating collective behavior is a delicate matter, and these events are still too recent to make definitive judgments easy. But if a rapid comparison is made, it can be seen clearly that the little pacific peoples with their old democratic traditions were the ones that reacted with the most firmness and unanimity. In the Netherlands, in February 1941, the first deportation caused such an uproar that a general strike of several days' duration, something inconceivable under the Nazi boot, broke out spontaneously. In Denmark the deportations were blocked by the active cooperation of the whole population; the Germans, as we have seen, did not dare impose the yellow star on the Jews because of the attitude of King Christian X. (Remember, too, that in tiny, far-off Bulgaria, great popular demonstrations took place at the time of the deportations, to the cry of "We want the Jews back.") These weak countries, whose very history had sheltered them from the excesses and temptations of imperialist ambitions, once more gave the world proof of their balance and maturity.

THE CHRISTIAN CHURCHES: DOGMA AND REALITY

The shocked response of people to the Nazi persecutions of the Jews was essentially moral in nature, a spontaneous reflex of outraged conscience. The position taken by the established spiritual authorities could therefore not fail to be a determining factor in the situation. The churches were the only moral authority whose power grew rather than diminished amid the turmoil of Nazism,

(12) Cf. the previously mentioned report (p. 66) by Knochen, chief of the German police in France: "It has been shown that it is almost impossible to cultivate an ideologically based anti-Jewish feeling in the French, whereas economic inducements would more easily arouse sympathy for the anti-Jewish struggle (the internment of more than 100,000 foreign Jews living in Paris would give many Frenchmen a chance to raise themselves from the lower to the middle classes)."

especially as regards the Jews, since the popular conception of them which had taken shape in the course of centuries had always been associated in the popular mind with the first childhood impressions made upon it by the Christian Gospels and religious education.

The possibilties open in this connection to the monolithic organization of the Catholic Church, to which more than three-fourths of the population of the subjugated countries, with the exception of the USSR, belonged, were particularly great. In former days, during the Middle Ages, the attitude of Catholicism to the Jews had had two aspects. The official doctrine, as laid down by Saint Thomas Aquinas, commanded the preservation of Jewish lives; but at the same time it sanctioned all the exactions and humiliations visited upon stiff-necked Jewry. It is true that the Popes and Princes of the Church many times opposed the massacre of the Jews in the name of Christian charity; but it is also true that its theologians and thinkers accepted the oppressed condition of the Jews as natural and salutary. (13) Long before the Nazis introduced the yellow star, did not the Lateran Council of 1215 decree that Jews must wear the badge? As against the Church Triumphant, the Blindfold Synagogue had a special part to play: (14) the humbled and abased Jews were tangible proof of the truth of the Faith, of the grandeur and reality of the Christian dogma. Hence the incessant effort to humiliate the Jews on the one hand, and the principle of the inviolability of Jewish lives on the other. But

(13) Here is how Saint Thomas Aquinas summed up the general doctrine in an answer to the Duchess of Braban, who had asked him "to what extent she could impose exactions on the Jews":

". . . Although, according to the laws, the Jews' own fault has condemned them to perpetual servitude, and the lords may consider all their earthly goods as their own, with this proviso that they may not be deprived of the necessities of life . . ., it would appear that one must not impose any servitude on the Jews not suffered by them in years past, for it is departures from the usages of the past that are disquieting. You may, in observing such principles of moderation, follow the custom of your predecessors as regards the exactions to be imposed on the Jews, on condition, however, that there is nothing elsewhere that would forbid it." 13

(14) The juxtaposition of the Church Triumphant and the Veiled Synagogue is a theme that can be found on the façade of many cathedrals; the Church is represented as a dazzling young woman, the Synagogue as a figure with blindfolded eyes.

these two attitudes, whose compatibility had been ceaselessly called into question during centuries of massacres, proved impossible to reconcile, and our own age has seen the contradictions of the church doctrine violently explode.

Let us hasten to add that the church's tireless humanitarian efforts in the face of the Hitler terror, with the approval or under the stimulus of the Vatican, can never be forgotten. We do not know what were the exact instructions sent by the Holy See to the churches in the different countries, but the coincidence of effort at the time of the deportations is proof that such steps were taken. Mention has already been made of the intervention of the Slovakian clergy (cf. p. 160), who, as noted in the German report on the matter, acted under the influence of the Holy See. In Poland, there was an echo of such a stand by the Vatican in the ideas privately developed by Monseigneur Szepticki, Metropolitan of the Uniate Catholic Church of Galicia, (15) according to which "the extermination of the Jews was inadmissible." A witness to this confidential conversation hastened to tell the Germans about it, adding: "He (the Metropolitan) is expressing the same thoughts as the French, Belgian, and Dutch bishops, as if they had all received the same instructions from the Vatican." [14] However, in conformity with their surroundings, the clergy in the countries of Eastern Europe were nowhere near as bold in their defiance as the Western clergy; in France, the Netherlands, and elsewhere, a number of prelates, not content with cautious and diplomatic remonstrances, conducted public prayers for the Jews. A series of pamphlets, called *Témoignage chrétien* (Christian Witness), clandestinely continued the tradition of Charles Péguy, barring the way to racist contagion under the slogan, "France, take care lest you lose your soul"—this certainly was one of the finest pages of the French Resistance. It should be added that in the Vatican itself, the Pope personally aided and protected dozens of Rumanian Jews. When the Nazis made an exorbitant demand on the Jewish inhabitants of Rome in October 1943, he offered fifteen kilos of gold to make up the sum.

(15) The Uniate Catholic Church (Ruthenian) is as much subject to the supreme authority of the Holy See as all the other Catholic churches, from which it differs only in a few details of ritual (old Slavonic liturgy, etc.).

These humanitarian activities were necessarily carried on by the Vatican in a cautious and quiet way. The immense church interests which were the Pope's responsibility, the extensive means for blackmail which the Nazis enjoyed, on a scale commensurate with the Universal Church, probably account for his failure to issue that solemn and public declaration which the persecuted looked forward to so ardently. It is painful to have to say that all during the war, while the death factories ran full blast, the Papacy kept silent. However, it has to be recognized that public protests might have been immediately followed by pitiless retaliation, as experience on a local scale showed. (Thus, Jews converted to Catholicism in the Netherlands were deported along with the others, following an episcopal letter read in the Catholic Churches, while a reprieve was given to Protestant Jews, since the Protestant Church had refrained from public protest. A short-lived reprieve, it is true; some months later, they shared the usual fate.) What would have been the effect of a solemn condemnation pronounced by the supreme authority of Catholicism? The significance, in principle, of an intransigent attitude of opposition to Nazi treatment of the Jews on the part of the church would have been immense. Its particular and immediate consequences, for the activities and institutions of the Catholic Church as well as for the Jews themselves, are something which it is more hazardous to express an opinion about.

One may however wonder whether the attitude of Pius XI, author of the famous encyclical *Mit brennender Sorge*, would not have been firmer than that of his successor. Von Weizsäcker, Ambassador of the Third Reich to the Holy See, drew such a parallel when he reported on the Vatican's reactions to the mass deportation of Jews from Rome. In his first report, dated October 17, 1943, he warned his government as follows: "They say that the bishops of French cities, where similar incidents occurred, have taken a strong stand. The Pope, as supreme head of the Church and Bishop of Rome, cannot be more reticent than they. They are also drawing a parallel between the stronger character of Pius XI and that of the present Pope." In a second report, dated October 28, Weizsäcker congratulated himself on his apprehensions not having been borne out: "Although under pressure from all sides, the Pope has not let himself be drawn into any demonstrative censure of the deportation of the Jews from Rome. Although he must expect that this attitude will be criticized by our enemies, and exploited by the Protestants of the Anglo-Saxon countries in their propaganda against Catholicism, he has done everything he could in this delicate matter not to strain relations with the German government." (16)

If the Holy See had no choice but to be extremely cautious and vigilant during the time when the SS ruled Rome, one can also agree that the reading of such reports would scarcely have had the effect of restraining the murderous zeal of the rulers of the Third Reich.

But we have also to reckon with an even larger question involved in these considerations. As we have seen, in the different countries more or less under the rule of Nazi Germany, the deportations and massacres were preceded by a series of measures, or "Jewish statutes," calling for the segregation of the Jewish population and the imposition of all sorts of discriminations against them. We have also seen that these governments, though they recoiled from the last consequences of the "final solution," willingly and deliberately enacted legislation whose effect was to make Jews live under conditions like those they had had to endure in the Middle Ages. What was the attitude of the Holy See toward these measures, allowance being made for the fact that their consequences were not apparent until 1942?

However inhuman these anti-Jewish measures were in themselves, they were certainly not of such nature as to excite the same emotions as the atrocious end toward which they tended. But was that a valid excuse for supporting them? Yet, the "Jewish Statutes" in June, 1941 did not evoke a specific protest from the French Catholic episcopate (notwithstanding the good example of the Protestant Church of France). There is evidence that these statutes did not call forth any censure from the supreme governing circles of the Church. Léon Bérard, the Vichy Ambassador to the Holy See, was, indeed, expressly charged by Marshal Pétain with finding out what the opinion of Rome was on the matter, his report, all of whose statements he claimed to have verified with the authorized representatives of the church government, and which he took several weeks to prepare, stated that the "Statute" was in no way reprehensible from the Roman Catholic point of view, and that the Vatican had no intention of starting any "quarrel" over it.

After emphasizing the care and thoroughness with which he had verified his information, and citing in his support the writings of St. Thomas Aquinas, Ambassador Bérard concluded:

"As an authorized person at the Vatican informed me, they have no intention of quarreling with us over the Jewish statute. However, the representatives of the Holy See expressed two wishes to me, with the obvious desire that they be transmitted to the Chief of the French State:

"1) That no provisions on marriage be added to the law on the Jews. Here we should encounter difficulties of a religious order. The Vatican is very much aroused over the fact that Rumania has adopted marriage laws inspired by or imitating the Fascist legislation.

"2) That the precepts of justice and charity be considered in the application of the law. Those who spoke to me seemed to have in mind above all the matter of the liquidation of businesses in which Jews have an interest.

"Please excuse, Monsieur le Maréchal, my having written at such length. . . ."

It may be permissible to suppose that the Vichy diplomat went for his information to prelates whom he regarded as sympathetic to Vichy views, and that he interpreted it in a way that would incommode his master as little as possible; nevertheless, such a report would have been unthinkable if its author had had to face the formal and open disapproval of the Pope. It is not for a Jewish writer to pass judgment on the secular dogmas of another religion; but one cannot help being deeply troubled when one considers the enormous consequences that flowed from these dogmas.

Do not misunderstand the meaning of our emotion. We do not suggest that there was even a trace of anti-Semitism in the Pope's thought. If, unlike so many French bishops, he did not raise his voice, it was doubtless because his jurisdiction extended over all Europe, and he had to consider not only the serious dangers hanging over the Church, but also the state of mind of the faithful in all countries. Jacques Maudaule, a Catholic writer, has recently said that "the Church is a democracy," and that "it is almost impossible for the Pope to express an opinion unless he is forced to it by a kind of great movement of opinion arising in the masses and communicating itself to the priests from the faithful." [15] If the

Pope made no move, he perhaps did not feel sure of this "great movement of opinion arising in the masses." But then it would follow from this—and here is the gravest aspect of the matter—that the Vatican's silence only reflected the deep feeling of the Catholic masses of Europe. Here, one has reason to believe, is an essential element in the background of the causes that led on to genocide, its last necessary condition. Does not the catechism teach tens of millions of modern children that the Jews were the murderers of Jesus and therefore condemned until the Last Judgment?

Is it not true that a prayer recited on Good Friday speaks of the "perfidious Jews" and of "Jewish perfidy," (19) and that for generations, preachers from the "Eagle of Meaux"° down to lowly village priests have described the Jews as a "monstrous people, without hearth or home"? It must be pointed out, of course, that the present-day Catholic Church has begun a radical revision of its teachings on this subject. It seems that particularly the French clergy has launched a resolute attack on anti-Semitism, and even as this new edition of *Harvest of Hate* goes to press, it appears that reforms are imminent also in Rome. However, there had to be Auschwitz to put this process in motion, and who will ever be able to determine the role of childhood impressions, deeply etched upon the mind, in the events that led up to Auschwitz? (19A)

The problem, to be sure, does not concern Catholics alone, but all of Christianity. Without going back to the Middle Ages, one need only recall that as recently as a few decades ago Christian preachers in Germany, Austria, and elsewhere, whether they were called Lüger, Stöcker, or Monseigneur Jouin, were the leading heralds of European anti-Semitism. The seed they sowed has flourished, and the harvest their efforts reaped would doubtless have surprised even these imprudent clergymen. They did not realize

(19) The principal if not the only meaning of the Latin words *perfidi, perfidia* is "unbelief," "denial of faith." But in the missals used by the faithful they are generally translated as "perfidious" and "perfidy."

° I.e., Jacques Benigne Bossuet, Bishop of Meaux (1627-1704), one of the greatest orators in French history.

(19A) Note to 1974 edition. This passage was written in 1958. Since then, the historic decisions taken at Vatican II have resulted in so radical a revision of the Catholic attitude—in the Western countries and notably in France—toward the Jews that a detailed study of these latest developments would be beyond the scope of this volume.

how fundamentally anti-Christian anti-Semitism was; the pure destructive passions of genocide were still restrained in them. The measures that they advocated, ostracism or banishment, were only symbolic murders. But when moral barriers collapsed under the impact of Nazi preaching, and the genocidal passion was free to slake itself, the hatred of God slumbering in men's hearts awoke and stood revealed in the light of day; the same anti-Semitic movement that led to the slaughter of the Jews gave scope and license to an obscene revolt against God and the moral law. An open and implacable war was declared on the Christian tradition. Hitlerism's universal iconoclasm was only the logical consequence of Nazi anti-Semitism; by an atrocious demonstration *in vivo*, it tragically confirmed the penetrating insights of such great thinkers as Sigmund Freud and Jacques Maritain,[16] who saw in original anti-Semitism a "revolt of the ill-baptized" against the moral law, a frenzied and unavowed hatred of Christ and the Ten Commandments that in its furious search for satisfaction vented itself on the only object that was allowed to be fair and legal game, the baffling people of God. Here we have the *causa specifica* of anti-Semitism; (20) and so, by another route, we again find our way to the deep meaning of the Nazi explosion: Hitlerism attacked the Jews as the symbol of all established values, which it had marked down for destruction. Here one perceives the deep paradox of the Jews' Calvary: they were the first victims of the anti-Christ sacrificed, in the last analysis, for a cause that was hardly theirs.

The preceding pages are only an attempt to untangle the chief causes, old and new, from the multiplicity of factors that led to

(20) Obviously we do not mean to exclude all the other factors that act to pit Christian against Jew (and vice versa), which fall into the category of what sociologists call "group tensions"—conflicts of economic interest, national and religious hatreds, xenophobia, etc. But all these are insufficient to account for the persistence, intensity, and uniqueness of Jew-hatred through the ages.

During the interesting discussion already mentioned, after having stated that "there are minorities everywhere, but nobody has ever seen so constant and universal a persecution, which no profane explanation can account for," Jacques Maudaule gave this as his personal conviction: "I think that there is a mystery of anti-Semitism that complements the mystery of Israel; it is the reverse, if you will, of the election of Israel, and in the last analysis is a religious problem."

The phrase "religious problem" is open to many interpretations. There is perhaps no need to invoke the will of God in seeking to elucidate a phenomenon which can be adequately explained by the secret volitions of man.

genocide. Nothing is further from our intention than to slight the generous efforts put forth locally by the clergy of the Western countries, especially in France. Only at the top did the obstinate silence of the Vatican have its counterpart in the prudent reticence of Cardinal Suhard, Archbishop of Paris, and other high dignitaries (whereas the Archbishops of Lyon and Toulouse, as well as a number of bishops, made their protests heard). The lower clergy, on the other hand, and the monastic orders, rivaled one another in their energy and daring, and were the leaders in the efforts to save the Jews. Dozens of priests and humble monks paid with their lives for their devotion. In this work of human love one seems to see again the unyielding purity and the ardor of the first Christian martyrs.

JEWISH REACTIONS

More than three years after the end of the war, the wretched Jewish remnant of the concentration camps still vegetated in Germany, behind the fences of the Displaced Persons camps. No country wanted them. Jewish Palestine, whose inhabitants opened their arms to the survivors, was guarded by British cruisers. Were they going to wait and wait indefinitely in the very country of their agony? It needed the birth of the State of Israel to put an end to this.

Though there were only a few thousand Jewish survivors in the camps, there were innumerable Western Jews in the liberated countries whose eyes were concentrated fixedly on the tragic Jewish fate to which the end of the Third Reich had provided no *finis,* and which might so easily have been theirs. From the East, however, in a thin but steadily swelling stream, the Jews were beginning to move across frontiers and boundary lines, drawn by the magnet of Palestine. The German camps were the first stage of their journey. Of their own accord they were going to rejoin their brothers in Palestine, provided they could make their way out of the land of their Calvary.

Thus we see reappearing a difference, expressed in their very behavior, which has already been emphasized and which is absolutely essential to an understanding of the Jewish position. There is (or was, rather) the Eastern Jew, the "real Jew," marked off in every way from the men among whom he lived and possessing the chief characteristics of a separate and defined nationality, a true citizen of an imaginary country who fed on the memory of the lost Zion. His persistence through the centuries is one of the strangest puzzles of history, a puzzle to which the preceding pages provide at least a partial key. The doubly uprooted "assimilated" Jew of the West is only his pale reflection, a weak echo.

In the dense centers of Judaism as they were perpetuated in Eastern Europe, the intensity of persecution had its reaction in the strengthening of the Jewish conscience. The ways in which the Jews adapted themselves to the life around them were also unique; the internal cohesion of ghetto society increased proportionately with the external hostility. The ancestral faith and the teachings of the Law gave form, guidance, and support to Jewish life; its content, the idea of "chosenness," cemented the whole together with an unparalleled solidity. Secret pride at being the Chosen People through the ages strengthened the Jews' will to live. It can perhaps even be said that this pride got an additional, perverse nourishment from the fact that the Jewish people had given to the Christian world, which hated them so, the Saviour whom it adored. It should also be remembered here that this ghetto world, which had always been unarmed and today is no more, was distinguished by a devotion to the Book and to learning and by a renunciation of the instincts and their ardors—in a word, by a spirituality for which there is no parallel. Thus it was that a Jewish nation continued to exist, scattered over Eastern Europe, with its five-centuries-old center in Poland.

At the hour of its destruction the last representatives of Polish Judaism sent the Palestinian Jews this last despairing farewell:

In the last moment before their destruction, the last survivors of the Jewish people in Poland appealed to the whole world for help. They were not heard. We know that you, the Jews of Palestine, suffer cruelly at our incredible martyrdom. But may those who could have helped us, and failed to do so, know what we think of them. The blood of 3,000,000 Jews cries for vengeance, and will be avenged! And the punishment will not only strike the Nazi cannibals, but all who did nothing to save a condemned people. . . . May this last voice from the abyss reach the ears of all humanity! [21]

If these lines were addressed to the Palestinian Jews, it was because the latter were the only audience which the dying Jews of Europe felt any communion with, which had any real meaning for them. Jewish Palestine had real meaning for the Nazis, too: Was it not characteristic that, though the European Jews were helpless and unarmed, as early as 1939 the Nazis looked forward to the Jews of Palestine countering reprisal with reprisal? [22] Did not the redoubtable Eichmann direct his wrath particularly at the Jewish Zionists, "these elements of great biological value"? [23] So the circle closed quite naturally, and the Jewish reality was affirmed in Palestine just when the Jews of Europe were breathing their last.

From this agony the Jews learned a harsh and summary lesson. A people that had never possessed arms transformed themselves into a warrior nation. The nightmare of the recent past, of brothers and sisters sent to an atrocious and anonymous death, haunted the fighters—this explains their furious ardor. Jewish dynamism, which had been traditionally restrained and directed toward pacifist goals, now expressed itself in a directly aggressive way, showing all that violence and those military virtues which it had so long eschewed.

To be sure, settling in a new country was a factor; so was the experience of manual labor. But the change occurred in a few short years, and was induced above all by moral factors, the very ones that had led to the birth of Zionism. It was impelled by a feeling of solidarity and of Zion finally reconquered, receiving its final impetus from the European catastrophe. In the space of one generation a completely new Jew, physically and morally, was shaped, unpolished, primitive, and direct, closely tied to his ancestors and yet strangely different from them. A curious experiment—a falling off, some will say; an achievement, according to others—awakening the enthusiasm of all the Jews of the Dispersion. It came as a soothing balm to many a secretly tormented soul and relieved somewhat the Jewish "inferiority complex"; it also gave the lie, once and for all, to all the racial theories.

✱   ✱   ✱

Before going on to a cursory examination of the reactions of the assimilated Jews of the West, a word of caution about the necessarily schematic character of these generalizations. There were thousands of assimilated Jews in the East who were completely indifferent to Judaism. And there were Jews in the West who remained passionately attached to their ancestral traditions and modes of life. As for the life of the Jews of the USSR, it is a chapter apart. Moreover, the unfolding of the Jewish fate was closely tied to the structural changes taking place in the modern secular world; everywhere it seemed to be tending toward the same end of complete integration with the surrounding world; people little suspected the abyss yawning beneath the footbridge hastily thrown across from the ghetto to the outside world.

So deep, however, was the division between East and West that it seemed almost a difference in nature. The Jews of the West were branches cut from the historic and traditional trunk, but assimilated and integrated into their respective countries, often only sharing the name of Jew with those of the East. These Jews dressed, lived, and thought like their compatriots. They had the same interests, the same occupations, and the same ambitions; but to this was added a supreme ambition: to be recognized and treated everywhere as men of full worth and equal rights before the law. The last vestige of an ancient past—their talent for commerce and the professions—served as an easy pretext for attacking them. But these attacks were all the more baseless as the Jews had not monopolized or dominated any of these fields for ever so long a time. Their religion itself was no longer practised with sufficient zeal to make them stand out; it was maintained out of an obscure feeling of fidelity to self and ancestry, rather than from any deep mystical impulse. One can speak of a "weak form" of Judaism, as contrasted with its strong forms; one can also speak of "psychological" Jews, in opposition to the "real" Jews of the East, though it has to be kept in mind that this "psychological Jew" did not arise from any Jewish psychology alone, but was called forth primarily by the attitude of the surrounding world, which stubbornly recreates and perpetuates the type of the Jew, who, in turn, is conditioned and influenced by the image entertained of him. For what factor has more influence on the restless and melancholy Jewish psyche (and also on the striking Jewish determination to be faithful at all costs) than his piercing sense of being apart, of being the special object of hostile or curious glances? How paradoxical that a group already so far along toward being assimilated, that gives every promise of dissolving itself, should find itself defined, marked out, and kept alive by a pure trick of the mind, a mere idea! (22) In our secularized societies, this relentless and subtle game would in all likelihood have come to some kind of an end if there had not been the Jewish reality in the East, exercising a decisive influence as much by the continual influx of its "real" Jews as by the simple fact of its existence. For the Jew as well as for his antagonist, the encounter with a real Jew revived the memory of the archetype and all its associated emotions in a thousand different and contradictory ways. This image was projected on the assimilated European, who, though he was just like his compatriots, seemed to alter visibly when the image was superimposed on him.

The great collective hatreds that rend the world, whether originating in fear, cupidity, or the lust for power, always correspond in some sort to a real situation, to concrete collective interests. There is an enemy to destroy, riches to conquer. Around the nucleus of this interest also rally all the instincts of aggression and murder. The anti-Semitic passions of the Western world are perhaps the only emotions of this kind which, when we seek to discover their basis, seem to have no underlying interest to explain them. However deep we go into them, we find nothing but archaic vestiges, confused resentments, and illusory pretexts. Which accounts for the fact that their ultimate expression, Hitlerism, was the only attempt in history to condemn man for what he *is*, not for what he *does*; for his abstract entity, not for his concrete acts. (23)

The impossibility of the Jew's escaping or defending himself was an indispensable condition for his role of scapegoat; he was the target for pure and absolute hatred, for an aggressiveness unmotivated by any real interest. He responded to persecution with pleas and appeals to reason, but nothing was better calculated to increase the irrational hatred of his adversaries. A living reproach to the conscience of the modern world, he lived and endured with no sus-

(22) This is much the same thesis developed by J. P. Sartre in his *Réflexions sur la question juive*, with one essential exception: Though Sartre states at the beginning of his study, "I shall limit my description to the Jews of France," in fact he would seem to extend his conclusions to all Jews without exception, and ends up by denying the entire Jewish people "any feeling of historicity."

picion of his real significance, a man eager above all to live, but to whom the fullness of life was denied.

Thus there existed a bond between the Antwerp tailor, the Parisian banker, and the Salonikan longshoreman. The sentence passed on them by Hitler, their common destiny of death, gave them a solidarity in all their trials. The traumatic effect of this was certainly considerable, and the exacerbated Jewish sensibility emerged from its trials even sadder and more disquieted, more wounded. But once the torments had passed, it was impossible to discern an over-all collective reaction. All one sees is a confusing array of individual responses: Some Jews reject their Judaism, are converted, and change their names; others become Jewish nationalists and emigrate to Israel; still others make no choice at all and go back to their pre-war life. Perhaps the unique character of the bond that united these Jews is responsible for this diversity. Since the bond was based on no community of interests or ideas, having only a shaky foundation in long historical memories which are chiefly memories of a long martyrdom, it was unlikely that it could have resulted in any great collective resolution. (24)

However this may be, it is doubtless the existence of the State of Israel that will be the new essential factor in the development of the Jewish question in the years to come. One may even go so far as to suggest, as some people have already done, that now that the great reservoirs of East European Jews have dried up and the doors of Israel are open wide to any Jew choosing the Zionist solution, a sharp separation will take place between those who choose

(23) Cf. the ideas developed by J. Billig in his remarkable study, *L'Allemagne et le génocide, op. cit.*

(24) (Note: January, 1974). I did not think it necessary to make any changes in this passage, which seems to me an accurate reflection of the attitude that prevailed prior to 1967. The Six-Day War of June, 1967 changed the situation in that the majority of diaspora Jewry, shocked beyond expectation by the events, felt a strong bond of solidarity with Israel. A minority decided to settle in Israel; in the case of the others, it seems that the existence of a Jewish State has reinforced their sense of "Jewish identity," just as, in fact, I foresaw as early as 1950.

The Yom Kippur War of October, 1973 has reinforced these tendencies. In addition, as a result of the attitudes shown by most governments in Europe and elsewhere, it has created a feeling of isolation among many Jews in the diaspora.

the Jewish nationality and those who remain in their native lands and move further and further away from Judaism. With the dispersion approaching its end, will the Jewish problem solve itself by simply ceasing to exist? Put in this way, the problem has a false simplicity. It takes no account of the intensity of the emotional associations that still bind the peoples of Europe together, and, consequently, the Jews as well. Deeply rooted in people's hearts, these passions do not seem at all on the point of dying out or being absorbed. And as long as they persist, there will be excluded from these groups isolated individuals who will perpetuate the Jewish psychology and conscience. But the Jewish reality has made a choice: to create a homeland. This was its true response.

Sources and Documents Cited

THE DOCUMENTS QUOTED in this book are for the most part drawn from the archives of the Nuremberg Tribunal (International Military Tribunal for Major War Criminals and The American Military Tribunal). They are referred to by the numbers given them during the trial, consisting of a combination of letters and figures (for example, PS. 1601, NG. 2586, etc.) Photostats of these documents have been collected in the archives of the Center for Contemporary Jewish Documentation (CCJD), 27 rue Guénegaud, Paris, VI.

The originals of some of the documents from other sources may be found in the archives of the CCJD; in this case, they carry a classification number consisting of two Roman and Arabic numerals (for example, LXXXVIII, 65).

The references are indicated in customary fashion.

FOOTNOTES

CHAPTER ONE

1. Speech by Julius Streicher to the party congress at Nuremberg, September, 1936.
2. Interview granted to an English newspaperman (*Sunday Referee*, July 30, 1933).
3. Hermann Rauschning, *Hitler m'a dit*, Paris, Ed. "France," 1939, p. 272 ff.
4. Rauschning, *op. cit.*, p. 292.
5. *Idem.*
6. Père de Grandmaison, *Notions de sociologie*.
7. Rauschning, *op. cit.*, p. 277.
8. Rauschning, *op. cit.*, p. 276.
9. Robert Kanters, *Essai sur l'avenir de la religion*, Paris, Ed. Julliard, 1945, p. 107
10. Rauschning, *op. cit.*, p. 274.
11. This document, like those which follow, is taken from a 1933 Nazi col-

lection: "The Atrocity Propaganda Is Based on Lies, Say the German Jews Themselves." (B 1220)

12. J. Goebbels, "From the Kaiserhof Hotel to the Chancellery, Diary Extracts From January 1, 1932 to May 1, 1933." (B 2227)

13. *Nachrichtendienst der N.S.D.A.P.*, No. 24, August 1933; quoted from the *Collection de documents* published in Switzerland in 1936. (B 519)

14. *Idem.*

15. Minutes of the meeting of the Committee for the Four Year Plan, October 14, 1938. (PS 1449)

16. Secret report on the events and the directive of the party tribunal relative to the anti-Semitic manifestations of November 9, 1938. Munich, February 13, 1939. (PS 3063)

17. Report submitted by Heydrich to Goering on the plundering and destruction of November 9-10, 1938. Berlin, November 11, 1939. (PS 3058)

18. Rauschning, *op. cit.*, p. 274.

19. Karl Jaspers, *La Culpabilité Allemande*, Paris, Ed. de Minuit, 1948, p. 134.

20. Cf. footnote 16. (PS 3063)

21. Minutes of the Council of Ministers, November 12, 1938. (PS 1816)

22. Note on the transfer agreement (*Haavara-Abkommen*), Ministry of Foreign Affairs, Berlin, March 10, 1938. (NG 1889)

23. "The Jewish Question as a Factor in Foreign Policy in the Year 1938." Important fourteen-page report of January 25, 1939. (PS 3558)

CHAPTER TWO

1. Verdict of the Nuremberg International Tribunal, I, 288.

2. "The treatment of the populations of the ancient Polish territories, in conformity with the racial-political points of view," by Councillor Wetzel. Berlin, November 25, 1939. (PS 660)

3. Special delivery letter (*Schnellbrief*) to the heads of all action groups (*Einsatzgruppen*) from the security police, signed Heydrich. Berlin, September 21, 1939. (PS 3363)

4. Minutes of a conference called by Heydrich on January 30, 1940. (NO 5322)

5. Report entitled: "The War Economy in Poland, 1939–40." (EC 344)

6. Extract from a speech by Hans Frank. (PS 2233)

7. (NG 2490)

8. Note on "The Creation of a Ghetto in the City of Lodz," dated December 10, 1939, signed Ubelhor (cf. "Getto Lodzkie," *Dokumenty i Materialy* series, Warsaw, 1946, p. 26).

9. "The War Economy in Poland, 1939–40." (EC 344)

10. Extract from a speech by Hans Frank. (PS 2233)

11. *Laws and Ordinances of the Government General* series, submitted by the Public Ministry of the USSR at the Nuremberg trial. (USSR 93)

12. Various pieces of testimony (cf. the series of articles by Michel Mazor, "*la Cité engloutie*," in Nos. 34-36 of the *Monde juif*, Paris, August-October, 1950.)

13. *Idem.*

14. Notes for the report to the Commander-in-Chief of the Army (Oberbefehlshaber des Heeres), February 15, 1940. (NO 3011)

15. Felix Kersten, *Klerk en Beul*, Amsterdam, S. Meulenhoff, 1948.

16. Viktor Brack's deposition at "The Doctors' Trial" in Nuremberg. (Session of May 13, 1947)

17. Note from Rademacher, dated July 3, 1941. (NG 2586)

18. Recapitulatory note on "The Solution of the Jewish Question." Ministry of Foreign Affairs, Berlin, August 21, 1942. (NG 2586)

19. Note prepared by Dieter Wisliceny, on November 18, 1946, during his detention at Bratislava. (LXXXVIII, 65)

20. File on the "Madagascar Plan" sent by Dannecker to Rademacher on August 24, 1941. (NG 2586)

21. Minutes of a conference of "specialists on population questions and evacuation" held at Strasbourg, October 2-3, 1940. (NO 5589)

22. Report on the deportations of Jews of German nationality in Southern France. Karlsruhe, October 30, 1940; signature illegible. (NG 4933)

23. Report of SS Commandant Lischka at a staff conference of the military administration in France. February 3, 1941. (XXIV, 13)

24. *Idem.*

25. Report from Knochen to the RSHA, Paris, February 12, 1943. (L, 38)

26. "Treatment Applicable to Jews in the Occupied Zone." Note signed "Best" dealing with the "Measures Suggested by Ambassador Abetz to the Military Administration." Paris, August 19, 1940. (XXIV, 1a)

27. Report by Dannecker: "The Nature and Handling of the Jewish Question in France." Paris, July 1, 1941. (XXVI, 1)

28. Note from the office of the Commissioner General for Jewish Questions, September 9, 1942. (CVI, 103)

29. Extract from the letter sent to Marshal Pétain by General Boris, November 10, 1940. (K3 58a)

30. Extract from the letter sent to the Commissioner for Jewish Questions by Marc Haguenau. Moissac, July 31, 1941. (K3 1a)

31. Extract from a letter sent to the Chief Rabbi of Paris by the director of the Marshal's "Civil Section." Vichy, December 23, 1941. (K 367a)

32. Letter from Madame Nerson on the subject of the dismissal of Jacques Cahen, killed on the field of honor, addressed to Marshal Pétain (1/27/1941), followed by the reply of the director of the Marshal's civil section (1/31/1941). (K3 60a)

33. Circular letter from the RSHA on "The Attitude of Persons of German Blood Toward the Jews." Berlin, October 24, 1941. (L, 152)

34. Ministry of Food and Agriculture, decrees of March 11, 1940, October 24, 1940, December 6, 1940, May 26, 1941, June 18, 1941, and September 18, 1941. (PS 1347)

35. Circular letter from the Ministry of Finance, April 20, 1941. (PS 1347)

36. Proposed law on the "Juridical Incompetence of Jews." Berlin, August 13, 1942. (NG 151)

37. Letter from the head of the Wehrmacht Oberkommando to the head of the Chancellery of the Reich. Berlin, September 10, 1942. (NG 151)

38. Law published in the *Reichsgesetzblatt*, 372/1, 1943. (PS 1422)

39. Report of the Ministry of Justice dealing with criminality in the Greater German Reich during 1942. (NG 787)

40. This document, dated April 1943, is cited from the verdict given by the American Military Tribunal at Nuremberg in the so-called "Jurists' Trial." (p. 10,776 of the official English typescript) We do not know the subsequent course of this affair.

41. Memo submitted to Goebbels by Meyers-Christian on "How to Treat the Jewish Question in the German Press." (Weinreich, *op. cit.*)

42. Opinion given by the Ministry of the Interior on the subject of the "Final Solution of the Jewish Question." Berlin, March 16, 1942. (NG 2586)

43. Minutes of a conference called by the RSHA. (NG 2586)

44. *Ibid.*

CHAPTER THREE

1. Jacob Lestchinsky, *Balance Sheet of Extermination*, New York, Institute of Jewish Affairs, 1946.

2. Report of the Inquiry Commission on the "Aryanizations" carried out in the Franconia Gau and the abuses discovered in this connection. (PS 1757)

3. Report of J. Bürckel to Marshal Goering, Vienna, November 19, 1938. (PS 2237)

4. Speech by W. Funk, Reich Minister of the Economy, delivered November 15, 1938. (PS 3545)

5. Testimony of Abraham Weiss, director of the Institute of Judaism at Warsaw (quoted from *The Black Book of Polish Jewry*, New York, Roy, 1943).

6. *The Black Book of Polish Jewry, op. cit.*

7. Notes for the report to the Commander-in-chief of the Army (Oberbefehlshaber des Heeres), February 15, 1940. (NO 3011)

8. Report of Knochen to the German military administration in France. Paris, January 28, 1941. (V, 64)

9. "The Tasks Facing Reichsleiter Rosenberg's Einsatzstab." The note, prepared by a close collaborator of Rosenberg, is undated. (CXL, 69)

10. Report by Stabseinsatzführer Zeiss. Frauenberg, January 19, 1945. (CXL, 69)

11. Report by Stabseinsatzführer Anton. Belgrade, March 29, 1944. (CXL, 102)

12. Report by Pohl, April 29, 1943: "The Library for the Study of the Jewish Question." (CXL, 99)

13. Report by R. Scholtz, head of the Einsatzstab Rosenberg Bureau of Plastic Arts, dated July 1944. (CXL, 103)

14. Report by A. Rosenberg to the Führer, dated April 16, 1943. (PS 015)

15. Letter, marked "Private and Very Confidential," from Burges, official of the military administration in France, to Councillor of State Turner. Letter not dated (February 1941?). (PS 2523)

16. Report on Action M, signed by "The Chief of the Einsatzstab West." Not dated, probably prepared at the beginning of 1945. (PS 1649)

17. Letter from Speer, "Inspector-General of Construction in the Capital of the Reich," to Rosenberg. Berlin, January 26, 1942. (PS 1738)

18. Request made by Franz Rademacher to the Personnel Bureau of the Ministry of Foreign Affairs. Berlin, August 1, 1940. (NG 2879)

19. Counsellor of Legation Carlthéo Zeitschel to SS Obersturmführer Dannecker. Paris, June 20, 1941. (CXXV, 45)

20. Memorandum from SS General Fanslau, chief of Section A of the WVHA. Not dated, quoted in the accusation in the Oswald Pohl trial, session of April 8, 1947.

21. Account entitled "The Tasks, Organization, and Financial Plan for Service III (W) of the WVHA." (NO 542)

22. Nuremberg War Crimes Tribunal, "The Concentration Camps" proceedings (trial of Oswald Pohl and accomplices), session of March 10, 1947.

23. Letter from Jerouchim Apfel, in the collection of Mme. N. Novitch.

24. Circular from Himmler on "The Use of Jewish Labor in the Occupied Eastern Territories." Berlin, August 13, 1943. (PS 1931)

25. Note on the forced labor camps for Jews, submitted to Himmler by Globocnik on June 21, 1943. (NO 485)

26. Nuremberg Tribunal, trial of Oswald Pohl and accomplices, session of March 10, 1947.

27. Engineer R. Lautrich to the administration of the Lodz ghetto. Hohensalza, July 13, 1943 (according to the series *Dokumenty i Materialy*, "Obozy," I, 310-12, Lodz, 1946).

28. "Economic Aspect of the Reinhardt Action," report submitted to Himmler by Globocnik. (NO 057)

29. "Top Secret for Commands: the Utilization of Property on the Occasion of the Evacuation and Transfer of Jews." An order sent to SS administrations by SS General Frank. (NO 724)

30. Nuremberg Tribunal, trial of Oswald Pohl and accomplices, session of April 8, 1947.

31. Affidavit by Oswald Pohl. Nuremberg, April 2, 1947. (NO 2714)

32. Letter sent to Pohl by R. Brandt, chief of Himmler's staff, dated December 3, 1943. (NO 2754)

33. Letter from the Winter Relief Delegate for "Gau Wartheland" sent to the German administrator of the Lodz ghetto. Posnania, January 16, 1943. (*Dokumenty i Materialy* series, "Akcje," Warsaw, 1946, II, 168 ff.)

34. WVHA circular to concentration camp commanders. Oranienburg, July 11, 1942. (NO 394)

35. Undated report by Globocnik on "The Administrative Liquidation of the Reinhardt Action." (NO 059)

36. Cf. letter of Pohl to Himmler, dated January 15, 1944. (NO 5368)

37. Nuremberg Tribunal, trial of Oswald Pohl and accomplices, session of April 8, 1947.

38. P. Friedman, *This Was Oswiecim*, London, 1946; cf. also O. Lengyel, *Five Chimneys*, New York, 1947.

39. R 107 and L 018.

40. Speech delivered by H. Himmler in Posnania before a group of high SS chiefs, October 4, 1943. (PS 1919)

41. Report to Knochen by Dannecker on the subject of the deportation from France of 5,000 Jews. Paris, March 10, 1942. (RF 1216). Memorandum from Wagner on the subject of the deportation of the Jews from Bulgaria. Berlin, April 3, 1943. (NG 4180)

42. P. Friedman, *op. cit.*

43. Report by Carl, regional superintendent of Slutsk, to the Superintendent General of White Russia at Minsk. Slutsk, October 30, 1941. (PS 1104)

44. From *Dokumenty i Matarialy*, Jewish Historical Commission, Warsaw, 1946, II, "Akcje," 144-45.

CHAPTER FOUR

1. *Bleter far Geszichte* (periodical of the Polish Jewish Historical Commission, January-March, 1948, I).

2. These statistics, as well as most of those which follow, are taken principally from the following sources: Friedman, *The Extermination of the Polish Jews under the German Occupation from 1939 to 1945* (consulted in manuscript form); *The Black Book of Polish Jewry*, New York, Roy, 1943; *Hitler's Ten Year War on the Jews*, New York, Institute of Jewish Affairs, 1943.

3. Mary Berg, *Le Ghetto de Varsovie*, Paris, Albin Michel, Paris, 1947. *The Black Book of Polish Jewry* gives the figure of 1,761 Jews converted in January 1940.

4. There were 334 Jewish deaths in Warsaw in June 1939, 1,094 in April 1940, 4,290 in June 1941, and 5,700 in September 1941 (*Hitler's Ten Year War on the Jews*, New York, 1943). In April 1941, there were 361 births and 81 marriages (*Black Book of Polish Jewry*). A medical commission had been created to study the pathological evolution of the famine; according to its estimates, the population of the ghetto would have taken five years to disappear at the rate given. (Testimony of Doctor Israel Rothbalsam, from the collection of Mme. Novitch.)

5. Mary Berg, *Le Ghetto de Varsovie*, Albin Michel; S. Rothbalsam, *Souvenirs d'un médecin juif*, from the collection of Mme. Novitch.

6. Mary Berg, *op. cit.*, p. 65-66, 98.

7. Testimony by Doctor Israel Rothbalsam, transcribed by Mme. Novitch. Cf. also the article in *Figaro Littéraire*.

8. *Journal de Mary Berg, op. cit.*, p. 156.

9. *Idem*, p. 169.

10. *Idem*.

11. Document quoted by J. Kermisz in *Powstanie w getcie Warszawskim*, p. 29.

12. J. Tenenbaum, *In Search of a Lost People*, New York, 1948, p. 67 ff.

13. Report from Biebow, commissioner of the ghetto (Leiter des Ghetoverwaltung) to Ventzki, burgomaster of Litzmannstadt (Lodz), April 19, 1943. From *Dokumenty i Materialy, op. cit.*, III: "Getto Lodzkie," Warsaw, Jewish Historical Commission of Poland, 1946.

14. This information on Ch. Rumkowski is taken from a study by Solomon F. Bloom, "The Dictator of the Lodz Ghetto," *Commentary*, New York, February 1949.

15. *Black Book of Polish Jewry*, p. 77. Since Cracow was the seat of the German administration of the Government General and Frank's residence, its ghetto began to be liquidated in the summer of 1940; 50,000 Jews were sent to other ghettos in August and October of that year.

16. *Journal de Mary Berg, op. cit.*, p. 157.

17. The accounts of Mme. Rabinowitch and Mme. Bronke, from the collection of Mme. Novitch.

18. *Black Book of Polish Jewry*, p. 100. The special inquiry commission of the USSR (minutes No. 47) gives the figure of 136,000 inhabitants.

19. Dvorjetski, *Le Ghetto de Vilna*, Geneva, Union OSE, 1946.

20. Dvorjetski, "La Liaison clandestine entre les ghettos," *Le Monde Juif*, No. 18, April 1949.

21. Figures taken from the bulletin of the Czech Ministry of Information, Prague, State Office of Statistics, 1945. Cf. also the report of the Inspector for Statistics of the Reich, Berlin, April 19, 1943. (NG 5194)

CHAPTER FIVE

1. A decisive role has been attributed to Bormann by Viktor Brack, administrator of the "euthanasia program" for the mentally ill, who played a key part in the development of the extermination proceedings ("The Doctors' Trial," Nuremberg Tribunal, session of May 13, 1947).

2. *Le Journal de Docteur Goebbels*, Paris, Cheval Aile, 1949, p. 246. The authenticity of the document, whose original is in the Hoover War Library, is incontestable.

3. Report from Councillor of the Legation Rademacher to Ambassador Bielefeld, Berlin, February 10, 1942. (NG 5770)

4. Directive from Goering to SS-Gruppenführer Heydrich. Berlin, July 31, 1941. (PS 710)

5. Dannecker, *op. cit.* (RF 1210)

6. Article published in *Das Reich*, Goebbel's weekly paper, November 25, 1941. Cf. on this subject the comments of Dieter Wisliceny.

7. Diary of Hans Frank, vol. 1941/IV. (PS 2233)

8. "Secret Business of the Reich": minutes of the conference held January 20, 1942, at Berlin, Am Grossen Wannsee 56/58, on the subject of the final solution of the Jewish question. A copy of the minutes, as well as a certain number of other documents of considerable interest, has been found in the archives of the Ministry of Foreign Affairs, and it is this important file, NG 2586, which will often be quoted later.

9. Note sent by Luther, director of the department of the interior in the Ministry of Foreign Affairs, to Weizsäcker, Undersecretary of State at the Ministry. Berlin, September 24, 1942. (PS 3688)

10. Secret circular letter from Himmler, dated October 9, 1942. (NO 1611)

11. Party decree 66/881, October 9, 1942; "Preparatory Measures for the Solution of the Jewish Problem in Europe." (PS 3244)

CHAPTER SIX

1. Trial of the *Einsatzgruppen* at the Nuremberg Tribunal, interrogation of Ohlendorff (session of October 13, 1947).

2. *Einsatzgruppe* A, account of general activity up to October 15, 1941. Berlin, January 31, 1942. (L 180)

3. *Idem.*

4. *Idem.*

5. *Idem.*

6. Report of the chief of the security police and the SD. Berlin, August 9, 1941. (NO 2947)

7. General report of Group A; section relative to White Russia. Berlin, June 30, 1942. (PS 2273)

8. *Einsatzgruppen* trial, interrogation of Hauptsturmführer Schubert, session of January 6, 1947.

9. Affidavit by interpreter Metzner. Augsburg, September 10, 1947. (NO 5558)

10. *Einsatzgruppen* trial, interrogation of Ohlendorff, session of October 15, 1947.

11. Activity report of the Kommandantur for the period July 1-5, 1942. Bachtchissarai, July 16, 1942. (NOKW 1698)

12. Affidavit by Adolf Rube, former secretary of the criminal police at the Minsk Kommandantur, Karlsruhe, October 23, 1947. (NO 5498)

13. Report of SS Untersturmführer Doctor Becker to SS Obersturmbannführer Rauff. Kiev, May 16, 1942. (PS 501)

14. Affidavit by Hermann Graebe. (PS 2992)

15. Report by Kommandant Sauer on the extermination of 26,200 Jews in Pinsk, October 29, 30, 31, and November 1, 1942. (USSR 119a)

16. *Einsatzgruppen* trial, interrogation of SS Sturmführer Gustav Noske, session of December 4, 1947.

17. Deposition of SS Gruppenführer Bach-Zelewski before the International Tribunal of Major International War Criminals, session of January 7, 1946.

18. Documents NO 5654 and 5655.

19. All these quotations, as well as those following, have been put together, forming a kind of anthology, in the verdict of the American Tribunal, which tried some twenty former members of the *Einsatzgruppen* at Nuremberg in 1947.

20. *Einsatzgruppen* trial, interrogation of Blobel, session of October 30, 1947.

21. *Einsatzgruppen* trial, interrogation of Ohlendorff, session of October 14, 1947.

22. *Einsatzgruppen* trial, interrogation of Graf, session of January 7, 1948.

23. Report on the situation and the activity of the security police and SD action groups in the USSR. Berlin, July 31, 1941, p. 4. (NO 2651)

24. Affidavit by Haensch. Nuremberg, July 8, 1947. (NO 5972)

25. *Einsatzgruppen* trial, interrogation of Graf, session of January 7, 1948.

26. Minutes No. 47 of the special inquiry commission of the USSR, session of December 23, 1944, p. 7.

27. Previously quoted affidavit by Metzner. Augsburg, September 10, 1947. (NO 5558)

28. Document previously quoted: "Party Decree 66/881, October 9, 1942. Preparatory Measures for the Solution of the Jewish Problem in Europe." (PS 3244)

29. Directive of the headquarters of the group of southern armies: "Struggle Against Elements Hostile to the Reich." Headquarters, September 24, 1941. (NOKW 1608)

30. Secret circular of the commander of the 6th army, signed von Reichenau. Headquarters, October 10, 1941. (D 411)

31. *Einsatzgruppen* trial, interrogation of Blobel, session of October 28, 1947.

32. Report by Major Rossler. Kassel, January 3, 1942. (USSR 293)

33. Head Commissioner of Baranovitche, February 10, 1942. (PS 3667)

34. Journal of the 10th Division, August 5, 1942. (NOKW 2150)

35. "Report of the Representative of the Ministry of Occupied Territories in the East to the Commander-in-Chief of the Center Army Group," addressed to the headquarters of the Ministry in Berlin, dated December 15, 1941. (PS 1682)

36. Report of the Reich Commissioner for the East to the Minister of Occupied Eastern Territories. Riga, June 18, 1943. (R 135)

37. Report from the Slutsk regional commissioner to the Commissioner General of White Russia at Minsk. Slutsk, October 30, 1941. (PS 1104)

38. Report of "the Inspector of Armament" in the Ukraine to the head of the economic services of the Wehrmacht Oberkommando, General Thomas. With the Army, December 2, 1941. (PS 3257)

39. General Report of *Einsatzgruppe* A. Berlin, June 30, 1942. (PS 2273)

40. Account No. 6 of the activity of the *Einsatzgruppen*, between October 1-15, 1941. (R 102)

41. Deposition of Ohlendorff during the trial of the major war criminals, session of January 3, 1946. (NO 3392)

42. Report on the anti-partisan struggle from September 1-December 1, 1942, dated December 26, 1942. (NO 1128)

43. Affidavit of SS Sturmbannführer Wilhelm Höttl. Nuremberg, November 6, 1945. (PS 2738)

44. Jacob Lestchinsky, *Crisis, Catastrophe and Survival*, New York, Institute of Jewish Affairs, 1948.

45. *Einsatzgruppen* trial, interrogation of Blobel, session of November 2, 1947.

46. Account by Wisliceny, *doc. cit.*

47. *Einsatzgruppen* trial, deposition of Blobel, session of November 1, 1947.

48. Account by Wisliceny, *doc. cit.*

49. Written deposition by Rudolf Hoess. Minden, March 14, 1946. (D 749)

CHAPTER SEVEN

1. Letter from Himmler to Berger. Reval (Esthonia), July 28, 1942. (NO 626)

2. Account by Wisliceny. Bratislava, November 18, 1946. (LXXXVIII, 65)

3. Account by Wisliceny, *doc. cit.*; cf. also a note signed Dannecker, dated Paris, July 21, 1942.

4. Berlin, September 16, 1942. (NG 2586)

5. Note signed Dannecker, on the "Future Deportation of the Jews of France." Paris, June 15, 1942. (XXVI, 29)

6. Report made by the Paris IVb at the request of SS Gruppenführer Oberg, "Supreme Chief of the SS and Police in France." Paris, September 3, 1942. (RF 1227)

7. Account by Wisliceny, *doc. cit.*

8. Directive from Himmler to the RSHA. Headquarters of the SS Reichsführer, April 9, 1943. (NO 5197)

9. Instructions given by R. Brandt, Himmler's secretary, to Kornherr, "Inspector for Statistics." With the Army, April 10, 1942. (NO 5196)

10. Secret circular of the military administration in France. Paris, May 13, 1942. (RF 1215)

11. Note on the "Fundamental Principles of the Policy Followed in the Jewish Question Since the Assumption of Power." Berlin, August 21, 1942. (NG 2586)

12. Diplomatic dispatch sent by Rintelen to Luther. Feldmark, August 20, 1942. (NG 3559)

13. In particular, in Hungary in 1944, at the time of his interviews with directors of the Jewish community (cf. Kästner's report on the activity of the Budapest Jewish Rescue Committee, B 1252).

14. Anonymous testimony collected by Hans Klee in Switzerland at the end of 1943. (LXX, 70)

15. Confidential letter from Kube to Lohse, dated December 16, 1941. (PS 3665)

16. Report from SS Sturmbannführer Brand to SS Obergruppenführer von dem Bach, dated July 25, 1943. (NO 2262)

17. Report from Kube to Lohse, Minsk, July 31, 1942. (PS 3428)

18. Report from Globocnik to Himmler on "Operation Reinhardt." Trieste, January 5, 1942. "The documents relative to 'Operation Reinhardt' must be destroyed soon; all documents referring to other activities in this matter have already been destroyed." (NO 064)

19. Testimony by David Mekler, from the collection of Mme. Novitch.

20. Letter from Himmler to SS Obergruppenführer Krüger, July 19, 1942. (NO 5574)

21. Testimony by Mrs. Bronka and Mr. and Mrs. Rabinowicz, from the collection of Mme. Novitch.

22. Message from the SS Reichsführer to SS Obergruppenführer Krüger. During the campaign, February 16, 1943. (NO 2494)

23. Report by SS Gruppenführer Katzmann to SS Obergruppenführer Krüger on "The Solution of the Jewish Question in Galicia," dated June 30, 1943. (L 018)

24. Letter from the "Hoherer SS und Polizeiführer" of the Lublin district to the governor of the district, forwarded to "the Krakow-Kobierzyn State Clinic;" Lublin, September 4, 1942, from K. Kermisz *Akcje i Vyssiedlenia*, Jewish Polish Historical Commission, Warsaw, 1946.

25. From the collection of Mme. Novitch.

26. Previously cited report from Katzmann to Krüger. (L 018)

27. From Jacob Littner, *Erinnerungen aus einem Erdloch*, Kluger, Munich, 1948.

28. Telegram from Benzler to the Ministry of Foreign Affairs. Belgrade, September 8, 1941. (NG 2723)

29. Memo from Luther to von Weizsäcker, Berlin, October 2, 1941. (NG 3354)

30. This is the figure given by Wisliceny, *doc. cit.*

31. *In memoriam*, published by M. Molho, rabbi of the Salonika community, Salonika, 1948, p. 82; *Les Crimes allemands en Pologne*, Commission of Inquiry Into the German Crimes, Warsaw, 1948 (p. 89).

32. According to M. Molho, the number of these fictitious marriages eventually rose to one hundred daily. (p. 88)

33. This phrase of Hoess's was reported by Wisliceny, *doc. cit.*

34. Affidavit by Erwin Lenz. Berlin, May 10, 1947. (NOKW 1715)

35. Memo from Undersecretary of State Luther on "The Principles of the Anti-Jewish Policy." Berlin, August 21, 1942. (NG 2586)

36. *Idem.*

37. Account of Wisliceny, *doc. cit.*

38. Note from Luther on his interview with the Hungarian Ambassador Sztojay. Berlin, October 6, 1942. (NG 1800)

39. Report by R. Kästner. (B 1252)

40. Account by Wisliceny, Bratislava, November 18, 1946. (LXXXVIII, 67)

41. *Idem.* Cf. also W. Höttl's affidavit, where he refers to Eichmann's "mission to Rumania," from which "he probably would not return." (PS 2738)

42. Report on the situation by the SD and security police action groups in the USSR. Berlin, July 31, 1941, p. 18. (NO 2651)

43. Instructions sent to von Killinger, German Ambassador to Rumania. Berlin, November 11, 1942. (NG 2193)

44. Report by Charles Kolb, representative of the International Committee of the Red Cross in Rumania, on his trip to Transnistria, December 11-21, 1943. Bucharest, January 14, 1943. (Kolb gives the following figures: 206,700 deportees from Bessarabia; 88,600 from Bucovina, or a total of 295,300; 54,300 survivors in December 1943. However, Kolb notes that the first two figures are based on a 1930 census; that from June 1940 to June 1941 the territories in question had formed part of the USSR; and that on the eve of the German attack part of the Jewish population had been evacuated by the Russians.)

45. Report from von Killinger to his government. Bucharest, December 12, 1942. (NG 3986)

46. Account by Haim Benadov, member of the Central Consistory of Bulgarian Jews, presented to the European Conference of Documentation Centers and Jewish Historical Commissions. Paris, December 1947.

47. Report from Beckerle, German Ambassador at Sofia, to his government. Sofia, June 7, 1942. (NG 2357)

48. Telegram from Eichmann to Knochen, head of the SD in France. Berlin, February 24, 1943. (Cf. our previously cited work, *La Condition des Juifs en France sous l'occupation italienne.*)

49. Report from Knochen to the RSHA. Paris, February 22, 1943. (I, 38)

50. Report on the action taken by the Italian Ministry of Foreign Affairs in the interests of foreign Jews in Italy and Italian Jews living abroad during the period between the start of the racist policy in Italy and the Cassibile Armistice. The report, a copy of which has been sent us, was drawn up at Rome in 1945.

51. Cf. the report previously cited. The principal artisans of the Italian action were Vitetti, director general of the Ministry, Vidau, his successor, and Professor Perassi, chief of the legal division.

52. Ciano's name heads the list in a report that Laval sent to the prefect of the Alpes-Maritimes (II, 186), as well as in a report sent to Knochen by Schweblin, former director of Vichy's anti-Jewish police. (I, 51)

53. Note from the Italian government to the government of the Reich, November 17, 1942, quoted from the report on Italian activity previously cited.

54. Letter from General Avarna di Gualtieri, representing the Italian Supreme Command at Vichy, to General Bridoux. Vichy, April 27, 1943. (I, 47)

55. Cf. in particular a memo submitted to Mussolini on July 23, 1943 (*op. cit.* on Italian activities.)

56. Report drawn up by a high officer of the Italian Second Army (stationed in Croatia), dated November 3, 1942 (cf. *op. cit.* on Italian activities).

57. "The details contained in this document were such that they could not fail to arouse a feeling of horror in the most cynical heart. It was sent by the spokesman of Bastianini to the Chief of State, accompanied by a few lines which openly stated that no country, not even Germany, its ally, could hope to associate Italy, the birthplace of Christianity and moral law, with such crimes, for which the Italian people could one day be called to account." (*op. cit.* on Italian activities, p. 62)

58. Details furnished by Colonel Vitale, president of the Research Committee of Deported Jews, in his report submitted to the European Conference of Documentation Centers and Jewish Historical Commissions. Paris, December 1947.

59. Letter from Eichmann to the Ministry of Foreign Affairs (attention of

the Councillor of the Legation Rademacher). Berlin, June 22, 1942. (NG 183)
60. H. Wielek, *De Oorlog die Hitler won*, Amsterdam, 1947, p. 139-63.
61. Georges Wellers, *De Drancy à Auschwitz*, Paris, Ed. du Centre. 1946. (p. 48-60)
62. Note on the treatment of Jews of foreign nationality within the German orbit of power (*im deutschen Machtbereich*), signed Rademacher. Berlin, February 20, 1943. (NG 2586)
63. Report from Bene to the Ministry of Foreign Affairs. The Hague, August 13, 1942. (NG 2631)
64. H. Wielek, *op. cit.*, p. 335.
65. Report by SS Obersturmführer Röthke. Paris, July 18, 1942. (XXV b, 80)
66. Statistical report signed Ahnert, prepared at the request of SS General Oberg. Paris, September 3, 1942. (RF 1227)
67. *La Persécution antisémitique en Belgique*, Liege, Thomé, 1947, p. 30.
68. Report by Bene previously cited; cf. n. 63.
69. Report from Röthke to Dannecker concerning his telephone conversation with Eichmann. Paris, July 15, 1942. (RF 1226)
70. H. Wielek, *op. cit.*, p. 321. Röthke wrote on September 4, 1943, in France: "It is necessary to associate French anti-Semites with us and to denounce the camouflaged Jews. Money should not play any part in this (proposition: 100 francs per Jew)."
71. Dannecker's draft of "The Future Organization of Deportations in France." Paris, July 8, 1942. (XXVb, 55)
72. *La Persécution antisémitique en Belgique*, p. 28.
73. S. Ven den Bergh, *Deportation*, Bussum, 1946. In Dutch.
74. H. Wielek, *op. cit.*, p. 286-96.
75. *Idem*, p. 312-13.
76. E. d'Aron, *Examen ethno-racial*, Paris, November 16, 1942. (XXXVI, 104)
77. Report submitted to Himmler by the RSHA. Berlin, November 24, 1942. (NO 2408)
78. Georges Wellers, *op. cit.*, p. 99-100.
79. *Idem*, p. 68. The word probably was "invented" by children in the infirmary of the Drancy camp.
80. *Idem*, p. 70-71.
81. *Idem*, p. 47.
82. Report by Röthke, on "The Present State of the Jewish Question in France," Paris, March 6, 1943. (RF 1230)
83. File found in the IVb archives in Paris: "Proposed Decree on the Denationalization of French Jews Nationalized After 1927." Cf. also Roger Berg, p. 87-91.
84. Note by Röthke on "The Present State of the Jewish Question in France." Paris, July 21, 1943. (I, 54)

CHAPTER EIGHT

1. The victims were forced to get down into a ditch containing quicklime. Water was then sprayed into the ditch, making the quicklime boil. This procedure is described in *Les Crimes allemandes en Pologne*, published by the Inquiry Commission of the Polish Government, I, 170-74, as well as by Karski, *Mon témoignage devant le monde*, Paris, Self, 1948, p. 308 ff.

2. According to the testimony of Karl Brandt, the message sent by Hitler to Bouhler and himself gave them full power to introduce euthanasia. Prepared in October 1939 it had been pre-dated September 1. (Interrogation of Karl Brandt before the Nuremberg Tribunal, "The Doctors' Trial," session of February 4, 1947.)

3. Deposition by Fritz Mennecke, "The Doctors' Trial," session of January 17, 1947.

4. Article by Professor Kranz in the April 1940 issue of the *N.S. Volksdienst.*

5. Interrogation of K. Brandt, "The Doctors' Trial," session of February 5, 1947.

6. Report by the Advocate General (Oberstaatsanwalt) of Cologne to the Minister of Justice. Cologne, October 20, 1941. (NO 845)

7. The description of the technique and procedures of euthanasia was given at length by Viktor Brack, during "The Doctors' Trial," at several sessions in May 1947. (Cf., for the same information, the deposition of witnesses like the nurse Pauline Kneissler, session of January 13, 1947.)

8. Letter from Doctor Hölzel to Professor Pfannmüller. Schwartzsee, Kitzbühel, August 20, 1940. (NO 1313)

9. Interrogation of K. Brandt, "The Doctors' Trial," session of February 4, 1947.

10. Deposition by Fritz Mennecke, "The Doctors' Trial," session of January 17, 1947.

11. Letter from Mennecke to his wife, Mathilde, Weimar, February 25, 1947, "Elephant Hotel," 8:58 p.m. (NO 907) Mennecke dated his letters to the minute.

12. Affidavit of Julius Muthig. Nuremberg, April 17, 1947. (NO 2799)

13. Report from Kreisleiter Wolf to the Gauleiter. Ansbach, March 6, 1941. (D 906)

14. Report from Kreisleiter Walz to the Administration of the Franconia Gau. Lauf, December 30, 1940. (NO 796)

15. Secret report from the Kreisleiter to the administration of the Kreis, in Weissenberg. Langlau, February 24, 1941. (D 906)

16. Memo on the planned transfer of inmates of homes and poorhouses, submitted by Pastor P. Braune, director of charitable institutions of Hoffnungsthal, and vice president of the Löbethal Committee. July 9, 1940. (NO 823)

17. Letter from the Bishop of Limburg to the Minister of Justice of the Reich. Limburg, August 13, 1941. (PS 615)

18. Interrogation of K. Brandt, "The Doctors' Trial," session of February 4, 1947. Affidavit V. Brack. Nuremberg, October 14, 1946. (NO 425)

19. Report sent by Wetzel to the Reich Commissioner for "Ostland" on "The Solution of the Jewish Question." Berlin, October 25, 1941. (NO 365)

20. Trial of the major war criminals, interrogation of Konrad Morgen, session of August 8, 1946.

21. Interrogation of V. Brack during "The Doctors' Trial," session of May 14, 1947.

22. *German crimes in Poland,* complete edition (in Polish), IV, 97.

23. Testimony of Kurt Gerstein. (PS 1553)

24. *Les Crimes allemands en Pologne,* French edition, Warsaw, 1948, p. 106-32.

25. *Het doedenboek van Auschwitz,* s'Gravenhage, Dutch Red Cross, 1947.

26. Testimony of Rothbalsam from the collection of Mme. A. Novitch.

27. Report by a Jewish deportee, returned to Slovakia. August 17, 1943. (LXX, 77)

28. *Sobibor*, s'Gravenhage, Dutch Red Cross, 1947.

29. The recollections of this sole survivor, Rudolf Reder, have been published under the title *Belzec*. (Cracow, 1946)

30. *Les Crimes allemands en Pologne, op. cit.*, p. 110, 120, 127.

31. Affidavit by Rudolf Hoess. Nuremberg, May 17, 1946. (NI 034)

32. Affidavit by Rudolf Hoess. Nuremberg, April 5, 1946. (PS 3868)

33. Affidavit by Rudolf Hoess. Muenchen, March 14, 1946. (D 749)

34. Trial of the major war criminals, interrogation of Konrad Morgen, session of August 8, 1946.

35. Affidavit by Rudolf Hoess, *doc. cit.* (PS 3868)

36. From the account by Franz Ziereis (mortally wounded attempting escape). Mauthausen, May 23, 1945. (PS 1515)

37. *Les Crimes allemands en Pologne, op. cit.*, p. 22-23.

38. P. Friedman, *This Was Oswiecim*, London, U. I. R. A., 1946, p. 19.

39. Affidavit by Rudolf Hoess, *doc. cit.*, (D. 749)

40. *Idem*.

41. *Idem*.

42. *Idem*.

43. *Idem*.

44. *Les Crimes allemands en Pologne, op. cit.*, p. 93.

45. *This Was Oswiecim, op. cit.*, p. 19.

46. *Témoignages strasbourgeois*, Paris, Les Belles-Lettres, 1947. Testimony of Dr. Robert Levy, *Auschwitz II—Birkenau*, p. 464. Hoess affidavit, *doc. cit.*

47. *Les Crimes allemands en Pologne, op. cit.*, p. 97. It should be pointed out that, according to R. Hoess, the maximum capacity of the crematoria reached only 4,000 per twenty-four hours.

48. Testimony of Georges Wellers.

49. Testimony of R. Levy. *Témoignages strasbourgeois, op. cit.*, p. 464.

50. *Idem*.

51. Testimony of Klein, *Témoignages strasbourgeois*, p. 433.

52. According to testimony in *Het doedenbock van Auschwitz* (*op. cit.*, p. 16), the order to suspend exterminations and to dismantle the crematoria arrived from Berlin on November 2, 1944. P. Friedman, *This Was Oswiecim*, p. 77, gives the date of September 2, 1944; this is certainly an error.

53. *This Was Oswiecim*, p. 78.

54. Joseph Tenenbaum, *In Search of a Lost People*, New York, Beechhurst Press, 1948, p. 141.

55. Trial of the major war criminals, deposition of D. Wisliceny, session of January 3, 1946.

56. Testimony of R. Waitz. *Témoignages strasbourgeois*, p. 469-70.

57. *Auschwitz, deil II: de deportatietransporten van 15 jilu 1942 tot en met 24 Augustus 1942*. This is the second part of the excellent study by the Dutch Red Cross previously cited.

58. Affidavit by Friedrich Entress, one of the SS doctors at Auschwitz. Nuremberg, April 14, 1947. (NO 2368)

59. *Les Crimes allemands en Pologne, op. cit.*, p. 98.

60. Affidavit by R. Hoess. (PS 3868)

61. *Idem*. (D 749)

62. G. Wellers, "La Révolte du sonderkommando à Auschwitz," *Le Monde Juif*, no. 18, April 1949.

63. *Idem.*

64. Testimony of R. Waitz, *Témoignages strasbourgeois*, p. 493.

65. Georges Wellers, *De Drancy à Auschwitz*, *op. cit.*, p. 202.

66. *Témoignages sur Auschwitz*, Paris, Ed. de l'amicale des anciens déportés d'Auschwitz. Paris, 1946.

67. *Idem.* Hafner's account, p. 71.

68. Affidavit of Peters. Frankfort, August 27, 1947. (NI 12111)

69. "The Trial of Cyklon B" (*Tesch and accomplices*), London, His Majesty's Stationery Office, 1947.

70. Affidavit of Alfred Zawn, former accountant for the Testa company. Nuremberg, October 18, 1947. (NI 11937)

71. Peters' affidavit, *doc. cit.*

72. Diary of Kremer, complete photostat. (NO 3408)

73. G. M. Gilbert, *Nuremberg Diary*, New York, Farrar, Strauss, 1947, p. 260.

74. *Idem*, p. 251.

75. Report from Röthke to Dannecker, *doc. cit.* (RF 1226)

76. The *Danziger Vorposten* of May 13, 1944. Article signed "Lobsack."

77. *Der Angriff*, May 14, 1944.

78. Affidavit by SS Rottenführer Perry Broad. Nuremberg, October 20, 1947. (NI 11984)

79. Affidavit by R. Diels. Nuremberg, October 20, 1947. (NI 11957)

80. Deposition of SS Obergruppenführer Bach-Zelewski, trial of the RuSHA (*Rasse und Siedlungshauptamt*), session of October 24, 1947.

81. Note from the personal file of R. Hoess in the SS administration (NO 2124)

82. Speech delivered by Himmler at Posnania, October 4, 1943. (PS 1919)

83. Letter sent by the "Head of the Central Administration for the Waffen SS and the Police Buildings at Auschwitz" to the SS Sturmbannführer Caesar, "Head of the Agricultural Enterprises for the Auschwitz Concentration Camp." Auschwitz, November 6, 1943. (NO 4463)

84. Affidavit by Gerhard Wiebeck. Dachau, February, 28, 1947. (NO 2331)

85. Testimony of M. Klein, *Témoignages strasbourgeois*, *op. cit.*, p. 448.

86. Testimony of J. Hofstein, *Témoignages strasbourgeois*, p. 515.

87. *Het doedenboek van Auschwitz*, *op. cit.*

88. In this connection cf., for example, Rolf Weinstock, *Das wahre Gesicht Hitlerdeutschlands*, Singen, 1948, as well as P. Loheac, *Un médecin français en déportation*, Paris, Bonne Presse, 1949.

89. Testimony of R. Waitz, *Témoignages strasbourgeois*, p. 491.

90. Bruno Bettelheim, *A Study of Gestapo Aims and of the Effects of Gestapo Methods on the Personality and Behavior of Concentration Camp Inmates*, Washington, 1945.

91. Testimony of G. Stroka, *Témoignages strasbourgeois*, p. 89.

CHAPTER NINE

1. Report made to the Commandant of the SD and security police at Zhitomir entitled: "Incident at the Time of the Special Treatment (*Sonderbehandlung*) Today." Berditchev, December 24, 1942. (USSR 311)

2. Contract between SS Gruppenführer Globocnik and Walther C. Toebbens. Lublin, January 31, 1943. (CXCVIII, 1)

3. Cf. the reports of SS Gruppenführer Stroop ("The Jewish Quarter in Warsaw Is No More"). (PS 1061)

4. Report of Veesenmayer, German Ambassador to Hungary. Budapest, July 25, 1944. (NG 1806)

5. These considerations by the German High Command were revealed by SS General Stroop after his capture. (*Bleter far Geszichte*, nos. 3-4, Warsaw, August-December, 1948, p. 167)

6. Report by Stroop previously cited. (PS 1061)

7. From J. Tenenbaum, *In Search of a Lost People*, New York, Beechhurst Press, 1948.

8. Telegram from Stroop, April 24, 1943. (PS 1061)

9. Report by Stroop previously cited (introduction and commentary). (PS 1061)

10. *Le Journal du Docteur Goebbels*, Paris, Cheval Aile, 1949, p. 332, 347, 373.

11. From A. Sutzkever, "Vilner Ghetto" (in Yiddish), quoted in Leo Schwartz, *The Root and the Bough*, New York, Rinehart, 1949.

12. From J. Wulf, preface to *Pamietnik Justyny*, Warsaw, 1945.

13. From J. Tenenbaum, *In Search of a Lost People*, op. cit., p. 96-99.

14. Report of SS Gruppenführer Katzmann, June 30, 1943, doc. cit. (L 018)

15. Report of the chief of the SD and the security police. Berlin, June 12, 1942. (NO 5158)

16. Report of the chief of the SD and the security police. Berlin, May 1, 1942. (PS 3943)

17. *Ruch Podziemny w Obozach i Gettach*, p. 110-18.

18. Report of the chief of the SD and the security police. Berlin, June 12, 1942. (NO 5158)

19. Activity report No. 5 of the security police and SD action groups in the USSR for the period September 15-30, 1941, p. 14. (NO 2655)

20. Activity report for Commando XIa at Nikolaiev for August 18-31, 1941. (NO 2066)

21. *Le Journal du Docteur Goebbels, op. cit.*, p. 97.

22. Report of the Prosecutor for the People's Tribunal of the Reich to the Minister of Justice. Berlin, October 3, 1942. (NG 683)

23. Testimony of Chief Rabbi Cohen of Bordeaux. (XX, 14)

24. Cf. Marie Syrkin, *Blessed is the Match, the Story of the Jewish Resistance*, Philadelphia, The Jewish Publication Society of America, 1947.

CHAPTER TEN

1. Cf. the brochure by J. I. Schneersohn, rabbi of Lubawicz (New York, May 1946), and K. Abshagen, *Le Dossier Canaris*, Paris, P. A. Chauvane, 1949, p. 150.

2. Cf. Himmler's personal letters, several of which were published by Captain Albert Zoller, in particular in *France-Soir*, September 19, 1948.

3. Trevor-Roper, *Last Days of Hitler*, New York, Macmillan, 1947.

4. S. Goudsmith, *La Mission Alsos*, Paris, Artheme Fayard, 1948, p. 204.

5. The fact is notorious. Cf. Trevor-Roper, *op. cit.; see also*, in reference to the Russian expeditions, certain depositions in the "Einsatzgruppen Trial," especially that of Biberstein.

6. Trial of Weizsäcker and accomplices, deposition of Bach-Zelewski, session of March 25, 1948.

7. Letter from Himmler to his adjutant, Sievers. Himmler's GHQ, March 1944. Cf. David Rousset, *Le Pitre ne rit pas*, Paris, Le Pavois, 1949, p. 225.

8. Letter from Himmler to SS General Pohl. Himmler's GHQ, April 25, 1944. (NO 640)

9. Confession of Franz Ziereis, former commandant of the Mauthausen camp, made on May 24, 1945; deposition of former inmate Hans Marsalek. Nuremberg, April 8, 1946. (PS 1515)

10. Deposition of Viktor Brack, "The Doctors' Trial," session of May 14, 1947.

11. Note sent by V. Brack to the SS Reichsführer, dated March 28, 1941. (NO 203)

12. Deposition of V. Brack, "The Doctors' Trial," session of March 14, 1947.

13. Letter sent to Reichsführer Himmler by Doctor Pokorny. Komotau, October 1941. (NO 035)

14. Letter to Reichsführer Himmler from Oberführer K. Gerland, Vice Gauleiter of the Lower Danube province. Vienna, August 24, 1942. (NO 039)

15. Letter from Himmler to Professor Clauberg. The Führer's Headquarters, July 10, 1942. (NO 213)

16. Letter to Himmler from Blankenburg, Brack's deputy at the Führer's Chancellery. Berlin, April 29, 1944. (NO 208)

17. Expert opinion of Dr. Karl Wilhelm Friedrich Taubock, in charge of research in physiology and biochemistry at the I. G. Farben laboratories. Nuremberg, June 18, 1947. (NO 3963)

18. Report of the chief of the SD and the security police to the SS Reichsführer. Berlin, November 24, 1942. (NO 2408)

19. *Idem.*

20. Copies of messages sent by Mrs. Gisi Fleischmann in Switzerland. (LXX, 83; LXX, 84)

21. On the role of the Grand Mufti, see S. Wiesenthal, *Grossmufti-Grossagent der Axe*, Vienna, Ried-Verlag, 1947, and Pearlman, *Mufti of Jerusalem, the Story of Haj-Amin el Hussein*, London, Gollancz, 1947, as well as the depositions of Dieter Wisliceny, Bratislava, November 18, 1946.

22. Note dated July 22, 1944, signed Biss. (LXX, 13)

23. Cf. Count F. Bernadotte, *La Fin*, Lausanne, Marguerat, 1945.

24. Letter from the SS Reichsführer to Dr. Kersten. Berlin, March 21, 1945. Cf. the photostat of the letter in *Klerk en Beul, op cit.*

25. Deposition of Oswald Pohl during his trial at Nuremberg, session of May 19, 1947.

26. Report of the Budapest Jewish Rescue Committee, prepared by Kästner, p. 172. *See also* the note drawn up by K. Becher after his capture, and the notes of Dieter Wisliceny.

27. The Morgenthau memoirs, published under the title, "The Morgenthau Diaries," *Collier's Magazine*, November 1, 1947.

28. Report from Morgenthau to President Franklin D. Roosevelt, January 16, 1944.

29. Report submitted by Wetzel to the "Ministry of Eastern Occupied Territories," on the organization of the occupied regions of the USSR. Berlin, April 1942. (NG 2325)

30. From a speech by Goebbels delivered about the middle of May 1943. (NG 1531)

CHAPTER ELEVEN

1. Extract from the memo entitled "The Gypsy Question," drawn up in August 1938 by Portschy, Gauleiter of the province of Styria, which he submitted to Lammers, Chief of the Chancellery of the Reich, February 9, 1939. (NG 845)

2. Secret circular from the SS Reichsführer. Berlin, March 10, 1944. (PS 664)

3. Dora E. Yates, secretary of the Gypsy Lore Society in London. "Hitler and the Gypsies," *Commentary*, November 1949.

4. Affidavit of SS Obersturmführer Heinz Schubert. Nuremberg, February 24, 1947.

5. Dora E. Yates, *art. cit.*

6. Thoughts and suggestions on "Plan East" prepared for the SS Reichsführer by Professor Wetzel. Berlin, April 27, 1942. (NG 2325)

7. Minutes of a conference held on July 16, 1941, by the Führer. (L 221)

8. Report from Lohse to Rosenberg. Riga, June 18, 1942. (R 135)

9. Directives for the anti-partisan struggle, signed Keitel, dated December 16, 1942. (NO 631)

10. Directives of Keitel, September 16, 1941. (C 148)

11. Personal letter from Rosenberg to Marshal Keitel. Berlin, February 28, 1942. (PS 081)

12. The text of this speech delivered in Wewelsburg has not been found. Mention of it was made by SS General Bach-Zelewski. Trial of the major war criminals, session of January 7, 1946.

13. Speech by Himmler to a conference of SS Generals at Bad Schachen, October 14, 1943. (L 70)

14. Diary of Frank, conference of May 30, 1940. (PS 2233)

15. *German crimes in Poland, op. cit.*, II, 44-46; *Mass Executions in Poland in the Period 1939–45.*

16. Report from the representative of the Ministry of Foreign Affairs to the "Protector of the Reich" in Bohemia and Moravia. Prague, October 5, 1940. (D 739)

17. Letter from Thierack to Bormann. Berlin, October 11, 1942. (NG 558)

18. Circular III/2B of the RuSHA, February 26, 1942. (NO 3758)

19. Circular decree from the SS Reichsführer on the use of Eastern labor. Berlin, February 20, 1942. (PS 3040)

20. Circular decree from the SS Reichsführer on the suppression of major crimes and the forbidden sexual relations of labor in the East. Berlin, February 16, 1944. (NO 1365)

21. Account of an interministerial conference held May 27, 1941, at the Ministry of the Interior of the Reich. (NG 844)

22. Letter from Bormann to Rosenberg. Führer's Headquarters, July 23, 1942. (NO 1878)

23. Wetzel's previously cited memo, April 27, 1942. (NG 2325)

24. This document, whose exact date cannot be established, was quoted in the verdict given at the RuSHA trial at Nuremberg.

25. Note drawn up at the headquarters of the political administration of the Wehrmacht, signed Brandenburg. Berlin, June 12, 1944. (PS 031)

26. On the tracking down of children kidnapped by the Nazis, cf. Dorothy Macardle, *Children of Europe*, London, V. Gollancz, 1949, p. 235-40.

27. Wetzel's previously cited memo, April 27, 1942. (NG 2325)

28. Report prepared by Wetzel, November 25, 1939, in collaboration with Hecht, "director of the Section for Ethnic Germans and Minorities." (PS 560)

29. Letter from Franz von Homeyer, director of the General Commissariat of the Crimea, to Director General Paul Dargel. Mélitopol, March 23, 1943. (CXLIV, 482)

30. L'Economie de guerre en Pologne en 1939–40. (EC 344)

31. German crimes in Poland, op. cit., p. 67-85.

32. Report by Greifelt, director of the Commission for Strengthening Germanism, on the "Treatment and Assignment of Persons Evacuated from Alsace, Lorraine, and Luxemburg," Berlin, October 3, 1942. (NO 5028)

33. Letter from Berndt, director in the Ministry of Propaganda of the Reich, to the SS Reichsführer. Berlin, May 20, 1942. (NO 2472)

34. Letter from SS General Berger to Himmler, dated June 21, 1944. (NO 2245)

35. Stenographic account of the speech delivered by Reichsmarshal Goering before the Reich Commissioners for Occupied Territories. Berlin, August 6, 1942. (USSR 170)

36. The story of the project for the total deportation of the Dutch population is told in F. Kersten's book, Klerk en Beul, op. cit. Documentation in the Rijksinstituut voor Oorlogedocumentatie in Amsterdam, and an inquiry made by that Dutch State institution, lend great weight to Dr. Kersten's story.

37. Cf. in the (London) Times of November 6, 1945, the "Orders and Instructions for the Establishment of a Military Government in England After the Projected Invasion in 1940."

CHAPTER TWELVE

1. Note on the arrest of Canon Lichtenberg, archives of the Ministry of Foreign Affairs (NG 4447); cf. also H. Rothfels, Opposition allemande contre Hitler, Chicago, 1948, (Krefeld, 1949), p. 42.

2. Testimony of Israel Rothbalsam, from the collection of Mme. Novitch.

3. This refers to the last "free" elections, which took place March 5, 1933, one week after the Reichstag fire. The exact results were: Nazi Party: 288 seats; National Party (Hugenberg): 52; Bourgeois Bloc: 33; Center: 73; Social-Democrats: 121.

4. Müller-Claudius, L'Antisémitisme et la fatalité allemande, Frankfort, Knecht, 1948, p. 166-74. The inquiry which the author began in the fall of 1942, had, obviously, to be carried on with extreme care. He took care to bring up indirectly "the solution of the Jewish question" during a series of private conversations; sixty-one people, of all professions and social classes, were thus questioned. Most were members of the Nazi Party; but, on analyzing the results, the author thought himself justified (for good reasons, we think) in applying them to the whole German population.

5. Enno Kind, "La Résistance allemande," quoted from Les Temps Modernes, Paris, August-September, 1949, p. 229.

6. Nuremberg Tribunal, "The Concentration Camps Trial," session of May 15, 1947. It is significant that the fact in question was revealed by one of the defenders of the accused, Paul Ratz. "I am going to show that the removal of gold teeth from inmates dead of natural causes in no way constitutes a criminal action. German professional publications have actively de-

bated the basis for this measure since 1925. At that time, distinguished German dentists were already lending active support to it. . . ." (Page 1241 of the official English typescript)

7. A. Leroy-Beaulieu, *Israel chez les Nations*, Paris, 1893, preface, p. iii.

8. Dated September 2, 1899, the "spiritual testament" of Mommsen was made public only thirty years after his death. It was published in 1948 by the magazine *Die Wandlung*, p. 69-70.

9. Cf. S. Freud, *Totem and Taboo*, from which we have taken this observation ("The Treatment of Enemies," Vienna, 1925, 4th German edition, 1925, p. 47-53). Cf. also J. G. Frazer's classic work, *The Golden Bough*.

10. Protest sent by Archbishop Sapieha to Governor General Frank, Cracow, November 2, 1942. (USSR 93)

11. Extract from a report (cited above) by a Wehrmacht officer. "Notes and Observations Made During a Trip Into the Eastern Zone of Operations." Berlin, October 23, 1941 (NDKW 3047)

12. Activity report of "action groups" No. 45. Berlin, December 12, 1941. (NO 2828)

13. Saint Thomas Aquinas, *De regimine Judaeorum*, 2, in *Opyscule omnia*, Paris, J. Perrier, 1949, I, 213-14. The text is probably from 1261.

14. Frederic's account of his trip to Poland and particularly of his conversation with Metropolitan Szepticki. Berlin, September 19, 1943. (CXLV a-60)

15. During a debate on "Judeo-Christian Friendship," organized by The Friends of Jewish Thought. We quote from the typescript published in Nos. 3-4 of *L'Amitié judéo-chrétienne*, p. 28, December 1949.

16. Cf. Freud in *Moses and Monotheism*, Paris, NRF, 1948, p. 238 ff, and Maritain in *Le Droit raciste et l'assaut de la civilisation*, New York, Maison Française, 1943. This thesis has been developed by the American Jewish writer Maurice Samuel, in *The Great Hatred*, London, Gollancz, 1948.

17. Mass celebrated in July 1944 in the city of Weszprem with the bishop's authorization. Report sent to Berlin by Veesenmayer, German ambassador to Hungary, July 20, 1944. (NG 5613)

18. Comprehensive report for Action Group A. Berlin, October 31, 1931, p. 127. (L 180)

19. Information published by the *Neue Zeitung*, Munich, May 17, 1947, and reproduced in the work by Müller-Claudius previously cited, *L'Antisémitisme et la fatalité allemande*, p. 34.

20. Cf. "Les Eglises Protestantes pendant la Guerre et l'Occupation," Actes de l'Assemblée Générale du Protestantisme Français, held at Nîmes, October 22-26, 1945, Paris, Fédération Protestante de France, 1946.

21. Appeal of the National Committee for Jewish Resistance in Poland, dated November 15, 1943, at Warsaw and sent to the Jews in Palestine. From the collection of Mme. Novitch.

22. Note from the German Ministry of Foreign Affairs, dated September 7, 1939, signed Schaumburg. Schaumburg suggested "counter-measures against the Jews (German) in order to assure indirect protection for Germans in Palestine." (NG 1923)

23. Report from Veesenmayer, German ambassador to Hungary to his government. Budapest, June 25, 1944. (NG 1806)

Notes

Note

Total Number of Jewish Victims of Racial Persecution
During World War II

(From *Revue d'histoire de la deuxième guerre mondiale*,
No. 24, October, 1956)

Most of the publications dealing with racial persecution during the last war have set the total number of Jews destroyed by the Nazis at six million. However, this figure, which has appeared in numerous publications in many lands, is generally quoted without any documentary or statistical support. The question then is: where did the figure of six million originate, and how reliable is it?

We believe we will not be in error if we suggest that it was first cited at the Nuremberg trials; hence also its wide currency. The following statement appears on Page 496 of the judgment of the International Military Tribunal: "Adolf Eichmann, who had been put in charge of this program [of extermination] by Hitler, has estimated that the policy pursued resulted in the killing of six million Jews, of whom four million were killed in the extermination camps." (1) The source of this information is not given, but a study of the official record of the hearings reveals that the Tribunal based its conclusion on two second-hand sources—the testimony of the SS officers Wilhelm Hoettl and Dieter Wisliceny, both of whom confirmed Eichmann's figure. It could be argued, of course, that a figure with such incomplete support should be viewed with some reservations. (The very wording of the judgment: "Eichmann . . . has estimated . . ." reflects a note of caution.) But on what source could Eichmann himself have based his figures? Might he not have exaggerated? His friend Dieter Wisliceny testified before the International Military Tribunal that Eichmann "said he would leap laughing into the

(1) *Trial of the Major War Criminals Before the International Military Tribunal*, Nuremberg, Official Text in the English Language, session of September 30, 1946, Vol. XXII, p. 496.

grave because the feeling that he had six million people on his conscience would be for him a source of extraordinary satisfaction." (2)

On the other hand, the very nature of the operations involved in a planned program of extermination—police roundups, the organizing of transports, and the transfer of the victims by train to Auschwitz or to one of the four extermination camps in Poland—should make it fairly simple to establish the total number of deportees who set out on the journey from which there was no return. All the testimony taken from surviving deportees includes references to endless roll calls for the purpose of verifying the number of prisoners first at the time of their departure, and again when they arrived at their destination. It would be surprising if such statistics should not have been compiled, as was done most meticulously in the case of such possessions as furniture, watches or fountain pens taken from the victims. And while this detailed information has not been located to-date (except in the cases of France, the Netherlands and Hungary) (3), there are available comprehensive statistical studies, which were worked out very efficiently, were surely based on primary sources and should permit a closer investigation of the problem.

In March, 1943, Himmler ordered Dr. Richard Korherr, the "Inspector of Statistics to the *Reichsführer SS*," to prepare a report on the "final solution of the Jewish problem." It is significant that, in his order, Himmler specified that the report should use the term "evacuation," not "special treatment" (*Sonderbehandlung*) of Jews. Korherr gave Himmler two reports, one of 17 pages, dated March 27, 1943, and a digest of six pages, dated April 19, 1943, (4) the latter intended for Hitler himself. (It seems that these two documents were discovered by the Allied War Crimes Service too late to be used in the Nuremberg trials.) The report

(2) *Trial of the Major War Criminals Before the International Military Tribunal*, Nuremberg, Official Text in the English Language, session of January 3, 1946, Vol. IV, p. 371, Cross-Examination of D. Wisliceny. *Translator's Note*: Actually, the text in the Tribunal's record, which I have personally inspected, reads "five million" not "six million."

(3) *France*: series of 76 files, containing, transport by transport, the lists of persons deported from the camp in Drancy (in the archives of the *Centre de documentation juive contemporaine*); *Netherlands*: lists of deportees from Westerbork (cf. the two sections on "Auschwitz," published by the Dutch Red Cross, s'Gravenshage, 1947); *Hungary*: series of reports from the German embassy in Budapest covering the period from April to July, 1944 (archives of the C.D.J.C., CLXXXIX, 1–219.)

(4) Report by Korherr, *Inspekteur für Statistik*, entitled, *Die Endlösung der europäischen Judenfrage* (The Final Solution of the Jewish Problem in Europe; archives of the C.D.J.C., Documents CXXXVIII a, 72 and 73).

of April 19 (for its complete text, see Appendix) ends with the following passage:

> *Balance Sheet of European Jewry:* According to the data cited above, the decrease of European Jewry to-date should amount to *4 million.* Aside from Russia, which has about 4 million [Jews], larger Jewish populations on the European continent now exist only in Hungary (750,000) and Rumania (300,000), and perhaps also in France. If, in addition to the decline cited above, we count Jewish emigration and the excess of mortality among Jews in the Central and Western European countries outside Germany, along with inevitable duplications due to Jewish population movements, the decrease of the Jewish population of Europe between 1937 and the beginning of 1943 may be estimated at 4.5 million. This total includes only partially the incidence of death among Soviet Jews in the occupied Eastern territories; it does not include any of the deaths in the rest of European Russia and in the battle zone.

Thus, according to very precise data available to the statisticians of the Third Reich at the time, the "decrease of European Jewry" by December 31, 1942 already amounted to 4 million, not counting "deaths in the rest of European Russia and in the battle zone." At this point, Hungarian Jewry was still intact (according to German documents, 430,000 Hungarian Jews were deported to Auschwitz between April and July, 1944) (5) and important ghettoes and labor camps still existed in the *General-gouvernement* of Poland; i.e., German-occupied Poland. (According to the Korherr report, an estimated 297,914 Jews were still living in the *Generalgouvernement* of Poland alone.) The hunt for Jews throughout Europe was to continue unabated for another two years.

On the basis of the Korherr report alone, it could be stated almost with certainty that the total number of Jews killed must have been between 5 and 7 million; the most likely total still would be 6 million. This total includes only losses by violent death, gassing or shooting; it does not take into account the *demographic deficit* added between 1939 and 1945 which resulted from the almost total cessation of births in Jewish families, the almost total extermination of children—only strong adults in the prime of life stood a good chance of surviving in the camps—and so forth. In all likelihood professional statisticians, on the basis of their demographic procedures, will conclude that under the circumstances the "actual losses" of the Jewish people between 1933 and 1945 totalled about 8 million.

(5) Cf. the reports of the German embassy in Budapest cited earlier, and particularly the report (July 7, 1944) of Ambassador Veesenmayer (C. D. J. C. archives, CLXXXIX, 40).

There are two other methods of statistical assessment which are less reliable than the one cited above but which, it should be noted, both tend to yield the same total: a loss of 6 million due to violent death.

One of these methods is to compile the figures by sites of extermination; i.e., the five death camps (Auschwitz, Belzec, Treblinka, Sobibor and Chelmno) and the "open-air killings" during the "chaotic exterminations" in Russia.

In 1945–46 the official Polish government commission formed to investigate German crimes in Poland made a thorough study for the four last-mentioned camps, interviewing both the survivors and the railroad employes who worked on the railroad lines leading to the camps. This study yielded the following figures:

Belzec 600,000
Treblinka 700,000
Sobibor...300,000
Chelmno...250,000

Total   1,850,000 (6)

As regards the gigantic human charnel house that was Auschwitz, its commander, Rudolf Hoess, testifying before the Nuremberg tribunal, said that 2.5 million Jews had been destroyed there. (7) However, it seems that this figure includes also inmates other than Jews, such as gypsies, Russians or *Aryan* Poles. We will therefore put the total conservatively at 2 million.

As for the "chaotic exterminations" in Russia, the SS *Einsatzgruppen* (SS killing squads) submitted weekly statistical reports to the *Reichssicherheitshauptamt* (Main National Security Office) in Berlin. However, only part of these reports have been recovered. Those reports which were found enabled the American tribunal in Nuremberg to

---

(6) Report of the official Polish government commission for the investigation of German crimes in Poland (English edition: *German Crimes in Poland*, Warsaw, 1948, pp. 130–32). If we bear in mind the cross-checking methods employed by the commission, and also the period during which the investigation took place (1945–46), these figures would seem acceptable.

(7) *Trial of the Major War Criminals before the International Military Tribunal*, Nuremberg, Official Text in the English Language, session of April 15, 1946, Vol. XI, p. 397, cross-examination of R. Hoess. When asked by Dr. Kaufmann, "Is it furthermore true that Eichmann stated to you that in Auschwitz a total sum of more than 2 million Jews had been destroyed?" Hoess replied, "Yes."

arrive at a definite total of over 1 million victims, (8) while Eichmann, who evidently had all the pertinent data in his possession, said there had been 2 million. (9)

We then arrive at a total of 5,300,000, not counting the innumerable deaths from starvation, disease, etc. in the vast ghettoes of Poland and in the many labor camps all over Europe. (For instance, it will be noted that our statistics do not include the notorious Camp Maidanek, because the Polish Commission on War Crimes did not class it as an extermination camp in the strict sense of the term.)

The second of the two methods, which has been used by specialists in Jewish demography, notably the New York economist and statistician Jacob Lestchinsky, compares the available Jewish population figures in various European countries before the war and after the war, respectively. In this manner some of the international Jewish organizations, such as the World Jewish Congress, have consistently arrived (since 1945) at the total of 6 million. (10)

It is clear, then, that lacking a very precise statistical balance sheet we have no alternative but to accept this total conclusively as the most probable one, even if some of its components might be subject to reservations. (11)

(8) Telford Taylor (former U.S. Chief of Counsel for the prosecution at the Nuremberg trials), *Nuremberg Trials*, New York, 1949, Carnegie Endowment for International Peace, p. 328.

(9) Affidavit of W. Hoettl, cf. *Trial of the Major War Criminals Before the International Military Tribunal*, Nuremberg, Official Text in the English Language, session of December 14, 1945, Vol. III, p. 569: "Approximately 4 million Jews had been killed in the various concentration camps, while an additional 2 million met death in other ways, the major part of which were shot by operational squads of the Security Police during the campaign against Russia."

(10) See J. Lestchinsky, *Le Bilan de l'extermination*, World Jewish Congress, 1946; *Catastrophe and Survival, A Jewish Balance Sheet*, New York, Institute of Jewish Affairs, 1948.

(11) Particularly in the case of France, for which the Ministry for Prisoners, Deportees and Repatriates has placed the number of victims at 100,000 and sometimes as high as 120,000 (cf., for instance, the figures reprinted in Roger Berg, *La Persecution Raciale*, Paris, 1947) In reality, the total number of deportees from the Drancy camp was about 62,000, to which we must add the transports organized directly at Pithiviers (about 5,000 deportees), at Beaune-la-Rolande (about 4,000), at Compiègne (one or two transports), at Lyon-Montluc (1,200) and at Toulouse Caffarelli (1,200), along with deportations from the *departements* of Nord and Pas-de-Calais that were made via Camp Malines in Belgium (2,000 at most). Killings in local massacres, particularly during the German retreat, must also be taken into account. The totals for losses of this type are not fully known. However, they should not amount to more than several thousand.

Accordingly, the total number of victims would be, at the most, 85,000.

Finally, it should be noted that a British researcher, Gerald Reitlinger, in his work *The Final Solution* (London, 1953 and Cranbury, N.J., 1968), questions the total of 6 million. He asserts that many of the figures were deliberately inflated for psychological reasons—both by the Nazis, who were motivated by an urge to boast of their crimes, and by the Jews, who were influenced by the pessimism typical of victims. He therefore strongly questions some of the figures given by the Nazis. By systematically re-examining the figures given for each country, adopting the lowest figure in each case by way of hypothesis, he arrives at a total between a minimum of 4,200,000 and a maximum of 4,600,000. His heaviest corrections are in the figures for Eastern Poland and the Soviet Union proper. In the case of these two regions, estimates are complicated by population movements during and after the war, and by the total absence of reliable statistical data on the present Jewish population there.

In our opinion, one who devotes time and effort to making such corrections solely on the basis of psychological considerations must be motivated by similar considerations himself. In Reitlinger's case this could be explained by the typical British penchant for understatement. No doubt there always will be some uncertainty about the exact total of victims claimed by the racist madness. However, the estimated data available are sufficiently abundant and reliable for us to be able to accept, as the most probable numer, the "classic" total of 6 million.

L. POLIAKOV

Appendix

Statistical Report prepared by Korherr (April 19, 1943)

THE FINAL SOLUTION OF THE JEWISH PROBLEM IN EUROPE (12)

Introductory Note: Jewish statistics must always be treated with a degree of caution because any statistical survey dealing with Jews must be expected to show inaccuracies peculiar to the subject. These errors stem from the nature and development of Jewry, its delimitation, its constant wanderings over thousands of years, innumerable conversions to Judaism on the one hand and secessions on the other, attempts at assimilation, miscegenation with host peoples; but above all, the inaccuracies are due to the efforts of the Jews to evade statistical assessment.

Finally, partly out of considerations of expediency, partly because Jewish race and Jewish religion largely coincide, and partly because they were influenced by religious concepts dating from the last century, statisticians until quite recently dealt with the Jews according to religious rather than racial criteria. The statistical study of Jews according to race presents great difficulties, particularly because of the superficial decline of Jewry resulting from secession, conversion, racial miscegenation in the distant past, and from attempts of Jews to conceal their identity. These difficulties are reflected in the failure of the statistical survey of racial Jews (*Rassejuden*) made in Austria in 1923 and the statistical investigation of half-Jews and quarter-Jews in the German census of 1939. Generally speaking, figures given in Jewish statistics should be regarded as minimum figures, with error increasing in inverse proportion to the amount of Jewish blood present.

Any attempt at a reliable statistical survey of numbers and movements of the Jewish population in the Eastern territories since the outbreak of World War II poses almost insuperable problems because there is no way of keeping track of the mass Jewish population movements caused by the war.

(12) Document No. NO-5193. Translated from the German.

BALANCE SHEET OF JEWRY

The World. The world's total Jewish population during the last decade has been estimated at between 15 and 18 million, sometimes even at much more than 20 million. According to the Reich Bureau of Statistics the total in 1937 was *17 million*.

Europe. Of the above total, some *10.3 million (60 per cent)* were living *in Europe* in 1937, and 5.1 million (30 per cent) in America. Ca. 1880, the percentage of Jews living in Europe was still 88; that living in America only 3.

In Europe Jews were, and are, particularly numerous in the former Polish-Russian and Baltic regions, between the Baltic Sea and the Gulf of Finland and the Black Sea and the Sea of Azov; also in the trading centers of Central and Western Europe, in the Rhine region and on the shores of the Mediterranean Sea.

Germany. The figures on the balance sheet of Jewry in the Reich vary following the respective assumption of power in various regions. Only after the [National Socialist] assumption of power in each case did a large-scale drain set in. Prior to these points in time some areas actually experienced increases in Jewish population due to the outflow of Jews from regions that had become part of the Reich.

A comparison of Jewish population figures at the time of the [National Socialist] assumption of power in the various regions with the figures as of December 31, 1942 yields the following data:

Region	Date of [National Socialist] Assumption of Power	No. Jews prior to [National Socialist] Assumption of power	No. Jews as of 12/31/42
Old Reich	1/30/1933	561,000 }	51,327
Sudetenland	9/29/1938	30,000 }	
Austria	3/13/38	220,000	8,102
Bohemia and Moravia	3/16/1939	118,000	15,550
Eastern territories (including Bialystok)	Sept. 1939 (June 1940)	790,000	233,210
Generalgouvernement (including Lvov)	Sept. 1939 (June 1940)	2,000,000	297,914
Totals	—	3,719,000	606,103

In some instances, the figures given for the time prior to the [National Socialist] assumption of power overlap. Thus, on the eve of the union of the Sudetenland with the Reich, the bulk of the Sudetenland's 30,000 Jews (27,000 Jews by religion) quickly passed into the Protectorate without having to cross frontiers or losing any of their wealth. As a consequence, some of these Jews appear also in the 1939 Jewish population figures for Bohemia and Moravia. By May 17, 1939 there were only 2,649 Jews left in the Sudetenland.

It has been possible to establish, or to estimate, the Jewish population in the Reich territory, including the Protectorate and the *Generalgouvernement*, on the eve of World War II.

	No. Jews as of 5/17/1939	Compared with No. Jews as of 12/31/1942
Old Reich	233,973 ⎫	51,327
Sudetenland	2,649 ⎬	
Austria	94,270	8,102
Bohemia and Moravia	110,000	15,550
Eastern Territories	ca. 790,000	233,210
Generalgouvernement	ca. 2,000,000	297,914
Totals	3,120,892	606,103

Prior to the war, the Old Reich and Austria had already disposed of more than half of their Jewish populations, which were .civilized and sterile; this occurred above all through emigration. In the East, on the other hand, the disintegration of the Jewish masses, which posed a threat because of their fecundity, set in only during the war, and especially following the evacuation measures of 1942.

Thus, between 1933 and 1943, the Jewish population in the expanded Reich territory, that is, the territory under National Socialist rule, has decreased by 3.1 million. In the Old Reich, only one-twelfth still remain; in Austria, only one twenty-seventh; in *Generalgouvernement* and in Bohemia and Moravia about one-seventh; and in the Eastern territories only one-third to one-fourth.

EMIGRATION. EXCESS OF MORTALITY AND EVACUATION.

This decline is the result of a concurrence of emigration, excess of mortality and evacuation, plus other negligible changes such as official secession, official acceptance as a first-degree *Mischling* [half-breed], additions, emendations of records, etc., as shown in the table on the facing page.

The balance sheet for the *Old Reich, Austria, and Bohemia and Moravia* is as follows:

Jewish population at time of [National Socialist] assumption of power:	929.000
Changes resulting from:	
Emigration .	–557,357
Excess of Mortality	– 82,776
Evacuation	–217,748
Additions, etc.	+ 3,860
	–854,021
Total Jewish population as of 12/31/42	74,979

The extraordinarily high excess of mortality among the Jews in the Old Reich, for instance, due to the abnormal superannuation and lack of vitality of the Jews, is attributable to their low birth rate as well as to their high mortality: during the first quarter of 1943 a total of 22 births were registered as against 1,113 deaths. The figures of emigration and excess of mortality (chaotic wartime conditions!) in the Eastern territories and the *Generalgouvernement* are not verifiable. They were computed on the basis of the initial and final population figures, and of evacuation figures.

Between 1/1/1943 and 3/31/1943 a total of 113,015 Jews were evacuated from the Reich territory, including Bohemia and Moravia, the newly-incorporated Eastern territories and the district of Bialystok, to the East, and 8,025 Jews were resettled at the ghetto for aged Jews in Theresienstadt, resulting in another sharp decrease in the number of Jews still remaining in Germany, particularly in the Eastern territories.

Mixed Marriages. As of 12/31/1942 the Jewish population in the Reich territory of 1939 included a considerable number of Jews living in mixed marriages:

Territory	Period from ..... to 12/31/42	Decrease (–) or Increase (+) in Jewish Population due to				
		Emigration	Excess of Mortality	Evacuation (13)	Misc.	Total
Old Reich (with Sudetenland)	1/30/33 (9/29/38)	-382,534	-61,193	-100,516	+4,570	-539,673
Austria	3/13/38	-149,124	-14,509	- 47,555	- 710	-211,898
Bohemia and Moravia	3/16/39	- 25,699	- 7,074	- 69.677	—	-102,450
Eastern Territories (incl. Bialystok)	Sept. '39 (June '40)	-334,673		-222,117	—	-556,790
Generalgouvernement (incl. Lvov)	Sept. '39 (June '40)	-427,920		-1,274,166	—	-1,702,086
Totals		-1,402,726		-1,714,031	+3.860	-3,112,897

(13) It must be remembered that "evacuation" is tantamount to "extermination." In most instances, "excess of mortality . . ." probably has the same connotation.

	No. Jews as of 12/31/42	Of these, no. living in mixed marriages	Remainder
Old Reich...............	51,327	16,760	34,567
Austria.................	8,102	4,803	3,299
Bohemia and Moravia.......	15,550	6,211	9,339
Totals..................	74,979	27,774	47,205

In the interval between 12/31/1942 and 4/1/1943 the number of Jews in the Old Reich has further decreased from 51,327 to 31,910. Of these 31,910 Jews more than half, that is, 16,668, are living in mixed marriages; of these, 12,117 in privileged mixed marriages and 4,551 in unlicensed mixed marriages. Finally, as happens consistently also in other censuses, the record might include an even larger number of Jews who eventually will have to be written off an unfindable. The Jewish population in the old Reich territory (not including the Eastern territories) is nearing its end.

Assignments to Labor Service. At the beginning of 1943, 21,659 of the Jews living in the Reich territory were assigned to essential war work. Added to this total assigned to essential war work were 18,435 Jews of Soviet nationality in the military district of Königsberg, 50,570 stateless and foreign Jews at Camp Schmelt (Breslau) plus 95,112 former Polish Jews in the ghettoes and camps of the military district of Poznan.

Concentration Camps. As of 12/31/1942 a total of *9,127 Jews* were in concentration camps and 458 in prisons.

The quartering strength of Jews in the concentration camps was as follows:

Lublin..................7,342   Mauthausen/Gusen...........79
Auschwitz..............1,412(14)   Sachsenhausen.................46
Buchenwald..............227   Stutthof..........................18
                       Ravensbrück.....................3

Ghetto for Aged Jews. At the beginning of 1943, a total of 49,392 Jews were living in Theresienstadt, the only ghetto for aged Jews; they were deducted from the total Jewish population figures.

(14) This total of 1,412 inmates for Auschwitz is certainly less than the true total, because this camp contained a very high proportion of "work Jews," who could be "revived" as new transports came in. (cf. pp. 197 ff.)

Evacuation from Other European Countries: Evacuations of Jews were carried out as follows in the territories in the German sphere of power and influence beyond the borders of the Reich:

Country	Prior to 12/31/42	First Quarter of 1943
France (area occupied prior to 11/10/42	41,911	7,995
Netherlands...................................	38,571	13,832
Belgium......................................	16,886	1,616
Norway.......................................	532	158
Greece ....:...............	–	13,435
Slovakia.....................................	56,691	854
Croatia	4,927	–
Bulgaria.....................................	–	11,364
Russian territories, including former Baltic countries, since the start of the Eastern campaign................................	633,300(15)	–
Totals	792,818	49,254

Balance Sheet of European Jewry: According to the data cited above, the decrease of European Jewry to-date should amount to *4 million*. Aside from Russia, which has about *4 million*, larger Jewish populations on the European continent now exist only in Hungary (750,000) and Rumania (300,000), and perhaps also in France. If, in addition to the decline cited above, we count Jewish emigration and the excess of mortality [over births] among Jews in the Central and Western European countries outside Germany, along with inevitable duplications due to Jewish population movements, the decrease of the Jewish population of Europe between 1937 and the beginning of 1943 may be estimated at 4.5 million. This total includes only partially the incidence of death among Soviet Jewry in the occupied Eastern territories; it does not include any of the deaths in the rest of European Russia and in the battle zone. We must add to this the migrations of Jews within Russia into the Asiatic part of the country. Like those figures, the number of Jews who emigrated overseas from European countries outside the German sphere of influence is largely unknown.

(15) Partial figure, as can be seen from the following commentary.

It seems that since *1933, that is, during the first decade of National Socialist rule, European Jewry has lost almost one-half of its population.* Of this lost half, only about half, or one-fourth of Europe's total Jewish population in 1937, has migrated to other continents.

Index

345

THE DEATH BRIGADE
(previously published as *The Janowska Road*)
Leon W. Wells

THE DEATH BRIGADE records the experiences of a young Jew in the city of Lvov, Poland, from 1941 to 1945. Interned by the Germans in the Janowska concentration camp, he escaped, was recaptured and assigned to the Death Brigade which worked to obliterate traces of the mass executions of the inmates. He escaped a second time and went into hiding until the liberation.

"One must read these pages over and over again, year after year. . . . The story of Leon Wells stands as an unsurpassable record of the borderless extremes of the human capacity for evil, and for endurance; it is a modern counterpart of Job, confronting not God, but Man."   —Meyer Levin

"His story is a unique account, not merely because it is a fascinating historical document, but because of the high quality of his writing and its universal human appeal. It is not just a recital of evidence, it reads like a drama. The characters of the persons he writes about, friends or foes, are vividly etched. Details are skillfully woven into a broad picture that tells of the tragedy of a people."   —*America*

"An overpowering classic of survival, of one man's will to live, to tell the story."   —*Detroit Free Press*

Dr. Wells testified at the Nuremberg trials and the Eichmann trial. He now lives in the United States, and is a physicist and inventor in the field of optics.

320 pp. • 5¼" x 8½"
ISBN 0-89604-000-3 • $4.95 paperback

THE HOLOCAUST KINGDOM
A Memoir
Alexander Donat

This unique memoir of a Polish-Jewish family that survived
the Warsaw Ghetto and Hitler's death camps reaches
beyond the story of one man to tell the saga of a doomed
people.

"Extraordinary—marvelous. So fair, so balanced, so just, so true.
It moved me greatly. It should be read by everyone."
—Saul Bellow

"I have read hundreds of eyewitness accounts on the holocaust-
kingdom: this one surpasses them all. . . . A powerful work of art.
It should be read and re-read."   —Elie Wiesel

"An unforgettable picture of the Jewish martyrdom . . . and the
tragedy of the Jewish resistance."   —Irving Howe

"Donat's survival story possesses excitement in triple degree. For
depth of perception, dramatic intensity and documentary value it
stands as high as any volume ever published. Never—and I
include such books as *The Wall*—has the story of the Warsaw
Ghetto been told as understandably, as vividly, as in THE
HOLOCAUST KINGDOM. The survival story of their child in the home
of a Polish underground fighter, and a Catholic orphanage . . .
makes scenes of *Gone With the Wind* fade by comparison."
—Meyer Levin

"Here the Warsaw ghetto and concentration camp take on a
terrible personal meaning . . . Incredible dignity and almost
impenetrable courage mark the Jewish martyrs whom we read
about in these pages."
—Malcolm Boyd in *The Christian Century*

"A superior book . . . a book to be given to those teenagers
whose reading matter preoccupies so many parents."
—Michele Murray in *National Catholic Reporter*

"Recommended for all libraries."   —*Library Journal*

"No one who wants to understand these events can afford to
miss this chronicle of man's will to survive."
—Gertrude Samuels in *The New York Times Book Review*

368 pp. • 5¼" x 8½"
ISBN 0-89604-001-1 • $ 5.95 paperback

THEIR BROTHERS' KEEPERS

The Christian Heroes and Heroines Who Helped
the Oppressed Escape the Nazi Terror

Philip Friedman

With a Foreword by Rev. John A. O'Brien, S.J.

"Those who despair of humanity should be the first to read Philip
Friedman's account of the heroic acts of Christians in various
European countries who saved Jews during the Nazi terror. In
each case, non-Jewish lives were risked, and in many cases lost,
for the sake of compassion and conscience. Those who tend to be
fatalistic before overwhelming force should read this book for the
examples of effective resistance, whether by an individual or a
clandestine group or by an entire nation as in the case of the
Finns and the Danes."
　　　—Meyer Levin in *The New York Times Book Review*

"Dr. Friedman's well-documented and deeply moving recital of
the rescue of prospective Jewish victims by Christians, often at the
risk of their own lives, sheds a few rays of light on the Nazi
nightmare. Itself a major document of human solidarity, this story
testifies to the survival of the spirit of heroism, as well as martyrdom, in behalf of humanitarian ideals."　　　—Salo W. Baron

"I wish many people would read this book, for it gave me the
feeling that if all of us had the courage to protest immediately
when we feel something is wrong, we perhaps could prevent such
tragedies as Hitler brought about."　　　—Eleanor Roosevelt

A native of Poland, Dr. Friedman survived the Holocaust
and emigrated to the United States. He has authored many
books, essays, and articles on Jewish history.

232 pp.　•　5¼" x 8½"

ISBN 0-89604-002-X　•　$ 4.95 paperback

JUSTICE IN JERUSALEM

Gideon Hausner

With an Introduction by Barbara W. Tuchman

Gideon Hausner had been Attorney General of Israel for only two weeks when, on May 23, 1960, Prime Minister Ben-Gurion informed a stunned Knesset that Adolf Eichmann had been found and would be brought to trial for his crimes against the Jews. In this revealing and deeply moving book, Mr. Hausner tells the complete story of his role in preparing and conducting the prosecution's case against Eichmann.

"A brilliant lawyer's brief, an attempt to lay out the whole record."   —*Newsweek*

550 pp. • 5¼" x 8½"
ISBN 0-89604-003-8 • $6.95 paperback

GHETTO DIARY

Janusz Korczak

With an Introduction by Aaron Zeitlin

By education and profession a pediatrician, by talent a successful writer, by temperament and conviction a teacher and educator, by passion a charismatic leader and apostle of child welfare, Janusz Korczak spent his last years in the Warsaw Ghetto as the head of an orphanage of 200 children. Though he had many offers of personal rescue from the German extermination machine, he refused to desert his children in their mortal predicament. Instead he accompanied his charges to the Umschlagplatz and Treblinka (August 5, 1942), where he and they were murdered.

UNESCO (United Nations Educational, Scientific and Cultural Organization) has proclaimed 1978 the International Janusz Korczak Year, to commemorate the hundredth birthday of Korczak, who has become a kind of patron saint of teachers and physicians all over the world.

192 pp. • 5¼" x 8½"
ISBN 0-89604-004-6 • $8.95 hardcover